Measuring Entrepreneurship

INTERNATIONAL STUDIES IN ENTREPRENEURSHIP

Series Editors:
Zoltan J. Acs
George Mason University
Fairfax, VA, USA

David B. Audretsch
Indiana University
Bloomington, IN, USA

Books in the series:
Black, G.
  The Geography of Small Firm Innovation
Tubke, A.
  Success Factors of Corporate Spin-Offs
Corbetta, G., Huse, M., Ravasi, D.
  Crossroads of Entrepreneurship
Hansen, T., Solgaard, H.S.
  New Perspectives in Retailing and Store Patronage Behavior
Davidsson, P.
  Researching Entrepreneurship
Fornahl, D., Audretsch D., Zellner, C.
  The Role of Labour Mobility and Informal Networks for Knowledge Transfer
Audretsch D., Grimm, H., Wessner, C.
  Local Heroes in the Global Village
Landstrom, H.
  Pioneers in Entrepreneurship and Small Business Research
Lundstrom, A., Stevenson, L.
  Entrepreneurship Policy: Theory and Practice
Elfring, T.
  Corporate Entrepreneurship
van Stel, A.
  Empirical Analysis of Entrepreneurship and Economic Growth
Fritsch, M., Schmude, J.
  Entrepreneurship in the Region
Reynolds, P. D.
  Entrepreneurship in the United States
Congregado, E.
  Measuring Entrepreneurship

Measuring Entrepreneurship

Building a Statistical System

Edited by

Emilio Congregado

University of Huelva
Spain

Emilio Congregado

University of Huelva
Department of Economics and Statistics
11 Plaza de la Merced
Huelva, 21071
Spain

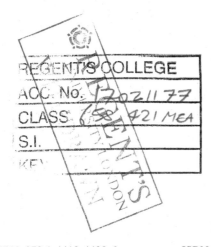

ISBN: 978-1-4419-4430-6   e-ISBN: 978-0-387-72288-7

To Ana, Patricia and Rafael

Foreword

Entrepreneurship is playing an increasingly important role in the political agenda. This phenomenon is due to the increasing influence of politics on the entrepreneurial promotion of growth and employment objectives. This results in the need to satisfy the new demand for statistical information in two ways. On the one hand, quantitative information -stock and flow analysis, on the other hand, qualitative information –which tries to assess the ability to create wealth and employment and to innovate and export, among others. Consequently, searching a systematic set of indicators that allows us to understand the basic entrepreneurship dimensions in order to diagnose, forecast, and monitor entrepreneurial networks, is crucial for both the research agenda and the political action agenda. However, the lack of this kind of statistical information is clear if we review some statistical subsystems on entrepreneurship on a comparison basis. The few essays on the subject are still in an initial stage. The reference theoretical framework to set the key dimensions to be analysed is to be established yet. The search for indicators and even the articulation of specific statistics have become crucial in order to make progress in the applied research, and to design, implement, and assess the different measurements of public intervention on this subject. Thus, the development of a set of indicators that allow us to satisfactorily capture the different dimensions of the entrepreneurial network for a specific sector or territory becomes a basic element to assist progress in entrepreneurship knowledge. A short time ago, the only progress in the articulation of indicators –with a certain dose of comparability- was related to the quantitative aspect of the individual entrepreneurship network. Using Labour Force Surveys, the number of self-employed people began to be used as a proxy for the number of people that carry out an entrepreneurial function within a specific territory or sector. Thus, the International Labour Office began to collect information on the percentage of self-employed people in some countries. Similarly, and using a common methodology to measure, Eurostat included these self-employment rates in its divulgation plans for the EU-15 countries. Together with these attempts at measurement, some countries and institutions have made isolated efforts in the field of structural statistics. Nevertheless, and regardless of the varying levels of success with which these efforts have been carried out, the main task is the articulation and systematisation of the available indicators, as well as the search for new statistical information sources that allow us to capture not only the quantitative composition of a specific territory or sector's entrepreneurial network, but also its quality. The aim is to learn the entrepreneurial network's capacity to contribute to economic growth, to take advantage of the profit opportunities, to create employment, and to help in innovation processes by giving the systems the required amount of comparability. This should be achieved by using common methodologies to obtain indicators to be implemented in the network. In this sense, during the last few years, some events and projects have assisted the development of statistics on entrepreneurship. Firstly, the Ministerial Conference held in Istanbul in 2004, and the Workshop on Small and Medium Enterprises and Entrepreneurship held in Paris in 2005, endorsed the need to gather more statistical information on entrepreneurship. Secondly, the Centre for Economic and Business Research's (FORA, Danish department of the Ministry of Economy and Business Affairs) effort stands out due to its pioneering character, which has highlighted the development of a complete system of indicators on entrepreneurship in its entrepreneurial promotion strategy. In this context, cognizant that we should be one of these first institutions and organizations who try to satisfy this new demand for statistical information, during the last 18 months the Institute of Statistics of Andalusia, together with a group of researchers from different universities, coordinated by the Department of Economics and Statistics at the University of Huelva, has carried out a project encompassing the viability, content and scope of a subsystem of regional entrepreneurial competitiveness indicators. The groundbreaking character of the project is due to its spatial area of application. In this sense, we have to stress that this is the first attempt with these features within a Self-Government Region, and even at the regional level in all of Europe. This results in an additional challenge, since territorial disintegration of indicators implies one more obstacle to be added to those mentioned above. Therefore, the weak consolidation of the subject, the small number of countries that have real statistical systems on entrepreneurship, and the necessity of providing the system with the required amount of future comparability, lead us compulsorily to the need of implementing our proposal in the ongoing international experiences framework, and to the necessity of including this proposal in a widely agreed conceptual framework. This work is the result of shared reflections of both a group of researchers who are the core of research on entrepreneurship, and also of people in charge of projects with similar features carried out at international level. This process serves to provide us with the most consolidated items in other subsystems, and enables the consideration of regional systems needs by people in charge of national and supranational organizations. Lastly, I would like to thank all the researchers and international experts on this subject for their collaboration and interest, and also for their effort to develop the different studies which result in this publication.

José Antonio Griñán Martínez
Counsellor of Economy and Treasury (Junta de Andalucía)

Preface

This book is part of a joint project carried out by the Andalusian Statistics Institute (IEA, Consejería de Economía y Hacienda) and the University of Huelva, in order to contribute to the design of a complete system of indicators on entrepreneurship and competitiveness. All regions or countries (Andalusia not being an exception) obviously have the aim of being one of the most entrepreneurial economies, in order to enhance economic growth and employment. In this sense, providing policy makers with a guide of propositions, policy areas and data for monitoring and forecasting should be an essential element of our region's strategy to promote entrepreneurship. In fact, the existence of a well-established system of entrepreneurship indicators ought to be a necessary condition, a prerequisite, for the design and monitoring of any entrepreneurial policy. In addition, the body of propositions derived from the economics of entrepreneurship, as in any other field of economic analysis, should be based on a set of available and appropriate indicators.

With this aim, the Andalusian Statistical Institute is promoting the development of a system of indicators, guided by two main principles: to give an appropriate answer to the demand of statistical resources in the field of entrepreneurship, using the current state of entrepreneurship research as a guide; and to integrate this system in the context of other international or national projects with similar objectives in order to contribute to comparability. The first principle has some powerful implications on the design of an articulated entrepreneurship statistical system. The existence of a gap between the economic theory and the available data for testing their main propisitions, and the empirical research has been a well-recognised fact in the economics of entrepreneurship. Up until recently, researchers have been forced to make imaginative efforts to advance in entrepreneurship empirics. The lack of an articulated system of entrepreneurial indicators has even limited the scope of several researches. In fact, statistical information contained in structural business statistics has been revealed as insufficient for entrepreneurship research purposes. In parallel to that, the natural available statistical source has been the labour force survey or any other household surveys –data from Household Panels or Social Security- where the interviewee gives his/her own answer about his/her status in employment, and occupation. Consequently, self-employment has been considered as the best way to proxy entrepreneurship and "The Economics of Entrepreneurship" has been replaced gradually by "The Economics of Self-employment". These surveys, planned and designed to take into account different aspects of labour market, have presented an excellent basis on which to increase awareness of the effects of some individual socio-economic variables on the decision to become an entrepreneur. However, these surveys have presented two main limitations: on the one hand, with the exception of some economic areas such as Europe, the lack of comparability –since a common methodology has not existed- has limited the scope of the main results obtained and even the admissible essays; on the other hand, some relevant dimensions revealed as crucial in entrepreneurship research have had to be excluded within questionnaires.

Recently, international institutions such as the Organisation for Economic Co-operation and Development, the International Labour Office, and a set of national agencies have been leading a process, still in progress, of trying to adapt statistics on entrepreneurship to fit the researchers and policy makers' needs. In this task, at least the following three factors are crucial: i) the previous consensus of the definition of entrepreneurship –perhaps comprehensive of different approaches-, decreasing the high degree of controversy on the theoretical framework; In fact, the existence of eclectic approaches to entrepreneurship, abandoning the useful theoretical tools of economic analysis, has caused the inexistence of an articulated statistical demand on Statistical Agencies, and a wide range of surveys and indicators designed for fragmentary purposes; ii) to detect the key dimensions to advancing empirical research, taking into account the possibility of integrating this information into the existing human population surveys thus enhancing the battery of questions and the sample size when it is necessary; iii) to advance international comparability, through a general agreement on a common methodology.

In this context, we are agreeing on the necessity of beginning by fixing the current state of entrepreneurship research with a specific perspective: to clarify the main dimensions we must try to capture, to detect the main statistics and indicators available, to analyse the statistical researcher's demands, and finally, to collect similar experiences, in progress, devoted to standardizing entrepreneurship statistics and indicators. To carry out this task, and sponsored by the IEA, we held last February, in Punta Umbría (Spain) an international workshop in which a set of researchers discussed, from different perspectives, the current, state-of-the-art research on entrepreneurship, focusing on the methods, the data demands and the potential weaknesses of different indicators and sources.The concept of entrepreneurship, the main topics and approaches to empirical research, the disposable statistical sources and indicators, and some pioneering essays to develop entrepreneurship indicators were some of the themes treated. In sum, the objective and scope of this publication is to serve as a starting point in the design of a complete entrepreneurship statistical system by means of a comprehensive exposition of the data and indicators more appropriate to different approaches to entrepreneurship research.

Emilio Congregado
Huelva
March 2007

Acknowledgments

At this point, we want to thank the Andalusian Statistical Institute for their financial support, but especially for their sensibility towards social demands, assuming a key role as a promoter of this pioneer project, placing it at the cutting edge of this research topic.

Finally, I would like to express my gratitude to all participants for their disposal and interest. This project was, from the beginning, a great –and pleasant- challenge, which has been, thanks to the participants' work, easy to carry out. This book is yours.

Contents

Contributors

Ahmad, Nadim, Manager of the OECD's Structural Business Databases
Statistics Directorate of the OECD
Paris
France

Carmona, Mónica, Lecturer in Marketing
Department of Business Administration and Marketing, University of Huelva
Plaza de la Merced, 11, 21071, Huelva
Spain

Cerdán, Mario, Lecturer in Accounting and Finance
Department of Accounting and Finances, University of Huelva
Plaza de la Merced, 11, 21071, Huelva
Spain

Congregado, Emilio, Senior Lecturer in Economics
Department of Economics and Statistics, University of Huelva
Plaza de la Merced, 11, 21071, Huelva
Spain

Davis, Tim, Manager of the OECD's Entrepreneurship Indicators Project
Statistics Directorate of the OECD
Paris
France

Golpe, Antonio A., Lecturer in Economics
Department of Economics and Statistics, University of Huelva
Plaza de la Merced, 11, 21071, Huelva
Spain

Hessels, Jolanda, Researcher
EIM Business and Policy Research
Zoetermeer
The Netherlands

Larsen, Morten, Head of Section
  FORA Ministry of Economics and Business Affairs
  Division for Research and Analysis
  Denmark

Máñez, Juan A., Senior Lecturer in Economics
  Department of Applied Economics II, University of Valencia, and LINEEX,
  Av. dels Tarongers s/n, 46022, Valencia
  Spain

Menudo, José M., Lecturer in Economics
  Department of Economics, University Pablo de Olavide,
  Ctra. Utrera, Km.1, 41013, Utrera (Sevilla)
  Spain

Millán, José M., Lecturer in Economics
  Department of Economics and Statistics, University of Huelva
  Plaza de la Merced, 11, 21071, Huelva
  Spain

O'kean, José M., Professor of Economics
  Department of Economics, University Pablo de Olavide,
  Ctra. Utrera, Km.1, 41013, Utrera (Sevilla)
  Spain

Parker, Simon C., Professor of Economics
  Durham University, Max Planck Institute for Economics and IZA,
  Durham, Jena and Bonn
  UK and Germany

Rochina-Barrachina, María E., Senior Lecturer in Economics
  Department of Applied Economics II, University of Valencia, and LINEEX,
  Av. dels Tarongers s/n, 46022, Valencia
  Spain

Román, Concepción, Lecturer in Economics
  Department of Economics and Statistics, University of Huelva
  Plaza de la Merced, 11, 21071, Huelva
  Spain

Sanchis, Juan A., Senior Lecturer in Economics
  Department of Applied Economics II, University of Valencia, and LINEEX,
  Av. dels Tarongers s/n, 46022, Valencia
  Spain

Schuetze, Herbert J., Juan Antonio, Assistant Professor
  Department of Economics, University of Victoria,
  PO Box 1700 STN CSC,
  Victoria, BC V8W 2Y2
  Canada

Van Stel, André, Researcher
EIM Business and Policy Research, Erasmus University Rotterdam and
Cranfield University School of Management
Zoetermeer, Rotterdam, Cranfield
The Netherlands and UK

Chapter 1
Introduction and Outline

Emilio Congregado

Despite the fact that entrepreneurship has always remained in the agenda of researchers and policy makers, it is very far from being considered a topic belonging to the core. However, in recent years we have been witnessing a renewed interest in the economics of entrepreneurship.

There exist several factors explaining this fact: i) first of all, self-employment has been considered as a way to reduce the high and persistent unemployment rates in the few last decades. So governments have turned into the primary advocates of propositions and results on which basis they have designed different kinds of incentives for attracting a higher proportion of individuals towards self-employment. As a direct result, researchers have exhaustively explored the determinants of the self-employment rate, in order to create guidelines for a development policy; ii) economists have been able to integrate entrepreneurship into economic theory by using an operational approach, which identifies entrepreneurship with self-employment. This process has allowed progress in the formalisation and derivation of propositions in a similar manner to the rest of economics and has brought entrepreneurship closer to labour economics; and iii) from an empirical perspective, these demands have given rise to an exhaustive microeconometric work. Using micro data from household panels or even from labour force surveys the impact of a wide range of individual socio-economic characteristics and of some aggregate economic variables on occupational choice have been explored. This last kind of work has permitted the quantification of the effect of different tax incentives, the analyses of the role of liquidity constraints or revealed the need to establish certain measures of positive discrimination in favour of women or immigrants, among others.

However, this rapprochement between entrepreneurship and economics coexists with "eclectic" and "sociological" views, putting a certain predicament upon politicians and statistical agencies on the basis of the supposed multidisciplinary character of entrepreneurship. This multidisciplinary approach, far from being positive, may only contribute to the waste of efforts and resources. A clear understanding

Emilio Congregado
University of Huelva
Congregado@hu.es

of this hostility towards other approaches is necessary. Currently, it is crucial to have a system of indicators on entrepreneurship which are able to respond to the demands of researchers and policy-makers, and for this reason, it is important to clear up this topic a little. For example: if we review the literature included under the heading of entrepreneurship we can observe a wide range of positions on this matter, from works included in labour economics to views typically related to business economics or even by sociologists. One view, widely held in the field of entrepreneurship is that it is a diffuse concept, with several dimensions, and thus very difficult to measure. However, as in other economic fields, we abstracted some factors in order to make an operative concept. In this way, self-employment is revealed as the operative concept which has allowed the integration of entrepreneurship in labour economics. To a certain extent, only when researchers have used occupational choice models and job search models for explaining the supply of entrepreneurship -perhaps self-employment-, has entre-preneurship begun to be a more consolidated topic and their propositions have begun to be taken into account by the mainstream.

This work seeks to forge a closer relationship with this type of audience, attempting to bring the economics of entrepreneurship and its statistical demands to institutions. In other words, this book has a conscious bias towards the economics of entrepreneurship, revealing their statistical need for a double perspective: of topics and of the econometric tools available. Although several chapters contain indicators and statistical sources usually suitable in business demography, the exposition of the subjects, tools and data sources of the economics of entrepreneurship constitute the core of this book.

Following the current economic theory, entrepreneurial activity can be defined on the basis of the performance of at least one of these four functions: i) to reduce inefficiencies, always present in the firm (Leibenstein, 1969,1979); ii) to detect the potential profit opportunities (Kirzner, 1973, 1979, 1985); iii) to face the uncertainty (Knight, 1929), and, iv) to innovate (Schumpeter, 1913).[1] Therefore if we want to take a broad view of entrepreneurship and to collect the four vectors forming the entrepreneurial activity, we must find indicators showing the different dimensions considered. In order to carry out this task researchers have adopted a positive attitude consisting of an exhaustive search of indicators from the available statistical sources.

The current approach to measure entrepreneurial stock in a country, region or sector has been the use of some indicators from labour force surveys or from business registers. Although their pertinence could be discussed within the function of our previous conceptualisation of entrepreneurship both types of sources have been intensely explored in order to quantify the entrepreneurial network.

Labour force surveys contain information about the occupational work force, and organise it by professional category. Using this information, it is possible to

---

[1] In this sense, we will consider as a member of the entrepreneurial network anyone who carries out at least one of these vectors, independently of the kind of link they have with the firm property or the way they perform their task.

establish the first numbers regarding the amount of people who are performing an entrepreneurial activity within a certain work sphere. Another possibility is given by the exploitation of information from business registries. In this case, the objectives and scopes must be radically different. Some of the dimensions which may be analysed are the number of firms or establishments, and their characteristics: size, type of activity and duration. However, using these kinds of sources we lose sight of the agent.

In sum, the purpose of this book is to make recent advances in the theory and application of the economics of entrepreneurship more accessible to advanced undergraduate students and even to the non-technical public, emphasizing the data demands to advance the future research agenda and to allow better monitoring of any strategy to promote entrepreneurship. So, the main objective of this book is to delve deeper into this topic, from this perspective: stating the main sources and indicators available to take in as many quantitative as qualitative aspects related to the measurement of entrepreneurship, discussing their pertinence and their availability in order to realize international comparisons, as a way to detect the statistical needs derived from empirical research.

In order to carry out this task the book is divided into three main parts. Part I is concerned with the economic theory of entrepreneurship and with the current empirical research agenda, emphasising the limitations induced by indicators and data sources.

In Chapter 2, by Professor Simon C. Parker, the current research agenda is reviewed in terms of the needs of empirical research. Professor Parker analyses how to measure entrepreneurship using the sources of available data, and presents an exhaustive discussion on how the use of more powerful econometric tools can help in the progress of several important empirical issues, and about how the performance in the measurement of some variables is constrained by the deficiencies of current statistical sources.

An important concept discussed in Chapter 3 is that of an entrepreneurial network, which represents a comprehensive view of the economic theory of entrepreneurship. As we have mentioned before, one of the most important questions in order to develop an efficient entrepreneurship statistical system is to clarify the entrepreneurship concept. In this chapter, José María O'Kean and José Manuel Menudo, suggest the use of a general vision of the entrepreneurial network, distinguishing three different levels of variables that permit us to measure the quantities and qualities of entrepreneurial activities: individual actions, firms and industrial perspectives, and macroeconomic visions. The authors offer a comprehensive understanding of the entrepreneurial network, which is especially useful for applied studies that clarify the role of different entrepreneurial productive figures, differentiating between the individual and the corporative entrepreneurial network. They also offer a wider vision introducing key agents that to a lesser extent develop the content of the entrepreneurial function such as consultant and business promotion agencies.

Part II concentrates on the general statistical sources and indicators of entrepreneurship, including some essays to measure entrepreneurship using specific and non-specific statistics, and reviews some recent attempts to construct a common system of indicators of entrepreneurship.

Chapter 4, by Tim Davis, presents a practical approach to the development of internationally-comparable indicators on entrepreneurship. As noted in the chapter, the need for better international statistics on entrepreneurship and SMEs has been identified in OECD research and forums for some time. Like the Huelva Workshop itself, the Statistics Directorate of the OECD wants to develop both more and better indicators of entrepreneurship, its determinants and impacts. This chapter presents the underlying rationale for developing entrepreneurship indicators, some priorities for aspects of entrepreneurship to be covered and the general approach to be followed by the OECD.

Chapter 5 is devoted to the COMPENDIA data base. This data base, built by André van Stel, contains business ownership rates for 23 OECD countries from 1972 onwards. This data base has been an important contribution to cross-country entrepreneurship research, representing a pioneer attempt to construct an international data base with comparable data.

In Chapter 6 José María Millán et al. try to collect, describe and evaluate all the potential sources –each of them pursuing different goals- in order to study the "entrepreneurship phenomenon" using Spanish statistical sources. Thus, the traditional existing data bases together with the new ones now appearing are contributing to improve the knowledge of the labour market situation –self-employment included. Although in this sense the available information might be considered quite accurate, in order to reach the particular goals of each source this information becomes incomplete and even erratic if we intend to analyse entrepreneurial activity by it. As a consequence, if we accept that entrepreneurs play a relevant role in explaining economic growth and reducing unemployment, this situation is at least disconcerting.

Chapter 7, by Nadim Ahmad, provides a survey of a range of databases in different OECD Directorates providing information related to entrepreneurship where special attention is given to structural business statistics. The chapter also considers a number of comparability problems and an exposition of the new work areas with relation to: business demography, the development of micro-level data, and an essay which links trade and business registers.

A general strategy used to measure and monitor entrepreneurship, based on the Danish experience, is presented in Chapter 8 by Morten Larsen. This work presents the methodology used to produce a composite indicator, The Danish Entrepreneurship Index, which was built in order to capture entrepreneurship as defined as the *entry and exit of firms and the creation of high growth firms.*

Part III concentrates on five applied areas of empirical entrepreneurship research, detecting proxies used and statistical needs for future research agendas.

In Chapter 9, André van Stel and Antonio Golpe, use time series analysis techniques to explore the relationship between economic growth and entrepreneurship in Spain using the Spanish Labour Force Survey.

In Chapter 10, by Herbert J. Schuetze, the emphasis is on understanding the interplay between tax policy and entrepreneurial activity. The purposes of this chapter are to illustrate the current state of knowledge regarding the impacts of taxation on entrepreneurship, to identify areas in which additional research is particularly warranted and pinpoint the data requirements necessary to fill in these gaps in the literature. While this literature has provided a great deal of knowledge regarding the effects of tax policy on entrepreneurship, the work is far from complete. A number of the shortcomings in the literature are results of a lack of quality data focused on self-employment outcomes.

Chapter 11, by Juan A. Máñez, María E. Rochina and Juan A. Sanchis, provides a survey of a range of statistical techniques used to analyse entrepreneurial success, using structural business data. Special attention is given to applying survival analysis to individual data, including a wide range of potential applications to entrepreneurship research.

An approach to a specific kind of human capital is given by Emilio Congregado, Mónica Carmona and Concepción Román in Chapter 12, where attention is concentrated on the potential proxies available in order to capture entrepreneurial human capital stock and some dimensions related to the different ways in which the entrepreneurial human capital accumulation process can operate. The chapter also considers a number of procedures used to test for intergenerational transmission of entrepreneurial human capital.

Chapter 13, by Jolanda Hessels and van Stel, investigates whether the presence of export oriented entrepreneurs is a more important determinant of national economic growth than entrepreneurial activity in general. Using cross-country data from the Global Entrepreneurship Monitor the author tests the extent to which the export orientation of entrepreneurs is reflected in GDP growth.

Chapter 14 reviews one of the most recent topics in entrepreneurship: the role of labour market institutions. Golpe, Millán and Román study, from a statistical perspective, the variables and proxies used to analyse the impact of these institutions in the different types of transitions within the labour market.

In Chapter 15, Carmona, Cerdán and Millán analyse the role of liquidity constraints in the problem of occupational choice, in order to examine how the level of development in financial institutions favours or hinders the emergence of new entrepreneurs.

Finally, Chapter 16 proposes a theoretical framework in order to determine the various dimensions to be taken into account when creating a statistical system of entrepreneurship. Thus, in a summarizing attempt Congregado et al. outline the difficulty of integrating the different approaches in the entrepreneurship phenomenom.

Part I
The Current State: Entrepreneurship in Theory and Practice

Chapter 2
Statistical Issues in Applied Entrepreneurship Research: Data, Methods and Challenges

Simon C Parker

2.1 Introduction

This chapter discusses aspects of the statistical measurement of entrepreneurship, and the use of statistical methods in explaining the role of entrepreneurship in modern economies. The discussion is conducted with reference to topical issues in current entrepreneurship research. The chapter is divided into five sections, the first two sections each containing three components, relating to data measurement, the statistical methods required to analyse the phenomena of interest, and a brief list of issues that remain to be addressed. I first discuss the measurement of entrepreneurship at an aggregate level. Two main classes of measure are in common usage at present. I argue that this is an advantageous situation on balance, as the various measures capture different aspects of what entrepreneurship entails. The econometric methods required to analyse the determinants of international differences in entrepreneurship, and time series variations within countries, are also discussed in this section, as are several outstanding issues that remain to be addressed.

Section 3 discusses interpersonal comparisons in entrepreneurship, in terms of what makes some individuals more likely than others to become entrepreneurs. I argue that panel data sets should be used for this purpose whenever possible. Section 4 treats statistical measurement of entrepreneurship at the regional level, and emphasises the ongoing challenges statisticians face in advancing our core knowledge at this level of analysis. Section 5 offers a brief overview of policy issues, pointing out where progress has been made in the statistical analysis of public policy's interface with entrepreneurship, and where more work is needed. The final section concludes the chapter.

Simon C Parker
Durham University
s.c.parker@durham.ac.uk

E. Congregado, *Measuring Entrepreneurship.*
© Springer 2008

2.2 International comparisons

2.2.1 Data: How to measure entrepreneurship?

The first question is how to define entrepreneurship for the purposes of making international comparisons. At present, there are broadly two available approaches and data sets. The first defines of entrepreneurship as self-employment, which can be implemented at the aggregate country-level using publicly available OECD *Labour Force Statistics* data. The second approach defines entrepreneurship as the formation and operation of new firms, and is implemented in the Global Entrepreneurship Monitor (GEM), a joint project between London Business School of the UK, and Babson College of the US. Table 2.1 lists some characteristics of the two measures and data sets.

As the table shows, both existing measures and approaches have their merits and demerits. The OECD data go back to the 1960s; useable international comparisons on a large panel of countries go back as far as 1972 (Parker and Robson, 2004); and the series continues to be published. There are some problems of comparability between countries, though algorithms are now being developed by Andre van Stel at Erasmus University in the Netherlands to resolve these problems. In contrast, we currently only have a limited number of years of GEM data, which precludes meaningful time series analyses of entrepreneurship. GEM data have the advantage of greater comparability across countries, and the TEA flow index dovetails with business studies research which equates entrepreneurship with new venture creation. However, a sometimes overlooked drawback of TEA is that by focusing only on new

Table 2.1 Comparison of OECD and GEM data on entrepreneurship

Data set:	OECD(Labour Force Statistics)	GEM
Definition of entrepreneurship	Self-employment	New venture creation (Total Entrepreneurial Activity index, TEA)
Type of measure	Stock	(In)flow: all individuals owning businesses more than 42 months old are discarded from TEA
Advantages	Long time series Includes established as well as new entrepreneurs	Focuses specifically on entry (flow) Considerable cross-country comparability Disaggregate as well as aggregate level data
Disadvantages	Self-employment includes part-time and hobby (non-entrepreneurial) firms Data are not strictly comparable across countries	By omitting older firms, TEA overstates entrepreneurship and is volatile (sensitive to the business cycle) Also includes non-entrepreneurial firms Short time-series

firms, it is overly sensitive to the state of the business cycle. While the movement of countries up and down the TEA "league table" no doubt makes good headlines, it is less clear why firms over 42 months old cease to be entrepreneurial as a matter of course; numerous counter-examples doubtless spring to mind.

In my opinion, the existence of more than one practical entrepreneurship measure is an advantage rather than a limitation. The researcher has greater choice to employ an empirical measure that relates more closely to their theoretical construct, whatever that may be. Unless one adopts an evangelical view that stock or inflow are intrinsically important, both measures contain different information that makes them complements rather than substitutes. Some researchers have recognised this, suggesting that researchers might choose to use a mixture of entrepreneurship measures in their empirical research (Gartner and Shane 1995). Note however that OECD and GEM data the only sources of data that can be used to make international comparisons of entrepreneurship. Other cross-country data sources exist, including the European Community Household Panel (Garcia-Mainar and Montuenga-Gomez 2005).

2.2.2 *Statistical methods*

The great advantage of cross-country data sets with a time dimension, such as the OECD *Labour Force Statistics*, is that they facilitate time series analysis. Thus, the researcher can analyse not only static differences between countries, but also trends and cycles in entrepreneurship within countries, as well as cross-country differences in those trends and cycles. Long spans of data are necessary if the researcher is to explain entrepreneurship in terms of slow-changing underlying factors, such as in the economic (e.g., technical change) or policy/institutional (e.g., tax) environment. With time series data for several countries, the statistical power of econometric analysis is enhanced, as both time-series and cross-sectional variations can be harnessed to identify underlying processes (Blanchflower 2000; Parker and Robson 2004). The use of time series data does however require the researcher to abandon the simple ordinary least squares estimator, which generates potentially spurious results when data are non-stationary; superior cointegration methods should be used instead (Parker 1996; Parker and Robson 2004).

2.2.3 *Issues that remain to be addressed*

There are several ways that the statistical analysis of international comparisons of entrepreneurship can be improved. First, cleaner and more comparable cross-country data are needed. GEM has made a valuable contribution in this regard, albeit from a particular viewpoint; it is to be hoped that the comparable OECD LFS data will also become widely available on an updated basis some day. Second, researchers can do much more to disseminate appropriate econometric (cointegration) techniques, especially those relating to time series data and panels with a large time series dimension. Third, the current literature presently contains numerous reduced form analyses of entrepreneurship and growth; there is ample scope for structural empirical modelling, which recognises that not only might entrepreneurship feed into growth (as some early GEM reports asserted), but also that entrepreneurship might in turn respond positively to more favourable growth conditions. Endogeneity of entrepreneurship is obviously the issue here ? which should not be surprising: presumably that is the reason why we study it! Structural approaches contain the promise of uncovering the causal linkages between entrepreneurship and growth, a topic of growing interest (Acs et al. 2004; van Stel et al. 2005; Wong et al. 2005; and see below).

2.3 Interpersonal Comparisons

2.3.1 Data and Measurement Issues

Studies about individuals' choices to become entrepreneurs can be grouped into three categories, according to the dependent variable used in their empirical analyses. These relate to individual's choice of employment status (self-employed/business owner or employee); the individual's choice of whether to start a new venture; and the entrepreneur's choice of whether to continue or terminate the present business.

Large-scale micro data sets have been widely available for many years now, fuelling dramatic growth in what is now a vast applied literature on the determinants of entrepreneurship status, entry, and survival (see Parker, 2004, for a review of this literature). Much has now been learned about the salient factors behind these processes; rather than repeat a summary of them here, I will instead concentrate on two limitations of current data sets: the absence of a longitudinal component, and measurement problem in key variables of interest.

Longitudinal surveys, which compile data on individuals by following them through time, are gradually becoming more widely available. The best known longitudinal (panel) data sets in use in applied entrepreneurship research are the National Longitudinal Survey and the Panel Survey of Income Dynamics (both US); the British Household Panel Survey and National Child Development Survey (both UK); and the European Community Household Panel. Several of these data sets, such as PSID and BHPS, are ongoing panels which "top up" respondents who leave the panel with new replacements. It is now becoming clear that panel data sets are essential for understanding the individual-specific factors that drive entrepreneurship as an occupational choice. As well as facilitating the analysis of individual-level career dynamics, panel data enjoy two key advantages over static cross section surveys: they can control for *state dependence* and *unobserved heterogeneity*, both of which appear to be integral aspects of these choices (Henley 2004; Hochguertel 2005). To explain these concepts, consider the following econometric model of occupational choice:

$$s_{it} = X_{it}\beta + \gamma s_{it-1} + \mu_i + u_{it} \tag{2.1}$$

Here, s_{it} represents the decision of individual i about whether to be self-employed at time t: this depends on whether they were self-employed at time t-1 (via the parameter γ); on a vector of observable characteristics at t, X_{it}; and on a person-specific idiosyncratic fixed effect, μ_i. The u_{it} is a random error term. State-dependence is the tendency of individuals to continue what they were doing in the past; this is reflected in the γs_{it-1} term. Unobserved heterogeneity is the set of idiosyncratic person-specific factors that make some people innately more likely to be entrepreneurs, for reasons that we cannot measure directly. This is represented by the fixed effect μ_i. When models of this sort have been estimated, these two constructs are found to make important qualitative differences to key parameters of interest, many of which reside in β (see, e.g., Henley 2004; Hochguertel 2005). Put bluntly, without taking account of state dependence and unobserved heterogeneity, the researcher is at risk of generating misleading inferences about the determinants of entrepreneurship. Whether or not panel data are available, statisticians and researchers must pay close attention to measurement error when seeking to understand the individual-level determinants of entrepreneurship. Key to this is obtaining reliable income data for entrepreneurs. For example, in one canonical model of entrepreneurial occupational choice, an important driver of switching propensities is suggested to be relative incomes (Rees and Shah 1986; Taylor 1996; Parker 2003). Yet in conventional sample surveys, self-employed people are known to be reluctant to respond to questions about their income and wealth, and drastically under-report their incomes when they do respond (Pissarides and Weber 1989; Lyssiotou et al. 2004). Statisticians tasked with obtaining individual-level entrepreneurship data need to find better ways of eliciting truthful responses, if at all possible. This is desirable for several reasons, not just for helping researchers identify entrepreneurial selection effects. The levels and inequality of entrepreneurial incomes are of policy interest in their own right (Parker 1997, 1999; Hamilton 2000); and returns to entrepreneurship appear to affect effort and labour supply decisions of entrepreneurs (Bitler et al. 2005; Parker et al. 2005).

High quality asset data are available in the US, where entrepreneurs are observed to play a central role in the accumulation of savings and wealth. Recent calculations reveal that entrepreneurs hold nearly 40% of total net worth in the US (Gentry and Hubbard 2004), while half of the richest 5% of American families own businesses (Quadrini 2000). In addition, entrepreneurial families account for one third of all stockholdings (Heaton and Lucas 2000). Numbers like these suggest that entrepreneurial wealth-holding is important enough to merit serious investment of statistical resources in acquiring better data, especially outside the US where wealth data are patchier. Better data could be used to shed light on issues which are still imperfectly understood, including the "private equity premium puzzle" in business ownership (Moskowitz and Vissing-Jorgensen 2002; Hintermaier and Steinberger 2005); entrepreneurs' investment decisions (Carroll et al. 2000); and entrepreneurs' retirement decisions (Parker and Rougier 2006).

2.3.2 Estimation Issues

There are several statistical estimation issues which crop up when individual-level data are used to analyse entrepreneurial choices. One is endogeneity, especially of human capital and assets. Neither human capital nor assets are random draws; individuals, including entrepreneurs, purposively choose their values; neglecting this can seriously bias regression model parameters purporting to shed light on drivers of entrepreneurship. A good practical example of this is supplied by Parker and van Praag (2006), who show that the inappropriate use of OLS biases substantially downwards rates of return to entrepreneurs' schooling in the presence of borrowing constraints. Other researchers are also recognising the importance of dealing with endogeneity, including Garcia-Mainar and Montuenga-Gomez (2005) in the context of human capital, and Hurst and Lusardi (2004) in the context of wealth. More however remains to be done to spread good practice across the research community, entailing the use of Instrumental Variables (IV) or Generalised Method of Moments (GMM) estimators.

Other statistical estimation issues include the need to control for self-selection into occupations when analysing entrepreneurial outcomes; controlling for tastes (where possible), such as risk aversion; and using non-parametric as well as parametric estimation where this is appropriate. Sample survey data on risk attitudes are potentially valuable, although the accuracy of survey responses to hypothetical questions about gambles is questionable; recent papers that utilise such data in entrepreneurship research include Ekelund et al. (2005) and Kanniainen and Vesala (2005). Non-parametric methods have also become more popular, with Paulson et al.(2006) combining these methods with reduced form and structural parametric estimation in an analysis of borrowing constraints. The advantage of non-parametric methods is to weaken essentially uninteresting assumptions about model structure to generalise the applicability of the researchers' results.

2.3.3 Issues that Remain to be Addressed

There are several ways that improved data can potentially advance our understanding of entrepreneurship. One involves digging deeper inside firms, matching firm-level with individual-level data. We have at present some tantalising evidence about how the inflexibility of incumbent firms' routines can inhibit the development of new ideas inside those firms (see, e.g., Henderson 1993)—requiring new venture creation (entrepreneurship) to exploit those ideas. We are already seeing the emergence of a research agenda which connects firms' decisions with those of employees who quit to pursue new opportunities in entrepreneurship (Gompers et al. 2005). However, this research agenda is still in its infancy, and further development is inevitable. Another area where novel sources of data would be helpful is in relation to credit markets. Some suggestive evidence by Blanchflower et al. (2003) points to the existence of racial discrimination by banks against borrowers; more bank file data are needed to further explore this and related issues, including the relevance and predictive power of conventional theories of credit rationing and asymmetric information (Parker 2002). Ongoing research is also beginning to make more ambitious linkages between hitherto separate topics in entrepreneurship research, for example between human capital, loan decisions and entrepreneurs' performance (Parker and van Praag 2006); and between borrowing constraints and business transfers (Caselli and Gennaioli 2005). Statisticians charged with compiling new entrepreneurial data sets need to recognise the growing demands of researchers for data that break down conventional boundaries in the growing drive for unification of the entrepreneurship field.

What should be clear from the discussion so far is that European researchers are generally less well served than their American counterparts, in terms of their access to high quality data on contemporary issues in entrepreneurship research. There is a case for European statistical agencies to compile more and better European data (preferably in the form of an ongoing cross-country panel data) which bear on the issues we have treated here. As well as obtaining data specifically on wealth accumulation, I would appeal for better data on borrowing constraints (rather than simple measures of asset values, which has been the norm in the literature to date); on business angels and their investments; on high growth firms ("gazelles"); on career histories of entrepreneurs that link firms with workers; and on non-profit entrepreneurs and the nature of their enterprises.

2.4 Regional Comparisons

A lively area of ongoing entrepreneurship research connects aspects of geography, economic growth and entrepreneurship. Work by Acs et al. (2004) and Audretsch and Fritsch (2002) relates spillovers, clusters and growth at the regional level, and evidence is now accumulating that regions with higher levels of new venture creation also have higher average economic growth rates. One possible explanation of this linkage is that entrepreneurs exploit knowledge spillovers in local clusters to generate that growth; an alternative explanation is that small forms are "hothouses", where future entrepreneurs learn from owner-manager "role models" (Wagner 2004).

A statistical (data) problem immediately surfaces: what is the appropriate unit of analysis for which to collect and analyse data? Applies research in this area has tended to work at the level of the firm (small or new) or the province/locality, rather than at the level of the individual. This in turn raises further questions, about the appropriate definitions of small and new firms (e.g., "what is small?"), and where the local boundaries can be drawn. To date, researchers have tended not to worry overly about the sensitivity of their results to these definitions. That may need to change.

As elsewhere in this chapter, some outstanding statistical estimation issues emerge. While the emphasis in the knowledge spillover research has focused on the effects of entrepreneurship on growth, reverse causality is also possible. Indeed, this seems more likely than not, since firm formation activities are known to be more frequent in high-growth periods (Audretsch and Fritsch 1994; Reynolds 1994). This consideration, and the importance of treating lag structures carefully as spillover effects take time to transmit changes in value and employment (Audretsch and Fritsch 2002), again suggest the need for structural modelling; though little of that has been attempted (at least to my knowledge) to date.

Topics deserving further statistical analysis include the effects of local unemployment on the propensity to start new firms and spillover externalities. The available evidence on local unemployment conditions is mixed, with for example Henley (2004) and Acs and Armington (2004) detecting no effects using UK and US data respectively, while Niittykangas and Tervo (2005) report positive effects using a panel of Finnish data. Arguably, finer-grained panel data are needed to resolve this issue. Second, we still lack detailed micro evidence of spillover externalities. The proxies that have been used in the literature have been useful certainly, but rather crude (Audretsch and Feldman, 1996). Third, it is still unclear whether it is better to start up in local rather than national markets, with conflicting evidence coming from Brüderl et al. (1992) and Bhide (2000), among others. These are not issues on which a consensus looks likely to emerge any time soon; greater clarification would however be welcome.

2.5 Policy Issues

While theoretical models of entrepreneurship proliferate policy recommendations, rigorous quantitative analyses of government interventions are scarcer. Fortunately, robust policy evaluation methods are beginning to emerge, and disseminate through the literature. One example is matching approaches which compare outcomes for program participants and members of control groups. For instance, Meager et al. (2003) used this approach to assess a British business support scheme for youths called the Prince's Trust, while Almus (2004) also used one to evaluate start-up loan assistance programmes in Germany in the 1990s. Another example is to control for selection bias into government programmes, as in Wren and Storey (2002) in the context of the UK's Enterprise Initiative scheme. However, despite the welcome improvement in the rigour of statistical evaluation methods, further work remains to be done to develop and disseminate these methods in the wider scholarly community. Some intrinsically difficult problems remain, including evaluating the true additionality of programs, such as loan guarantee schemes (Riding and Haines 2001); and estimating the externalities generated by entrepreneurs—although there have been some ambitious efforts along these lines (Nordhaus 2004).

On a positive note, solid progress is now being made on several empirical fronts in the policy domain. For example, it is becoming clear that courts play a central role in enforcing loan contracts, which has important direct effects on the efficiency of entrepreneurship (Jappelli et al. 2005; Zazzaro 2005). Also, less draconian bankruptcy laws do seem to promote entrepreneurship (Fan and White, 2003; Berkowitz and White 2004). Research using time series data have detected generally negative effects from government regulations on entrepreneurship (Kanniainen and Vesala 2005; Torrini 2005). The evidence on taxation and entrepreneurship is reviewed in another chapter, by Herb Schuetze;[1] here again, empirical work seems to be clarifying the role of policy in practice.

2.6 Summary

To summarise, it is clear that progress has been and continues to be made in many areas of statistical data collection and analysis in applied entrepreneurship research. Throughout the chapter, I have tried to balance a generally favourable view towards this progress with an attempt to identify areas where further improvements are needed. There are certainly some cases where theory has overtaken the current state of the art in statistical measurement, and where the latter needs to catch up, including competing theories of entrepreneurial start-up finance; social capital of entrepreneurs; and the distinction between productive and unproductive entrepreneurship. I would expect to see individual researchers rising to some of these challenges, by compiling their own data suited to the particular task at hand. It is not practical to expect statistical agencies to obtain these data themselves, though they may in the future play a greater role in commissioning and distributing novel large scale data sets, to promote their more widespread utilisation.

What of the future for statistical methods in applied entrepreneurship research? I would expect to see greater use of experimental methods in entrepreneurship research, rather than continued almost exclusive reliance on questionnaire-based instruments; a recent example of this is Coelho et al (2004). There are several areas where experimental evidence could help to distinguish between rival theories, including models of credit markets, and entrepreneurial learning frameworks. Future researchers might also want to control empirically for individuals' measured preferences and cognitive biases, as exemplified by Landier and Thesma (2003), for example. However, I hope that future researchers rein back efforts to model entrepreneurs' attitudes and perceptions; the danger here is of "cheap talk", whereby entrepreneurs give systematically misleading responses to survey interviewers.

Another statistical method I see becoming more popular in applied entrepreneurship research in the future is the use of simulation and calibration methods. As theories of entrepreneurship become more complicated, and broader linkages are made between previously disparate topics, tractable structural modelling will become more complex and maybe even impossible. We have already seen several examples of simulation and calibration methods in the economics of entrepreneurship, including the evaluation of government credit programs (Gale 1991; Li 2002); the optimal taxation of entrepreneurs (Parker 1999); entrepreneurs' life cycle savings

---

[1] Chapter 10

and investment decisions (Quadrini 2000; Meh 2005); and entrepreneurs' asset portfolio decisions (Polkovnichenko 2003; Hintermaier and Steinberger 2005). This trend looks set to continue. Finally, for the reasons outlined throughout in this chapter, I foresee greater usage in applied entrepreneurship research of panel data and more sophisticated statistical estimators, such as instrumental variables and policy evaluation methods. What seems certain is that future researchers operating at the empirical frontiers of this field will need superior statistical training as never before.

References

Acs Z, Armington C (2004) The impact of geographic differences in human capital on service firm formation rates. Journal of Urban Economics 56:244–78

Acs Z, Audretsch D, Braunerhjelm P, Carlsson B (2004) The missing link: The knowledge filter and entrepreneurship in endogenous growth. CEPR Discussion Paper No. 4783 (www.cepr.org/pubs/dps/DP4783.asp)

Almus M (2004) Job creation through public start-up assistance? Applied Economics 36:2015–24

Audretsch D, Feldman M (1996) R&D spillovers and the geography of innovation and production. American Economic Review 86:630–40

Audretsch D, Fritsch M (1994) The geography of firm births in Germany. Regional Studies 28:359–65

Audretsch D, Fritsch M (2002) Growth regimes over time and space. Regional Studies 36:113–24

Berkowitz J, White MJ (2004) Bankruptcy and small firms' access to credit. Rand Journal of Economics 35:69–84

Bhide AV (2000) The Origin and Evolution of New Businesses. Oxford University Press, Oxford

Bitler MP, Moskowitz TJ, Vissing-Jorgensen A (2005) Testing agency theory with entrepreneur effort and wealth. Journal of Finance 60:539–76

Blanchflower D (2000) Self-employment in OECD countries. Labour Economics 7:471–505

Blanchflower D, Levine PB, Zimmerman DJ (2003) Discrimination in the small-business credit market. Review of Economics & Statistics 85:930–43

Brüderl J, Preisendörfer P, Ziegler R (1992) Survival chances of newly founded business organisations. American Sociological Review 57:227–42

Carroll R, Holtz-Eakin D, Rider M, Rosen HS (2000) Entrepreneurs, income taxes and investment, in Does Atlas Shrug? In: Slemrod JB (ed) The Economic Consequences of Taxing the Rich. Russell Sage, New York, pp 427–55

Caselli F, Gennaioli N (2005) Credit constraints, competition, and meritocracy. Journal of the European Economics Association 3:679–89

Coelho MP, de Meza D, Reyniers DJ (2004) Irrational exuberance, entrepreneurial finance and public policy. International Tax & Public Finance 11:391–417

Ekelund J, Johansson E, Järvelin MJ, Lichtermann D (2005) Self-employment and risk aversion—evidence from psychological test data. Labour Economics 12:649–59

Fan W, White MJ (2003) Personal bankruptcy and the level of entrepreneurial activity. Journal of Law & Economics 46:543–67

Gale WG (1991) Economic effects of federal credit programs. American Economic Review 81:133–52

Garcia-Mainar I, Montuenga-Gomez VM (2005) Education returns of wage earners and self-employed workers: Portugal vs. Spain. Economics of Education Review 24:161–70

Gartner WB, Shane SA (1995) Measuring entrepreneurship over time. Journal of Business Venturing 10:283–301

Gentry WM, Hubbard RG (2004) Entrepreneurship and household saving. BEP Advances in Economic Analysis & Policy 4(1):1–55

Gompers P, Lerner J, Scharfstein D (2005) Entrepreneurial spawning: Public corporations and the genesis of new ventures, 1986 to 1999. Journal of Finance 60:577–614

Hamilton BH (2000) Does entrepreneurship pay? An empirical analysis of the returns to self-employment. Journal of Political Economy 108:604–31

Heaton J, Lucas D (2000) Portfolio choice and asset prices: the importance of en-trepreneurial risk. Journal of Finance 55:1163–98

Henderson R (1993) Underinvestment and incompetence as responses to radical innovation Evidence from the photolithographic alignment equipment industry. Rand Journal of Economics 24(2):248–70

Hintermaier T, Steinberger T (2005) Occupational choice and the private equity premium puzzle. Journal of Economic Dynamics & Control 29:1765–83

Hochguertel S (2005) The dynamics of self-employment and household wealth: new evidence from panel data. Mimeo Department of Economics Free University of Amsterdam May 25

Hurst E, Lusardi A (2004) Liquidity constraints, household wealth, and entrepreneurship. Journal of Political Economy 112:319–47

Jappelli T, Pagano M, Bianco M (2005) Courts and banks: Effects of judicial enforcement on credit markets. Journal of Money Credit & Banking 37(2):223–44

Kanniainen V, Vesala T (2005) Entrepreneurship and labour market institutions. Economic Modelling 22:828–47

Landier A, Thesma D (2003) Financial Contracting with Optimistic Entrepreneurs: Theory and Evidence. Paper presented at AFA 2004 San Diego Meetings. http://ssrn.com/abstract=479581

Li W, (2002) Entrepreneurship and government subsidies: a general equilibrium analysis. Journal of Economic Dynamics & Control 26:1815–44

Lyssiotou P, Pashardes P, Stengos T (2004) Estimates of the black economy based on consumer demand approaches. Economic Journal 114:622–40

Meager N, Bates P, Cowling M (2003) An evaluation of business start-up support for young people. National Institute for Economic Research 59:59–72

Meh A (2005) Entrepreneurship, wealth inequality and taxation. Review of Economic Dynamics 8:688–719

Moskowitz TJ, Vissing-Jorgensen A (2002) The returns to entrepreneurial investment: a private equity premium puzzle? American Economic Review 92:745–78

Niittytkangas H, Tervo H (2005) Spatial variations in intergenerational transmission of self-employment. Regional Studies 39:319–32

Nordhaus WD (2004) Schumpeterian profits in the American economy: Theory and measurement. NBER Working Paper No. 10433 NBER Cambridge MA

Parker SC (1996) A time series model of self-employment under uncertainty. Economica 63:459–75

Parker SC (1997) The distribution of self-employment income in the United Kingdom, 1976–1991. Economic Journal 107:455–66

Parker SC (1999) The optimal linear taxation of employment and self-employment incomes. Journal of Public Economics 73:107–23

Parker SC (2002) Do banks ration credit to new enterprises? And should governments intervene? Scottish Journal of Political Economy 49:162–95

Parker SC (2003) Does tax evasion affect occupational choice? Oxford Bulletin of Economics & Statistics 65:379–94

Parker SC, van Praag CM (2006) Schooling, capital constraints and entrepreneurial performance: The endogenous triangle. Journal of Business & Economic Statistics (Forthcoming)

Parker SC, Robson MT (2004) Explaining international variations in self-employment: evidence from a panel of OECD countries. Southern Economic Journal 71:287–301

Parker SC, Rougier J (2006) Self-employment and the retirement decision. Applied Economics (Forthcoming)

Parker SC, Belghitar Y, Barmby T (2005) Wage uncertainty and self-employed labour supply. Economic Journal 115:C190–C207

Paulson AL, Townsend R, Karaivanov A (2006) Distinguishing limited liability from moral hazard in a model of entrepreneurship. Journal of Political Economy 114:100–44

Pissarides CA, Weber G (1989) An expenditure-based estimate of Britain's black economy. Journal of Public Economics 39:17–32

Polkovnichenko V (2003) Human capital and the private equity premium. Review of Economic Dynamics 6:831–45

Quadrini V (2000) Entrepreneurship, saving, and social mobility. Review of Economic Dynamics 3:1–40

Rees H, Shah A (1986) An empirical analysis of self-employment in the UK. Journal of Applied Econometrics 1:95–108

Reynolds PD (1994) Autonomous firm dynamics and economic growth in the United States 1986–1990. Regional Studies 28:429–42

Riding AL, Haines Jr G (2001) Loan guarantees: Costs of default and benefits to small firms. Journal of Business Venturing 16:595–612

Stel A van, Carree M, Thurik AR (2005) The effect of entrepreneurial activity on national economic growth. Small Business Economics 24:311–21

Taylor MP (1996) Earnings, independence or unemployment: why become self-employed? Oxford Bulletin of Economics & Statistics 58:253–66

Torrini R (2005) Cross-country differences in self-employment rates: The role of institutions. Labour Economics 12:661–83

Wagner J (2004) Are young and small firms hothouses for nascent entrepreneurs? Evidence from German micro data. Working Paper No. 301 University of Lüneburg.

Wong PK, Ho YP, Autio E (2005) Entrepreneurship, innovation and economic growth: Evidence from GEM data. Small Business Economics 24:335–50

Wren C, Storey DJ (2002) Evaluating the effect of 'soft' business support upon small firms' performance. Oxford Economic Papers 54:334–65

Zazzaro A (2005) Should courts enforce credit contracts strictly? Economic Journal 115:166–84

Chapter 3
Entrepreneurial Tools

José María O'kean and José Manuel Menudo

Abstract The required tools for the analysis of the entrepreneur and their economic actions are absence and some confusion does exist which impedes theoretical development and empirical testing. The aim of this article is to set out a collection of analytical tools which in turn makes it difficult to draw-up economic policy used to foster entrepreneurship. For this purpose, the present paper given attention to the identification of the nature of the entrepreneur and his economic function; to study the composition and quality of the entrepreneurial network and the factors which affect the appearance of said economic agents.

3.1 Introduction

The economy is a tool-box; but the set of tools is not complete. The appropriate tools for the analysis of the entrepreneur and their economic actions are notable for their absence (Fellner 1983; Barreto 1989).

Numerous authors have rummaged in the box searching for the appropriate tools, or have even tried to create other new ones.[1] Nevertheless it is certain that even amongst those researchers engaged in this area of economic investigation that we term "entrepreneurship", no methodological agreement exists regarding the research programme and its heuristic that might help us avoid the confusion that often arises (Machlup 1967).

It is true that the entrepreneur is a difficult agent to observe in its pure state (Shapiro 1983). It is perhaps for this reason that there appears to be lack of empirical data on the composition of the entrepreneurial network, as well as on the possible indicators of the qualities of the said network.

José M O'kean
Universidad Pablo de Olavide
jmokean@upo.es

[1] See Baumol (1995), Kilby (1971), Kirzner (1973), Casson (1982), Wu (1989), Schultz (1990), Adaman and Devine (2002), amongst others.

Also problems exist in detecting the nature of the entrepreneurial function. At times, this function appears in a moment of innovation and after, as occurs with the "Schumpeterian phantom", disappears for a long period of time. Other times, it is the prey, as Kilby affirms, which everyone says they have seen but no one has been able to capture.

Many have written about the relevance of entrepreneurs in a period of economic growth and their role at the heart of economic activity within market systems.[2] And there exist countless articles on how economic theory has forgotten the entrepreneur.[3] Also, it is certain that we can find serious studies on entrepreneurial action,[4] but which have not been accepted as constituting general economic theory by the academics working in this field.

The truth is that the tool-box continues to be relatively empty and some confusion does exist which impedes theoretical development and empirical testing, which in turn makes it difficult to draw-up economic policy for the promotion of entrepreneurial activity.

Nevertheless, we believe the literature neglects the existence of some tools, more or less accepted, that could be utilised to generate an economic theory of the entrepreneur that could be integrated, without too much distress, into economic analysis.

The aim of this article is to set out a series of themes relevant for the elaboration of a general theory of the entrepreneur and, accordingly, to establish a collection of analytical tools with which to deepen our understanding of the role of the entrepreneur and perhaps to facilitate the development of future research in the field.

The present paper is structured along different study themes in which, in each case, the initial hypothesis and proposed tools will be set out. In essence it seeks to advance in the identification of the nature of the entrepreneur and his economic function; to study the composition and quality of the entrepreneurial network and the factors which affect the appearance of said economic agents.

---

[2] The work of Treadway (1969) y Hawawini (1984), are examples of models of entrepreneurial behaviour amidst uncertainty, while the work of Williams (1983), Grabowski y Vernon (1987), Romer (1990) and Segerstrom (1991), amongst others, represents attempts to create a model around the Schumpeterian innovative entrepreneur. Chandler (1990), Scherer and Ross (1990), Dosi (1988), Thurik (1996) and Carree (2002) demonstrate the influence of entrepreneurial activity in the changes in the productive structure towards those that favour economic growth. Also the empirical literature shows the effects of entrepreneurial activity on economic growth (Leff, 1979; Wennekers and Thurik, 1999; Carree and Thurik, 2003).

[3] See Baumol (1968), Kilby (1971), Kirzner (1973), Casson (1982), Blaug (1986) or Schultz (1990).

[4] One can cite the work of Wilken (1979), Baumol (1983), Casson (1982), Kilby (1982), Jones and Svejnar (1985), Roskamp (1979), Kilhstrom and Laffont (1979), Chamley (1983), Bond (1986), amongst others.

3.2 Entrepreneurs: Agents and Productive Figures

3.2.1 Initial Hypothesis

We consider that it is possible to introduce the figure of the entrepreneur into diverse theoretical constructions—the theory of oligopoly and monopoly, the theory of innovation and growth, welfare economics, the theory of organization, management science, statistical description, operational research and consultation—if we correctly differentiate between the various productive factors.[5]

In our paper we accept as our initial hypothesis, following the tradition of Cantillon, Say, Marshall and Walras amongst other authors (O'kean and Menudo 2003), that entrepreneurial activity constitutes an additional productive factor, along with natural recourses, labour and capital (Schultz 1975; Baumol 1990; and Casson 1982, 1997).

3.2.2 Factors, Agents and Income

If we accept entrepreneurial activity as constituting a further productive factor, the resultant four productive factors determine other productive agents that have property rights or the availability of these factors. Thus, four productive agents can be identified: owners of natural resources, workers, capital and entrepreneurs. These four factors bestow on their owners four distinct incomes: natural resource rents, work salaries, interest or rents form capital and entrepreneurial earnings.

Table 3.1 allows us to differentiate between the productive factors, the agents that are owners of these factors or develop this productive action, and the income that these productive agents receive. In this way we can emphasize four production factors, four productive agents and four incomes, where "entrepreneurial earnings" refers to the income received for the carrying out of the entrepreneurial function, later defined.

Table 3.1 Factors, agents and incomes

Productive Factors	Productive Agents	Incomes
Land, Natural resources	Landowner, Owner	Rent
Labour	Worker	Salary
Capital	Capitalist	Interest
Entrepreneurial function	Entrepreneur	Entrepreneurial earnings

---

[5] There also exist writings that do not consider entrepreneurial activity as a factor of production (Abraham and Gurzynski 1987), considering that entrepreneurial activity and the decision-making process as unconsciousness (Harper 2003). The entrepreneurial activity is more than a stock of knowledge, and without rejecting these approaches, our objective is to develop theoretical arguments with a strong basis and general applicability that will go beyond the hunches and impulses found in all decision-making.

3.2.3 Productive Figures

The main difficulty in studying the entrepreneurial function derives from the impossibility of visually isolating the entrepreneurial agent. In reality what can visualised is what we call productive figures, which tend to be physical persons that bring together diverse productive agents and therefore the property or the availability of diverse production factors. Thus, the owner is the person in which the role of capitalist and entrepreneur coincide; the manager refers to that person who is both entrepreneur and worker; the self-employed person a fusion of entrepreneur, worker and capitalist; and we can call farmer the physical person who combines the four productive factors and the four productive agents.

Table 3.2 illustrates some of these possible productive figures, and in this way we differentiate between owner (entrepreneur and capitalist), the manager (entrepreneur and worker), the self-employed or artisan (entrepreneur, capitalist and worker) and the farmer (in which the four productive agents coincide), applying a terminology to these productive figures which has a certain classic ring to it but which still remains useful for our objective.

Undoubtedly the productive entrepreneurial "agent" is often confused with the "productive figure" of the owner and this causes considerable confusion regarding entrepreneurial activity and principally about the origins of the incomes it generates. In general, the accumulation of interests or capital rents and entrepreneurial earnings coincide in the figure of the owner.[6] And for this reason it could be convenient to use the term "profit", as payment from the productive figure which includes the entrepreneurial agent, but always bearing in mind that said term also refers to different incomes as payment of different factors.

This productive figure tool can permit a more efficient empirical approach to the study of the managerial/entrepreneurial function, accepting that in general our analysis is concerned with productive figures rather than agents.

Table 3.2 Agents and productive figures

Productive Figures	Owner	Manager	Artisan Self-employed	Farmer
Owner				
Worker				
Capitalist				
Entrepreneur				

---

[6] As we all know, the concept of profit is conceived in different ways according to the perspective adopted. Thus, it may refer to book profit, tax profit or financial gain and includes all the productive activity costs, including those of opportunity. According to the property structure, conditioned by the productive figure (self employed, owner, corporate entity), the size of the profits will differ. In addition, if we accept one of the basic hypothesis of entrepreneurial theory, such as the existence of market disequilibrium, which leads to profit opportunities, the concept of profit must open the way for the creation of a surplus, which will be appropriated by some economic agent or other, according to the definition of the firm's property rights.

3.3 Entrepreneurial Function Vectors

Without doubt the biggest advance and agreement reached in entrepreneurial theory is due to the greater importance given to studying the role of the entrepreneurial function (functional hypothesis) instead of concentrating on identifying the figure of the entrepreneur (indicative hypothesis), which until now has been an unfruitful line of investigation.

From the various contributions it can be concluded that the entrepreneurial function is composed of four vectors or theoretical principals, with perhaps the addition of one other that could be of use. This structuring in vectors permits us to combine the different theoretical contributions in a compatible way, with the aim of developing a single entrepreneurial function. Thus, we avoid the controversies over which concept of the entrepreneur is the most important or useful (Kirzner, 1979b). Each vector implies a study area where specialists employ their own concepts. The integration of these vectors claims to understand what the specialists working in the other areas are doing so as fuse them together to form a single and generic entrepreneurial function.

Amongst the main vectors four grand theories on the managerial/entrepreneurial function stand out:

(a) *Leibenstein' entrepreneur responsible for reducing those inefficiencies that are always existent in the company's production processes.*
We can briefly sum up Leibenstein's contribution (1969, 1979) in an entrepreneurial scenario characterised by the permanent existence of inefficiencies brought about by transaction costs, the lack of specification inherent in labour contracts and gaps in knowledge. These inefficiencies incur costs far superior to the theoretically minimal ones. The firms do not minimize their costs and a degree of inefficiency exists (X-Inefficiency) that has to be reduced. The entrepreneur for Leibenstein is the agent permanently responsible for reducing the degree of inefficiency in his firm. It is here that the first role of the entrepreneurial function can be identified.

(b) *Kirzner's entrepreneur who seizes the profit opportunities that always exist in the market.*
The second theory we consider is devised by Kirzner (1973, 1979a, 1985), who thinks that the entrepreneurial function is more justified in the market process than in the firm and in an environment of insufficient information. This lack of information means existing profit opportunities are only surmised by the most perceptive. Detecting these profit opportunities and undertaking the necessary actions to take advantage of them constitute, for Kirzner, the essence of the entrepreneurial function. Entrepreneurs are therefore agents that contribute significantly to the process of market equilibrium and amongst their qualities one should stress their permanent state of alert in an environment in which information is not perfect.

(c) *Knight's entrepreneur that faces up to uncertainty by predicting the future.*

The introduction of time and uncertainty regarding the future, constitute the basis of Knight's theory (1921) on the entrepreneur and the third vector of the entrepreneurial function. To understand this theory it is necessary to differentiate between a situation of risk and a situation of uncertainty. Faced with a situation of risk, the agent responsible knows the possible scenarios and calculates the possibilities of said scenarios occurring. Faced with a situation of uncertainty the scenarios are unknown and its possibilities non-existent. In general decisions that have implications over a long period of time are subject to situations of uncertainty. The entrepreneur is the agent responsible for converting a situation of uncertainty into a situation of risk. He tackles uncertainty, he determines the possible scenarios that could arise and analyses the probability of their occurring. The agent who is the owner of the financial resources will be the one who assumes the risk. Knight's entrepreneur will have to venture to prophesize on the future and will act accordingly; his function is none other than to confront risk. The scenario where he acts is not a situation of imperfect information which he perceives and other economic agents ignore, as Kirzner claimed, but rather one where he will evaluate the future environment, a situation in which there is no information.

(d) *Schumpeter's innovative entrepreneur.*

The fourth entrepreneurial function theory is the aforementioned contribution of Schumpeter's innovative entrepreneur. The Schumpeterian entrepreneur operates within the context of a cyclical process of economic development. The entrepreneur is an agent that destroys the equilibrium with the process of creative destruction. This action is the essence of economic development since it provokes adaptive responses by the rest of the agents. The nature of the creative response consists of companies, industries or economies acting outside the existing practical field. This is characterised by the fact that the aforementioned ordinary inference rules on pre-existing data cannot be applied; because it models the following course of events and their results over the long term; and thirdly, it has evidently linked, to a greater or lesser extent, to: the quality of personal available in a society, the relative quality of the personal, that is to say, the quality available in a determined area of activity relative to the quality simultaneously available in other fields, and the decisions, actions and way individuals behave (Schumpeter 1947).

For Schumpeter (1912) there exist five types of innovation: introducing a new good or distinct quality of this good; introducing of a new production method; opening a new market; securing the exploitation of a new source of raw materials or semi-manufactured goods; and creating a new industrial organisation.

The Schumpeterian entrepreneurial theory has become the most characteristic of all the existing proposals, in the frustrated attempt to introduce the entrepreneur into conventional economic theory (see Blaug 1983).

His innovative entrepreneur is pretty different from the capitalist, manager, owner, or even the company itself, although several of these facets do coincide in the same physical person (Schumpeter 1947). His function does not consist especially in invent anything nor create in any way the conditions that the company exploits.[7] In consists of achieving results (Schumpeter 1950).

The dynamic process brought about by the innovative entrepreneur is well known, and leads to a new market equilibrium and the gradual disappearance of the extraordinary profits responsible for the "adaptive response". For Schumpeter, strictly speaking, the imitator is not the entrepreneur, and the innovative agent, will cease to be considered as such if he does not carry out new combinations in practise effectively (Schumpeter 1912).

It is for this reason that we have referred to the Schumpeterian ghost, to the extent that for Schumpeter an agent is only an entrepreneur when he innovates but ceases to be one when he takes on other, non-innovative, activities. This presupposes, by definition, that the entrepreneurial function is excellent and that entrepreneurs are invisible most of the time.

(e) *Finally we can define a fifth entrepreneurial function; typical of the way of the entrepreneur behaves in politicized markets*, where the State intervenes to alter the economic environment, for its own benefit or for that of a particular group. The essence of this theory lies in the relevance of the State in the modern economy. As a result of its actions new economic environments and new profit opportunities arise. In general, the entrepreneurial agent will keep an eye the totality of actions that constitute the economic policy of the different governments. Some entrepreneurs will even be tempted to influence strategic public agents—those that take the really relevant decisions—so that the actions carried by the public agencies favour their own interests. If these actions constitute part of the entrepreneurial function, or is merely rent-seeking, is a good subject for discussion; similarly if this activity is legal or whether it borders corruption. But they exist. There are many entrepreneurial agents that apparently "waste time" maintaining this type of relations. This vector allows us to appreciate the importance of the institutional representation of entrepreneurial interests, if its representatives manage, through concerted public action, to guarantee a more favourable economic environment for its associates whose interests they represent (see O'kean 1991).

3.4 Entrepreneurial Network

How to step from the functional hypothesis to the indicative hypothesis? That is to say, to step from studying what the entrepreneur *does*, to studying who the entrepreneur *is*. For us the entrepreneur is the one who performs one or all of the entrepreneurial function vectors, an action that results in the design and implementa-

---

[7] Regarding the debate between the functional and indicative approaches see Casson (1982), Sánchez Gil (1966) and O'kean (1991).

tion of the company's competitive strategy. This assumption, due to its importance, requires a brief explanation.

Firstly, we think that the entrepreneurial agent is that or those that design or implement the company's strategy. This permits us to overcome the traditional limitations of the indicative hypothesis, and, at the same time, to conceive that in some companies the entrepreneur is an individual agent, while in others the entrepreneurial function is carried out by various people, by way of the staff or management team.

The strategic design, once again, will deal with reducing inefficiencies, innovation, searching for new profit opportunities, or the definition of future scenarios. Understanding some of these vectors, through the design or implementation of the competitive entrepreneurial strategy, contributes to the performance of the entrepreneurial function.

On the other hand, as we will see below, being a entrepreneur does not mean being an "excellent entrepreneur". If these vectors are not undertaken with excellence, the quality of the entrepreneurial function will be carried out poorly, but will still be carried out.

3.4.1 Composition of the Entrepreneurial Network

The group of agents that perform the entrepreneurial function, be it in a certain sector, region or country constitute the entrepreneurial network of said sector, region or country. It permits us to conceive the entrepreneurial network as being composed of two types of entrepreneurial agents: individual entrepreneurs, and in the case of larger firms, corporate entrepreneurs, in which the entrepreneurial function is carried out by diverse natural persons. Amongst the individual entrepreneur we can even differentiate between employers and the self-employed (own-account worker), as we have done in fig. 3.1, two professional categories on which we can find homogenous statistical data in the quarterly labour market surveys, carried out by the national statistics office.

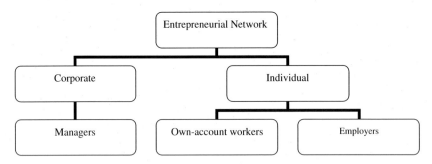

Fig. 3.1 Entrepreneurial network

3.4.2 *Quality of the Entrepreneurial Network*

Not all entrepreneurs carry out their activities to the same level of quality. We disagree, as we have indicated, with those, such as Schumpeter or Schultz amongst others, that think that the entrepreneur is only considered as such when he performs a certain vector of entrepreneurial function with *excellence*, ceasing to be so once his activity converts itself into a routine. For this reason we consider necessary to distinguish between four categories within the entrepreneurial network, dealing with its quality, as we did in fig. 3.2, differentiating between, an excellent entrepreneurial network, imitator, routine, and inexistent or insufficient (see O'kean 1991).

While the first category of the network would be that which is capable of designing and implementing innovative strategies, which reduce inefficiencies, confront uncertainty and perceive and grab new profit opportunities, the second would be characterized by agents who study the competitive strategies of the best, and copy them. The entrepreneurial network would be routine when it is predominantly made up of companies that, year after year, continue to manage their entrepreneurial without appreciable change. Finally, if, on studying a region or country, a lack of entrepreneurial activity is noted, the entrepreneurial network is then to be considered vacuous or insufficient for the economy's employment and growth requirements.

The entrepreneurial network categories also permit us to suggest a sequence of entrepreneurial promotion policy, that could invigorate a routine network, shifting it towards imitation and finally towards excellence or directly confront the inexistent/insufficient entrepreneurial network scenario. Frequently entrepreneurial promotion policies are designed without really knowing the quality of the entrepreneurial network, and seek to attain a degree of excellence, which given the initial network, cannot be achieved immediately.

Undoubtedly the indicators of entrepreneurial network quality is of the tasks yet to completed and the work of Sweeny (1987), amongst others, can serve as a reference, although one has to recognise that perhaps this may be one of the most complex tasks pending.

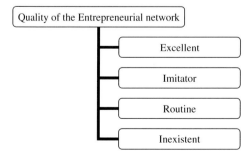

Fig. 3.2 Quality of the entrepreneurial network

3.5 Variables that Affect the Appearance of Entrepreneurs

What determines that a entrepreneurial network is sufficient with respect to its components, and excellent regarding its quality? This is a key question in economic development and of concern to all economists working on this topic. It is also the most relevant question from an economic policy point of view.

If the entrepreneurial function represents another production factor, the logical thing would be to use the same focus in its analysis as with the rest of the factors and consider the functioning of the entrepreneurial market. But attempts to systematise the entrepreneurial market have been diverse and fairly unsuccessful.[8] The most difficult question is to determine the demand of the entrepreneurial function, since in the individual entrepreneur (the most characteristic), the same person physical person is at the same time, both the supply and the demand, and this clashes with the traditional market vision in which the suppliers and customers compete amongst themselves.

A way to advance in the study of the factors that determine the appearance of entrepreneurs is to consider, on one hand, the factors which affect the desire to carry out this activity (that would be the demand), and on the other hand, the costs and necessary requirements to carry out his function (that we could identify as the supply).[9]

To determine why the different economic agents wish to be entrepreneurs we can apply Kirzner's theory on the entrepreneurial function and affirm that the expected benefits of carrying out the entrepreneurial function are the main incentive to be entrepreneurs. Whether it was reducing entrepreneurial inefficiencies, recognising market disequilibrium that could reap profit opportunities, confronting uncertainty or innovating, the economic agents will decide to be entrepreneurs if they can obtain profits, company earnings to be exact, which is how we have called their specific income.

What does the possibility of seizing these company profits depend on?

1. Firstly, the general economic conditions, and, naturally, the macroeconomic policy is relevant. (see Audretsch, Wennekers and Verheul 2002)
2. Secondly, the degree of economic competition, given that if the information tends to be perfect, entrepreneurial agents will be in better conditions to detect profit opportunities and to initiate actions to seize said profits, that in regulated or imperfect markets. (see Lumpkin and Dess 1996; Thurik 2003).
3. On the quality of the entrepreneurial network itself, since an excellent entrepreneurial network will better detect entrepreneurial opportunities than

---

[8] See Kilby (1971), Hammeed (1974), Casson (1982), Schultz (1980), Kaiser (1990) and O'kean (2000).

[9] The development of these question can be seen in our work referred to above, in which the factors that influence the desire to be entrepreneurs such as expected income are presented as entrepreneurial demand and costs and requirements as the supply in the entrepreneurial market, noting that the term market is used as a theoretical tool; see O'kean (2000).

another of poor quality (Aldrich and Zimmer 1986). Policies for the promotion of entrepreneurs, accumulated experience and improved entrepreneurial management knowledge, can help to improve the quality of the entrepreneurial network (O'kean et al. 1988; Audrestsch et al. 2001).

4. Finally, technological change can leave an excellent entrepreneurial network obsolete, incapable of detecting new opportunities, new business, and an environment that nobody understands (Tansik andWolf 1996).

And with regard to supply, costs, and requirements, what does the entrepreneurial network's size depend on?

1. Firstly on psychological and social factors that make a sufficient number of suitably well-qualified agents decide to be entrepreneurs.[10] Education, social recognition, and, on occasions, values and even religious ideas affect the desire to be entrepreneurs (Lavoie 1991; Tiessen 1997).[11] Also channels for social advancement, and if entrepreneurial activity is the only way, marginalised social groups can rise up the social ladder (see Ulijn and Brown 2002).

2. On the necessary intellectual knowledge and the cost of acquiring it. Although one has to bear in mind that this knowledge, acquired in Universities and Business Schools, only represents a small percentage of the knowledge necessary to carry out the entrepreneurial function (see Murphy et al. 1991; Arenius and De Clercq 2005)

3. On required non-intellectual knowledge, that is much more important, and mainly is the result of experience and as such is a question of time and the right environment. The case methods followed in some Business Schools is a way of helping to acquire this knowledge (see Harper 2003).

4. On the availability of property laws governing the productive recourses necessary to carry out the entrepreneurial function (Hayek 1960, Rizzo 1985). This implies that the entrepreneur does not have to be the owner of the capital resources, but must be able gain access to them.

5. On the salary level that could be obtained in an equivalent job position given the candidate's profile and education, as an opportunity costs (Casson 2001). One would have to add a bonus to this salary for the greater dedication, responsibility and professional risk involved in being a entrepreneur.

6. On the total administrative paperwork that needs to be completed to be able to carry out entrepreneurial action.

7. Finally on transaction costs in the economy, that allows entrepreneurial activity to proceed in a swift and fluid manner, or on the contrary submits it to restrictions and barriers which hinder its completion (Williamson 1979).

---

[10] For an extensive review of the literature on the psychological factors of entrepreneurial activity see Brockhaus (1982), Gilad (1986), Ginsberg and Buchholtz (1989), Kets de Vries (1977) and Harper (2003).

[11] For a reference on the role of culture in productive activity, especially in those aspects relative to entrepreneurial activity see Casson (2000).

From this collection of variables, one can conclude that it is possible to outline an entrepreneurial promotion policy which affects some of these variables, when the policy-makers consider that the situation is critical. A society may have an insufficient, poor quality network owing to psychological and sociological factors, a lack of intellectual and non-intellectual knowledge, elevated transaction costs etc. Knowing the characteristics of the entrepreneurial network in which one wishes to act, is an unavoidable pre-requisite, and it does not appear that some successful experiences in a particular entrepreneurial network are transferable to another different productive network. Thus, for example, facilitating a population's access to finance makes no sense if they have no desire to be entrepreneurs or do not possess the necessary knowledge to take on this economic function.

3.6 Concluding Remarks

The economic theory on the entrepreneurial function is in need of some common analytical tools, and which help avoid confusion. In our opinion it is possible to establish some basic assumptions that could contribute to advancement in this direction.

We believe that we must accept the entrepreneurial function as another productive factor, and include it therefore in the production functions and in growth theory and recognise its importance within distribution theory (although this still requires effort in accepting the entrepreneurial market as a theoretical abstraction).

The difference between productive agent and productive figure could be very useful. It avoids confusion and may contribute to indispensable statistical research in order to know the economic reality and to be able to check theories and policies.

With regard to this differentiation, to distinguish between profit and entrepreneurial earnings is equally useful, the former being the total payments received by the productive figure in which the entrepreneurial agent is integrated and the latter concept the entrepreneurial agent's specific payment.

Considering the function as a sum of vectors in which we can integrate different theories can avoid debates which often produce more heat than light. The four vectors outlined which correspond to the theories forwarded by Leibenstein, Kirzner, Knight and Schumpeter represents a fairly common starting point.

The delimitation of the entrepreneurial network in its different typographies is the first step towards the study of the facts and to produce relevant statistics. Differentiating between individual entrepreneurs and corporations, and between employers and the self-employed, represents an interesting advance and permits the use of initial statistics via the quarterly survey of the labour market, carried out by national statistics.

Understanding that the entrepreneurial network is of varying quality, and accepting that an entrepreneurial agent is an entrepreneur even when he may not carry out, with excellence, some of the vectors that constitute the entrepreneurial function, opens up an interesting field of investigation which advances in a barrage of indicators about the quality of the network and advises policy-makers responsible for entrepreneurial promotion to adapt policies to suit the reality of the network on which they wish to intervene.

Knowing the variables that influence the appearance of entrepreneurs—accepting as a basis our proposed tools, and which are not yet complete—is the starting point for whatever entrepreneurial promotion activity. A factor for growth whose importance fortunately almost nobody brings into question.

Advancement in the study of the entrepreneurial function requires a common effort in the theoretical sphere and to complete the economic analytical tool-box. Entrepreneurial action is too important an economic activity for Economics and Business Administration students not to be able to find the entrepreneur in any introductory text to the subject. We must continue to advance in this research programme.

Acknowledgments We are grateful for inspiring remarks made by several participants of different meetings. Any remaining errors are nevertheless our responsibility.

References

Abraham H, Gurzynski Z (1987) The Entrepreneur as an non-factor. South African Journal of Economy 55(2):114–120

Adaman F, Devine P (2002) A reconsideration of the theory of entrepreneurship: a participatory approach. Review of Political Economy 14(3):329–55

Aldrich H, Zimmer C (1986) Entrepreneurship Through Social Networks. In: Greenfield SM, Strickon A (eds) Entrepreneurship and Social Change. Ballinger, NY, pp 45–53

Arenius P, De-Clercq D (2003) A Network-Based Approach on Opportunity Recognition. Small Business Economics 24(3):249–65

Audretsch D, Thurik AR, Verheul I, Wennekers AR (eds) (2002) Entrepreneurship: Determinants and Policy in a European-US Comparation. Kluwer Academic Publisher; Boston

Barreto H (1989) The Entrepreneur in Microeconomic Theory: Disappearance and Explanation. Routledge, London

Baumol W (1968) Entrepreneurship in Economic Theory. American Economic Review 58:64–71

Baumol W (1983) Toward Operational Models of Entrepreneurship. In: Ronen J (ed) Entrepreneurship. Lexington Books, MA, pp 29–48

Baumol W (1990) Entrepreneurship, Productive, Unproductive, and Destructive. Journal of Political Economy, 98(5):893–921

Baumol W (1995) Formal Entrepreneurship Theory in Economics: Existence and Bounds. In: Bull I, Thomas H, Willard G (eds) Entrepreneurship Perspectives on theory building. Pergamon, Oxford, pp 17–38

Bond EW (1986) Entrepreneurial Ability, Income Distribution, and International Trade. Journal of International Economics 20:343–356

Blaug M (1983) Marx, Schumpeter y la teoría del empresario. Revista de Occidente V (21–22): 117–130

Blaug M (1986) Economic History and the History of Economics. Wheatsheaf Books, Brighton

Brandstätter H (1997) Becoming an entrepreneur - A question of personality structure? Journal of Economic Psychology 18(2):157–177

Brockhaus RH (1982) The Psychology of the Entrepreneur. In: Kent CA, Sexton DL, Verper KH (eds) Encyclopedia of Entrepreneurship. Prentice Hall, New York, pp 39–57

Bull I, Thomas H, Willard G (1995) Toward a theory of entrepreneurship. In: Bull I, Thomas H, Willard G (eds) Entrepreneurship Perspectives on theory building. Pergamon, Oxford, pp1–16

Carree MA (2002) Industrial restructuring and economic growth. Small Business economics 18(4):243–55

Carree MA, Thurik AR (2003) The impact of entrepreneurship on economic growth. In Audretsch DB, Acs ZJ (eds) Handbook of Entrepreneurship Research. Kluwer Academic Publishers, Boston

Casson M (1982) The entrepreneur: An economic theory. Barnes & Noble Books, Totowa NJ

Casson M (1997) Information and organization: A new perspective on the theory of the Firm. Oxford University Press, New York

Casson M (2000) The Economics of Business Culture. Oxford Clarendon Press

Casson M (2001) Information and Organization: A new perspective on the Theory of the Firm. Oxford University Press, New York

Chamley C (1983) Entrepreneurial abilities and Liabilities in a Model of Self-selection. The Bell Journal of Economics 44(1):70–80

Chandler AD Jr (1990) Scale and Scope: The Dynamics of Industrial Capitalism. Harvard University, Cambridge, MA

Dosi G (1988) Sources, Procedures and microeconomic effects of innovation. Journal of Economic Literature 26(11):20–71

Fellner W (1983) Entrepreneurship in Economic Theory: The "Scientific Method" and Vicarious Introspection. In: Backman J (ed) Entrepreneurship and the Outlook for America. Collier Macmillan, New York, pp 25–54

Gilad B (1986) Entrepreneurial decision making: Some behavioural consideration. Gilad & Karsh: Handbook of economic behaviour vol. A. Greenwich JAI Press 1986, London

Ginsberg A, Buchholtz A (1989) Are Entrepreneurs a Breed Apart? A Look at the Future. Journal of General Management 15(2):32–40

Grabowski HG, Vernon JM (1987) Pioneers, Imitators, and Generics-A Simulation Model of Schumpeterian Competition. Quarterly Journal of Economics 102(3):491–525

Hamilton RT, Harper DA (1994) The Entrepreneur in Theory and Practice. Journal of Economic Studies 21(6):3–18

Harper D (2003) Foundations of Entrepreneurship and Economic Development. Routledge, London

Hawawini G (1984) Uncertainty and the production decisions of owner-managed and labor-managed firms. Oxford Economic-Papers 36(1):119–30

Hayek FA von (1937) Economics and Knowledge. Econometrica 4:33–54

Hayek FA von (1960) The Constitution of Liberty. Routledge, London

Hérbert RF, Link AN (1982) The entrepreneur. Praeger Publisher, New York

Jones DC, Svejnar J (1985) Participation, Profit Sharing, Worker Ownership and Efficiency in Italian Producer Cooperative. Economica 52(28):449–65

Kaiser CP (1990) Entrepreneurship and resource: Allocation. Eastern Economic Journal 16(1):9–20

Kets de Vries MFR (1977) The Entrepreneurial Personality: A Person at the Crossroads. Journal of Management Studies 4:34–57

Kilby P (1971) Hunting the Heffalump. Entrepreneurship and Economic Development. The Free Press, New York, pp 1–40

Kilby P (1993) An Entrepreneurial Problem. American Economic Review 73(2):106–111

Kilhstrom RE, Laffont JJ (1979) A General Equilibrium Entrepreneurial Theory of Firm Formation Based on Risk Aversion. Journal of Political Economy 87(4):719–49

Kirzner I (1973) Competencia y función empresarial. Unión Editorial, Madrid

Kirzner I (1979a) Perception, Opportunity and Profit. The University of Chicago Press, Chicago

Kirzner I (1979b) Comment: X-Inefficiency, Error, and the Scope for Entrepreneurship. In: Rizzo MJ (ed) Time Uncertainty and Disequilibrium Exploration of Austrian Themes. Lexington Books, Lexington MA, pp 140–51

Kirzner I (1985) Discovery and the Capitalist Process. The University of Chicago Press, Chicago

Knight F (1921) Riesgo, Incertidumbre y Beneficio. Aguilar, Madrid

Lumpkin GT, Dess GG (1996) Clarifying the entrepreneurial orientation construct and linking it to performance. Academic of Management Review 21:135–72

Lavoie D (1991) The Discovery and Interpretation of Profit Opportunities: Culture and the Kirzne-
    rian Entrepreneur. In: Berger B (ed) The Culture of Entrepreneurship. Institute for Contempo-
    rary Studies Press, San Francisco, pp 33–51
Leff N (1979) Entrepreneurship and Economic Development: The Problem Revisted. Journal of
    Economic Literature 17(1):46–64
Leibenstein H (1969) Entrepreneurship and Development. American Economic Review 58(2):
    72–83
Leibenstein H (1979) The General X-Efficiency Paradigm and the Role of the Entrepreneur. In:
    Rizzio MJ (ed) Time Uncertainty and Disequilibrium. Lexington, MA, pp 127–39
Machlup F (1967) Theories of the Firm: Marginalist, Behavioral, Managerial. American Economic
    Review 57(1):1–33
Murphy KM, Shleifer A, Vishny R (1991) The Allocation of Talent: Implications for Growth. The
    Quarterly Journal of Economics 106(2):503–30
O'kean JM, Barzelay M, Stone A (1988) Promoción empresarial: estrategias. Información Comer-
    cial Española 663:92–103
O'kean JM (1991) Empresario y Entorno Económico. Deusto, Bilbao
O'kean JM (2000) La teoría económica de la función empresarial: el mercado de empresarios.
    Alianza, Madrid
O'kean JM, Menudo J M (2003) La théorie de la fonction entrepreneurial chez J.-B. Say. La tradi-
    tion Cantillon-Turgot-Say. Potier JP, Tiran A (eds): Jean-Baptiste Say. Nouveaux Regards sur
    son Oeuvre Economica Paris 2003 577–603
Rizzo MJ (1985) Rules versus Cost-Benefits Analysis in the Common Law. Cato Journal 4(3):
    865–84
Romer PM (1990) Endogenous Technological Change. Journal of Political Economy 98(5): 71–102
Roskamp KW (1979) A Neo-Classical Macro-Economic Model: Entrepreneurs Bankers, Innova-
    tions and Excess Profits. Kredit-und-Kapital 12(1):42–55
Sánchez M (1966) Naturaleza y evolución de la función empresarial. Aguilar, Madrid
Segerstrom PS (1991) Innovation, Imitation, and Economic Growth. Journal of political economy
    99(4):807–27
Shapiro M (1983) The Entrepreneurial Individual in the Large Organization. In: Backman J (ed)
    Entrepreneurship and the Outlook for America. Collier Macmillan, New York, pp 55–82
Scherer FM, Ross D (1990) Industrial Market Structure and Economic Performance. Houghton
    Mifflin Company, Boston, MA
Schultz TW (1975) The Value of the Ability to Deal with Disequilibria. Journal of Economic
    Literature 13(3):827–846
Schultz TW (1980) Investment in entrepreneurial ability. Scandinavian Journal of Economics
    82:437–448
Schumpeter JA (1912) Teoría del desenvolvimiento económico. Fondo de Cultura Económica,
    México, 1976
Schumpeter JA (1950) Capitalismo, Socialismo y Democracia. Orbis, Barcelona, 1983
Sweeny GP (1987) Innovation, Entrepreneurs and Regional Development. London Printer
Tansik AD, Wolf G (1996) Entrepreneurial Roles in the Process of Tecnological Innovation. In:
    Libecap G (ed) Entreneurship and Innovation: The impact of Venture capital on the Develop-
    ment of new enterprise. Jai Press, London
Tiessen JH (1997) Individualism, Collectivism, and Entrepreneurship: A Framework for Interna-
    tional Comparative Research. Journal of Business Venturing 12(5):367–84.
Thurik AR (1996) Small firms, entrepreneuship and economic growth. In: Admiraal PH (ed) Small
    Business in the Modern Economy. Blackwell Publishers, Oxford
Thurik AR (2003) Entrepreneurship and Unemployment in the UK. Scottish Journal of Political
    Economy 50(3):264–90
Treadway AB (1969) On Rational Entrepreneurial Behaviour and the Demand for Investment.
    Review of Economic Studies 36:106 227–39
Ulijn J, Brown T (eds) (2002) Innovation, Entrepreneurship and Culture: The interaction between
    Technology, Progress and Economic Growth. Edward Elgar, Cheltenham

Wu SY (1989) Production, entrepreneurship and profit. Blackwell, Cambridge.
Wennekers S, Thurik R (1999) Linking Entrepreneurship and Economic Growth. Small Business
    Economics 13(1):27–55
Williams EE (1983) Entrepreneurship, Innovation and Economic Growth. Technovation 2:3–15
Williamson OE (1979) Transaction Cost Economics: The Governance of Contractual Relation.
    Journal of Law and Economics 22:233–261

Part II
Measurement: Dimensions, Indicators and Statistical Sources

Chapter 4
Understanding Entrepreneurship: Developing Indicators for International Comparisons and Assessments

Tim Davis

Abstract Everyone thinks entrepreneurship is important, including the OECD. There is a fairly extensive body of theoretical literature on entrepreneurship, its determinants and impacts but relatively little empirical work has been done by government policy analysts to analyse and compare entrepreneurship measures. In part this is due to the fact that limited data is available, especially international data.

Researchers argue about the link between entrepreneurship and growth, but everyone wants entrepreneurship even if the link to growth is not clear. There are myriad definitions that describe the notion of entrepreneurship in terms of high-level principles, but those definitions are not easily reflected through statistical measures. Some relatively straight-forward measures exist, but they do not necessarily reflect the entrepreneurship objectives that policy-makers want to pursue.

While virtually all countries are interested in entrepreneurship, the policy objectives that different countries pursue through entrepreneurship differ considerably. Some promote entrepreneurship for employment creation; others see it as a tool for improving productivity and international competitiveness. Nevertheless, most countries have shown a strong desire to understand entrepreneurship and to compare themselves to others so they can determine where it makes sense to copy successful policies, and where it does not.

The OECD has identified numerous government policy interests related to entrepreneurship and is proceeding to produce a periodic "Scoreboard" of internationally-comparable entrepreneurship indicators to assist evidence-based policy making. Data for the OECD Entrepreneurship Scoreboard will be drawn from both existing and new sources. A Manual for Measurement will be produced, to include definitions, methodologies and a framework of indicators.

Tim Davis
The OECD Entrepreneurship Indicators Project Tim Davis, Statistics Directorate, OECD
tim.davis@oecd.org

E. Congregado, *Measuring Entrepreneurship.*   39
© Springer 2008

4.1 Introduction

4.1.1 Background

For many years, economists and policymakers have identified "entrepreneurs" as important drivers for employment, innovation and economic growth. While it is generally accepted that entrepreneurship is "good", the links between entrepreneurship and various facets of economic growth are less well understood. The interest of both developed and developing countries in how government policies and other national "business environment" factors influence the rates and types of entrepreneurship has increased considerably in recent years.

While there is considerable interest in entrepreneurship throughout OECD countries, there is, as yet, neither an overall entrepreneurship statistical framework, including concepts and definitions, nor an agreed-to list of key indicators that are required to improve the collective understanding of entrepreneurship and its impacts. This situation has been due, in part, to financial constraints and also to differing statistical priorities among member countries. The OECD began to focus attention on entrepreneurship as part of its "Jobs Strategy" in the latter part of the 1990s and there have been some specific efforts to assemble information on entrepreneurship as part of Country Surveys and a number of targeted analytical pieces on entrepreneurship and/or growth. A brief summary of the OECD's work related to entrepreneurship is provided in the section "Highlights of Entrepreneurship Activities and Research at the OECD", below.

In addition to this analytical work, the OECD also maintains some SME- and entrepreneurship-related information in databases such as those on structural business statistics and labour force activities for member countries. Furthermore, data on R&D and innovation in databases maintained by Directorate for Science, Technology and Industry (DSTI) also might provide some useful insights into entrepreneurial behaviour in countries, though the inability to classify much of this information by firm size or age, or link it to an "entrepreneur", limits the utility of this data for entrepreneurship studies. Hence, in order to fully contribute to the policy debate and facilitate the development of specific evidence-based entrepreneurship policies there is a need for a more focussed and comprehensive programme of data on entrepreneurship.

In 2004, a number of developments conspired to give important impetus to the work on the development of new entrepreneurship statistics. An OECD Ministerial Meeting in Istanbul in 2004 called for countries to develop more robust statistics on entrepreneurship and SMEs to improve policy development and monitoring.[1] Also, a number of key OECD countries, led by Denmark, formed a small Consortium entitled the International Consortium for Dynamic Entrepreneurship Benchmarking.

---

[1] The Istanbul Ministerial also resulted in the creation of the Centre for Entrepreneurship, SMEs and Local Development at the OECD and this body, in turn, has been a strong voice for better international entrepreneurship data.

The countries all demonstrated their commitment to improving entrepreneurship data through financial contributions and the Consortium, in turn, provided some financial and research support to help the OECD advance its indicator work. Finally, the Kauffman Foundation of the United States, which has long supported practical research aimed at facilitating successful entrepreneurship, also offered financial resources.

An Expert Workshop, *Understanding Entrepreneurship: Issues and Numbers* was held in October 2005 and it provided considerable input from leading entrepreneurship researchers and policy analysts. Participants confirmed the importance of entrepreneurship and the need for comparable international indicators.

4.1.2 The Importance of Entrepreneurship

In recent years, entrepreneurship has been receiving a lot of attention from governments, academics, business support groups and others. Nurturing entrepreneurship is an explicit policy priority for many OECD countries, whether they already have significant levels of entrepreneurship or they are seen to be trailing the leaders in this domain.

Entrepreneurship programmes exist throughout the OECD. Ireland encourages expatriates to return to set up firms while Japan assists those in older age groups to be entrepreneurial. The European Community (EC) issued a Green Paper on entrepreneurship in 2003, detailing benefits and encouraging joint work on common practices. The EC followed with an Action Plan on entrepreneurship in 2004 and, subsequently, they regularly monitor progress on factors that affect entrepreneurship as well as on specific pro-entrepreneurship activities of member countries.[2] The UK has also repeatedly stressed the importance of entrepreneurship and has numerous support mechanisms in place. The Danish interest in, and attention to, entrepreneurship is well documented and they have taken the lead to engage other OECD countries in an International Consortium to support common understanding of issues and to tackle international measurement issues. In North America, Canada and the United States have public sector programs in place to support entrepreneurship, and many quasi-public or private bodies also support the development and growth of new and/or small businesses. Numerous countries use entrepreneurship as a component of regional development or assistance to depressed areas.

For many, the benefits of entrepreneurship are clear. Entrepreneurship is viewed as a critical activity to regenerate and sustain economic growth in strong economies and also as a means of boosting employment and productivity in depressed regions or in developing countries. The dynamic process of new firm creation introduces and disperses innovative products, processes and organisational structures throughout the economy. As firms enter and exit the market, theory suggests that the new arrivals will be more efficient than those they displace. Furthermore, existing firms

---

[2] Commission of the European Communities, 2003, 2004

that are not driven out are forced to innovate and become more productive to compete. Empirical support for this process of "creative destruction", first described by Schumpeter, has been provided by numerous studies by the OECD and others.[3] Entrepreneurship is a major force in economic dynamism.

At the OECD Expert Workshop in 2005, numerous aspects of the importance of entrepreneurship were identified by presenters, but two were underscored. The first relates to links between entrepreneurship and economic growth. The second concerns the role that entrepreneurship could play in improving the economic and social position of groups within society.

There is some debate about whether entrepreneurship causes economic growth or whether it is a facilitator or enabler of economic change. The link between entrepreneurship, productivity and economic growth was examined. The evidence appeared to be that both entry and exit played a very powerful role in enhancing productivity. If anything it appeared that if entrepreneurship led to the more rapid exit of low productivity firms, that this was particularly desirable when they were replaced by new firms that were more productive. Whilst that debate continues Workshop participants agreed that economic growth was assisted by a positive entrepreneurial climate.

It was recognised that entrepreneurship could also play an important social function. Some ethnic minorities, throughout history, have seen entrepreneurship as a way of escaping from disadvantage, particularly the case for recent immigrants. In other cases women have often not been able to be considered as equals in the male-controlled corporate structure and have seen entrepreneurship as an appropriate and desirable employment opportunity.

The U.S. record of high employment, high productivity and high economic growth is envied by many other countries. Many observers suggest that entrepreneurship and new firm creation (and turnover) are major factors behind the differences in economic performance. However, rates of firm exit and entry are not significantly different in the United States than, say, in Europe. What may be different, though, is the way the new firms grow in the U.S., and how they displace the former leaders. In this regard, it appears that the U.S. and Europe are moving apart. Eight out of the largest 25 firms in America in 1998 did not exist, or were very small, in 1960 while the largest 25 European firms in 1998 were already large in 1960. And this turnover at the top continues at a brisk pace in the American economy. It took 20 years to replace 1/3 of the Fortune 500 companies listed in 1960 yet only 4 years to replace 1/3 of those listed in 1998.[4]

Countries have not only shown interest in understanding entrepreneurship and its determinants within their borders, they have also expressed the desire to share and compare ideas and information concerning entrepreneurship. Nurturing entrepreneurship is non-competitive across countries. Successful entrepreneurial activity in one country does not reduce opportunities for entrepreneurship in another.

---

[3] Conway et al. (2005)

[4] Commission of the European Communities, 2003

"Entrepreneurship has always been important, but its role stands out in the present time of innovative change. Fostering a climate to help instil greater dynamism in the creation and expansion of firms is fundamental."[5]

4.1.3 Entrepreneurship and Job Creation

One of the questions that continue to arise concerns the role of small or new businesses in job creation. The fact that the issue is raised at all indicates significant changes in thinking over time. In North America, throughout the post-war years and well into the 1960s, governments and the public showed complete faith in the large corporation as the source of jobs and growth. Small firms were granted little attention and were considered as extras playing minor, bit parts in the economic theatre.

Now, a few decades later, many consider small and new businesses as the dominant force in the economy. This change in thinking began with the pioneering longitudinal studies of job creation in the U.S. by David Birch first released in 1979. His research, which showed that small firms created more jobs than large ones, was initially dismissed by many and his methods and sources were discredited. Canadian research in the early 1980s[6] showed results similar to those of Birch, and elicited similar reactions. Today, numerous studies have looked at job creation from many perspectives and the notion that SMEs create the majority of new jobs has become conventional wisdom for many—though not all. And even those who still favour the small-business-job-machine image realise that the net, national job creation figures are an oversimplification that hides the true nature of job creation and how dynamics change over time in response to various factors.

While debate about sources of jobs continues, it appears that differences are often due to concepts and measuring methods rather than any underlying differences in data. If a firm is categorised as small, upon entry, and then all subsequent employment growth is assigned to that original category, then virtually 100% of employment growth will be due to small firms. After all, virtually all firms were small at entry. But such a definition may not be helpful in a policy context. Approaches that will facilitate development of small firms will have little applicability to large corporations even though those corporations were once in the small category. Perhaps different measures of job creation are appropriate for different policy instruments.

While new firms are undoubtedly important, it is likely that established firms in most developed economies still generated the majority of gross new jobs. Evidence for Canada and the U.S. is illustrative in this regard.

One of the indisputable truths that has emerged from the job creation research is that slow changing total job figures, and even annual net job change figures, mask tremendous turbulence in job markets by geography and by sector as well as in the

---

[5] OECD 2001 new economy beyond the hype

[6] Canadian Federation of Independent Business

overall economy. Indeed, even within the firm, net job figures may hide the creation and destruction that takes place in different occupations.

Evidence confirms that the Schumpeterian process of creative destruction does indeed raise productivity and efficiency. Canadian studies shows that new firms are more productive and pay higher wages than exiting firms in a variety of industries. But new firm creation is not the sole contributor to productivity and employment growth. Existing firms also exhibit churn as some grow while others contract, without any entry or exit. Indeed, even within firms there is undoubtedly both expansion and contraction going on all the time, but very few measures would capture that internal churning since firm dynamics start with net figures at the firm level.

4.1.4 Highlights of Entrepreneurship Activities and Research at the OECD

The OECD has a long history of interest in entrepreneurship, but work has generally consisted of ad hoc, special studies or brief references to entrepreneurship in larger analytical works. Several papers by the DSTI and the Economics Department (ECO) have explored the relationship between new firm creation and economic performance. From time to time, data have also been assembled on particular aspects of entrepreneurship or on factors that may be related to levels or rates of entrepreneurship. For example, some SME data is maintained within the OECD business statistics data base and the Firm Level Data Project attempted to harmonise firm entry and exit data for ten OECD countries. A brief overview of some of the activities is provided below.

In 1992 the OECD Industry Committee requested compilation of statistics in support of more policy-oriented, empirical work on SMEs. The sustained high levels of unemployment across the OECD in the early nineties prompted analysts to focus attention on the relation between enterprise size and employment creation. Much of this work was presented at an OECD High-Level Workshop on SMEs: Employment, Innovation and Growth in 1995. An overview of the quantitative studies was presented in an OECD Working Paper in 1996 (Schreyer 1996).

Various analytical studies in recent years have also illustrated the OECD emphasis on entrepreneurship. Among them, Fostering Entrepreneurship: The OECD Jobs Strategy (1998), the Final Report of the OECD Growth Project, (2001), Firm Dynamics work by ECO, a study of Entrepreneurship and Local Development, by Alistair Nolan of the Local Economic and Employment Development Programme (LEED) (2003) and the work on Micro-Policies for Growth and Productivity (2005) are worth noting.

The OECD Jobs Strategy was a further initiative designed to find solutions to the high levels of unemployment that persisted in many OECD countries throughout the nineties. Entrepreneurship emerged as one of the promising ways of stimulating job creation without distorting market forces and the study Fostering Entrepreneurship (1998) was an effort to understand the factors that effect entrepreneurship both in general and in specific country situations. While recognising that no accepted standard for measuring entrepreneurship had been established, the study nonetheless determined that levels or rates of entrepreneurship varied considerably across OECD countries. The five-country study (Australia, The Netherlands, Spain, Sweden and the US) concluded that none of the countries had a perfect environment for entrepreneurship and thus that all could learn from the experiences of others. Based on the analysis of these five countries, a series of broad policy guidelines were enunciated. While the broad guidelines establish an excellent framework for further empirical examination, the work was never extended across a larger number of countries, in part due to a lack of international data.

In 2002, an OECD study of firm dynamics[7] using a new firm-level database revealed some interesting features of firm dynamics across OECD countries. Perhaps not surprisingly, it was found that burdensome regulation and costly workforce adjustment diminished the entry of new, small firms. It was also noted that in the US, entrant firms were smaller, and initially less productive, than those in Europe. Surviving firms in the US, however, expanded more rapidly than those in Europe.

The objective of the OECD Growth Project was to investigate the causes of differences in growth performance in OECD countries. The final report identified and investigated areas of major impact and strongly endorsed the positive role of entrepreneurship. In particular, the study showed that start-up businesses in the field of ICT and new technology sectors contributed strongly to productivity growth. Among the five key policy recommendations was one calling for action to stimulate firm creation and a variety of factors affecting creation rates were examined. As a result, additional recommendations on improving access to finance, reducing administrative burdens, removing barriers to entry, reducing bankruptcy and insolvency costs, improving entrepreneurship education and management training and promoting entrepreneurship spirit, were all advised.

The LEED study analysed many contributions of entrepreneurship to local development but cautioned against naïve expectations that entrepreneurship programmes would provide for quick solutions to problems such as unemployment. Indeed, the study noted that employment creation through entrepreneurship was often modest and was rarely a solution to the social exclusion of large numbers of persons with marginal skills. Nevertheless, the study argued that other benefits of entrepreneurship promotion, including reductions in the duration of unemployment and increases in productivity and incomes, provided suitable rationale for cost-effective measures to foster entrepreneurship. In keeping with findings of other OECD studies, the author noted that the principal rational for entrepreneurship policies must be to address factors that impede the proper functioning of markets, rather than introduce measures to replace the role of markets.

In order to support solid evidenced-based policy and allow assessments and adjustments as required, the study noted that goals of entrepreneurship policy and

---

[7] Scarpetta et al. (2002)

strategy must be clear and explicit. This will not only enhance assessment of feasibility but also help to avoid duplicative or conflicting programmes. The enquiries suggested that policy decisions and assessments were often based on limited empirical evidence and the study noted the paucity of data for specifically examining local entrepreneurship issues. It was recommended that the OECD promote longitudinal studies, designed to include micro-enterprises that are missed in other official statistics, which are conducted at the local level, though using consistent methodologies across countries. By centralising the statistical development work, the study argued, costs for individual countries would be minimised but the value of the resulting policy-relevant data would be maximised, given the ability to make international comparisons.

The study on Micro-Policies for Growth and Productivity, sought to identify the critical and successful policy areas for each of the micro-drivers of growth—entrepreneurship, information and communications technology (ICT), innovation and human capital—through a quantitative benchmarking methodology. This work established some pioneering methodologies for better understanding entrepreneurship in particular and it also highlighted some weaknesses in currently-available indicators.

Finally, the OECD Bologna Process, which was launched with the first Ministerial Conference in 2000, is a very significant initiative by the Organisation to broadened the dialogue on SMEs and entrepreneurship and stimulate more meaningful interchange between analysts and policy makers. A second Ministerial Conference in Istanbul in 2004 stressed the need for evidence-based policy making and called for efforts to strengthen the statistical base for cross-country, comparative analysis. Specifically, it was recommended that "An internationally comparable set of indicators should be developed for monitoring the level of entrepreneurial activity and the entrepreneurial environment in each country."[8]

4.1.5 Entrepreneurship Policies

What are the questions facing policy-makers in OECD countries? Are they convinced of the value of entrepreneurship and are they now trying to find the right balance of policies to enhance entrepreneurial activity? Are there still unanswered questions about the importance of entrepreneurship?

Entrepreneurship appears to be of considerable interest to policy-makers everywhere, whether they are convinced that entrepreneurs are the dominant force in economic development or just significant contributors. But there are many different perspectives on entrepreneurship, often within the same country. For example, entrepreneurship is often linked to regional development programs. Stimulating the creation of new firms is seen as a tool to boost employment and output of depressed

---

[8] Fostering Entrepreneurship and Firm Creation as a Driver of Growth in a Global Economy, OECD, 2004

regions. In other examples, entrepreneurship is a key element of strategies designed to facilitate the participation of certain target groups, such as women or minorities, in the economy. Finally, programs aimed at boosting competitiveness often identify high-growth entrepreneurship as a key to innovation and productivity growth. In each of these cases, there is a different concept of who is an entrepreneur.

While many countries have embraced entrepreneurship as a means of reviving or sustaining economic growth, there remain many questions about the impact of entrepreneurship itself as well as about the best means to encourage entrepreneurial activities. Are there different types of entrepreneurship and, if so, are some entrepreneurial pursuits more beneficial for economic prosperity than others? Can the process of entrepreneurship itself be rendered more efficient and more productive?

For many, there is still need to better understand the role of the entrepreneur, who is commonly associated with new and/or small firms, in job creation and economic growth. Others are convinced of the direct link between entrepreneurship and job creation and they want to determine the best way to encourage entrepreneurship and move beyond firm creation to firm growth.

If increasing levels of entrepreneurship are sought in all countries, do countries have common goals? What are the policy goals of governments in the area of entrepreneurship? Is the goal simply to maximise the number of new entrants? Since evidence suggests that the churning effect of entry and exit is beneficial, should policy facilitate exit as well? Once established, is it better for a firm to prosper and grow for a long period of time or do new dynamic firms quickly become old less productive firms that should, in turn, exit to make way for another more dynamic entrant? Many definitions of entrepreneurship effectively assume that the entrepreneur's activities do not warrant further study after the firm is a few years old. Few measures try to capture the contributions of the serial entrepreneur, whether he is repeatedly starting brand new firms or launching new initiatives within an existing corporate structure.

If government policy interests relate to job and productivity growth, are established entrepreneurs as valuable as new ones? Isn't it likely that a dynamic entrepreneur will continue to hatch bright ideas and develop them into growing businesses? Or, isn't it likely that the entrepreneur will innovate and raise productivity both within an existing firm as well as through new firms?

The role of venture capital and other forms of financing, in stimulating entrepreneurship and firm growth also raises policy questions that warrant further study. Additional policy issues concern the relationships between government research labs and businesses that might commercialise such work. Views are often sharply divided on this point both across and within countries. Some feel that individuals should not benefit from knowledge creation funded by all taxpayers; others applaud such initiatives and point out the ongoing benefits to society of job growth, increased output and even greater tax payments.

Finally, a fundamental policy question relates to the very notion of a "government role" in entrepreneurship. For some, the answer is self-evident: "Governments have no role. Entrepreneurship is about individuals taking actions on their own." But others argue that such an approach is unrealistic in a complex economic system that already has myriad regulations and programmes in place. Thus, for many, there is considerable room for governments to facilitate entrepreneurship in a non-interventionist way. A smooth-running market economy is the best way to encourage entrepreneurship, rather than direct support. For example, the "business-friendly" infrastructure in the U.S. is supported by competition law that discourage monopolies and unfair competition as well as by intellectual property rights that protect a firm's valuable, but often intangible, knowledge assets.

Some countries have established firm policy agendas concerning entrepreneurship. Others are still considering options and priorities. Policy makers in Europe, for example, have concluded that differences in levels, rates and perhaps even types of entrepreneurship between Europe and the U.S. are significant factors in the U.S.'s record of low unemployment, high productivity, high per capita income and high rates of growth. The European Union as a whole, and many of the member states on their own, have fixed on a clear policy agenda that embraces entrepreneurship as a means of addressing problems such as continuing high levels of unemployment and lagging productivity growth. Through its Green Paper on Entrepreneurship (2003) and its Action Plan the EC has identified five key policy areas that will help make Europe more entrepreneurial:

- Entrepreneurial mindsets or attitudes
- Encouraging more people to become entrepreneurs
- Gearing entrepreneurs for growth and competitiveness
- Improving finance
- Making administration and regulation more SME-friendly

The challenge now for analysts and policy makers in Europe and elsewhere is to find the key factors that will lead to improvements in each of these areas to determine how to influence those factors to operate in a way that is conducive to entrepreneurship without introducing market distortions.

Despite the abundance of entrepreneurship policies and the explosion of entrepreneurship research in recent years, there still seems to be a disconnect between research and policy. Perhaps the most comprehensive reviews of entrepreneurship policy have been done by Lundström and Stevenson and they have characterised SME Policy as an area where "a great deal of trail and error persists", and noted that it "lacks a theoretical base."[9] Indeed, many countries rely on case studies and best practices, rather than empirical evidence, to assess the impact of their entrepreneurship programmes. Myriad statistics are used to show a need to boost or at least maintain the level of entrepreneurship; but very few of these statistics are commonly defined or collected across countries to allow for international comparisons.

---

[9] Lundstrom and Stevenson (2002)

4.1.6 Entrepreneurship Concepts and Definitions

A Brief History of Entrepreneurship Definitions

Scholars have dedicated almost three centuries to the attempt to define the concept of entrepreneurship. The lack of consensus may, in part, be due to the fact that entrepreneurship isn't neatly contained within any single academic domain. Indeed, many disciplines have contributed their perspectives on the concept of entrepreneurship, including psychology (Shaver and Scott 1991), sociology (Reynolds 1991, Thorton 1999), economics (Cantillon 1730, Marshall 1890, Knight 1921, Schumpeter 1934, 1949) and management (Stevenson 1985).Given the heightened interest in entrepreneurship in recent years, it is unlikely this multi-disciplinary interest will diminish any time soon.

The French economist Richard Cantillon[10] is generally accredited with being the first to coin the term "entrepreneurship" in about 1730. Loosely, he defined entrepreneurship as self-employment of any sort, and entrepreneurs as risk-takers, in the sense that they purchased goods at certain prices in the present to sell at uncertain prices in the future.

Many eminent economists elaborated on Cantillon's contribution, adding leadership and recognizing entrepreneurship, through organization, as a fourth factor of production, but the key tenets of risk taking and profit were nearly always retained as important features of entrepreneurship. Early on, Adam Smith (1776) wrote about entrepreneurship when he observed that division of labour discouraged innovation because of repetition. Alfred Marshall (1890) identified entrepreneurship as a crucial factor of production alongside land, capital and labour. Say (1803) stressed the importance of management vs. ownership in an enterprise and identified the entrepreneur as the manager.

It was not until Joseph Schumpeter's definition of an entrepreneur in 1934 however, that the more modern interpretation, relating entrepreneurship, additionally, to innovation, entered the mainstream. Schumpeter defined entrepreneurs as innovators who implement entrepreneurial change within markets, where entrepreneurial change has 5 manifestations: 1) the introduction of a new (or improved) good; 2) the introduction of a new method of production; 3) the opening of a new market; 4) the exploitation of a new source of supply; and 5) the re-engineering/organization of business management processes. Schumpeter's definition therefore equates entrepreneurship with innovation in the business sense; that is identifying market opportunities and using innovative approaches to exploit them.

However although Schumpeter's definition embodies a characteristic of entrepreneurship that is widely recognized today, namely, innovation, it still retains some ambiguity that has meant the debate regarding a definition of entrepreneurs/hip continues; although, to some extent, this reflects the definition of innovation, in particular whether it relates to incremental or quantum changes. Indeed some (Drucker 1985) have argued that entrepreneurship reflects merely the creation of a

---

[10] The word *entrepreneur* itself derives from the French verb *entreprendre*, meaning 'to undertake'.

new organization and that any individual who starts a new business venture is an entrepreneur; even those that fail to make a profit. Although, it could be argued that this corresponds to Schumpeter's 'opening of a new market'.

The debate still continues but it is perhaps best summed up by the economist Peter Kilby[11] who in 1971 compared those who study entrepreneurship to characters in Winnie The Pooh hunting for the mysterious and elusive Heffalump. Like the economists and scholars, familiar with entrepreneurs and their contribution to economic growth, and who have attempted over the years to define an entrepreneur, the hunters in Winnie the Pooh all claimed to know about the Heffalump but none could agree on its characteristics.

Measuring Entrepreneurship

While the academic debate over the concept of entrepreneurship is interesting, the real focus of the entrepreneurship indicators work is measures that will inform the development of good policy. Even in cases where a fairly clear definition has been enunciated, it is difficult to find a measurement tool that matches the terminology that has been chosen. For example, the European Commission has defined entrepreneurship as "the mindset and process needed to create and develop economic activity by blending risk-taking, creativity and/or innovation with sound management, within a new or existing organisation". While conceptually appealing, it would be difficult to convey this notion on a questionnaire in a way that would invite consistent interpretation by all respondents.

The practical definition, or measure, of entrepreneurship that one chooses will ultimately depend on the nature of the policy objective. If policy makers are interested in employment creation, they may focus on a measure that seems most directly linked to jobs, such as self-employment or new firm creation, no matter what the size or growth rate of the firm. If the policy objective is competitiveness or productivity growth, however, a measure of entrepreneurship that distinguishes high growth or innovative firms may be preferred. In this case, the firm population of interest may exclude zero-employee firms (self employment), or even very small firms, from the population of young businesses in order to get a better count of the growth business population.

Relevant measures will also depend on the national context and structure of the business population. For many in the United States, new firm creation is paramount and efforts are made to ensure that only pure, new firm creations are measured. In France, however, while new firm creation is carefully measured, so too are "reprises" which involve the takeover of some or all of the factors of production of an existing firm. Since the growth and survival characteristics of the population of reprises are different, and often superior, to those of the pure-birth firms, tracking of both populations is worthwhile. Given that the demographic profile of today's business owners suggests that many existing firms may be closed or offered for sale, it is likely that

---

[11] Kilby (1971)

more countries will want to track take-overs, mergers, revivals and other forms of business continuity or resumption, as well as pure births.

Finally, there is a debate about whether studies of entrepreneurship should be limited to the activities of small and medium-sized firms. Understanding the determinants and characteristics of growth firms may be more important than focussing on a single concept of entrepreneurship.

Although a single definition of entrepreneurship across OECD countries may not be feasible, or even desirable, it is important to have consistent definitions of the individual measures that will be assembled to understand entrepreneurship and the factors that influence those measures. The OECD Programme will define concepts such as firm birth, self employment and high growth as well as specific concepts relating to firm financing. A particular goal of the Programme will be to ensure that terminology is distinct and clear and that definitions are applied consistently across countries.

4.1.7 Existing Entrepreneurship Data

While few, if any, meet all the requirements of analysts and policymakers for internationally-comparable data, there are numerous statistics relating to entrepreneurship already produced by governmental, quasi-governmental and private institutions. Many of these data sets are purely national and some focus only on special niche activities or a specific subset of the population. Other projects, though, have gathered data in numerous countries. Perhaps most well known is the GEM (Global Entrepreneurship Monitor) Project that has gathered information through both household surveys and specialist interviews since 1998.

In Europe, Eurostat has recently implemented the first "Factors of Business Success" (FoBS) survey, in a number of EU countries, and the European Commission's Eurobarometer has measured attitudes towards various aspects of entrepreneurship in both Europe and the USA. Other countries have also attempted to assess the entrepreneurial climate through similar attitudinal surveys.

Other programs measure important drivers or determinants of entrepreneurship such as access to finance or administrative and regulatory burden. Canada has a well established periodic survey that measures SMEs' access to finance through both supply-side and demand-side surveys. The US Federal Reserve carries out a periodic survey of small business finances (SSBF) and the University of Warwick recently conducted the first major study of SME finances in the UK.

An inventory of existing entrepreneurship data sources has been developed by the Entrepreneurship Indicators Project at the OECD and it will be included in a forthcoming Project Report. That inventory is not designed to be exhaustive but rather to identify model questions or best practices for extension of existing concepts and methods across a larger number of countries.

4.2 An OECD Programme for International Entrepreneurship Indicators

4.2.1 A Collaborative Approach to Assembling and Developing Data

The importance of entrepreneurship to both developed and developing countries is clear and numerous efforts are either underway or under development to produce data to measure entrepreneurship and to shed light on the factors that encourage both entry into entrepreneurship and firm growth. But these efforts are largely undertaken in isolation. There have been relatively few attempts to develop comparable international indicators and even at the national level the linkages between entrepreneurship policies and entrepreneurship data have not been clear. There is an active community of academic researchers who present theoretical and some empirical work relating to entrepreneurship but there have been few forums for discussions of comparable international entrepreneurship data by statistical offices and perhaps fewer still that bring government entrepreneurship policy people together with data producers. The OECD will work with countries and other international organisations to develop entrepreneurship indicators that will enhance the comparability of existing data and develop new data to fill gaps in a co-ordinated manner.

In summary, the OECD Programme comprises the following elements, which are elaborated further below:

- A regular Scoreboard or Compendium on Entrepreneurship;
- A Manual for entrepreneurship measurement;
- Compilation of standard, international data based on existing and new sources; and,
- An OECD Network for international entrepreneurship data development.

An International Scoreboard on Entrepreneurship

A planned compilation of internationally-comparable data will address current and emerging policy issues relevant to both OECD and non-OECD countries. The Scoreboard will present entrepreneurship-related data in three general areas: First measures of level or rates of entrepreneurship, such as the number of start-ups in a period, will be presented. Second, various determinants of entrepreneurship, reflecting capacities and characteristics of entrepreneurs and the entrepreneurial climate or conditions of the countries, will be portrayed. Such "determinant" measures will include rates of taxation, measures of regulatory burden or educational and employment characteristics of both entrepreneurs and of the population as a whole. Finally, measures of performance for both firms and the economy as a whole, such as employment or productivity growth, will be included.

The Scoreboard will benchmark relative performance according to various indicators but it is not intended to provide a single composite measure or overall ranking of countries. There are numerous complex factors relating to entrepreneurship, competitiveness and overall economic performance and no single measure can guide policy-making decisions or determine "success". Furthermore, since policy objectives differ across countries the importance of high or low values of certain indicators may also differ across countries. It is not even clear that a high or low value on a given indicator will have the same implications in terms of performance in different countries. Some of the world's wealthiest countries, with high GDP growth rates and high per capita income display very low rates of entrepreneurship, at least by some current measures.

A Manual for Measurement of Entrepreneurship

There is an extensive body of academic research on entrepreneurship and its impact on economic growth and employment, particularly dating from the 1980s. In order to understand entrepreneurship and how it varies across economies, several theoretical models have postulated relationships between various factors that establish entrepreneurship opportunities, supply of entrepreneurial talent, and enabling framework conditions. The interaction of all these factors in turn determines levels and types of entrepreneurial activities in an economy, viewed from various perspectives including new firm creation, survival or growth. As discussed earlier, there have also been numerous efforts to define entrepreneurship in both theoretical and practical terms. For example, measurement of entrepreneurship, based on the number of people involved in starting new firms, has been undertaken in a consistent manner, for a large number of countries, over a number of survey cycles by the Global Entrepreneurship Monitor (GEM) program. Also, a number of national surveys exist that shed light on particular aspects of entrepreneurship or factors that may determine the amount and type of entrepreneurship that takes place in a country. Most of these initiatives have remained isolated, however, and few attempts have been made to compare experiences and develop agreement amongst National Statistics Offices on key definitions, survey methods and measurement priorities.

The OECD Measurement Manual will include lists of minimum to ideal entrepreneurship indicators for consistent, ongoing cross-country measurement, standard concepts and definitions, and model questionnaires. Since the goal is the production of harmonised data, relevant for policy use, the work will be based, wherever possible, on definitions and methodologies already tested within countries.

Concepts and Definitions

An essential step in the preparation of a Measurement Manual is development of the definitions and concepts of the various items to be measured. If, for example, one wishes to compute the number or rate of "new firms" in an economy, and compare results across countries, a clear definition of what a new firm is, and what goes into the numerator and denominator, are required. Other conceptual details relating to thresholds, time periods and coverage must also be considered. Key concepts such as the entrepreneur, firm birth, firm death, firm size categories and high growth firms will be required for even the most basic set of indicators. Moreover, concepts involved in counting new firms, such as registration thresholds, or in measuring the self employed need to be established. Also of interest for international comparisons are the factors influencing entrepreneurship such as access to finance, regulatory and administrative burden or business education and advice. In many cases other OECD or international organisations have already considered and established definitions.

While firm births are important, for many countries the revival or resumption of a firm, through purchase or takeover of some or all the factors of production, is also important. Furthermore, interest in these "reprises", as they are called in French, will likely grow in the coming years since the demographic profile of today's business owners suggests that significant turnovers of firms will occur. Another priority for many countries is the consistent measurement of various aspects of financing of entrepreneurship and SMEs, including the very concept of a "financing gap".

It is not proposed, at this stage, that the OECD establish a single definition for entrepreneurship. As the earlier discussion on definitions concluded, the term entrepreneurship has been widely used and loosely defined, if at all. It is unlikely that countries will want to focus on a single notion of entrepreneurship as a policy objective; rather they will be interested, for example, in boosting firm start-up rates, increasing the proportion of high-growth firms, and increasing resumptions or revivals as a means of lowering firm closures. It is more important that they focus on quality measures for all these items than that they attempt to identify any one of them as the representative indicator for "entrepreneurship".

A number of proposed definitions have already been developed by the OECD Statistics Directorate as part of a Framework for Business Demography.[12]

A Multi-Source Approach to Collecting and Developing Entrepreneurship Data

Data will be assembled for the OECD Entrepreneurship Indicators Programme from a variety of existing and new sources.

Existing Data in OECD and Other Databases

An example of existing data is the labour force information collected and maintained by the OECD. While few analysts would agree that one can measure entrepreneurship simply by counting the number of self-employed, data on business ownership (or self-employment) paint at least a partial picture of the level or rate of entrepreneurial activity in a country or region. The OECD data on self-employment are not strictly comparable, given different definitions and measurement in countries, and additional harmonisation work is required.[13] The OECD also has structural business statistics by size class that will allow presentation of a profile of the SME sector in a country. Here too, while few would simply equate SMEs

---

[12] See chapter 7.

[13] The EIM Research Group in The Netherlands has already done considerable work to harmonise the OECD self employment data across countries and the approach utilised is sound.

and entrepreneurship, comparable data on the size and nature of the SMEs across countries does contribute to an understanding of the entrepreneurial nature of a country. Other examples of relevant, existing data include innovation, R&D and investment. Furthermore GDP growth rates, productivity measures and other macro statistics will be useful in monitoring the possible impacts of different rates of entrepreneurship.

Register-Based Data

As noted earlier, one approach to measurement of entrepreneurship favoured by many analysts is to determine the number or rate of new firms being created within an economy, sector or geographic region. As is the case with other measures, there is not universal agreement that new firm formation is the best measure of entrepreneurship but it is certainly widely used and oft-quoted, in one form or another. The GEM estimates of nascent entrepreneurship, discussed above, serve as a proxy for new firm creation as they measure new entrepreneurs rather than new firms. Virtually all OECD countries, however, maintain complete registers of all businesses that can be used to produce a wide variety of accurate measures on firm entry, exit and growth, by industry and region. Unfortunately, in the past, there has been little standardisation of the definitions, registration methods, or thresholds for business registration across countries so, while accurate measures were available for national measurement, no cross country comparisons of register-based data were possible. Furthermore, since the business registers are generally assembled to assist with the collection of survey data and were not intended to be used as sources of data themselves, demands for improvements to the registers to enable better data outputs are not treated with the highest priority. This situation has begun to change in recent years. In Europe, Eurostat has worked with a number of EU countries on a voluntary program to produce standard outputs on business demography. While there are still gaps in the data outputs, and not all EU member countries are participating, the work is very promising. The EU Regulation on statistical business registers, requiring all countries to comply with Eurostat standards for coverage and content, is also being revised. The version expected to be introduced in 2006 will widen coverage, introduce new variables, and require the recoding of overseas links. Given the recent expansion of the EU, this will be a major step towards increased harmonisation of register-based data in Europe. In addition, the OECD Statistics Directorate has undertaken a study of all the factors that reduce comparability of register based data on firm dynamics[14] and is developing a framework for business demography that will facilitate comparability across OECD, EU and non member economies.[15] This work is proceeding in parallel with the OECD's Entrepreneurship Indicators Project and the business demography programme will constitute an important source of entrepreneurship indicators.

---

[14] Vale (2006)

[15] Ahmad (2007)

New OECD-Led Entrepreneurship Surveys

While the collaborative activities discussed above will be instrumental in building a foundation for quality, comparable entrepreneurship data, it is already known that there are many topics of interest to policy makers for which no internationally-comparable data exists. Also, many countries are considering developing, or are already developing, additional national data on entrepreneurship. While these initiatives will be useful for understanding entrepreneurship within the national context, the value of the data will be much greater if it can be compared to measures for a number of other countries. However, there is currently no international forum where NSOs can meet to learn of entrepreneurship statistics activities underway in other countries and collaborate to benefit from each others experiences and to ensure that data is collected on a common basis and disseminated in a multi-country format. To help fill data gaps and to enhance the value of current or planned data collections, the OECD proposal includes a programme to co-ordinate international entrepreneurship surveys. The principal objective of this initiative would be to conduct a periodic, standard entrepreneurship survey in all participating countries.

While a number of useful variables concerning entrepreneurship attitudes and the level of entrepreneurial activity are collected through household surveys, the relatively small proportion of entrepreneurs in the total population yields a small sample for more in-depth analysis of entrepreneur and firm characteristics. Also, as discussed above, harmonised business registers are an important element of this overall for better entrepreneurship data. The registers show great promise as a source of firm data, especially on new firm birth and basic evolution, but they reveal little or nothing about the entrepreneur and they can't provide any details on things such as financing, innovation, networks, marketing and organisational structures. Ideally, a periodic firm survey would be conducted by the NSOs with samples drawn from the same official Business Registers that are used to provide the Business Demography data discussed above.

The target populations for co-ordinated international entrepreneurship surveys would vary depending on the specific topics of interest for each survey cycle. Nevertheless, even while an international survey might target different populations at different points in time, it would be very important to establish clear definitions of the populations of interest and to apply them consistently over countries and over time. Thus, for example, the survey might target high-growth firms, newly-created firms, young-but-established firms or even older firms but each of these would be clearly defined. Furthermore, when a specific sub-population is targeted, such as high-growth firms within a certain age or size category, it will also be important to collect data for the entire population of firms in that age or size category so that data for a control group is also available.

4.2.2 Advantages of OECD-led International Measurement

There are numerous advantages to assembling and/or collecting entrepreneurship data within an OECD-co-ordinated international indicators program, rather than through national data activities alone. A co-ordinated effort has advantages for identification and prioritisation of policy-relevant statistical activities, for development and implementation of measurements themselves and for the presentation and distribution of results. The OECD is an ideal forum for bringing together the appropriate country representatives and other international experts to agree on the data required for entrepreneurship policy and on the approach to producing the required data on an internationally-comparable basis.

There are obvious benefits of international comparisons based on standardised concepts, definitions and measurement tools. Existing data show that there are significant differences in levels of entrepreneurship between countries. But, since little comparable data exists across a large number of countries on the underlying conditions and stimuli that generate entrepreneurship, it is difficult to undertake multi-country analysis and share best practices. By establishing definitions of entrepreneurship that are relevant to the policy interests of all participating countries, and measuring the factors that may encourage or discourage entrepreneurship using common questionnaires and other measurement tools, countries can determine how their practices, and outcomes differ. Policies will always differ, but sound international data can help countries determine the costs and benefits of different policies in terms of their impact on entrepreneurship.

A co-ordinated, joint effort can also yield economies of scale in the development of the tools and questions. Rather than each country grappling independently with issues of target population, survey frames, data collection methodology, questions and questionnaire design, work could be distributed among participating countries and common approaches adapted through pooling of expertise. In addition to cost savings such an approach will permit exploitation of synergies of expert collaboration.

The National Statistics Offices (NSOs) are important partners in the development of entrepreneurship indicators. They already collect data on various aspects of firm behaviour that will be useful for deriving some entrepreneurship-relevant data and their methodological expertise and practical experience will be invaluable in establishing any new entrepreneurship surveys. Furthermore, the NSOs normally maintain the statistical business registers that will be central to the development of improved business demography data that will contribute to the indicator programme. The OECD's direct links to NSOs will facilitate the development of entrepreneurship indicators.

4.2.3 Priority Topics for New Data Collection

While a systematic review of country data needs has not yet been completed, topics that are of highest priority for countries include high growth entrepreneurship, financing, innovation, use of ICTs and other technology, and entrepreneurship education. Also of interest is the impact of administrative and regulatory environment on both the creation and growth of firms. While many users are seeking coherent international data, a number of analysts have noted the paucity of regional or local data as well. The notes below illustrate why topics such as the characteristics and determinants of high growth firms and the financing of entrepreneurship and SMEs are among the priority areas for improving entrepreneurship data.

High Growth Firms

There are still debates about the contribution of new firm entrants to net employment growth but there is little disagreement about the fact that a relatively small proportion of firms that are growing rapidly account for the majority of new jobs. The Canadian Growth Firms Project, for example, showed that 2.7% of firms met the criteria for "leading growth firms" and they accounted for 60% of job growth between 1997 and 2000.[16] Naturally, governments are particularly interested in this category of firms and want to understand determinants of and obstacles to, high growth. But while there are numerous examinations of high growth firms throughout OECD countries, there is no agreement whatsoever on just what high growth means. What are the appropriate metrics and thresholds to measure growth? Many studies focus solely on growth in employment, often because it is more readily available on business dynamics databases than other suggested measures such as payroll, sales, revenue, profit, or productivity.

To date, many studies have been limited to identifying the number of growth firms and their contributions to growth, measured in terms of employment or some other metric. Policy makers wish to go beyond this basic analysis to understand the characteristics of the firms, and perhaps the entrepreneurs, as well as the determinants of growth.

The United States is often viewed as the epitome of entrepreneurship with high rates of new firm creation and more young, large firms than other countries. But some comparisons show that the start-up rate is not all that different across countries, while growth performance after start-up is. The OECD (Scarpetta 2002) found that US firm entrants were smaller than their European counterparts but, once over the initial start-up phase, they expanded rapidly while European firms remained small. Figure 4.1 compares US start-up rates to those of a number of European countries, while Fig. 4.2 compares the distribution of SMEs by size class in the US and Europe. While the size classes presented are different in the two pie charts they nonetheless reveal that Europe has a much higher proportion of micro firms (under 9 or 10 employees, and a much smaller proportion in all size classes above that.

Since firm growth rates vary considerably across countries an international comparison of factors and results is very much of interest to those designing policies and programmes. It will be important, though, to ensure that any data collected on high growth firms and their entrepreneurs is matched with data on the non-high growth firms to permit meaningful analysis.

---

[16] Growth Firm Workshop Synopsis, Industry Canada, Sept 29, 2004

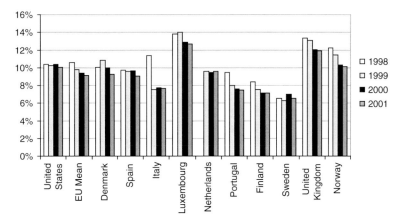

Fig. 4.1 A Comparison of US and European Business Start-Up Rates
Sources: United States—Firm Size Data—Small Business Administration. EU Mean—Mean start-up rate for the European countries shown. Other countries—Eurostat (The full Eurostat data set includes several other countries, but only those for which data are available for at least three of the above years are shown)

Financing of Entrepreneurship and SMEs

Since SMEs comprise 95% or more of all companies across OECD countries, it is not surprising that financing of entrepreneurship and SMEs continues to be a focus of attention of SME lobby groups, government policy analysts, academic researchers and other stakeholders. Yet, it appears to be an area conventional wisdom has been challenged in a number of cases. In Canada, concerns about bank financing of SMEs let to a major government effort involving statistical data collection and policy analysis. The "SME Financing Data Initiative" showed that 82% of SMEs obtained the financing they sought in 2000. That proportion dropped to 74% in 2001, a year of much slower economic growth. Only 23% of Canadian SMEs

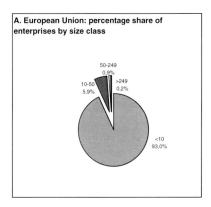
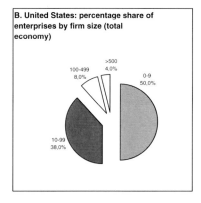

Fig. 4.2 Share of Business Firms by Size Class, United States and Europe
Sources: Joint OECD/Eurostat database on SME statistics

requested debt financing in 2000, though that proportion varied by size of firm with larger SMEs more likely to request debt.[17] Similar finding were evident from recent studies for the UK and for the EU as a whole, though in both cases questions were raised about differential rates of successful access to financing by gender and by ethnic group.[18]

Given the apparent success of entrepreneurs in obtaining debt financing, in at least some OECD countries, questions have turned from supply of debt financing to demand. Why is it that entrepreneurs and SMEs make little use of debt financing and would greater use of debt financing have an impact on the evolution and growth of entrepreneurial firms? What affects the capacity of firms to access and use debt financing?

A survey of both OECD and non-OECD countries, undertaken for the Global Conference on *Better Financing for Entrepreneurship and SME Growth* in Brazil in March 2006 demonstrated above all that data for analysis and international comparisons were largely unavailable. Indeed, the preparatory work done for that Global Conference underscored the dearth of international data on SME and entrepreneurship financing and the Conference ASction Statement called for the OECD to address the situation.

Since many OECD countries are particularly interested in boosting the number of high growth entrepreneurs, there is growing interest in equity financing and questions about why equity financing rates seem to vary across countries. The role of venture capital and other forms of financing, in stimulating entrepreneurship and firm growth has been of particular interest. Many countries feel that they must develop venture capital markets in order to rival American firm growth records. Studies have often noted that the lack of established venture capital markets is one reason why European countries sometimes show high rates of star-ups but lag behind the USA in firm growth. But, in the U.S., only 17% of venture capital goes into companies that are in the early stages of development; most venture capital goes into expansion phase or later stage firms. Also, most firms on the Inc. list of 500 fastest growing firms did not get venture capital.[19]

The Survey for the Global Conference also revealed a lack of comparable data on venture capital across countries. There is a need to establish standard concepts and definitions and collect data on a consistent basis to permit international comparisons and analysis.

---

[17] Statistics Canada, "Financing of Small and Medium Enterprises", The Daily, January 15, 2002

[18] Eurobarometer, "SME Access to Finance; Executive Summary" European Commission, Directorate-General for Enterprise and Industry, October 2005; and Fraser, Stuart, "Finance for Small and Medium-Sized Enterprises; A Report on the 2004 UK Survey of SME Finances", Warwick Business School, 2005

[19] Carl Schramm, Foreign Affairs, Vol 83, No. 4

4.3 Summary

A number of countries have led the way with measures of entrepreneurship and its determinants but consultations and research have revealed a lack of detailed data for international comparisons and analysis. The OECD provides an ideal forum to bring together existing data and help develop new data in a consistent and comparable manner. The OECD proposes to collaborate with other organisations as well as with the national statistical organisations to develop an international program of entrepreneurship indicators.

Acknowledgments The views expressed in this paper are those of the author and do not necessarily reflect the views of the OECD or its member countries.

References

Acs Z, Arenius P, Hay M, Minniti M (2004) Global Entrepreneurship Monitor, 2004 Executive Report. Global Entrepreneurship Monitor Babson College and London Business School

Ahmad N (2006) A Proposed Framework For Business Demography Statistics. Internal Working Paper Statistics Directorate OECD March 2006

Audretsch DB, Santarelli E, Vivarelli M (1999) Start-Up Size And Industrial Dynamics: Some Evidence From Italian Manufacturing. International Journal of Industrial Organization 17(7): 965–983

Audretsch DB, Thurik R (2001a) Linking Entrepreneurship to Growth. STI Working papers 2001/2 OECD, Paris

Audretsch DB (2002) Entrepreneurship: A Survey of the Literature. Prepared for the European Commission Enterprise Directorate

Autio E (2005) Report on High-Expectation Entrepreneurship. Global Entrepreneurship Monitor Babson College and London Business School

Bartelsman EJ, Scarpetta S, Schivardi F (2003) Comparative Analysis of Firm Demo-graphics And Survival: Micro-Level Evidence For The OECD Countries. OECD Economics Dept Working Paper 2002

Birch D (1979) The Job Generation Process. Department Of Urban Studies And Planning MIT press, Cambridge, MA

Bygrave W (1989) The Entrepreneurship Paradigm (II): Chaos And Catastrophes Among Quantum Jumps. Entrepreneurship Theory And Practice 14 (2):2–30

Brusco S (1986) Small Firms And Industrial Districts: The Experience Of Italy. In: Keeble D, Wever E (eds) New Firms And Regional Development In Europe. Kroom Helm, London, pp 184–202

Casson M (1990) Entrepreneurship. International Library of Critical Writings in Economics, Edward Elgar, London

Casson M (2003) The Entrepreneur-An Economic Theory. Edward Elgar Press (first edition 1982)

Conway P (2005) Product Market Regulation And Productivity Growth. OECD Economics Department Working Papers Paris

Drucker P (1985) Innovation and Entrepreneurship. Butterworth-Heinemann, Oxford

European Commission (2003) Green Paper, Entrepreneurship in Europe. Brussels

European Commission (2003) The Summary Report, The Public Debate Following the Green Paper on Entrepreneurship in Europe. Brussels

European Commission (2004) Action Plan: The European Agenda for Entrepreneurship. Brussels

Eurostat (2004) Business Demography In Europe- Results For 10 Member States And Norway. European Commission, Luxembourg

Gartner W (1989) Who is an entrepreneur? Is the wrong question. Entrepreneurship Theory And Practice 13(4) 47–68

Hébert R, Link A (1989) In Search Of The Meaning Of Entrepreneurship. Small Business Economics 1:39–49

Iversen J, Jørgensen R, Malchow-Møller N, Schjerning B (2005) Defining And Measuring Entrepreneurship. Discussion Paper 2005–17 CEBR- Center for Economic and Business Research

Karlsson C, Friis C, Paulsson T (2004) Relating Entrepreneurship To Economic Growth. In: Johansson B, Karlsson C, Stough RR (eds) The Emerging Digital Economy: Entrepreneurship Clusters and Policy. Springer-Verlag, Berlin

Kauffman Foundation (2004) State Entrepreneurship Policies and Programmes. Ewing Marion Kauffman Foundation

Knight F (1971) Risk, Uncertainty And Profit. University of Chicago, Chicago (1st edition 1921)

Knight K (1967) A Descriptive Model Of The Intra-Firm Innovation Process. Journal of Business of the University of Chicago Vol 40

Langlois R (1991) Schumpeter And The Obsolescence Of The Entrepreneur Working Paper 91– 1503 University of Connecticut 13.

Lundström A, Stevenson L (2001) Entrepreneurship Policy For The Future. Swedish Foundation for Small Business Research, Stockholm

Lundström A, Stevenson L (2002) On The Road To Entrepreneurship Policy. Swedish Foundation for Small Business Research, Stockholm

Lundström A, Stevenson L (2005) Entrepreneurship Policy: Theory and Practice. International Studies in Entrepreneurship, Springer

Marshall A (1890) Principles of Economics. Prometheus (reprinted in 1997), UK

Mata J (1994) Firm Growth During Infancy. Small Business Economics 6(1):27–40

Michelsen VN, Hoffman A (2005) A General Policy Framework for Entrepreneurship. Ministry of Economic and Business Affairs-Division for Research and Analysis (FORA)

Nolan A (2003) Entrepreneurship and Local Economic Development. OECD, Paris

OECD (1997) Globalisation and SMEs. Vol 1&2, Paris.

OECD (1998) Fostering Entrepreneurship and Women Entrepreneurs. In SMEs. Paris

OECD (2001b) Business Views On Red Tape: Administrative and Regulatory Burdens on SMEs. Paris

OECD (2001a) Drivers Of Growth. Paris

OECD (2005) SME & Entrepreneurship Outlook. CFE, Paris

OECD (2005) Micro-Policies for Growth and Productivity. Paris

Pilat D (2002) Factors of Success and Entrepreneurship. Strategies for Statistical Development. Paper for SWIC OECD, Paris

Reynolds P (1991) Sociology and Entrepreneurship: Concepts and Contributions. Entrepreneurship Theory and Practice 16(2):47–70

Reynolds P (1999) Creative Destruction: Source of Symptom of Economic Growth? In: Acs Z, Carlsson B, Karlsson C (eds.) Entrepreneurship, small and medium-sized enterprises and the macro economy. Cambridge University press, Cambridge, pp 97–136

Reynolds P, Bygrave W, Autio E et al (2003) Global Entrepreneurship Monitor, 2003 Executive Report. Global Entrepreneurship Monitor, Babson College and London Business School

Reynolds P, Bosma NS, Autio E (2005) Global Entrepreneurship Monitor-data collection design and implementation 1998–2003. Small Business Economics 24(3):205–231

Say JB (1803) A Treatise On Political Economy. Transaction Publishers (reprinted in 2001)

Scarpetta S, Hemmings P, Tressel T, Woo J (2002) The Role of Policy and Institutions for Productivity and Firm Dynamics: Evidence from Micro and Industry Data. OECD Economics Department Working Paper No. 329 2002

Schreyer P (1996) SMEs and Employment Creation: Overview of Selected Quantitative Studies in OECD Member Countries. STI Working Papers 1996/4 OECD, Paris

Storey DJ (1994) Understanding the Small Business Sector. Rutledge, London

Storey DJ (2003) Entrepreneurship, Small and Medium Sized Enterprises and Public Policies. In: Acs ZJ, Audretsch DB (eds) Handbook of Entrepreneurship Research. Kluwer Academic Publishers, London, pp 473–511

Thurik R (1996) Small Firms, Entrepreneurship and Economic Growth. In: Admiraal P (ed) Small Business in the Modern Economy. De Vries Lectures in Economics, Blackwell Publishers, Oxford

Van Stel A, Stunnenberg V (2004) Linking Business Ownership And Perceived Administrative Complexity- An Empirical Analysis Of 18 OECD Countries. Max Planck Institute of Economics Group for Entrepreneurship Growth and Public Policy No. 3504

Vale S (2006) International Comparison of Start-up Rates. Internal Working Paper Statistics Directorate OECD January 2006

Wennekers S, Thurik R (1999) Linking Entrepreneurship and Economic Growth. Small Business Economics 13:27–55

Wennekers S (2005) Determinants and Effects Of New Business Creation Using Global Entrepreneurship Monitor Data. Small Business Economics 24(3):193–203

Chapter 5
The COMPENDIA Data Base: COMParative ENtrepreneurship Data for International Analysis

André van Stel

Abstract This chapter presents a harmonized data set over the period 1972-2004, containing two-yearly data on the number of non-agricultural business owners and the size of the labour force for 23 OECD countries, as well as the quotient of these two variables which is called the business ownership rate of a country. The data set is called COMPENDIA and has been constructed by EIM Business and Policy Research, using OECD statistics as well as other relevant sources. We make an attempt to make business ownership rates comparable across countries and over time.

5.1 Introduction[1]

In present times there is renewed attention for the role of entrepreneurship in the economy. This is reflected by an increasing amount of research in the field of entrepreneurship. Much of this research is qualitative in nature. Far less entrepreneurship research is quantitative. In particular, there are relatively few studies which use data bases with internationally comparable figures on entrepreneurship.

Operationalizing entrepreneurship for empirical measurement is difficult (Storey, 1991). The degree of difficulty involved increases exponentially when cross-country comparisons are made. Systematic measurement conducive to cross-country comparisons is limited (Audretsch, 2003). Nevertheless, cross-country data bases on entrepreneurship are important in understanding the role of entrepreneurship in economic processes. The measure most often used to operationalize the extent of entrepreneurship in a country is the number of self-employed individuals or business

André van Stel

EIM Business and Policy Research, Zoetermeer, The Netherlands and Erasmus University Rotterdam, The Netherlands

ast@eim.nl

[1] This chapter is reprinted from: Stel, André van (2005), COMPENDIA: Harmonizing Business Ownership Data Across Countries and Over Time, *International Entrepreneurship and Management Journal* 1 (1), pp. 105–123, with kind permission of Springer Science and Business Media, Inc.

owners, largely because they are measured in most countries, and measured in comprehensive ways facilitating comparisons across countries and over time (Blau, 1987). But even for this measure of entrepreneurship, cross-country comparability is a major problem. The numbers of self-employed reported in *OECD Labour Force Statistics* -one of the most important data sources on the subject- are not comparable across countries as each country supplies figures according to its own self-employment definition. In particular, the extent to which owner/managers of incorporated businesses (OMIBs) are included in the self-employment counts differs across countries. This problem is not very well-known.[2] However, in chapter 5 of *OECD Employment Outlook June 2000*, attention is being paid to this particular subject, and an overview of self-employment definitions used in various (OECD) countries is provided.

In recent years, EIM has made an attempt to construct an international data base with self-employment figures for 23 OECD countries that are comparable across countries. The 23 countries are the 15 countries of the (old) European Union plus Iceland, Norway, Switzerland, the United States, Japan, Canada, Australia and New Zealand. The data base is called COMPENDIA (COMParative ENtrepreneurship Data for International Analysis). The data base currently contains figures for the period 1972-2004 (even years only), and is updated every two years.

To arrive at such a uniform data base, we first established the exact definition per country used in OECD Labour Force Statistics. Next, we have chosen a self-employment definition to be used in our uniform data base. In choosing a definition, we acknowledge that business ownership (self-employment) and entrepreneurship are related but not synonymous concepts. Entrepreneurship in a 'Schumpeterian sense' refers to the activity of introducing 'new combinations' of productive means in the market place. Entrepreneurship in a broad economic sense (business ownership or self-employment) means owning and managing a business, or otherwise working on one's own account. Thus, on the one hand Schumpeterian entrepreneurs are a small fraction of the business owners, while on the other hand some entrepreneurs (so-called intrapreneurs) do not work on their own account (Wennekers and Thurik, 1999).

In COMPENDIA we have chosen a strict application of the broad entrepreneurship definition given above. This involves inclusion of owner/managers of both unincorporated and incorporated businesses but exclusion of unpaid family workers. Following statistical convention, our definition also excludes so-called 'sideowners' (self-employment as a secondary activity). For countries not following the COMPENDIA definition in OECD Labour Force Statistics, we made a correction to arrive at an estimate for the number of self-employed persons according to the

---

[2] For instance, during a panel discussion of policy makers at the "First GEM Research Conference" (Berlin, April 2004), participants expressed their surprise because—contrary to what is commonly believed– Germany had relatively more self-employed individuals than the United States, according to OECD statistics. However, this can be explained by the fact that for Germany, OMIBs are included in the OECD self-employment count, whereas for the US, they are excluded. Hence the data are not comparable between the two countries.

required definition. In the present chapter, we provide explanation on the COMPEN-DIA data base. We describe in detail what the self-employment figures represent, how the figures were obtained and what corrections were made to the raw data. We pay special attention to the United States, as this country alone accounts for about 30% of all self-employed reported in the COMPENDIA data base.

The organization of this chapter is as follows. In section 2, we discuss the self-employment (business ownership) definition used in COMPENDIA. Also, we discuss the data on self-employment published in OECD Labour Force Statistics, which form the main source for our data base. In section 3 we discuss the general method that –in principle– is used for each country to correct the raw LFS data.[3] As an illustration of the many data problems that may arise when constructing a times series on the number of business owners, section 4 discusses in detail the construction of the COMPENDIA times series for the United States. Section 5 presents the business ownership rates for the 23 countries and provides some explanation on general trends in business ownership that can be observed across countries. The final section is used for discussion.

5.2 Definitions and Main Data Source

In this section we describe the self-employment (business ownership) definition used in COMPENDIA, *i.e.*, which groups of workers are included in the self-employment count? We also mention the sector classification used in COMPENDIA and we give a short overview of harmonization problems that have to be solved. Finally, we describe how business ownership data are scaled in COMPENDIA, to arrive at comparable figures across countries. We start this section with a description of self-employment data in OECD Labour Force Statistics.

Self-employment Data in OECD Labour Force Statistics

OECD Labour Force Statistics forms the basis for our data set on the number of self-employed per country. In this annual publication, in the chapter Country Tables, for every country there is a table called 'Professional status and break-down by activities'. In this table, total employment is divided in three professional statuses: a) employees, b) employers and persons working on own account, and c) unpaid family workers. In principle, we use the category 'employers and persons working on own account'. At all events, this category includes all *unincorporated* self-employed individuals (sole proprietors and partners). However, as far as *incorporated* self-employed are involved (owner/managers of incorporated businesses), there is a uniformity problem. In some countries they are counted as self-employed and in other countries they are counted as employee. The latter

---

[3] In the remainder of this chapter the full name 'OECD Labour Force Statistics' and the abbreviation 'LFS' will be used interchangeably.

case may prevail because formally, owner/managers of incorporated businesses are employees of their own businesses. The different statistical treatment of incorporated self-employed in different countries forms the main harmonization problem to be dealt with in COMPENDIA, and we will discuss this problem in detail in section 3.

In LFS, professional status applies to the *primary activity* of a person. For example, a person who works as an employee in some business for four days a week, and runs his own business for one day a week (*i.e.*, the person is self-employed as *secondary activity*) is counted in the a)-category rather than in the b)-category mentioned above.[4] In other words, the data in the professional status classification in LFS relate to the main job. In COMPENDIA, we follow this practice and we exclude the so-called side owners (*secondary activity*) from our self-employment count.

Which Groups of Workers are Included in COMPENDIA?

In constructing a data set on numbers of self-employed, we have to decide which groups of workers are included in the self-employment count, and which are not. In particular, we have to deal with the following two cases: unpaid family workers and owner/managers of incorporated businesses. In some studies, these groups of workers are counted as self-employed, and in other studies they are counted as employees. As regards unpaid family workers, we consider these workers not relevant for measuring the extent of 'entrepreneurship'. These people do not own the business they work for, and thus do not bear responsibility and risk in the same way as 'real' self-employed individuals do. We exclude this group of workers from our self-employment count. As regards owner/managers of incorporated businesses, we do consider this group as highly relevant, because in an 'entrepreneurial' sense, this group is not essentially different from the unincorporated self-employed. We include the incorporated self-employed in our self-employment definition.

Which Sector Classification is Used in COMPENDIA?

In LFS, the employment status division is applied separately for the agriculture, hunting, forestry and fishing industries on the one hand and the 'non-agricultural activities' on the other hand.[5] This two-sector classification is also used in COM-PENDIA. The agricultural industries are structurally different from the rest of the economy, in that self-employment is the natural employment status in these industries. Therefore, in this chapter, we concentrate on the number of self-employed in the non-agricultural industries.[6]

---

[4] The minimum weekly amount of time that a person has to work in order to be included in the (self-) employment count of LFS is one hour (OECD 2002, pp. xi–xii).

[5] The 'agricultural industries' are thus defined to include agriculture, hunting, forestry and fishing.

[6] The number of self-employed in agriculture, hunting, forestry and fishing as well as the number of non-agricultural self-employed can be found at www.eim.net.

Summarizing we use the following self-employment (business ownership) definition in the present chapter: *the total number of unincorporated and incorporated self-employed outside the agriculture, hunting, forestry and fishing industries, who carry out self-employment as their primary employment activity.* We use the terms business owners and self-employed interchangeably, to indicate that we also include owner/managers of incorporated businesses in our self-employment notion.

Harmonizing the OECD Labour Force Statistics Data

In constructing a harmonized data set for the number of business owners across countries and over time, two types of comparability problems can be identified. The *first* problem involves comparability across countries, *i.e.*, different countries using different self-employment definitions. Having chosen a self-employment definition to be used in our data set, COMPENDIA, we have to adjust the raw LFS data for those countries which use a different definition in LFS. The corrections that we apply mainly involve corrections for the numbers of incorporated self-employed in certain countries. We aim at applying the same method for each country to ensure comparability. This general method is described in section 3. The *second* problem involves comparability over time, *i.e.*, the occurrence of trend breaks in LFS. A trend break may occur if the set-up of the labour force survey in a country changes from a certain year onwards. Also changes in self-employment definitions over time or changes in industrial classifications may introduce trend breaks. These trend breaks are corrected for in COMPENDIA and the corrections are described in section 4 for the United States. For the corrections made for the remaining 22 countries we refer to van Stel (2003).

Scaling the Business Ownership Data

In order to compare self-employment figures across countries in a meaningful way, some form of scaling must be applied. A common scaling variable is the size of the labour force. In COMPENDIA, the number of self-employed (business owners) in a country as a fraction of total labour force is indicated as the country's business ownership rate. Total labour force consists of employees, self-employed persons (including OMIBs), unpaid family workers, people employed by the Army and unemployed persons. Data on total labour force are also obtained from OECD Labour Force Statistics. For this variable, comparability problems of the raw LFS figures across countries and over time occur less often than for the variable self-employment. However, in some cases, corrections were still needed, and these are described in van Stel (2003).

5.3 Harmonizing Self-Employment Data In Compendia

In this section we give a general description of the data collection and data construction of the number of business owners for the 23 countries in the data base, for the period 1972-2004. As mentioned, our business ownership definition includes unincorporated self-employed as well as owner/managers of incorporated businesses (OMIBs). We exclude the agricultural industries. In principle, we use the numbers reported in OECD Labour Force Statistics. At all events, this item includes all unincorporated self-employed. However, the extent of inclusion of OMIBs in the reported numbers varies per country, due to different set-up of labor force surveys in different countries. This involves issues as whether classification in employment status categories is done by the interviewer or by the respondent, the degree of guidance that is given by the interviewer on the term 'self-employment', the number of categories which respondents can choose from, etcetera. For details on these labour force surveys, see OECD (2000), Annex 5A.

Estimating the 1994 Level of the Number of OMIBs

The countries thus differ in the extent to which OMIBs are included in the official statistics. In *OECD Employment Outlook June 2000*, p. 158, countries are categorized in five types as regards the inclusion of OMIBs in OECD Labour Force Statistics:

1. excluding (all) OMIBs,
2. classification of OMIBs is unclear,
3. including (all) OMIBs,
4. including most OMIBs,
5. excluding most OMIBs.

Our desired definition is the third one: including (all) OMIBs. For countries not following this definition, *i.e.*, those countries which are categorized as 1), 2), 4), or 5), we make an estimation of the number of OMIBs *in 1994* using the following procedure.

Estimation Procedure for European Countries in COMPENDIA

We use as the total number of business owners (unincorporated as well as incorporated self-employed) the maximum of

a. the reported number of self-employed in OECD Labour Force Statistics 1981-2001, and
b. the number of 'non-primary private enterprises' with less than 50 employees, from the data base that is constructed in the framework of *The European Observatory for SMEs: Sixth Report* (KPMG/ENSR 2000).[7] This data base is largely based on the Eurostat publication *Enterprises in Europe*, which contains harmonized information for the 18 European countries in our COMPENDIA data set on (among other variables) the number of enterprises, by industry and size-class.

---

[7] The term 'non-primary' is defined to exclude agriculture, hunting, forestry and fishing.

We use the number of enterprises with less than 50 employees because in larger companies the manager often does not have the control. Formally, this control rests with the shareholders. A second reason for not including *all* firms in the estimated number of business owners is that not all firms are independent. Dependent firms (subsidiary companies) by definition are not linked to self-employed individuals. By using the number of enterprises smaller than 50 employees, we do not take account of the fact that partnerships have more than one self-employed individual, and on the other hand, that individuals can have more than one corporation or that individuals can run a business as a side activity. However, the number of enterprises smaller than 50 employees should approximately equal the number of business owners, *by and large*.

The comparison is made for the year 1994. In case the number of enterprises exceeds the reported number of 'employers and persons working on own account', as reported by OECD Labour Force Statistics, we can derive a raise-factor that corrects for the number of OMIBs. *In principle*, for such countries we apply this raise-factor constantly, for the whole period 1972-2004. For those 1)-, 2)-, 4)-, or 5)-categorized countries for which the reported number of business owners in LFS exceeds the number of enterprises, we choose the number of LFS-reported business owners. Because such a country does not belong to category 3), we know that such an estimate does not include *all* OMIBs. But we also know that the number of enterprises is lower, and therefore we argue that it is likely that the vast majority of the OMIBs *is* included in the reported LFS number.

Estimation Procedure for Non-European Countries in COMPENDIA

For the five non-European countries in COMPENDIA, we look again at the categorization in *OECD Employment Outlook June 2000*. The above-mentioned *European Observatory for SMEs* does not contain data on non-European countries. Therefore in case the categorization is not '3) including (all) OMIBs', we must estimate the number of OMIBs in another way. We use country-specific sources and we refer to section four (United States) and van Stel (2003) (other countries) for a description. In all cases we apply a procedure that resembles the procedure for the European countries as closely as possible.

Expert Knowledge

For all countries in our data set it holds that we deviate from the above procedures in case we dispose of 'expert knowledge', *i.e.*, additional information from other sources. This is the case for the Netherlands, Iceland, Switzerland, and New Zealand. For the estimation of the number of OMIBs of these countries we refer to van Stel (2003).

Is the Development Over Time of Numbers of OMIBs Measured Independently?

In Table 5.1, the number of business owners including statistically non-identified OMIBs is estimated for 1994. For some countries this results in a raise-factor that corrects (for) the number of OMIBs. In principle, the raise-factor is applied constantly for the whole period 1972-2004. In a small number of countries, the

Table 5.1 Estimating the number of business owners including all OMIBs in 1994 for 23 OECD countries (all numbers expressed in thousands)[1]

Country	OMIB-categorization in OECD Employment Outlook June 2000	1. Number of business owners in OECD LFS1981-2001	2. Number of enterprises smaller than 50 employees	3. Number of business owners (1994) used in COM-PENDIA 2004.2	Raise-factor OMIBs (3./1.; only if 3.>1.)
Austria	unclear	230	281	281	1.22
Belgium	incl. all	498	498		
Denmark	incl. most	161	164	164	1.02
Finland	incl. most	193	167	194	
France	incl. most	1817[3]	2293	2293	1.26
Germany	incl. most	2938	3070	3070	1.04
Greece	incl. most	840	555	840	
Ireland	incl. most	145	72	162	
Italy	unclear	4117[3]	3681	4117	
Luxembourg	unclear	11.8[4]	13	13	1.10
Netherlands[2]	incl. most	596	699	1.17[6]	
Portugal	unclear	736	600	736	
Spain	incl. all	2052	2052		
Sweden	incl. most	340	335	340	
United Kingdom	incl. most	3002[3]	3136	3170	1.04
Iceland[2]	unclear	18.1	18.1		
Norway	excl. most	116	168	168	1.45
Switzerland[2]	N.A.	N.A.	292		
United States	excl. all	8955	13929	1.56[6]	
Japan	excl. all	6130	6950	1.13[6]	
Canada	incl. all	1804[5]	1804		
Australia	excl. all	984	1493		1.52
New Zealand[2]	unclear	226	226		

[1] Data on number of enterprises taken from *The European Observatory for SMEs: Sixth Report*; estimation of OMIBs for non-European countries based on country-specific sources. Finland and Ireland: 1994 number of business owners in COMPENDIA 2004.2 adjusted for post-1994 trend breaks.

[2] Expert knowledge: estimation of number of OMIBs deviates from usual procedure.

[3] OECD Labour Force Statistics, version 1978-1998. UK: raise-factor for COMPENDIA 2000.1 (1.04) has been applied to revised 1994 figure (3035, from LFS 1981-2001)

[4] Including unpaid family workers

[5] OECD Employment Outlook June 2000

[6] Raise-factor not used to construct the data, and only mentioned for purpose of illustration.

implicit assumption is that the development over time of the number of incorporated self-employed (ISE; or OMIBs) equals that of the number of unincorporated self-employed (USE). This may be an implausible assumption as the development over time of the numbers of these two groups may be quite different over such a long period of time. This is not a desirable characteristic of using such a procedure.[8]

However, for the majority of countries the actual assumption that lies behind our method of estimating the number of OMIBs, is not so strong. For example, when a country is categorized as 'including most OMIBs', the development over time of 'most' OMIBs *is* included in the published numbers of OECD Labour Force Statistics. The actual assumption that we make when applying a point estimate of the raise-factor constantly for the whole period, is that the proportion of *non-identified* OMIBs in the total number of business owners stays constant over time, and this is a less strong and hence more plausible assumption. Additionally, for the United States, we use independent information on the number of OMIBs for the whole period 1972-2004. The only assumption we make here is that the quotient (employer firms)/(*self-reported* incorporated self-employed according to Current Population Survey) stays constant over the period 1972-1986 (see section 4). This is not such a strong assumption, and hence the development over time of the number of estimated OMIBs for the US may be considered reliable. In Table 5.1 we give an overview of the results of applying the (missing) OMIBs estimation procedure described in this section. The number of enterprises is reported only when it is needed in the OMIB estimation procedure of that country. Hence, the number is not reported for countries with categorization 'including all OMIBs', or for countries where 'expert knowledge' is used. The number of enterprises is also not reported for the non-European countries. In principle, the mentioning of a raise-factor for a country in the last column of Table 5.1 implies that the factor is applied constantly for the whole period 1972-2004. However, in three cases (The Netherlands, United States and Japan), the raise-factor is mentioned for illustrative purposes only.

5.4 Measuring Business Ownership In The United States

As regards the number of self-employed individuals in the United States, many different sources report different figures. The official self-employment definition as practiced by the Bureau of the Census in its *Current Population Survey* (CPS) excludes the incorporated self-employed. The definition thus only includes the unincorporated self-employed which consist of sole proprietors and partners, see

---

[8] Note that for countries where the 1994 number of business owners in LFS exceeds the number of enterprises smaller than 50 employees, *i.e.*, countries that use the reported LFS numbers, the development over time of the number of ISE *is* measured independently of the development of the number of USE.

the *United States Small Business Administration* (SBA, 1997), p. 87.[9] As we also include the incorporated self-employed (ISE) in our COMPENDIA definition, we had to resort to other sources as regards the number of ISE.

The organization of this section is as follows. First, we discuss reported figures on (unincorporated) self-employed in various sources. Our estimation of the number of ISE is described in subsection 5.4.2. This subsection also includes a discussion on some specific measurement problems concerning ISE. Third, we present our business ownership series for the US, and we provide some explanation for the different developments over time of numbers of unincorporated and incorporated self-employed.

5.4.1 Unincorporated Self-Employed

The number of non-agricultural unincorporated self-employed in the United States can easily be obtained from OECD Labour Force Statistics (which are actually figures from the Current Population Survey). This number varies from 5.342 million in 1972 to 8.362 million in 2002[10].

5.4.2 Incorporated Self-Employed

In the previous section we saw that obtaining the number of unincorporated self-employed persons is relatively straightforward. This is not true however for the number of incorporated self-employed, *i.e.*, the number of owner/managers of incorporated businesses. As mentioned earlier, this type of self-employment is excluded from the figures in official statistics. As a result, information on the numbers of owner/managers is hard to find. However, there are two sources which report more or less comparable figures on the subject. These are Bregger (1996) and Carolyn Looff, as reported in SBA (1997), p. 90. In SBA (1997), p. 91, it is reported that the number of incorporated self-employed (the owner/managers) increased with 40% between 1976 and 1979 and with 33.3% between 1979 and 1983. Bregger, p. 8, reports that the number of self-employed owners of incorporated businesses rose from 1.5 mln in 1976 to 2.1 mln in 1979 and to 2.8 mln in 1982. Note that these figures correspond to the 40% and 33.3% increases as reported in SBA (1997). However, it is clear from the latter source that the 33.3% increase relates to a

---

[9] People who are self-employed as a secondary activity (side owners) are also not included in the Census definition, see SBA (1997), p. 87.

[10] Some sources, such as Bregger (1996), p. 4, Table 1, and SBA (1997), p. 90, Table 3.3 report slightly different figures for the number of non-agricultural self-employed. However, as it turns out, these differences relate to the definition of agriculture, i.e. whether or not the industries hunting, forestry and fishing are included in the sector 'agriculture' (as is the case in LFS). See van Stel (2003) for details.

four-year period and not to a three-year period.[11] So, we have a figure of 2.8 mln for all industries (including the agricultural sectors) in 1982 according to Bregger. In SBA (1987), p. 114, Table 4.3 -which is the same type of tabulation as the one of Carolyn Looff in SBA (1997), p. 90- a number of 2.59 million of incorporated self-employed (ISE) in May 1983 is reported for all *non-agricultural* industries. These figures seem to match quite well. Indeed the ratio 2.59/2.8 (non-agricultural ISE/total ISE) closely resembles the corresponding ratio for 1989 that can be derived from Bregger, p. 8, Table 5.5. Therefore, in order to construct a series of the number of incorporated self-employed between 1976 and 1994, we use the figures for 1983, 1988 and 1994 as provided by SBA (1987), p. 114, Table 4.3 and SBA (1997), p. 90, Table 3.3 (these two tabulations are consistent) and for 1976 and 1979 we apply the 40% and 33.3% increase figures to the 1983 figure of 2.59 mln. We can even go back until 1967.[12] For 1967, Fain (1980), p. 7, reports a number of 850,000 incorporated self-employed. This figure consistent with the figures for 1976 and 1979 reported by Bregger (1996). In order to correct for the agricultural owner/managers we again apply the relative growth rate (1.5/0.85 between 1967 and 1976, an increase of 76.4%) in order to arrive at an estimate of the number of non-agricultural incorporated self-employed in 1967. See Table 5.2.

Underestimation of Numbers of OMIBs

Although with help of data reported in SBA (1987 and 1997) we have been able to produce some preliminary figures for the number of owner/managers of incorporated businesses (OMIBs), it is important to note that these figures actually understate the real number of OMIBs. This is because legally, these workers are employees of their own businesses. Now, in the labour force survey people are asked whether they are employed by a government, a private company or a nonprofit orga-

Table 5.2 Incorporated self-employed US (non-agricultural), 1967-94, preliminary times series

Year	Number ($\times$ 1000)	Source / method
1967	786	increase 76.4% 1967-76, reported by Fain (1980)
1976	1388	increase 40.0% 1976-79, reported by SBA (1987), p. 112
1979	1943	increase 33.3% 1979-83, reported by SBA (1987), p. 112
1983	2590	SBA (1987), p. 114
1988	2984	SBA (1997), p. 90
1994	3955	SBA (1997), p. 90

Source: Own calculations, based on SBA

---

[11] The 33.3% increase actually relates to the period 1978-82 instead of 1979-83, and to *all* industries, see SBA (1987), p. 112, Table 4.2. Because the period analysed in that table is 1979-83, the relative changes were assumed equal for the two periods.

[12] From 1967 on, because of a change in the Current Population Survey in that year, it is possible to identify those workers who report themselves as self-employed but have incorporated their business. Before 1967, these workers could not be identified separately from other self-employed individuals. See Bregger (1996), p. 4, and Fain (1980), p. 7.

nization (in which cases they are classified as wage and salary workers) or whether they are self-employed. In the latter case, the following question is asked: "Is this business incorporated"? The people who answer 'yes' are still classified as wage and salary workers in the official statistics. It is these figures (the numbers of people who answer 'yes' on the incorporated business question) that are tabulated in SBA (1987 and 1997) and which figures we have taken over in Table 5.2. However, not *all* incorporated self-employed are detected by the extra question. Owner/managers who answer that they are wage and salary workers (because legally this is the case) are not identified as self-employed workers because no extra question is asked to people who respond that they are employed by a private company. So the reported numbers of incorporated self-employed only relate to people who responded (erroneously, for the purposes of the labour force survey) that they are self-employed. The figures do not include the owner/managers who (correctly, for those purposes) identify themselves as wage and salary workers. These owners cannot be identified. For more details about these questionnaires, see Bregger, p. 8, SBA (1997), p. 113, and OECD (2000), Annex 5A.

So, the reported figures are actually an understatement of the real number of incorporated self-employed. However, the magnitude of the understatement is unknown, see Fain (1980), p. 7: "Another group which cannot be separated and studied are those incorporated self-employed who report themselves initially as wage and salary employees. There is no way to determine how large this group might be or to know whether it has grown larger or smaller over time". The problem of the unidentified owner/managers who report themselves as wage and salary worker seems to prevail not only in the United States but also in other OECD countries. This is because in general, statistical definitions are based on legal employment statuses, see Hakim (1988), p. 422: "Working proprietors or managers of incorporated businesses are classified as employees in statistical surveys, because that is their status in law and for tax and social insurance purposes. However, these distinctions are not necessarily observed by respondents to the labour force surveys that provide the main source of data on self-employment, and errors cannot always be detected and corrected by statistical offices." So, because the official status of owner/managers is that of employee, labour force surveys do not bother to ask respondents who report themselves as employees whether or not they own an incorporated business. Therefore, their numbers are unknown, as Hakim (1988), p. 423, reports: "And we do not have any idea how many more working proprietors and managers of their own incorporated businesses are invisible in the statistics because they classified themselves –according to the rules– as employees of their own small firm".

While Fain (1980) and Hakim (1988) in principle report on the particular measurement problems in the United States and the United Kingdom, respectively, the problems prevail in many other (if not all) OECD countries as well. See for example OECD (1992), p. 185: "Data on the numbers of owner-managers of incorporated businesses are not widely available. In addition, their propensity to report themselves as self-employed is unknown". This implies that those owner/managers of incorporated businesses who report themselves as employee are not identified, consistent with Fain (1980) and Hakim (1988). See also OECD (2000), Annex 5A.

Correction Based on Number of Employer Firms

Because we want to obtain a plausible estimate of the number of incorporated self-employed, and we know that the series from Table 5.2 is too low, we make a correction on these series. For this purpose we use the number of employer firms, as yearly published in the *The State of Small Business, A Report of the President*, see for example SBA (1998), p. 118, Table A9, and SBA (1999), p. 205, Table A5. The number of employer firms is a conventional estimate for the number of OMIBs. See SBA (2000), p. 5: "Incorporated self-employment is generally defined as an employer firm [...]". In *The State of Small Business, A Report of the President*, the number of 'nonfarm' employer firms is published each year, both by size-class and by industry. The term 'farm' relates to agriculture in narrow sense here, i.e., excluding the industries hunting, forestry and fishing. Because we work with the broad definition of agriculture, we subtract the number of employer firms in the industry 'Agricultural services, Forestry, and Fishing' from the total number of 'nonfarm' employer firms. Next, because we try to use a method for the United States that is as uniform as possible with the method for the European countries, we take only the employer firms that are smaller than 50 employees.[13] This leads to the series in Table 5.3 below.

As we see from Table 5.3, the number of employer firms is measured from 1988 onwards. We have no information on the number of employer firms before that year. Therefore, for the year 1988, we compute the ratio employer firms / incorporated self-employed according to the labour force survey (see Table 5.2)

Table 5.3 Estimated number of incorporated self-employed (non-agricultural) in US, 1988-2004, based on number of employer firms ($\times$ 1000)

Year	Estimated number of incorporated self-employed ($\times$ 1000)
1988	4690
1990	4789
1992	4808
1994	4974
1996	5157
1998	5252
2000	5321
2002	5346
2004	5380

Source: Own calculations, based on SBA (1998), p. 118, Table A9 (years 1988-94); SBA (2000), p. A-2, Table 1.2 (years 1996-98); SBA (2001), p. A-3, Table 2 (year 2000); and SBA (2003), p. 12, Table 2 (year 2002).

---

[13] For this purpose the number of firms with employment size between 19 and 50 is approximated at 75% of the firms with size between 19 and 100.

and apply this factor to the series in Table 5.2 (for the years prior to 1988). The ratio equals 4690/2984 = 1.57. The implicit assumption is that about two third of the OMIB-respondents in the labour force survey classify themselves as self-employed while one third classify themselves as wage and salary employees. This may be plausible.[14]

5.4.3 Total Number of Self-Employed

Having constructed a series for the incorporated self-employed, we are now able to construct a series for the total self-employed, according to our definition (all incorporated and unincorporated self-employed but excluding the agricultural sectors, the secondary jobs and the unpaid family workers). For the unincorporated self-employed (USE) we use OECD Labour Force Statistics.[15] For the incorporated self-employed (ISE) we use the series from Table 5.3 for 1988 and later years, and the series from Table 5.2, with the correction factor applied to it, for the years prior to 1988. For the years between 1972 and 1988 that are not reported in Table 5.2, we interpolate. This results in the series presented in Table 5.4.

Table 5.4 Total number of US non-agricultural self-employed, 1972-2004 (× 1000)

	1972	1980	1988	1996	2004
USE (OECD LFS)	5342	6956	8474	8929	9370
ISE, uncorrected(see Table II)	1120	2104			
ISE, corrected (see Table III for 1988-2004, and apply factor 1.57 for period 1972-86)	1761	3308	4690	5157	5380
Total self-employed	7103	10264	13164	14086	14750
Labour force (OECD LFS)	88847	108544	123378	135231	148644
Business ownership rate	0.080	0.095	0.107	0.104	0.099

Source: Own calculations.

---

[14] In a description of labour force surveys in different countries, OECD (2000), p. 192, states that "It is assumed that when the procedure is self-assessment alone, OMIBs will mainly classify themselves as self-employed".

[15] We use LFS versions 1981-2001 and 1970-1990. For 1990 and 1992, we have used LFS 1974-1994, in order to take account of two (minor) trend breaks in 1990 and 1994 in LFS 1981-2001.

Different Trends for Incorporated and Unincorporated Business Owners

From Table 5.4, we see that the number of incorporated self-employed (ISE) has increased faster than the number of unincorporated self-employed (USE). For example, in the period 1980-2002, the number of ISE increased with an average of 2.3% per year. In the same period the average annual growth of the number of USE was 0.8%. Apparently, more self-employed individuals choose for incorporation of their business. Why does this occur? There can be many reasons, as Fain (1980), p. 7, reports: "The move towards incorporation is a function of many complex factors. A worker will usually incorporate his business for traditional benefits of the corporate structure, including limited liability, tax considerations, and the increased opportunity to raise capital through the sale of stocks and bonds". Simply put, when an unincorporated business expands, it becomes more attractive to incorporate the business. So, when small businesses perform well and expand, they will often choose for incorporation. In that case however, the status of the entrepreneur in the official statistics changes from self-employed to employee. See Bregger (1996), p. 8: "What undoubtedly occurs is that, as the small businesses expand and bring on employees, the owners incorporate their businesses, thereby shifting the class-of-worker classification to wage and salary employment. This type of transitional shuffling, while not readily measurable, is very likely an ongoing event [...]".

From the previous paragraph, it is clear that data on USE alone can be misleading. For example, if the number of USE stays constant or decreases, one cannot tell whether this is because business ownership really decreases, or whether many small businesses have incorporated their business and as a result are not considered self-employed any more in official statistics. The above example underlines the importance of including the owner/managers of incorporated businesses in the self-employment count.

5.5 Business Ownership Rates 1972-2004

In this section we present some data on (non-agricultural) business ownership from the COMPENDIA data base. The complete data base can be found at www.eim.net.[16] From Table 5.5 we see that in 2004 business ownership rates are high in Mediterranean countries, especially Greece and Italy, while they are relatively low in Scandinavian countries and Luxembourg. We also see that for the 23 OECD countries covered by the data set, there are over 46 million business owners, 47% of whom are in European countries, and 32% of whom are in the United States.

---

[16] The data base also contains data on the number of business owners in agriculture, as well as data on total labour force, employment and unemployment, real gross domestic product per capita, and the share of women in the labour force. All variables are available for the 23 countries from 1972 onwards.

Table 5.5 Business ownership rates in 23 OECD countries, 1972-2004

	1972	1980	1988	1996	2004	Share 2004
Austria	0.093	0.073	0.069	0.074	0.089	0.007
Belgium	0.105	0.098	0.109	0.119	0.111	0.011
Denmark	0.082	0.074	0.056	0.064	0.063	0.004
Finland	0.066	0.064	0.076	0.080	0.082	0.005
France	0.113	0.101	0.099	0.088	0.082	0.048
Germany (West)	0.076	0.066	0.070	0.082	0.093	0.081
Greece	0.161	0.182	0.186	0.197	0.196	0.020
Ireland	0.077	0.086	0.101	0.112	0.117	0.005
Italy	0.143	0.148	0.169	0.183	0.193	0.102
Luxembourg	0.107	0.087	0.075	0.067	0.053	0.000
The Netherlands	0.100	0.085	0.082	0.102	0.114	0.021
Portugal	0.113	0.119	0.116	0.156	0.133	0.015
Spain	0.118	0.110	0.123	0.130	0.126	0.055
Sweden	0.074	0.070	0.064	0.081	0.081	0.008
United Kingdom	0.078	0.074	0.101	0.111	0.114	0.074
Iceland	0.111	0.088	0.101	0.130	0.128	0.000
Norway	0.097	0.084	0.084	0.071	0.072	0.004
Switzerland	0.066	0.065	0.071	0.085	0.075	0.007
Europe-18	0.100	0.095	0.105	0.112	0.115	0.466
United States	0.080	0.095	0.107	0.104	0.099	0.316
Japan	0.125	0.131	0.123	0.101	0.091	0.129
Canada	0.079	0.087	0.106	0.128	0.121	0.046
Australia	0.126	0.168	0.164	0.155	0.169	0.037
New Zealand	0.106	0.090	0.114	0.139	0.144	0.006
23 Countries	0.098	0.102	0.110	0.109	0.107	1.000
Total number of business owners($\times$ 1000)	29401	34342	40666	44219	46623	

Source: COMPENDIA 2004.2.Business ownership rates refer to the number of non-agricultural self-employed (unincorporated as well as incorporated) as a fraction of the labour force.Germany refers to West-Germany until 1991.

Concerning developments over time, most countries display a U-shaped pattern of initial decline, followed by an increase of the business ownership rate. The decline is not always visible from Table 5.5 because the data start only in 1972. However, in the post World War II period business ownership rates declined constantly in most Western economies. Large firms exploited economies of scale in the production of new economic and technological knowledge, leaving little room for entrepreneurship and small businesses (Schumpeter, 1950). But from the 1970s onwards times have changed and the trend towards less self-employment has reversed, starting in the United States. There are several reasons for the revival of small business and self-employment in Western economies. Notably, in many sectors, new technologies have reduced the necessity of scale economies to arrive at competitive advantages (Meijaard, 2001). Developments like globalization, the ICT-revolution and the increased role of knowledge in the production process have led to increased dynamics and uncertainty in the world economy from the 1970s onwards. In turn, these developments have created room for (groups of) small firms to act as agents of change (Audretsch and Thurik, 2000). The bigger role in technological development for small and new firms is referred to by Audretsch and Thurik (2004) as a regime switch from the 'managed' to the 'entrepreneurial' economy.[17]

Many Western countries have experienced a shift from the 'managed' to the 'entrepreneurial' economy. However, the extent and timing of this shift has not been identical across countries (Audretsch et al., 2002). The first country to experience the transition from the 'managed' to the 'entrepreneurial' economy was the United States (Verheul et al., 2002). Indeed, from Table 5.5 it can be seen that the United States has the highest increase in business ownership rate between 1972 and 1980. The different extent and timing of the shift across countries is further illustrated by Fig. 5.1, where the development of the business ownership rate is depicted for the United States, the United Kingdom, France and Germany. As mentioned, the upswing in business ownership was first experienced by the United States in the 1970s. The United Kingdom followed in the 1980s. Still later, Germany follows. France however, has had a constantly decreasing business ownership rate.

Institutions and policies of countries play a role in the different extent and timing of the shift across countries. For instance, the steep increase in business ownership in the United Kingdom in the 1980s was stimulated by government policy aiming at maximising the number of new-firm startups in an attempt to fight unemployment (van Stel and Storey, 2004). In the 1990s however, UK policy changed towards a focus on incumbent businesses with 'growth potential', which may explain the

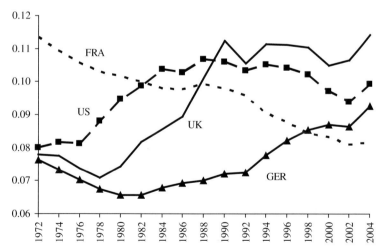

Fig. 5.1 Development in business ownership in four OECD countries, 1972-2004
Source: COMPENDIA 2004.2.Germany refers to West-Germany until 1991

---

[17] There are also other reasons for the revival of entrepreneurship such as an increased consumer demand for variety and the increased employment share of services in modern economies. See Carree *et al.* (2002) for an overview.

leveling off of the business ownership rate in the 1990s.[18] The constant decrease in France may be due to French policy, which for a long time focussed on large businesses, for instance by giving the majority of their orders to large businesses. Also, high tax burdens on SMEs and a discrepancy in social security between wage- and self-employed people create few incentives for entrepreneurship. A negative cultural attitude towards entrepreneurship probably also plays a role (Henriquez et al., 2002).

5.6 Discussion

In this chapter we presented the data set COMPENDIA. The data set contains harmonized information on numbers of business owners and the size of the labour force, for 23 OECD countries over the period 1972-2004. The quotient of these two variables is called the business ownership rate. These harmonized data are helpful for conducting quantitative research on entrepreneurship at the macro level. Our primary data source is *OECD Labour Force Statistics* and in COMPENDIA we have made an attempt to make business ownership rates comparable across countries and over time. The main problem in harmonizing business ownership data is the different statistical treatment of the incorporated self-employed, as this category of workers is classified as wage-and-salary workers in some countries, and as self-employed workers in other countries. We have chosen our business ownership definition to include the unincorporated *and* the incorporated self-employed, because both categories run their own businesses. Concerning self-employment definitions being in force in different countries, we based ourselves on the definitions reported in *OECD Employment Outlook June 2000*. Next, for countries not including *all* owner/managers of incorporated businesses in their self-employment count, we made corrections based on numbers of enterprises from *The European Observatory for SMEs: Sixth Report*, or, for some countries, specific information from national sources.

In making these corrections, we tried to approximate the (unknown) real numbers of business owners as closely as possible. Of course, the quality of the approximations depends on the plausibility of the corrections applied. In this respect, we should mention some limitations of our data set. *First*, for many countries, we apply a constant correction factor for OMIBs (computed in 1994) to the whole period 1972-2004. This is not ideal as, in reality, the number of OMIBs in proportion to the number of unincorporated self-employed may change over time. In many cases this drawback is however mitigated because our correction only relates to a smaller number of non-identified OMIBs. *Second*, for many countries, our correction factor for numbers of OMIBs is based on enterprise data, not on employment (*i.e.*, person-based) data. It is well-known that there are many difficulties in relating

---

[18] In the United States the leveling off may be due to shake out of industries that are in a more advanced stage than elsewhere in modern OECD countries (Audretsch and Thurik, 2004).

these two kinds of data sources. *Third*, for some countries little information on numbers of non-agricultural self-employed was available in OECD Labour Force Statistics, forcing us to use rather crude approximation methods. This holds especially for Switzerland and, prior to 1986, for New Zealand (see van Stel, 2003, for details). Despite these limitations we think that COMPENDIA provides the most reliable, comparative data set available today, regarding business ownership across industrialized countries and over time.

For harmonizing business ownership data across countries and over time, the ideal situation would be to use actual data on numbers of incorporated self-employed (as for some countries is already done in COMPENDIA 2004.2), but for many countries these numbers cannot be identified from the domestic labour force surveys being in force. For these countries, corrections based on numbers of enterprises are the best approximation possible. Nevertheless, in order to improve cross-country comparability of business ownership data, future research should concentrate on collecting actual data on numbers of incorporated self-employed. If not available from labour force surveys, such data may be obtained from other national sources like tax return data.

References

Audretsch DB (2003) Entrepreneurship: A Survey of the Literature. Enterprise Papers No. 14 Brussels: European Commission Enterprise Directorate-General

Audretsch DB, Thurik AR (2000) Capitalism and Democracy in the 21st Century: from the Managed to the Entrepreneurial Economy. Journal of Evolutionary Economics 10:17–34

Audretsch DB, Thurik AR (2004) A Model of the Entrepreneurial Economy. International Journal of Entrepreneurship Education, forthcoming

Audretsch DB, Carree MA, van Stel AJ, Thurik AR (2002) Impeded Industrial Restructuring: The Growth Penalty. Kyklos 55:81–98

Blau DM (1987) A Time Series: Analysis of Self-Employment in the United States. Journal of Political Economy 95:445–67

Bregger JE (1996) Measuring Self-Employment in the United States. Monthly Labor Review 119:3–9

Carree MA, van Stel AJ, Thurik AR, Wennekers ARM (2002) Economic Development and Business Ownership: An Analysis Using Data of 23 OECD Countries in the Period 1976-1996. Small Business Economics 19:271–90

Fain TS (1980) Self-employed Americans: their number has increased. Monthly Labor Review 103:3–8

Hakim C (1988) Self-employment in Britain: recent trends and current issues. Work, Employment and Society 2:421–50

Henriquez C, Verheul I, Van der Geest I, Bischoff C (2002) Determinants of Entrepreneurship in France. In: Audretsch DB, Thurik R, Verheul I, Wennekers S (ed) Entrepreneurship: Determinants and Policy in a European-US Comparison: 83-120. Boston/Dordrecht: Kluwer Academic Publishers

KPMG/ENSR (2000) The European Observatory for SMEs: Sixth Report, Zoetermeer, EIM

Meijaard J (2001) Making Sense of the New Economy. E-Commerce Research Forum 2 (5), Massachusetts Institute of Technology:27–57

OECD (1992) Employment Outlook. Paris

OECD (2000) Employment Outlook. Paris

OECD (2002) Labour Force Statistics. Paris

SBA (=United States Small Business Administration, Office of Advocacy) (1987) The State of Small Business, A Report of the President 1986. US Government Printing Office, Washington, DC

SBA (1997) The State of Small Business, A Report of the President 1996. US Government Printing Office, Washington, DC

SBA (1998) The State of Small Business, A Report of the President 1997. US Government Printing Office, Washington, DC

SBA (1999) The State of Small Business, A Report of the President 1998. US Government Printing Office, Washington, DC

SBA (2000) Small Business Economic Indicators. 1998 Washington, DC: SBA

SBA (2001) Small Business Economic Indicators. 2000 Washington, DC: SBA

SBA (2003) Small Business Economic Indicators. 2002 Washington, DC: SBA

Schumpeter JA (1950) Capitalism, Socialism and Democracy. Harper and Row, New York

Stel AJ van (2003) COMPENDIA 2000.2: A Harmonized Data Set of Business Ownership Rates in 23 OECD Countries. EIM Research Report H200302, Zoetermeer, NL: EIM; Internet: www.eim.net

Stel AJ van, Storey DJ (2004) The Link Between Firm Births and Job Creation: Is there a Upas Tree Effect? Regional Studies 38:893–909

Storey DJ (1991) The Birth of New Enterprises - Does Unemployment Matter? A Review of the Evidence. Small Business Economics 3:167–78

Verheul I, Bosma N, van der Nol F, Wong T (2002) Determinants of Entrepreneurship in the United States of America. In: Audretsch DB, Thurik R, Verheul I, Wennekers S (eds) Entrepreneurship: Determinants and Policy in a European-US Comparison: Kluwer Academic Publishers, Boston/Dordrecht, pp 209–45

Wennekers ARM, Thurik AR (1999) Linking Entrepreneurship and Economic Growth. Small Business Economics 13:27–55

Chapter 6
Entrepreneurship Analysis from a Human Population Surveys' Perspective

José María Millán, Concepción Román and Emilio Congregado

Abstract This paper tries to collect, describe and evaluate all the potential statistical sources—each pursuing different goals—in order to study self-employment in Spain. The improvement of traditional databases together with the recent incorporation of new statistical sources is bolstering the knowledge of today's labour market, self-employment included. Although the available information might be considered accurate for reaching the goals of each source, the information becomes incomplete and even erratic if we intend to analyse entrepreneurial activity by it.

6.1 Introduction

The study of entrepreneurship and its impact on economic activity has always been on the research agenda for economists. However, it has not been one of the most intensely explored topics. This shortcoming is heightened when we observe that most governments and institutions design and implement entrepreneurial support policies that are not sufficiently verified by empirical evidence. In this sense, most indicators assessing the entrepreneurial network have focused on its quantitative composition and, to a great extent, have been biased to the requirements of firm demography studies. Therefore, it's common to observe that most existing indicators are oriented to the quantification of firms, centres or establishments, and to measure their dimensions basically in terms of their number of workers. However, the economic analysis of entrepreneurship must also be taken on other grounds. For instance, the study of entrepreneurial activity requires indicators capturing the number of entrepreneurs in a particular sector (or geographic area) and accounting for the way they carry out their task. In conclusion, it is necessary to go deep into the causes that determine the choice of becoming self-employed as well as the duration and evolution of these business ventures. Therefore, suitable knowledge of relevant statistical sources (i.e. Human Population Surveys) and the continuous process of development, updating and improvement of these sources, constitutes a mandatory

José M Millán
Universidad de Huelva
jose.millan@dege.uhu.es

E. Congregado, *Measuring Entrepreneurship.*
© Springer 2008

85

requirement to test the basic propositions arising from the theoretical analysis of entrepreneurship.

The purpose of this paper is to identify and evaluate the information sources available to study entrepreneurship in Spain. The paper is organized as follows. In Section 2, we review some potential statistical sources. We also briefly present the Human Population Surveys available. In Section 3, we enumerate the exploitation techniques used in the Human Population Surveys. We also summarize the existing literature associated to these techniques and we devote special attention to works using Spanish data. In Section 4, we compare the Human Population Surveys focusing on the advantages and disadvantages of each survey and in the literature that has exploited them. Finally, Section 5 is reserved to conclusions and future perspectives for the Human Population Surveys in Spain.

6.2 Statistical Sources and Human Population Surveys

In regards to the Human Population Surveys, a brief review of the existing statistics shows us the extensive variety of available sources. First, there's the renowned Spanish Labour Force Survey (EPA), which addresses households and has been conducted by the National Statistical Institute (INE) since 1964. The EPA is the basic structural source yielding information about the characteristics of employment in Spain. It also provides information regarding unemployment and the population outside of the labour force. Its quarterly regularity also allows a follow up on the labour market situation.

There are other statistical sources, based on household data, that provide information on the working population (although their primary goals are not to measure employment): the Working and Living Conditions Survey (ECVT 85), the 1991 and 2001 Population Census, the 1991 Sociodemographic Survey, the Household Budget Survey (HBS), the Quality of Life at the Workplace Survey (ECVT) and the European Community Household Panel (ECHP).

The Working and Living Conditions Survey was conducted during the last quarter of 1985 by the Spanish Ministry of Labour. Its main purpose was to assess the informal economy and its importance within the labour market.

The main objective of the Population Census is to recount the entire population comprised in each of the Spanish's administrative units and population settlements. In addition, the Census intends to provide information on the population structure to facilitate the decision-making process' direction.

The Sociodemographic Survey was conducted in 1991 and complemented the same year's Population Census information, mainly regarding the life histories of those surveyed on topics such as educational and social background, migration, etc.

Conducted by the INE since 1958, the Household Budget Survey is a statistical operation with a long-standing tradition. Its main objective is to estimate the weights used in the Consumer Price Index.

Started up by the Ministry of Labour in 1999, the Quality of Life at the Workplace Survey (ECVT) is the unique nation-wide Spanish survey specifically designed to study the quality of life at the workplace.

The European Community Household Panel (ECHP) is a standardized survey for the EU-15 member states. Carried out between 1994 and 2001, it was conceived to study and monitor social cohesion, to study population needs and the impact of socioeconomic policies on households and individuals, and to help design new policies.

The European Statistics on Income and Living Conditions (EU-SILC), is an annual survey conducted to obtain information on household income, poverty and social exclusion. It started in 2004 as an improvement over the ECHP whose content needed to be updated in accordance with the new political demands and the need for faster data generation.

In 2001, the Spanish Central Bank decided to start the Spanish Survey of Household Finances (EFF).[1] The central purpose of this survey is to obtain detailed information concerning the financial position of Spanish households. The EFF is a unique statistical source in Spain that allows the linking of household revenues, assets, liabilities and expenditures.

Another important indicator of entrepreneurial activity is the affiliation to the Social Security system. Today's social security records are designed more for managerial purposes than to conduct population studies. Nevertheless, this situation has changed with a new database issued by the Ministry of Labour, the Continuous Survey of Work Histories, whose information is already available to research Centres.

Finally, there is the Global Entrepreneurship Monitor project (GEM)[2] which started in 1998. The GEM is an international research programme intending to generate harmonised annual data on entrepreneurship. It first started with 10 countries and currently covers 39 countries including Spain since 2000. The data it uses comes from a survey that aims at capturing the following dimensions: i) entrepreneurial activity; ii) attitudes and perceptions vis-à-vis entrepreneurship; iii) entrepreneurial environment; iv) a series of standardised questionnaires for experts.

6.3 The Use of Human Population Surveys in Empirical Research

Most textbooks approach the entrepreneurial phenomenon from a Business School perspective, setting aside any possible contributions derived from economic theory and empirical research. Nevertheless, the existing surveys on entrepreneurship

---

[1] See Bover (2004).

[2] For detailed information on the project see Reynolds, P. *et al.* (2005). On-line information on the International GEM project can be found at http://www.gemconsortium.org . On-line information on the Spanish GEM project is available at http://www.ie.edu/gem. For on-line information on the project for Andalucía visit http://www.gem-andalucia.org.

literature—Audretsch (2002), Blanchflower (2000, 2004a), Parker (2004) or Reize (2004) among others—refer to numerous works that overcome this deficiency. Their main contributions include the following models and techniques: discrete choice models, sample selection models and earnings functions, duration models, Cointegration estimators for time series, and decomposition techniques.

However, not all of these models are fit to use the micro-data offered by the Human Population Surveys (e.g. time series models) nor have they all been implemented with Spanish data (e.g. decomposition techniques).

The discrete choice models have been widely used to identify the factors inducing self-employment (such as the case of an unemployed individual becoming self-employed or an employee switching to self-employment). They may be divided into either binomial or multinomial models. In the former, the individual's decision is simply restricted to being self-employed or not, while the latter involves a wider range of choices. For instance, the individual may face the alternatives of being a paid-employed (employee), a self-employed with employees (employer) or a self-employed without employees (own-account worker).

Along these lines of research, the works by Evans and Leighton (1989), and Blanchflower and Oswald (1998) deserve special attention. In addition, some important works using Spanish data are: Alba-Ramírez (1994), based on the Working and Living Conditions Survey (ECVT 85), Carrasco (1999), based on the Household Budget Continuous Survey (HBCS); Aguado *et al.* (2003), Carrasco and Ejrnæs (2003), and Congregado *et al.* (2005), based on the European Community Household Panel (ECHP); and Congregado *et al.* (2003), based on the HBCS and the ECHP.

Sample selection models try to estimate the probabilities and expected profits associated to self-employed and paid-employed individuals controlling for possible selection bias. Selection bias may arise if self-employed individuals have special characteristics that make them more suitable for self-employment. In this case, controlling for the bias would allow to know whether the same individuals could improve their revenues in an alternative occupation.

Along these lines of research we may highlight the works by Taylor (1996) and Parker *et al.* (2005). The work by García and Montuenga (2004) also deserves special attention: using data from the ECHP, it compares the education returns of self-employed individuals and employees in Spain and Portugal.

Duration models seek to identify the variables affecting the duration of self-employment. These models use either Human Population Surveys (which provide information on the individual's self-employment spell) or firm registries (which provide information on the span between firm entry and exit). We may distinguish between two types of duration models: single-risk models and competing-risk models. Single-risk models are used when a transition can lead to only one destination or exit state (e.g. the transition from unemployment to employment) while competing-risk models allow for multiple destinations (e.g. the transition from unemployment to part-time or full-time employment). Using Human Population Surveys, Böheim and Taylor (2000) and Falter (2002) make special contributions in these directions.

Works using Spanish data that also deserve to be mentioned are: Carrasco (1999), which uses the HBCS; and Congregado *et al.* (2003), based on data from the ECHP.

Finally, decomposition techniques are used to explain differences between socioeconomic subgroups of the population (e.g. divided by gender or by ethnic background). These techniques allow us to determine whether the differences obtained in variables such as earnings and self-employment survival, are due to special characteristics of each subgroup or to possible discrimination. Some of the main works along these lines are Borjas and Bronars (1989) and Hundley (2001).

6.4 Entrepreneurship and Human Population Surveys

In this section we go further into the characteristics of the Human Population Surveys that make them suitable to study entrepreneurship in Spain. We also point out the exploitation possibilities offered by each survey in relation to the existing empirical approaches to entrepreneurial activity.

6.4.1 Spanish Labour Force Survey

Research on firm demography has intensively explored the indicators related to the number of firms or establishments in a particular geographic area or a specific economic sector. In Spain, studies in this direction have grown substantially since the establishment of the Central Companies Directory (CCD) and the Survey on Labour Juncture (ECL). Developed by the National Statistical Institute, the CCD is a statistical source that was preceded by the Economic Directories Integration Project (EDIP) of late 1989. In a unique information system the CCD consolidates data from all the Spanish firms and its local units that are situated in the national territory. The ECL was established in 1990 and is published quarterly by the Ministry of Labour. It uses data of over 12.000 establishments (all of them with more than 5 workers) gathered from the industrial, building and services sectors (Public Administration and Defence are excluded from the last one).

The statistical sources mentioned above are useful to study corporate entrepreneurial activity but fail to explain entrepreneurship from an individual perspective. To overcome this shortcoming and assess the whole entrepreneurial network (i.e. at individual and corporate levels) we must resort to the Spanish Labour Force Survey (EPA). This survey currently has a rotating panel sample (derived from the 2001 Population Census) of 65.000 households (covering approximately 200.000 persons). It is conducted quarterly and it allows a follow-up on the employment status and the type of occupation for the same persons during six consecutive quarters. The EPA itemizes working individuals into the following categories: employers (self-employed with employees), own-account workers (self-employed without employees), producers' cooperatives members, contributing family workers, employees and other. Thus, the number of employers and own-account workers constitutes a good proxy to quantify the individual entrepreneurial network.

Nevertheless, we are aware of the predominance of corporate firms in economic activity. In this kind of firms, there exists a clear separation between ownership and control and therefore the entrepreneurial activity may be carried out by corporate officers who are not necessarily firm shareholders. Therefore, in order to asses the whole entrepreneurial network we need indicators accounting for the corporate entrepreneurial activity. Again, the Spanish Labour Force Survey (together with the Population Census) may provide this kind of indicators. When classifying workers by occupation (National Classification of Occupations, CNO-94), there is a category for private and public business executives. The classification of workers by socioeconomic condition includes four categories: directors and heads of agrarian establishments, directors and managers of non-agrarian establishments, directive staff of the public administration and members of the state offices. Finally, when classifying (if applicable) the type of public administration the individual works at, there is a category for public companies and financial institutions. Therefore, the information pertaining these three classifications allows us to identify the private and public business executives. It is up to the researcher's criteria to either consider the hypothesis that no public worker is an entrepreneur, or to assume that those executives working for public companies or public financial institutions are involved in entrepreneurship. Therefore, it is possible to obtain approximate data on the individual and corporate entrepreneurial network, both at the national and regional level. The most significant shortcoming of this source derives from the fact that to a greater level of disaggregation corresponds a greater sample error.

Once we have clarified the way in which the EPA survey allows us to identify the entrepreneurial network in Spain, it is helpful to review the additional information provided in the survey that might be relevant to explain entrepreneurship. In addition to the personal and sociodemographic details of each household member in the sample, the survey provides extensive data on the individual's working situation: current employment (including working time and the economic sector of the activity according to the National Classification of Economic Activities, CNAE-93); job search and unemployment span (allowing to differentiate unemployment from voluntary unemployment); work experience (although referring only to the immediately previous job); educational background, etc.

Surprisingly, the EPA survey has rarely been used to study entrepreneurial activity. To a great extent, this is explained by the fact that the EPA does not include information on individual income and wealth (by contrast, this information is included in the rest of the European Labour Force Surveys). EUROSTAT tried to overcome this shortcoming by conducting pilot surveys in 2004 while expecting to begin the incorporation of the produced data to the EPA in the first quarter of 2005. However, the quality of the information collected did not meet the minimum reliability requirements and the project was put on hold. This is an important drawback since most of the existing literature emphasizes the key role played by liquidity constraints when deciding to start a business venture[3]. In this direction, three important works for the Spanish case are Carrasco (1999), and Congregado et al. (2003, 2005). Carrasco uses discrete choice models (binomial and multinomial) and data from the Household Budget Continuous Survey (HBCS) to show a positive correlation between family assets and the probability of switching from paid-employment to self-employment. For the multinomial case, i.e. when distinguishing between self-employed with employees (employer) and without employees (own-account worker), he shows that the correlation is positive for both cases although it is greater for the former. Congregado et al. (2003) obtain similar results when using data from the HBCS survey. However, when using data from the ECHP survey they find that the probability of switching to the own-account worker state is invariant to the individual's capital and labour income. Nevertheless, in Congregado et al. (2005) they include the last two waves of the ECHP and, contrary to their previous work, they obtain results consistent with Carrasco (1999).

Because of its characteristics, the EPA survey can be considered as an appropriate source to be exploited by discrete choice models, sample selection models and some decomposition techniques. In addition, given that it has been conducted quarterly since 1964, it allows us to adjust for the impact of the economic cycle, thus making it possible to test the hypothesis that aggregate economic conditions affect entrepreneurial activity. However, while the ECHP is a fixed-panel (i.e. there is no sample panel renovation), the EPA is a rotating-panel survey where the respondents remain in the sample during at most for six quarters. This fact together with the lack of information on current employment spell, makes it an inadequate survey to study self-employment through duration models. However, the EPA does collect information on the unemployment spell as a discrete variable since the respondent is asked to choose among intervals of different lengths to reflect the duration of his unemployment spell. This information, which may seem unimportant, becomes relevant when estimating unemployment duration models under two possible scenarios: when self-employment is the unique alternative to unemployment (single risk model) and when there are more alternatives (competing risk model). Finally the lack of information on individual income and wealth prevents us from exploiting the EPA through earnings functions techniques. However, Arellano and Meghir (1992) are able to estimate a labour supply function by combining two databases: One using the U.K. Family Expenditure Survey (equivalent to the HBCS in Spain) which has detailed information on individual income. The other using the U.K. Labour

---

[3] See Parker (2002) for a literature survey on this subject. Rees and Shah (1986), Evans and Jovanovic (1989), Evans and Leighton (1989), Dolton and Makepeace (1990), Fujii and Hawley (1991), Holtz-Eakin et al. (1994), Blanchflower and Oswald (1998), Clark and Drinkwater (2000), Bernhardt (1994), and Parker (2003) find evidence supporting the existence of liquidity constraints. By contrast, De Wit and Van Winden (1989, 1990, 1991), De Wit (1993), and Grilo and Thurik (2004) do not find evidence supporting their existence. Finally, Gill (1988), and Earle and Sakova (2000) find a negative effect of capital.

Force Survey (equivalent to the EPA) which provides the necessary information on working situation and job search. The fact that information on working time is included in both surveys makes them compatible to estimate the labour supply function.

Concerning the methodological changes experienced by the EPA, we point out the incorporation, since the second quarter of 1987, of a wider and more complex questionnaire that includes new definitions in accordance to the EUROSTAT criteria and the International Labour Organization (ILO)'s recommendations. With this reform, the EPA provides more complete and detailed information on subjects such as: underemployment; unemployment benefits; working time (full-time or part-time) and job contracts (temporary or indefinite). In addition the EPA began to use the National Classification of Economic Activities (CNAE-93) and the National Classification of Occupations (CNO-94; this classification introduced modifications in the socioeconomic condition categories), since the first quarter of 1993 and the second quarter of 1994, respectively. The educational variables used by the EPA (educational level, current studies and area of studies) are codified according to the National Classification of Education (CNED-2000) which substitutes the *ad hoc* classification used before.

Finally, there is a high degree of comparability between the EPA and the Labour Force Surveys conducted in the rest of the European Union. This is so because EUROSTAT provides the criteria to be adopted by the Communitarian Countries in order to homogenize the Labour Force Surveys conducted in each one of them. Moreover, it is important to point out that EUROSTAT carries out an annual survey, the European Union Labour Force Survey (EU-LFS), which includes the second quarter EPA of each year. In addition, two types of modules of survey questions are elaborated: standard modules (comprising questions to be permanently applied in the survey), and focal modules (consisting of questions to be applied in particular quarters).

6.4.1.1 Standard Modules

Facilitating the incorporation of young people into the labour market constitutes one of the most important points in the fight against unemployment in the European Union. To deal with this issue, EUROSTAT decided to elaborate a standard questionnaire on training and education to be applied gradually into the different surveys. In the EPA survey for instance, what was initially a single question concerning the level of completed studies, in 1998 turned into a module comprising questions on current or recent participation in training activities (level, type, duration, etc.) and on completed studies (level, year of completion, etc.). In order to achieve comparability across countries, the module also used the same codes stated in the International Standard Classification of Education (ISCED 1997). In this way, the module harmonisation facilitated the analysis of the transition process from school to the work force in the European Union.

6.4.1.2 Focal Modules

Following the lines established by the EU, since 1999 the EPA survey has incorporated, in its second quarter questionnaires, focal modules related to different topics of the labour market. Some of the topics treated in the focal modules were: labour hazards (1999); the transition process from school to labour market (2000); working relations, conditions and timetables (2001); disabled persons and employment (2002); education/training courses taken in the preceding 12 months (2003).

Due to its importance in the study of entrepreneurship, the 2000 module deserves special attention. The primary objective of this focal module was to determine the relation between the educational background of an individual and their first job obtained after leaving school, as well as the time spent during the job search. It also related the educational level of an individual to the ones of his progenitors. It's important to note that this focal module reinforces the effort carried out by EUROSTAT in the standard module previously discussed.

6.4.2 Working and Living Conditions Survey

The Working and Living Conditions Survey was carried out by the Ministry of Labour during the second half of 1985 to estimate the informal economy and its importance within the labour market. It used a sample of over 60.000 individuals collecting extensive information on the Spanish labour force. Moreover, it allowed us to distinguish between own-account workers and employers and, within this last group, those employing more than 5 workers. Without any doubt, its major drawback to assess current reality is its outdated data. Two important works exploiting this source are Alba-Ramírez (1994) and Gil, Martín and Serrat (1994). The first one uses discrete choice models to study how the unemployment spell affects the transition probability from paid-employment to self-employment. The results are later compared to the ones available for the United States. Furthermore, it estimates earnings functions for self-employed, employees and overall workers. On the other hand, Gil, Martín and Serrat estimate an unemployment duration model in which the possible exit states are self-employment and paid-employment (competing risk model) and they compare it to a simpler model where there is only one exit state (single risk model).

6.4.3 Population Census

A Demographic Census is the statistical project of greatest range that the National Statistics Office of any country must undertake periodically. The denomination, Demographic Census, includes three different censuses: Population, Housing and Building Census. Of these three, the Population Census is, without any doubt, the most important and long-standing. In Spain, the first modern Population Census took place in 1768 and since 1901 it is carried out every 10 years (before 1900, four population censuses where undertaken so that the 2001 Census is officially the sixteenth Spanish Population Census).

Today, the Population Census is conducted by the INE, and its main objective is the recount of the entire population comprised in the Spanish administrative units and population settlements. In addition, the census intends to provide information on the population structure to facilitate decision-making processes. Thus, by assessing the geographic, demographic, cultural, economic and social characteristics of the inhabitants, the structural image of the population provided serves as a guideline for the design of demographic, economic and social policies.

In accordance with international recommendations and in order to reach comparability with other countries' censuses, the Spanish Population Census covers all the persons whose habitual residence is in the Spanish territory. This includes individuals in exceptional circumstances on Census Day such as diplomatic personnel on official duty abroad and Spanish residents working temporarily abroad.

The 2001 census made considerable improvements over the 1991 census leading to a significant reduction in its workload and costs. Among these improvements were: a more efficient use of the information collected by the Municipal Registers of Inhabitants, the simplification of questions by eliminating marginal answer choices, and the exclusion of certain questions for being either too vague or because they were already included in other surveys conducted by the INE.

Finally, and with respect to the information provided by the census, besides the personal and sociodemographic details of each individual, it includes data on the individual's migration movements, education level, marital status, fecundity status and employment status. Concerning this last one, the census clearly differentiates employers from own-account workers and it includes the individual's occupation, workplace, economic activity and sector of employment. Given the above, the population census provides important information to study the labour force and entrepreneurial activity. However, it also presents some shortcomings: First, it lacks information on the individual's income thus giving rise to the problems already discussed for the EPA survey. Second, the long periods between censuses prevent assessing the situation in a continuous manner. And third, data is collected by self-registration (i.e. the respondent fills in the questionnaire) thus limiting the role of census officers in controlling the information obtained. Because of these shortcomings, duration models and earnings functions cannot be estimated. In addition, discrete choice models and sample selection models must be based on the participation in self-employment (but not on the transition decisions from one state to another because of the static condition of the census). Therefore, it is not surprising that this source has been seldom used to study entrepreneurial activity in Spain.

6.4.4 Sociodemographic Survey

The 1991 Sociodemographic Survey was carried out as a complement to the 1991 population census and it used a sample of over 160.000 individuals. The main drawback facing this survey is that it has not been updated. Besides the large amount of respondents, its big advantage is its retrospective feature: by means of a single interview it allows the reconstruction of each respondent's history of employment, geographical mobility, educational background, etc. This single-interview method has the advantage of avoiding the problems associated to fixed-panel surveys such as the ECHP, in maintaining the respondent's collaboration during extraordinarily long periods. By contrast, it has the shortcoming of being based on the respondent's memory.

The testimonies left by the respondents are of great significance since they reflect the history of the first 90 years of the 20th Century. In the eldest group, those born before 1911, 55% of the cases began to work before the age of 14 and 80% of the cases before the age of 16. This kind of information is no longer gathered by the surveys on labour activity such as the EPA because of the compulsory schooling covering those ages, which gives an idea of the transcendental change that has taken place in Spain over that period.

6.4.5 Household Budget Surveys

The Household Budget Surveys are among the most long-standing operations in Official Statistics. The first studies on household expenditure for Europe took place in the middle of the 19th century. They began in Spain in 1958 and have been providing information on the consumption expenditure of private households ever since. However, the relevance of this source for our purposes resides in the additional information the survey provides for each household member regarding demographic characteristics, education level, employment status, occupation, and income

The INE has traditionally carried out two types of HBS. The first type is constituted by the Household Budget Basic Surveys conducted in 1958, 1964–65, 1973–74, 1980–81 and 1990–91. Among their various goals, these surveys have provided estimations regarding the level and structure of annual household consumption and the weight structure of expenditure serving to calculate the Consumer's Price Index. The second type is formed by surveys the INE conducted quarterly to estimate household expenditure and its annual variation. These continuous surveys started with the Permanent Consumption Survey (EPC) which was carried out from the second quarter of 1977 until the last quarter of 1983. The EPC was designed as a panel of 2.000 households rotating every four quarters. Later on, from the first quarter of 1985 until the first quarter of 1997, the rotating-panel Household Budget Continuous Survey 1985, was carried out covering 3.200 households each quarter. In this case, the rotation speed was of 1/8 of the sample each quarter.

The coexistence over time of the two types of HBS presented some disadvantages, the most important being related to their costs. In order to optimize resources and in accordance to the European harmonisation recommendations of the Household Budget Surveys, the INE, under the coordination of EUROSTAT, unified the two types of surveys into the Household Budget Continuous Survey 1997 which started in the first quarter of 1997.[4] From then until the last quarter of 2005, approximately 8.000 households were interviewed maintaining the quarterly rotating-panel design (with a speed of rotation of 1/8 of the sample each quarter).

In response to the users' new demands and in accordance to the international recommendations by EUROSTAT, in 2006 a new survey was initiated, the HBCS 2006. Its main purpose is to ensure the maximum quality of the information provided on annual household consumption expenditure and its annual variations. The methodological design was simplified thus resulting in a considerable reduction in the respondent households' workload. The annual sample is designed to cover approximately 24.000 households, half of which are renewed each year. Every household in the sample will collaborate during 14 days in each of the two consecutive years. As a considerable improvement over the HBCS 1997, the information processing will take place in the provincial deputations of the INE where specific errors and inconsistencies will be controlled. This temporal and physical proximity to the respondent households will improve the quality of the provided information.

Having in mind the study of entrepreneurial activity, we will now proceed to point out the strengths and weaknesses of the HBCS' different versions. The main limitation of the HBCS 1997 with respect to its predecessor is the information it provided on household income. The HBCS 1985 data base offered detailed information on each household member's income and its source from the first quarter of 1985 until the first quarter of 1997, which allowed precise estimations of earnings to be carried out. On the contrary, the HBCS 1997 information on income referred to the household unit which makes it very difficult to impute the respective income to each one of its members. This shortcoming hinders the testing for the presence of liquidity constraints in any given discrete choice model. Therefore, the new European Statistics on Income and Living Conditions (EU-SILC) to be discussed later, constitutes the appropriate source to study household income in detail. Moreover, the information provided by the HBCS 1985 allows us to identify the employment status of the spouse of the head-of-household as employer, own-account worker, employee or unemployed; while the HBCS 1997 only distinguishes the spouses working from those not working. By contrast, the HBCS 1997 information provided on the head-of-household far surpasses its predecessor's. The HBCS 1985 information concerning the head-of-household's main activity was very limited, failing to identify its economic sector even at the most aggregated level (i.e. agriculture, industry and services). Since there are significant variances in the characteristics and behaviours of individuals working in different economic sectors, the impossibility of controlling effects in the activity's sector will induce a bias in the results of any econometric exercise on occupational choice. The HBCS 1997 clearly overcomes all these shortcomings by providing detailed

---

[4] With the incorporation of the 2001 Population Census data, the survey's results were revised starting in the first quarter of 1998. However, since the last two quarters of 1997 were not revised, the microdata files corresponding to these quarters are not comparable with the rest. For this reason, quarterly files are only available beginning in the first quarter of 1998.

information on the head-of-household's economic occupation and its economic sector, following the National Classification of Occupations (CNO-94) and the National Classification of Economic Activities (CNAE-93) with all the international comparability advantages that these classifications imply. The CNO-94 even allows the identification of the corporate entrepreneurial network, i.e. those corporate officers undertaking entrepreneurship. Additionally, and unlike the HBSC 1985, the HBCS 1997 includes head-of-household information on working hours and contract type, and it identifies whether his occupation belongs to the private or public sector.

Both surveys (HBCS 1985 and 1997) have the advantage of covering a considerable time span and, along with their quarterly periodicity, they allow for controlling the effects of the economic cycle on the entrepreneurial activity and, in particular, on the individual's decisions. However, it's a pity that the information on education refers only to the head-of-household thus biasing any possible results concerning the effects of education on entrepreneurship to this group of individuals. Finally, while the HBCS may be considered appropriate to assess entrepreneurial activity through discrete choice models, sample selection models and some decomposition techniques, it is inadequate in estimating self-employment duration models because its rotating panel feature allows for a two-year monitoring at maximum.

Regarding the changes introduced in the HBCS 2006, first, it is important to notice that these types of surveys have now gone beyond the pure economic scope, and have begun pursuing important social and socio-economic objectives as well. Switching from quarterly to annual periodicity certainly has a positive effect in cost reduction but it also represents an important disadvantage when studying the entrepreneurial network because the greater span between surveys prevents the implementation of discrete choice models and duration models. This could be overcome by designing the survey's questionnaire so as to accurately retrieve the information pertaining to the in-between surveys periods.

As we discussed earlier, some important works using the HBCS are Carrasco (1999) and Congregado et al. (2003). Carrasco uses the HBCS 1985 covering the period 1979–1990 to study the determinants of the individual's transition from different initial states (unemployed or paid-employed) to different final states (employer, own-account worker) through discrete choice models. In addition, he uses duration models to study the determinants of the duration in self-employment. For this last exercise, the HBCS' rotating panel feature prevents the observation of self-employment periods longer than two years. Moreover, the reduced number of observations forced the author to exclude durations of over three quarters clearly illustrating the limitations of the HBCS source to estimate duration models. Congregado et al. (2003) used both the HBCS 1985 and the HBCS covering the 90s decade, to study the same issues as in Carrasco (1999) but also to study the variables affecting the individual's decision to switch from own account worker (self-employed without employees) to employer (self-employed with employees), considering this decision as an indicator of entrepreneurial success.

6.4.6 Quality of Life at the Workplace Survey

The Quality of Life at the Workplace Survey (ECVT), started by the Spanish Ministry of Labour in 1999, is a sample survey of Spain's employed population, specifically designed to study the quality of life at the workplace at a national level. The ECVT collects objective information on working conditions at the workplace as well as subjective information concerning the personal perceptions that the employed individuals have of their working conditions and relations.

The survey has a sample size of 6.020 employed individuals (ages 16 and over) living in family dwellings. Its geographic scope covers the Spanish national territory with the exception of Ceuta and Melilla. The information provided by this survey is articulated in different modules covering working status, family arrangement, socioeconomic data and information on the quality of life at the workplace.

The module comprising working status provides information regarding the real situation the individual has at his workplace. This includes the size of the firm, type of contract and working time (part or full-time), years in the company, way in which he searched and obtained the job, secondary occupation (if applicable), etc. Concerning the possibility of assessing entrepreneurial activity, the survey allows the identification of self-employment by distinguishing paid-employed from self-employed individuals (but among this last group, it is not possible to identify those having employees). In addition, the National Classification of Occupations (CNO-94) also provides information on the individual's occupation that allows us to identify the corporate entrepreneurial network and the economic activity by applying the National Classification of Economic Activities (CNAE-93). This information is complemented by data on the individual's work experience such as the age and education level at which he started his first job, past occupations, unemployment situations, subsidies received, etc. There is also relevant data on the individual's family social mobility such as his birthplace and that of his progenitors, the educational and labour characteristics of his family, the current family structure and the working situation of the persons living with him.

The family arrangement module provides information on the individual's conjugal status, relationships, family size and type, among others. The socioeconomic module gathers information on the individual's gender, age, marital status, education level, company size, municipality size, etc. The individual is also asked to reveal his political and religious preferences.

Finally, the module on the quality of life at the workplace refers to the individual's attitudes towards his job and the level of satisfaction with it. It collects information on the job's levels of division, organization and communication; on the safety at work and on collective bargaining. It also gathers the individual's opinions on the level of alienation, participation, integration and autonomy at the workplace, and on his working time and retribution. In addition, the module evaluates the level of occupational training and its relation with job promotion.

Presently, the ECVT and the ECHP are the only nation-wide Spanish surveys providing information on the workers' level of satisfaction with their jobs. The ECHP, being a full panel survey, allows for the studying of the dynamic aspects in satisfaction levels. The ECVT, despite renewing the sample completely each year thus preventing controlling for the economic cycle, provides extensive information on the jobs' characteristics and is therefore particularly adequate for analysing the sources of job satisfaction. Even though the absence of income data prevents estimating earnings functions, the collected information may be exploited via sample selection models or discrete choice models to estimate the probability of being self-employed (but not the transition probability). Regarding the duration models, despite having information on the job tenure, we may only reconstruct incomplete durations (individuals that we do not observe to leave self-employment) but not complete durations (individuals that we observe leaving self-employment).

Briefly, the ECVT provides subjective information, absent from the majority of statistical sources, that might be a good complement in studying important aspects of job satisfaction in self-employment compared to paid-employment. However, it lacks the suitable structure and the appropriate sample size to be used as a source of reference in the analysis of the entrepreneurial activity.

6.4.7 European Community Household Panel

The European Community Household Panel (ECHP) is an EU-specific full panel survey using harmonized data of 76.500 households covering over 155.000 individuals in the 15 member states (7.200 households and 15.900 individuals for Spain). It constitutes one of the most important statistical instruments for the European Commission and it reinforces EUROSTAT's current statistical infrastructure. Its main objectives are to study and monitor the living and working conditions, social cohesion, population needs, the impact of socioeconomic policies, and to help in designing new policies for the member states.

The survey was designed in close consultation with the Member States through the denominated National Data Collection Units (NDUs). In most of the countries, the NDUs were formed by the National Statistical Institutes because of the required scientific and technological training.

The preliminary studies were mainly oriented to evaluate the possibility of efficiently using the data provided by pre-existing national and EU surveys with similar information that seemed to fulfil the stated objectives: the Spanish Labour Force Survey (EPA) and the Household Budget Survey (HBS), such as in Spain's case. Regarding the EPA, given its focus on the labour market, it seemed inconvenient to overload its questionnaires and very difficult to adapt it for multiple purposes. This, together with the lack of information on income, invalidated this survey as an instrument for the project. The use of the HBS was also discarded because of the specific requirement of absolute homogeneity across countries in the collected data as well as the necessity of widening it to other research areas.

Therefore, it was necessary to build a new statistical operation, coordinated by EUROSTAT and harmonized for the EU member states, but preserving statistical integration with the other household-addressed surveys (EPA, HBS). It was also considered that the new survey should go beyond the traditional snapshot of transversal information by allowing to capture longitudinal information, i.e. information pertaining to the same set of households and individuals through different periods in time. After several studies and preparatory conferences in the years 1990-1992, a pilot test was conducted in 1993. In 1994, the first wave of eight (initially only three waves were intended: 1994, 1995 and 1996) was conducted in all of the member states.

The ECHP uses the techniques of a full panel which are ideal for the fulfilment of the stated objectives but entail the difficulties associated to the follow-up of the individuals that remain in the sample during excessively long periods[5]. Given the non-existence of previous household full panels in the majority of the participating countries, the harmonization across countries was produced from the very beginning of the project. The panel follows-up on the same set of households and individuals allowing to study the changes in their lives produced by modifications in socioeconomic policies or in aggregate economic conditions, and to capture their reactions. Taking for granted that the effectiveness of a policy must be evaluated according to the way in which the affected react to it, the ECHP will provide very important indicators on the effects of socioeconomic policies framed in the Common Market.

The target population of the survey is formed by the set of private households and individuals living in principal family dwellings in the EU-15 territory (in Spain it is circumscribed to the whole Spanish territory with the exceptions of Ceuta and Melilla).

The information contained in this source has two different reference points that are complemented in a very interesting way: there are independent blocks of questions referring to households and individuals and there is a relationship file that allows us to easily relate the individuals in each household. Thus, on one hand the household file offers data on the composition and the characteristics of each household as well as detailed information on its income. On the other hand, the personal file comprises twelve sections whose brief data content description is as follows:

- General and demographic information: age, gender, marital status.
- Current employment: main activity, status in employment, type of contract (full-time/part-time), occupation in current job, main activity of the local unit of his company or organisation.
- Unemployment: number of times the person has been unemployed, unemployment spells that have exceeded 12 months.
- Search for a job: type of job search the individual has done, conditions in which he would accept to work.

---

[5] These difficulties may be overcome through retrospective studies such as the one conducted in the Sociodemographic Survey of 1991.

- Previous Jobs: whether the individual has worked or owned a business for at least 15 hours per week or not, date and reason for stopping in previous job, comparison between the present job or business with the previous one.
- Calendar of activities: monthly follow-up on the main activity status in the year prior to the interview.
- Income: main source of personal income in the year prior to the survey, current monthly net wage and salary earnings, income received from other sources.
- Education and training: highest level of general or higher education completed, age when the highest level of general or higher education was completed, current studies, and whether the individual has received vocational training paid for or organised by the employer, or not.
- Health: valuation of the individual's health condition, number of times he has consulted a general practitioner or medical specialist, whether he has a state financed health care system or a private medical insurance.
- Social Relations: frequency of relations with the individual's social circle (friends, relatives, neighbours), number of hours spent looking after children or persons (who need special help because of old age, illness or disability).
- Migration: this section analyses factors such as the migration trajectory of the individuals, their current region of residence and their arrival year to the region.
- Satisfaction with various aspects of life: degree of satisfaction with work or main activity, financial situation, housing situation, amount of leisure time.

The study of the labour market is one of the multiple topics that may benefit from the use of the ECHP source. In this sense, some of the important issues in the labour market that may be analysed are the transitions in school-active life (also treated in the standard module of the EPA since 1998), unemployment-employment, within employment, and employment-retirement. This allows the evaluation for instance of the effectiveness of professional training policies as well as the retirement policies. Nevertheless, we should point out that this type of transition analysis sometimes faces an insufficient sample size (e.g. when dealing with infrequent cases). The ECHP is also helpful in illustrating characteristics of the impact of social assistance policies and the role of employment assistance for women. Regarding long-duration unemployment and the return to labour activity thereafter, this source proves to be useful in studying its relation with human capital. As it might be expected, these issues may be redefined in terms of entrepreneurial activity. For the Spanish case, this has been done by the works of Aguado et al. (2003), Carrasco and Ejrnæs (2003) and Congregado et al. (2003, 2005). In all of them, the available information has been exploited through discrete choice models to study the variables leading an individual to choose to become self-employed. In addition, Congregado et al. (2003) develop a self-employment duration model in which, using the first 6 waves of the ECHP and based on the current year's information as well as on retrospective information, they are able to reconstruct self-employment durations of up to 15 years. Because of its characteristics, the panel also allows using sample selection models, decomposition techniques and to estimate earnings functions.

Notwithstanding, the difficulties faced by those who intend to study the entrepreneurial activity through this source deserve some attention. Via the ECHP we may identify self-employed individuals through the employment status stated in the current employment item. However, in order to distinguish among employers, self-employed with employees and own-account workers we must refer to the number of employees as a proxy. But this is obviously an approximation and it lacks the precision one would like to have. There is additional information on the individual's occupation and on the establishment he works at via the International Standard Classification of Occupations (ISCO-88) and the Nomenclature of Economic Activities (NACE-93). In the case of the ISCO-88 it is possible to identify the corporate entrepreneurial network or, in other words, the business executives.

As an additional disadvantage for the use of this source in Spain, the identification of the Spanish geographic zones is made according to the Nomenclature of Territorial Units for Statistics[6] level 1 (NUTS level 1), dividing its national territory in Northwest, Northeast, Madrid, Centre, East, South and Canary Islands. But this level of aggregation prevents us from studying the impact of the economic cycle because in Spain the economic-cycle indicators are generated at the aggregation level NUTS-2.

There exists nevertheless, a different and wider sample corresponding to the year 2000 that covers 15.600 households in Spain and that allows to use the NUTS level 2 classification. By using this sample it is possible to overcome the aforementioned problem but the households in the sample do not correspond to those of the full panel initiated in 1994. Therefore, the sample must be treated as a transversal cut over time thus allowing us to estimate the probability of being self-employed, but not the probability of transition from one state to another. In addition, the duration models cannot be implemented using this cut either.

Given all of the above, the ECHP constitutes a harmonised source that allows us to compare the characteristics of the entrepreneurial network at an international level. It includes information as relevant as the one referring to income (improving over the EPA information) and as limited as the one pertaining to the degree of satisfaction of the individuals with their jobs (only available in the ECVT). Nevertheless, for some of the information that will be obtained for the whole EU-territory, there are already more appropriate sources than the ECHP as, for example, the EPA or the HBS for the Spanish case. Concerning future perspectives, once the ECHP project was completed, a new instrument replaced it since 2004: the European Statistics on Income and Living Conditions (EU-SILC). We devote our next subsection to it.

---

[6] The NUTS is a three-level hierarchical classification in which each Member State is first divided in a number of regions (NUTS level 1), each of which is subdivided into smaller regions (NUTS level 2, corresponding to *Comunidades Autónomas* in Spain, *Regierungsbezirke* in Germany, *Régions* in France, *Regioni* in Italy, etc...), which in turn are subdivided again (NUTS level 3, corresponding to *Provincias* in Spain, *Kreise* in Germany, *Départements* in France, *Provincie* in Italy, etc...).

6.4.8 European Statistics on Income and Living Conditions

The European Statistics on Income and Living Conditions (EU-SILC) is an annual EU-harmonised survey coordinated by EUROSTAT that began in 2004 in Spain. It constitutes an appropriate source for the study of household income, income distribution and social exclusion. Between 1994 and 2001, the European Community Household Panel (ECHP) fulfilled these necessities. However, given that it was necessary to update its content in accordance to the new political demands, and that its functioning needed to be improved (mainly regarding the speed in data production), it was decided that ECHP be replaced by a new instrument with wider coverage; the EU-SILC.

Thus, the EU-SILC was launched in 2003 as a gentleman's agreement between six countries of the EU-15 (Belgium, Denmark, Greece, Ireland, Luxembourg and Austria) and Norway. In 2004, it was re-launched with a more demanding coordination and included most of the EU-15 countries (with the exception of Germany, the Netherlands and the United Kingdom) as well as Estonia, Norway, Iceland, and Turkey. In 2005 the remaining EU-25 member states were incorporated as well as Bulgaria and Rumania. Switzerland will join in 2007.

In Spain, the survey has a rotating panel design where one quarter of the sample is renewed each year allowing the observation of the studied variables' evolution. Around 15.000 households are interviewed and each household remains in the sample during four consecutive years. The households are distributed throughout the entire Spanish territory which allows us to have information at the NUTS-2 level (i.e. *Comunidades Autónomas*) for most of the included variables.

The main objective of the survey is to provide information on income, income distribution and social exclusion in Spain, and to allow comparisons with the other EU countries. It is expected that the survey will include different thematic modules in order to approach relevant social aspects such as social participation and the intergenerational transmission of poverty. More specifically, the EU-SILC is designed to collect data on: household income and economic situation; poverty and social exclusion; employment and labour activity; retirement, retirement benefits and socioeconomic situation of the aged; housing and its related costs; regional Development, and education, health and their impact in the socioeconomic status.

Household income constitutes an essential part in the EU-SILC for the analysis of the living conditions. It includes wage and salary earnings, benefits/losses from self-employment, social assistance, capital and poverty income, private transfers received, children's income, and after-tax income. Some comments regarding this variable should be pointed out. First, as in the ECHP, the income data refers to the year preceding the interview. Second, while the information on wage and salary earnings refers to the individual as well as to the household, the information pertaining to the benefits/losses from self-employment refers only to the household. Third, the survey only collects the monetary component of income (it does not include, for instance, the estimated owner-occupiers dwelling rent, the non-monetary income proceding from own production or the income in kind). These non-monetary components are expected to be incorporated beginning in 2007. Contrary to the ECHP where income was provided in net values, the EU-SILC provides gross income values. This allows for a greater degree of income comparability across Member States because it does not depend on the particular tax-scheme or on the Social Security contributions of each country. Given the initial difficulty in providing gross income data, some countries (Spain included) are allowed to provide net income data during the first years of the survey. Nevertheless, a net-gross conversion process was developed and has been applied since 2004 to obtain current gross wage and salary earnings (i.e. before tax deduction and before Social Security contributions).

The information on employment and Labour activity allows the classification of individuals according to their employment status in the following categories: self-employed with employees, self-employed without employees, employee and family worker. In addition, the survey offers information on the individual's type of occupation (in accordance to the International Standard Classification of Occupations ISCO-88), and on the activity of the establishment he/she works at (in accordance to the Nomenclature of Economic Activities NACE-2002). This will allow the identification of the entrepreneurial activity in a strict sense (i.e. the own-account workers with and without employees) but also the identification of the corporate entrepreneurial network (i.e. the business executives).

In addition to information above, the EU-SILC provides demographic data (age, gender, marital status, place of birth...), information on education, but not as detailed as in the ECHP (highest completed education level and age when completion, current studies...), information on current job (type of contract, number or working hours...), professional experience (characteristics of last main job such as employment status, occupation, type of contract...) job search data (again, not as detailed as in the ECHP) and personal information on general health condition and access to medical care.

This new source constitutes an enormous flow of information that will allow to study, through discrete choice models and sample selection models, all the transitions taking place in the Labour market. The abundant information on net and gross income together with the survey's extensive geographic coverage will allow the estimation of earning functions more accurately; allow for studying the influence of different fiscal schemes; and will provide data pertaining to the role that liquidity constraints play in individual decisions. This faster data availability (just one year after being generated) will allow for a faster redressing of the policies implemented thus gaining in efficiency. Because of its rotating panel feature, the EU-SILC will allow to verify with more reliability the role played by economic aggregate conditions in the individual decision making process. By contrast, the same rotating feature constitutes a disadvantage when trying to estimate duration models because the individuals remain in the sample for four years at most.

6.4.9 Spanish Survey of Household Finances

In 2001, the Spanish Central Bank decided to start the Spanish Survey of Household Finances (EFF), following the example set by other countries in which this type of survey has been conducted for many years. To be more precise, Italy's "Indagine sui bilanci delle famiglie" (IBF)[7] and, most notably, the United State's "Survey of Consumer Finances" (SCF)[8] were the ones that inspired the Spanish survey. The first wave, with a sample of 5.143 households, took place at the end of 2002. The second wave took place at the end of 2005, but from then on it is expected to be conducted every two years. The 2005 sample comprises a panel including the households previously interviewed in 2002, as well as a refreshment sample by wealth stratification. The fundamental objective of this survey is to collect detailed information on the patrimonial situation (i.e. real and financial assets' distribution, debt obligations, etc.) and financial decisions of households in Spain. The EFF-questionnaire is divided in nine main sections: 1) Demographic characteristics; 2) Real assets and associated debts; 3) Other debts; 4) Financial assets; 5) Pension plans and insurances; 6) Labour status and labour income (for all household members); 7)Non-labour income; 8) Means of payment; 9) Consumption and savings.

The EFF constitutes a unique Spanish statistical source linking income, assets, debt obligations and expenditures for each family unit. The most important characteristic of this sample might be the incorporation, through a collaboration system between the INE and the Taxation Agency, of an oversampling of households with a higher wealth level. Since a large proportion of the assets are held by a small fraction of the population, a random standard sample would not contain enough observations for most of the relevant analysis. To illustrate the oversample's importance consider the following: According to the aggregate information on tax statements, 40% of the total taxable wealth is held by 0.4% of the households. Therefore, in a random sample of 5.000 households one would expect to find at most 20 of these households while the EFF sample includes over 500 of them. Nevertheless, we should point out that the oversample does not include households from Navarre and the Basque Country because the Taxation Agency does not have personal fiscal data for those two Spanish Regions.

The EFF's questionnaire allows to clearly identify the entrepreneurs in a strict sense but the identification of the corporate entrepreneurial network is less reliable. In a first filter step, own-account workers are distinguished from the rest (i.e. employee, unemployed, retired, etc.). Then, occupied individuals are asked for their type of occupation (there is only one category grouping private business executives and public executives). The individuals are then asked for the economic sector of their activity and, depending on their working status (i.e. own-account worker, employee or unemployed) each is given a corresponding module.

The own-account worker module provides a big amount of information, including whether it is the individual's main occupation or not, weekly hours worked, number of persons working in the business and whether they are household members or not, the company's legal entity (i.e. entrepreneur—natural person- , corporation, limited liability company, other), working status (i.e. liberal professional,

---

[7] See Banca d'Italia (2000).

[8] See Aizcorbe, Kennickell and Moore (2003).

sole proprietor, business owner, partner in family firm, partner in non-family firm), profits/losses in the year prior to the interview, expected profits/losses for current year, profits share, the individual's shareholding of the firm, shareholding of the firm and the firm's market value.

The employee module provides information on weekly hours worked, part/full-time job, type of contract (i.e. indefinite, temporary, without contract, other), gross labour income, number of working years, initial salary when hired by the company (only if the individual is able to remember it), number of workers in the firm and the expectations of remaining in the firm.

Finally, the unemployed module provides information on the unemployment spell, the sources and the total amount of income and a question regarding the wage at which the individual would accept to work. Note that it would be interesting to exploit this information to test the job search theory based on reservation wages. [9]

In addition, the EFF provides information on demographic characteristics (i.e. age, gender, marital status, citizenship, place of birth, etc.), education (area of studies,[10] highest completed education level and age of completion), health condition, parents' main occupation in their lifes, real assets and related liabilities (including real state, means of transportation, jewelry, works of art, etc.), financial assets, pensions and insurance, household laboural and non-laboural revenues, laboural history of the household members, household consumption and savings (expenditures, savings destination, debt financing, risk aversion, extraordinary income, future expectations, etc.). Finally, information on the use of different means of payment, phone banking and e-banking is also collected.

We conclude this subsection by discussing some of the exploitation possibilities of the EFF source. First, the availability of information on income and its sources makes it suitable to estimate earnings functions. Second, despite being a rotating panel, its biannual feature as well as the lack of information on the immediate previous job[11] present some difficulties for the implementation of either discrete choice models or sample selection models in the analysis of transitions (nonetheless, it is suitable for participation analysis) . Third, because we ignore the sample rotation speed and the continuity of the project (believed to be indefinite) it is hard to evaluate whether it is suitable for the implementation of duration models or not. Therefore, the difficulty in estimating dynamic models prevents the controlling of the economic cycle's impact on individual decisions. Finally, given that entrepreneurs usually have a higher income, the oversampling of higher wealth level households turns this data base into an interesting source for the study of entrepreneurship.

---

[9] This theory tells us that the individual searching for a job would accept the job if the wage offered is greater or equal than his reservation wage. Therefore, there is some probability that the individual will not accept to work during some period and will continue to search. This implies that a fraction of the population will remain unemployed which partially explains the unemployment persistence.

[10] Only if possessing a college degree.

[11] The working history of the individual is from a general perspective, including the longest held job and whether the individual has been mainly self-employed or not.

6.4.10 Continuous Survey of Work Histories

Another important indicator of the entrepreneurial activity is the affiliation to the Social Security system. Managed by the General Treasury of the Social Security, the information proceeds from the statistical exploitation of the workers' historic files of affiliation to the different social security regimes. Nevertheless, we must clarify that up-to-date samples of this source have only been available to some researchers for conducting very concrete studies[12] on pensions, the influence of temporary help agencies (THAs), rates of employment and unemployment and profits distribution. We cannot forget that social security records are designed more for managerial purposes than to conduct population studies. Therefore, generating suitable data for researchers requires considerable technical work in identifying and documenting the relevant information before extracting it. This difficulty is overcome with the Continuous Survey of Work Histories, a new data base that is already available for research Centres conducting specific projects. The objective is to design a sample supplying the data needed for different kinds of research projects. Naturally, the data is anonymous and necessary precautions have been taken so that the personal information cannot be identified. This continuous survey will be updated every year with new information on the people already in the sample and with a proportion of new individuals who have joined the Social Security during the year. The original sample was taken from all the affiliated persons who were, in 2004, either paying to the social security or receiving contributive or unemployment benefits (irrespective of the length of the unemployment duration). The relevant information available through this source includes age, gender, region of work, whether the individual works for the State or not, type of contract, the company's economic activity (CNAE-93), the type of company (joint-stock, limited liability, etc.), the required qualification for the type of work (which is a good proxy for the education level), dates of activation and withdrawal from the social security system, quitting cause (voluntary, dismissal or retirement), unemployment benefits, and worker's taxable earnings base.

Regarding the advantages of this source, first we must point out that it uses real data rather than data obtained from a survey. Therefore, the information provided on the individual's work history allows for studying mobility in the labour market via discrete choice models and duration models with almost absolute precision and reliability.[13] The random sample offers 1.1 million anonymous work histories,

---

[12] See García-Fontes and Hopenhayn (1996), García-Pérez (1997), Jiménez-Martín and Sánchez (2000), Jiménez-Martín and Boldrin (2002), Bover *et al.* (2002), García-Pérez and Muñoz-Bullón (2005); among others.

[13] In this context, we must remember that a worker has to be part of a social security system all his life whether he is working or not. A worker becomes a member of a social security system on commencing work and even if he ceases to work he will continue to be entitled to social security. If, after ceasing work, a worker resumes working then he will be able to commence work again without the need to re-apply for another social security number because, as we have pointed out, once issued with a social security number ("membership" of the particular social security scheme) it is for life.

representing 4% of the reference population (27.4 million people). The sample will be updated by adding each year 4% of the newly incorporated persons to the social security system. Finally, while the elaboration of the EPA costs 13.5 million euros, the social security sample will have technically zero-cost, due to the fact that the information referring to the individual's work history is already available in the social security records.

Nevertheless, there are some disadvantages that are difficult to overcome. The most important is probably the one related to the individuals' wages. The available information refers to the taxable earnings base which allows to recover total wages in a simple way, except for the cases of very low or very high wages because in these cases payments are established by a minimum and a maximum base. The same problem is presented when the individual is subscribed to the own-account worker special regime, because most individuals in this regime declare according to the minimum base and therefore the information on their perceived income is not accurate. In addition, for partnership companies where the owners are wage earners, these owners appear as employees in the social security records while they appear as own-account workers in other employment statistics (i.e. the number of entrepreneurs is underestimated according to the social security records). Finally and like all the statistics generated from administrative registries, data on affiliation to the social security system is subject to variable legal norms which prevents from obtaining a homogenous series over time.

6.4.11 The Global Entrepreneurship Monitor Project

Finally, we point out the research project Global Entrepreneurship Monitor (GEM) jointly developed by Babson College (Massachussetts) and the London Business School. It was initiated in 1998 intending to generate harmonised annual data on entrepreneurship. It first started with 10 countries and currently covers 39 countries (including Spain since 2000) with a minimum of 2.000 individuals interviewed in each country. Since 2003 there is a regional version of the project, the Regional Entrepreneurship Monitor (REM), which increases and enriches the sample as well as the study's penetration.

Its main objective is to measure entrepreneurial activity in its initial stages for each of the participating countries (this is done in a harmonised way, thus allowing for cross-country comparability). In order to carry out this task, the Total early-stage Entrepreneurial Activity or TEA-index is constructed. This index identifies the starters and owner-managers of new businesses. The starters are those individuals between the ages of 18 and 64 that started a new business in the year prior to the interview and that have not paid more than three payrolls when interviewed. The owner-managers of a new business are those that have not paid salaries or wages for more than 42 months. The sum of the two measures serves to calculate the rates of entrepreneurial activity in each country.

But the GEM not only quantifies entrepreneurial activity, it also compiles information on the economic environment of the businesses and on the influence of sociological and psychological factors leading to entrepreneurship. Finally, the motivations of potential entrepreneurs are also analysed.

The exploitation possibilities of this source allows for cross-country comparability of entrepreneurial activity rates. However, the definition of entrepreneurial activity that it uses is not comparable with those on which other sources like EUROSTAT or the OECD are based. Also, duration models and earnings functions cannot be estimated because of the lack of panel data, retrospective information, and income data. In addition, discrete choice models and sample selection models can only be based on participation (but not in transitions from one state to another). Because all of the above, it is not surprising that besides the GEM national and regional reports, there are no other studies exploiting this source in Spain.

6.5 Conclusions and Future Perspectives

In this paper we have tried to identify and evaluate the information sources available to study entrepreneurship in Spain. We have seen that the analysis of entrepreneurial activity may be carried out through a wide variety of sources: both in quantitative terms, as in the firm demography studies; and in qualitative terms, through population surveys. We have covered the emergence of new statistical sources that, along with the improvement of the already existing ones, have contributed to enrich the information available to study the labour market.

Nevertheless, in spite of the different organizations' efforts in offering important and substantive amount of information, we see how the suitability of the sources is not fully adapted to the demands of entrepreneurial network analysts: the EPA still does not provide data on income, the ECHP project ended, the ECPF changed from quarterly to annual regularity, the Population Census and the ECVT still do not match the pursued goal, etc. Regarding the new emerging surveys, only the EU-SILC, in spite of its limitations, seems to get close to the ideal: the GEM project will only allow for cross-country comparability of entrepreneurial activity from a particular definition; the Continuous Survey of Work Histories will allow for a better definition of the transitions and the durations but it does not include many entrepreneurs and information is very limited; the EFF will provide enough explanatory information but fails to capture dynamic behaviour. Given that the National Statistical Plan 2005–2008[14] does not even mention the statistical information deficiencies on entrepreneurial activity, future perspectives are therefore not hopeful. Studies on entrepreneurship will still rely more on the skills and imagination of the researchers than on the suitability of the surveys.

Although the available information only allows carrying out a partial analyses of the entrepreneurship phenomenon, not all the blame can be put on data deficiencies.

---

[14] The National Statistical Plan is the main instrument organizing the statistical activity of the State General Administration. It contains the statistics that are to be carried out during the quadrennial period of reference.

In this sense, part of the problem comes from the fact that the economic analysis of entrepreneurship has not yet reached the degree of development necessary to reveal clear statistical necessities. As a result, there have been erratic uses of sources and indicators depending on the specific approach adopted: individual entrepreneurial network analysis, corporate entrepreneurial network analysis or firm demography studies. As we surpass these obstacles, a homogenization of the demands for this type of data should be created to improve the statistical measurements that would allow capturing the different dimensions in which entrepreneurship affects economic activity.

Acknowledgments The authors would like to thank José Ignacio García Pérez and our colleagues at the Universidad de Huelva, for their helpful comments and advice.

References

Aguado R, Congregado E, Millán JM (2003) Entrepreneurship, financiación e innovación. Revista de Economía Industrial 34(7):125–34

Aizcorbe A, Kennickell A, Moore KB (2003) Recent Changes in U.S. Family Finances: Evidence from the 1998 and 2001. Survey of Consumer Finances, Federal Reserve Bulletin

Alba-Ramírez A (1994) Self-employment in the midst of unemployment: The case of Spain and the United States. Applied Economics 26:189–205

Arellano M, Meghir C (1992) Female Labour Supply and On-the-Job-Search: An Empirical Model Estimated Using Complementary Data Sets. Review of Economic Studies 59(3):537–59

Audretsch DB (2002) Entrepreneurship: A Survey of the Literature. Prepared for the European Commission, Enterprise Directorate General

Banca d'Italia (2002) Supplements to the Statistical Bulletin. Methodological notes and statistical information. Italian Household Budgets in 2000

Bernhardt I (1994) Competitive advantage in self-employment and paid work. Canadian Journal of Economics 27:273–289

Blanchflower DG (2000) Self-employment in OECD countries. Labour Economics 7:471–505

Blanchflower DG (2004a) Self-employment: more may not be better. NBER Working Paper 10286 (Forthcoming Swedish Economic Policy Review)

Blanchflower DG, Oswald AJ (1998) What makes an entrepreneur. Journal of Labour Economics 16:26–60

Böheim R, Taylor MP (2000) Unemployment Duration and Exit States in Britain. ISER working papers 2000–01, Institute for Social and Economic Research

Borjas GJ, Bronars S (1989) Consumer discrimination and self-employment. Journal of Political Economy 97:581–605

Bover O, Bentolila S, Arellano M (2002) The Distribution of Earnings in Spain During the 1980s: The Effects of Skill, Unemployment, and Union Power. In: Cohen D, Piketty T, Saint-Paul G (eds) The Economics of Rising Inequalities. CEPR, Oxford University Press, London

Bover O (2004) The Spanish Survey of Household Finances (EFF): Description and Methods of the 2002 Wave. Occasional Paper n 0409, Banco de España

Carrasco R (1999) Transitions to and from self-employment in Spain: an empirical analysis. Oxford Bulletin of Economics and Statistics 61(3):315–41

Carrasco R, Ejrnæs M (2003) Self-employment in Denmark and Spain: institutions, economic conditions and gender differences. CAM Institute of Economics University of Copenhagen WP 2003–06

Clark K, Drinkwater S (2000) Pushed out or pulled in? Self-employment among minorities in England and Wales. Labour Economics 7:603–628

Congregado E, Golpe A, Millán JM (2003) Some Empirical Aspects of Self-Employment in Spain during the nineties. Seminario de Análisis Económico, Universidad de Huelva, SAE WP 20

Congregado E, Golpe A, Millán JM (2005) Determinantes de la oferta de empresarios. In: García J, Pérez J (eds) Cuestiones Clave de la Economía Española Perspectivas actuales 2004. Ed. Comares, pp 165–87

De Wit G (1993) Models of self-employment in a competitive market. Journal of Economic Surveys 7:367–97

De Wit G, van Winden F (1989) An empirical analysis of self-employment in the Netherlands. Small Business Economics 1:263–72

De Wit G, van Winden F (1990) An empirical analysis of self-employment in the Netherlands. Economic Letters 32:97–100

De Wit G, van Winden F (1991) An M-sector, N-group behavioural model of self-employment. Small Business Economics 3:49–66

Dolton PJ, Makepeace GH (1990) Self-employment among graduates. Bulletin of Economic Research 42:35–53

Earle JS, Sakova Z (2000) Business start-ups or disguised unemployment? Evidence on the character of self-employment from transition economies. Labour Economics 7:575–601

Evans DS, Jovanovic B (1989) An estimated model of entrepreneurial choice under liquidity constraints. Journal of Political Economy 97:808–27

Evans DS, Leighton LS (1989) Some empirical aspects of entrepreneurship. American Economic Review 79 (3):519–35

Falter JM (2002) Self-Employment entry and duration in Switzerland. Working paper, Employment Center, University of Geneva

Fujii ET, Hawley CB (1991) Empirical aspects of self-employment. Economics Letters 36: 323–29

García I, Montuenga VM (2004) Education returns of wage earners and self-employed workers: Portugal vs. Spain. Economics of Education Review 24: 161–70

García-Fontes W, Hopenhayn H (1996) Flexibilización y Volatilidad del Empleo. Moneda y Crédito 201:205–27

García-Pérez JI (1997) Las Tasas de Salida del Empleo y el Desempleo en España (1978–1993). Investigaciones Económicas 21(1):29–53

García-Pérez JI, Muñoz-Bullón F (2005) Are Temporary Help Agencies changing mobility patterns in the Spanish labour market? Spanish Economic Review 7(1):43–65

Gil FJ, Martín MJ, Serrat A (1994) Movilidad en el mercado de trabajo en España: un análisis econométrico de duración con riesgos en competencia. Investigaciones Económicas 18(3): 517–37

Gill AM (1988) Choice of employment status and the wages of employees and the self-employed: some further evidence. Journal of Applied Econometrics 3:229–34

Grilo I, Thurik AR (2004) Determinants of Entrepreneurship in Europe. ERIM Report Series Research in Management ERS-2004-106-ORG

Holtz-Eakin D, Joulfaian D, Rosen RH (1994) Entrepreneurial decisions and liquidity constraints. Rand Journal of Economics 25:334–47

Hundley G (2001) Why women earn less than men in self-employment. Journal of Labor Research 22:817–29

Jiménez-Martín S, Sánchez AR (2000) Incentivos y reglas de jubilación en España. Cuadernos Económicos de ICE 65

Jiménez-Martín S, Boldrin M (2002) Evaluating Spanish Pension Expenditure Under Alternative Reform Scenario. Working Paper ref 652, Universitat Pompeu Fabra (Forthcoming in a Chicago University press volume)

Parker SC (2002) Do banks ration credit to new enterprises? And should governments intervene? Scottish Journal of Political Economy 49:162–95

Parker SC (2003a) Does tax evasion affect occupational choice? Oxford Bulletin of Economics and Statistics 65:379–94

Parker SC (2004) The Economics of Self-Employment and Entrepreneurship. Cambridge University Press, Cambridge

Parker SC, Belguitar Y, Barmby T (2005) Wage uncertainty and self-employed labour supply. Economic Journal 115:190–207

Rees H, Shah A (1986) An empirical analysis of self-employment in the UK. Journal of Applied Econometrics 1:95–108

Reize F (2004) Leaving Unemployment for Self-Employment. An Empirical Study. ZEW Economics Studies 25, Physica-Verlag, Manheim

Reynolds P, Bosma N, Autio E; Hunt S, De Bono N, Servais I; López García P, Chin N (2005) Global Entrepreneurship Monitor: Data Collection Design and Implementation 1998–2003. Small Business Economics 24(3):205–31

Segarra A, Callejón M (2002) New firms' survival and market turbulence: new evidence from Spain. Review of Industrial Organization 20(1):1–14

Segarra A (dir.) et al (2002) La creación y la supervivencia de las empresas industriales. Civitas

Taylor MP (1996) Earnings, independence or unemployment: why become self-employed? Oxford Bulletin of Economics and Statistics 58:253–66

Chapter 7
A Proposed Framework for Business Demography Statistics

Nadim Ahmad

Abstract This chapter provides a step in that direction by proposing a framework of business demography indicators that can be applied across all OECD and large non OECD economies. The framework tries to provide a mechanism by which more comparable indicators of business demography can be produced across countries by considering both what is practically achievable and desirable. The framework deliberately sets out to measure business demographics. It does not therefore make proposals concerning other important indicators of entrepreneurship such as the characteristics of entrepreneurs (age, sex, education, previous entrepreneurial experience etc), entrepreneurial and related policies (government policy, bankruptcy regulations, access to finance, fiscal policy—personal and business taxes—business administrative burdens, employment laws, social security safety nets etc) or the characteristics of businesses that may predetermine success, such as research and development expenditure; although this work is being pursued as part of the OECD's Entrepreneurship Indicators Project (see Davis, 2006). That said, the framework is able to provide information on types of businesses, successful, young, old, sector specific, etc, that can be used to provide the frame for dedicated surveys that attempt to determine what makes businesses succeed or fail.

7.1 Introduction

The creation of new businesses and the decline of unproductive ones are often regarded key to business dynamism in OECD economies. Understanding business behaviour and (Schumpeterian) creative destruction, and identifying successful and failing businesses, as well as fostering entrepreneurship and innovation have become increasingly important objectives for policy makers in many OECD economies in

Nadim Ahmad

Manager of the OECD's Structural Business Databases, Statistics Directorate of the OECD, Paris, France,

Nadim.AHMAD@oecd.org

recent years.[1] Business churn *(i.e.* entry plus exit rates) is commonly viewed as a measure of the ability of economies to expand the boundaries of economic activity, to shift resources towards growing areas and away from declining areas, and to adjust the structure of production to meet consumers' changing needs. Moreover, higher rates of business creation and churning are generally held to benefit economic growth, job creation and poverty alleviation via increased productivity and innovation.[2]

The growing interest in these issues, and entrepreneurship more generally, has also influenced statistical development in this area. For example, as shown in Section 2, many national statistical offices now provide official statistics on the exit, entry and turnover of businesses. The Statistical Office of the European Union, Eurostat, has recently developed an enterprise demography database that includes many EU countries and little of this development has led to increased burdens on businesses, since much of the information is provided by existing data sources, for example business registers and administrative tax sources. This initiative has greatly improved the comparability of business demography data from European countries but comparisons of these statistics across non-EU countries are more complex (see Vale 2006). This largely reflects that fact that national definitions and concepts of business demography statistics usually reflect domestic data availability and the fact that internationally recognised definitions and concepts, with the notable exception of Eurostat, are largely non-existent. The OECD has also conducted one-off collections and studies of business demography statistics in the past (e.g. Bartelsman et al. 2003) on a harmonised basis, for the purposes of productivity and economic growth analysis, but these datasets also contained data that was not strictly harmonised for all countries (Brandt 2004).

Efforts have been made by the Global Entrepreneurship Monitor (GEM)[3] to develop an indicator of Early Stage Entrepreneurial Activity, formerly called the Total Entrepreneurial Activity (TEA) index, based on household interviews, that measures the number of entrepreneurs per capita (18-64 age group) that have started a business in the last 42 months. Useful as this measure is in providing some indication of the general level of new entrepreneurs it suffers through not being able to say much about the survival probability, employment, or growth potential of the newly created entrepreneurships; key issues of concern to policy makers interested in entrepreneurship. Moreover, a key issue concerns the types of entrepreneurs captured in the GEM survey. Many of the new start-ups will have very limited, if any, growth potential beyond satisfying the immediate, often subsistence, needs of the entrepreneur and, because these entrepreneurs are not tracked over time, the GEM approach is not able to identify the types and characteristics of businesses that are

---

[1] The Bologna Charter on SME Polices and the 'Bologna Process'; The 2nd OECD Ministerial Conference on SMEs, Istanbul 2004; European Commission Lisbon Summit and the "Lisbon Strategy', 2000.

[2] A number of studies also demonstrate strong correlations between turnover rates and GDP growth, see for example Barnes et al. 2002.

[3] See http://www.gemconsortium.org/ for more information.

likely to succeed. Additionally, because it is a household based survey it cannot truly be used to estimate the numbers of new enterprises, which could be particularly problematic if business creations by serial (multi business owning) entrepreneurs are significant. Equally the sample sizes and the respondent's perception of what constitutes a new business and the sector in which it operates are not always the same across countries.

The business demography database developed by Eurostat is better equipped to provide input into policy since: it is able to provide information on births, deaths and survivability at a relatively detailed sectoral level; uses common definitions for these variables as well as the definition of a business; and, is largely based on information coming from national business registers which, in theory, capture all new business entries and exits.[4] In addition, the database provides some information relating to the characteristics of the entrepreneurship; namely its legal form.

But more detailed information is required if one is to obtain a more comprehensive understanding of entrepreneurs and start-ups or, rather, the factors of success (and failure). For example: which start-ups are likely to grow fastest and provide the best long-term growth opportunities, and, specifically, what are the key characteristics that might determine success, such as foreign ownership, access to capital etc. Policy makers are also interested in the characteristics of entrepreneurship as outcomes too, and not only as inputs that might determine success, for example, increasing female or minority group entrepreneurship are policy objectives in many countries. Although this type of detailed information is not provided in the Eurostat database it can be attained indirectly, using survey based approaches that target successful and failed businesses;[5] an approach taken by Eurostat in their Factors of Business Success project and which is currently being considered by the OECD's Entrepreneurship Indicators Project.

The Eurostat framework and database has provided an important resource to compare business demography statistics internationally but, by design, the Eurostat framework has been developed in an EU context reflecting the needs, data availability and business statistics regulations applicable to EU countries. But business demography statistics between the Eurostat group of countries and other OECD economies, such as Australia, Canada, Iceland, Japan, Korea, Mexico, New Zealand Turkey and the United States, and other important global players, such as Brazil, China, and India, remain incomparable, see below (and Vale 2006). The OECD has an obvious role to play in bridging the gap between these countries. This document provides a step in that direction by proposing a framework of business demography indicators that can be applied across all OECD and large non OECD economies.

---

[4] In practice all business registers will operate with some form of threshold that excludes very small businesses operating, usually, below some employee or turnover threshold where registration, whether on a statistical or administrative register, is not required.

[5] Identifying and surveying failed businesses is more challenging, since, by their nature, they no longer exist.

The framework is broken down into 7 main sections. The first, Section 2, provides a brief overview of business demography statistics that are currently produced by international and national statistics institutes. Section 3 tackles a key issue, one that is central to any discussion on business demography indicators, head-on; namely the definition of a business. Section 4 provides a definition of business births; births being the expression used to describe pure creations of businesses. Section 5 provides a definition of the corollary to births, deaths. Section 6 provides definitions of birth and death rates by considering the populations (denominator) that should be used in defining these indicators. Section 7 provides definitions of survival rates and Section 8 considers the issues of high growth firms and young high growth firms (gazelles).

7.2 Overview and Comparison of current data sources

7.2.1 Comparability of Current National Statistics

The main motivation for the development of this framework is the perception that current national official estimates of statistics related to business demographics, such as start-up, exit and survival rates, numbers of high growth businesses, and definitions for small and medium businesses say are not comparable internationally. The picture is murkier still when non official sources of information are also considered, such as estimates derived from private databases, such as Dun and Bradstreet, or from survey based sources such as GEM. This plethora of competing sources, using different concepts, makes it very difficult for policy makers and analysts alike to use these data. However, national statistics offices have plenty of experience in developing national statistics, for example GDP, based on harmonised concepts and comparable sources, and, so, in principle, there exists tremendous scope for improvement in the comparability of business demography statistics. This section provides some assessment of this scope by comparing current data sources used by, or available to, national statistics institutes.

In practice most national statistics offices derive estimates of entries and exits using statistical business registers, and so the focus of this section will be on business register based information. That is not to say that survey based methods are not worth consideration. Much can be gained using survey based information but, in order to have good quality information, large sample sizes are required, and this is especially so if information on specific types of businesses are required; which can only be identified post, or during the survey. Business register information on the other hand is largely exhaustive in its coverage, certainly for non-micro businesses, and it provides the means by which specific businesses can be systematically targeted if follow-up investigations are desired.

But it is clear that even amongst countries that produce business demography statistics using business registers, significant methodological differences exist. There are a number of reasons why these differences exist. These can stem from very basic differences, such as the way in which businesses are defined, to more complex differences such as the way in which entries are identified and defined; which are affected by many factors, for example, the coverage of data sources used to measure entries, and the treatment of demographic events, such as mergers and take-overs, to name but two. The bottom line however is that the methodology used by national statistics institutions is driven primarily by national considerations rather than a desire for international comparability. A quote from a recent Australian paper on establishing a conceptual framework for business demography (ABS 2004) illustrates this well; "Whilst international comparability of the data is considered to be important, the overriding requirement is the provision of data in the Australian context". This is not stated as clearly by other national data providers, but appears to be a widely held view. Understanding the differences between national data sets is therefore a vital pre-condition to any meaningful analyses of them.

The main purpose of this proposed framework therefore is to provide a system of definitions that can improve the comparability of national statistics on business demographics. However, it will be some time before national statistics institutions will be in a position to produce statistics on the basis of such a framework and, as such, it is important to understand how and why current national estimates differ conceptually. This comprehension is equally invaluable in feeding in to the development of the framework itself; since it would be pointless developing a conceptual framework that could never be implemented in practice.

To provide a simple picture of the current degree of incomparability it is instructive to look at one of the most important business demography indicators commonly produced by national statistics offices: start-up rates (see Vale 2006), since a study of start-up rates reveals much about the incomparability of other business demography indicators, such as death rates, say, and related concepts such as the statistical units used to define businesses.

7.2.2 Start-Up Rates

The Chart 7.1 compares start-up rates across a number of OECD countries. It shows significant variation across countries, but at least part of this variation reflects conceptual differences and some care is needed in interpretation. For example, the increase in start-up rates for Slovakia in 2001 reflects changes to the coverage of source information, in this case business registers, which included unincorporated enterprises with no employees for the first time in the 2001 data.

In some countries, for example the United States, the estimates exclude businesses without employees from the scope of start-ups and businesses, whereas the Eurostat methodology includes these businesses. That said, although the harmonised framework developed by Eurostat stipulates the rules that should be used in defining births and the population from which they are sourced (via European regulations governing business registers), practical differences in the way concepts are constructed do exist between EU economies. This is partly because different approaches

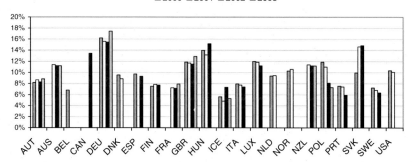

Fig. 7.1 Business Start-up Rates in Selected OECD Countries
Source: National statistical offices and Eurostat

are used in measuring enterprises, the statistical business unit adopted by Eurostat, but also because the development of business registers in some countries is continuing, and, as such, the coverage of activities is not currently identical across EU economies.

However the incomparability of national estimates of start-up rates can be established even without resorting to international comparisons. Vale, 2006, for example compares 5 start-up rates for the US, further showing that even where the rates appear to be similar, fundamental differences may still exist in the components (numerator and denominator) used in their construction; as shown in Figs. 7.2 (a), (b), and (c) below.

There are of course explanations for these differences, the key one being that not all entries are necessarily new businesses; some new entries reflect other demographic events, such as take-overs for example, and some of the US measures shown above try to correct for those entries that are not new businesses. Periodicity is another factor. One of the series shown above, for example, shows annualised quarterly data[6]. But different treatments of demographic events are not the only causes of difference; many others exist, as described in the typology below. The key point, however, is that an international framework is needed to describe how these factors can be treated in a consistent way across all countries.

---

[6] If start-up rates are calculated for sub-annual periods they can be averaged to produce annual totals, though these totals will be higher than those based on annual snap-shots due to better coverage of businesses that survive for less than one year. If sub-annual start-up data are only available in the form of birth rates, it is clearly more difficult to estimate the annual rate without further information about the net change in the population. Work to convert quarterly establishment start-up data from the Business Employment Dynamics series produced by the US Bureau of Labor Statistics to an annual basis has resulted in differences of over 40% between annualised start-ups and the combination of start-ups for the four separate quarters. This is a result of both the removal of short-lived businesses, and improvements to the 'purity' of the start-up estimates, removing entries that arise from other demographic events such as mergers say, by better linking establishments over time, (see Pinkston and Spletzer 2004).

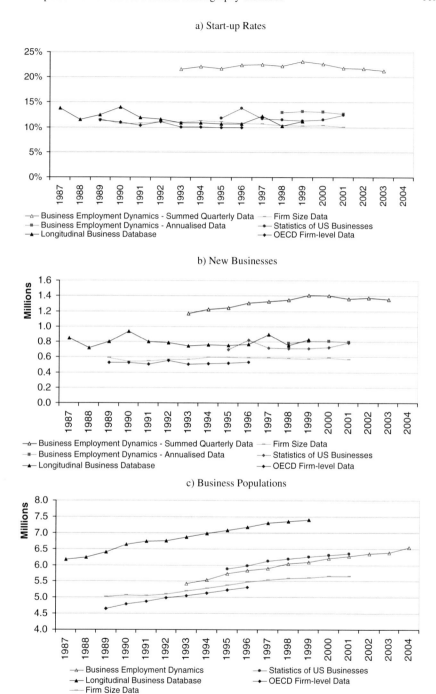

Fig. 7.2 Comparing Start-up Rates, New Businesses and Business Populations in the US

7.2.3 Typology of Factors Affecting Comparability

Nine main factors have been identified as affecting the conceptual comparability of business demography statistics.

- Units—what is the statistical unit used to measure businesses?
- Source—are the data taken from a register, a census or a survey? How reliable is the source?
- Coverage—to what extent are certain types of business included or excluded based on specific attributes (e.g. economic activity or legal form)?
- Thresholds—what explicit or implicit size thresholds apply to the source?
- Purity—to what extent can real births (and deaths) of businesses be distinguished from other demographic events, (such as mergers, take-overs, reactivations etc), that create new entries (and exits) but not births (or deaths); where births (deaths) reflect the creation (destruction) of combinations of new production factors, such as location, assets and employees, organisational structures etc.
- Timing—at what point are entries, exits, births and deaths identified?
- Periodicity—over what period are births and deaths measured, and how does this affect the measurement of very short-lived businesses?
- Type of Population—are businesses or people used in constructing the denominator for entry and exit rates?
- Temporal basis—is the population measured at a specific point in time, or does it consist of all units that were present at any time during a given period?

Various other factors affect business demographics such as the size of national economies, demand and supply constraints, the impact of tax, subsidy and other policies, the nature of the political system, and a wide range of other economic, political and social and cultural factors. None of these factors relate to the concepts and methodology used in constructing business demography statistics, and many of them account for the sort of variation in data that users are really interested in.

7.2.4 Inventory of Country Practices

The Table 7.1 provides a summary of business demography indicators currently produced by national statistics institutes in a number of OECD countries. It demonstrates that considerable differences exist in the purity, coverage, temporal basis and business units used across countries. It also provides information related to the Eurostat business demography framework, which many countries contribute to. The important point to recognise here is that, although the Eurostat framework prescribes recommended ways in which business demography indicators should be developed, the estimates provided by some countries are not yet compiled on this basis.

Table 7.1 Comparing Business Demography Statistics and their Sources

Country	Agency	Units	Source	Coverage
Australia	ABS Unternehmensneugrün	Legal	Register	Excludes non-market enterprises
Austria	dungen in Österreich 1993-2004	Enterprise.	Register	..
Belgium	Statistical Office	Legal	Register	Some specific legal, medical, financial, social and personal services are exempt from value-added tax. Public sector entities are included if they are registered for VAT
Canada	Statistical Office	Legal	Register	
Finland	Statistical Office	Enterprise	Register	Excludes foundations, housing companies, voluntary associations, public authorities and religious communities. The data cover state-owned enterprises, but not those owned by municipalities.
France	Statistical Office	Enterprises	Register	
Germany	Statistical Office	Local unit	Register	Excludes certain health, public administration, insurance and agricultural activities
Hungary	Statistical Office	Enterprise	Register	Includes all businesses with active registration and a tax number in the register, including most government bodies. There is no registration threshold so part-time businesses are included.
Japan	Statistical Office	Establishment	Census	Excludes sole-proprietor businesses in agriculture, forestry and fishing activities, or any businesses classified to domestic services, foreign governments or international agencies.
Netherlands	Statistical Office	Enterprises	Register	Excludes NACE categories (Sections A, B, E, L, M and N, and divisions 70, 73, 91 and 92).
NewZealand	Statistical Office	Legal unit	Register	The data exclude agriculture production (ANZSIC subdivision A01). They also exclude businesses of "little economic significance
Norway	Statistical Office	Enterprises	Register	Enterprises classified to public administration, agriculture, forestry and fishing are excluded, as are central and local government units

Table 7.1 continued

Country	Agency	Units	Source	Coverage
Spain	Statistical Office	Enterprises	Register	
Sweden	Statistical Office	Legal unit	Register	
Switzerland	Statistical Office	Enterprises	Register	Excludes in agriculture, forestry, fishing and public administration.
Turkey	Statistical Office	Business establishments excluding companies and cooperatives.	Register	..
United Kingdom	Statistical Office	Legal unit	Register	The data cover all economic activities and legal forms, though coverage is limited for certain activities that are exempt from VAT, particularly in the education and health sectors.
United States	Census Bureau	Establishment	Census	Excludes non-market sector and some public corporations.
..	Small Business Agency	Firm (Enterprise)	Census	See above
..	Census Bureau - longitudinal-	Establishment	Census	See above
Eurostat:	Enterprise	Register	Recommends NACE C to O, excluding L but practice varies by country	Recommends all active firms but practice varies by country

Country	Threshold	Purity	Timing	Periodicity	Temporal
Australia	50,000 Australian Dollars (approx. €31,000), with some exceptions, and some voluntary registrations	Excludes inactive businesses, changes in legal form, and reactivations, and identified take-overs.	Entries and Exits on the Register	Annual	Point-in-Time
Austria	..	New registrations are adjusted to remove re-registrations, dormant units, and multiple	Entries and Exits on the Register	Annual	Point-in-Time

Table 7.1 continued

Country	Threshold	Purity	Timing	Periodicity	Temporal
		registrations for the same enterprise. Adjustments are also made for registration lags.			
Belgium	No VAT registration threshold.	None	Entries and Exits on the Register	Annual	Point-in-Time
Canada	One or more employees		Entries and Exits on the Register	Annual	Live-During-Period
Finland	VAT registered and employers only	..	Entries and exits on the LEAP database	Annual	..
France		Excludes self employed reactivations and take-overs		Annual	..
Germany	Covers businesses with a turnover of at least €16,620 per year.	none	Entries and Exits on the register	Annual	..
Hungary	..	..		Half-yearly	Point-in-Time
Japan	..	..	New Establishments (based on location checks between censuses).	Five-yearly, annualised	
Netherlands	At least one person works in the enterprise for at least 15 hours a week	Tracks continuity, so excludes mergers, take-overs, reactivations etc		Annual	
New Zealand	Greater than $30,000 (approx €17,500) annual taxable expenses or sales and/or rolling mean employee count of greater than three		Exits and Entries on the Register	Annual	

Table 7.1 continued

Country	Threshold	Purity	Timing	Periodicity	Temporal
Norway	..	Excludes take-overs.		Annual	
Spain	..	Excludes	..		
Sweden		Reactivations			
			..		
Switzerland	..	Excludes reactivations and take-overs.	.		
Turkey	..	..	..		
United Kingdom	VAT registered and employing enterprises	..	Exits and Entries on the Register	Annual	
United States	Businesses without employees are excluded	..	..		
..	See above	..	..	Annual	point in time
..	See above	Adjusted for reactivations	..	Annual	point in time
Eurostat:	Excludes all continuing firms		Annual		

7.3 Defining Businesses

7.3.1 Business Definitions at the National Level

A fundamental requirement in measuring business entries (creation) and exits (destruction) concerns the definition of a business itself. The notion varies considerably, whether the interpretation is that of statistical offices or in the more general sense of that used by the man on the street or financial markets say. Statistical offices will typically define businesses according to their activity within national boundaries, although businesses are also, and increasingly so, measured in a global, multinational sense too; which corresponds more closely with the view of the general public, at least as far as multinationals go. That is not to say however that the definitions used by national statistical offices are consistent across countries[7]. Many businesses (parents) own or control other businesses (subsidiaries) operating within the same economy. Depending on the degree of control and the nature of economic activity, some statistical offices will consolidate parents with subsidiaries, others will not.

---

[7] Work by Eurostat (Herczog et al. 1998) for example, demonstrated that the operational definitions used for enterprises differed considerably for some firm configurations, across countries, both conceptually and, more commonly, in practice.

The rules that govern what statistical offices do largely reflect institutional and administrative arrangements that exist in each country. Not surprisingly these differ across countries and so too, therefore, do the definitions used for businesses. It's important to put these differences into context however and, perhaps, to explain why they have arisen and continue.

International definitions of businesses do exist. For example the System of National Accounts, Eurostat (EC Regulation 696/93) and the International Standard Industrial Classification of all Economic Activities (ISIC) all provide definitions. Although these three systems do not entirely converge, three main types of statistical unit emerge: Enterprises, Establishments (or local kind of activity unit) and Enterprise Groups. Legal units are usually the building blocks used in defining businesses in all of these measures but legal units are not themselves comparable across countries since they reflect national administrative and legal requirements that will differ across countries.

All OECD countries are able to produce structural business statistics on these bases (albeit with some differences in practice), often to meet the needs of international organisations, like the OECD, and often for their own needs for example in producing R&D statistics, which can only be practically produced at the Enterprise (and Enterprise Group) level, or the national accounts, which are typically based on establishment measures. However, the focus on business demography statistics by statistical offices is relatively new and, so, the business definitions used across countries differ.

Historically the main use of business statistics has been in providing inputs into the calculation of gross domestic product (GDP) and to separately identify the contribution to economic activity made by different (and as homogeneous as possible) industrial sectors. Businesses, in this context, have therefore been defined as reporting units in a way that facilitates the collection of statistics to meet these needs, whilst at the same time minimising the data burden on the businesses themselves. Whether a reporting unit is a subsidiary or not is only relevant if the subsidiary is not able to provide the information required, such as turnover, production, profits etc, to meet the needs of the statistical office. Typically, these reporting units are most effective when they correspond to business operating structures, which may or may not correspond to legal units, local units or establishments. It is usually possible to aggregate reporting units to give enterprise level data, though, for a few specific variables such as profits or overseas investment, the optimal reporting unit may sometimes correspond to a group of enterprises.

In collating business statistics as inputs into the national accounts for example, this approach works reasonably well, since in most cases it is able to provide the key economic aggregates needed at a detailed industry level whilst ensuring that businesses (reporting units) within each industry group are broadly homogeneous. This is especially true where local kind of activity units form the reporting unit and, although less so where enterprises are concerned, in all countries most enterprises correspond to local kind of activity units. In other words, the definition used for businesses in providing data for the national accounts, say, has only mattered in the sense that the more detailed the unit, the more homogeneous the industry activity measured - meaning that the business definition, in theory, only impacts on the distribution of value-added among industry groups; for total GDP the definition is of little theoretical relevance.

The needs of business demography statistics are however somewhat different. Because their main purpose is to provide information relating to the number of new businesses (entries), failures (exits) and growth, the definition of a business is of crucial importance since it impacts directly on entry, exit and growth rates. Indeed, as demonstrated below, the definition results in a trade-off between exit and entry figures and growth.

7.3.2 Selecting the Statistical Unit for Businesses

Consider an enterprise that initially comprises a single local kind of activity unit or establishment that then expands by creating another local kind of activity unit of the same size as the original unit but with effective operational control remaining at the enterprise level.

If businesses are defined as local kind of activity units this expansion results in an entry but no growth in the original business (establishment). If, on the other hand, businesses are defined as enterprises, no entries would have occurred but the original business unit would have doubled in size. Which of the approaches is better for policy purposes is not immediately obvious, since that depends on the policy focus. But a further expansion of the example can help to illustrate some consequences of each approach.

Consider now the outcome if the original enterprise grew by expanding its operations at the same (original) site. In this case, whether businesses are defined at the enterprise or local activity level, the result is the same; no births and 100% growth. Defining businesses as local kind of activity units or establishments therefore can result in an asymmetric treatment of growth dependent on location; which renders this approach inappropriate for policy makers interested in business demography statistics that paint a picture of the whole economy, as the results should be invariant, at least within economic borders, to where businesses choose to grow. That is not to say however that establishment based data cannot play a role in practice, since policy makers interested in investigating regional (state, county, local area) differences will not of course be able to use business demography data based solely at the national level. However even in these circumstances it is preferable to use the enterprise definition, albeit, where enterprises are defined on the basis of the economic borders of the regions; and, in practice, the smaller the region the more likely that enterprises and establishments align.

One could say that many enterprises are also part of larger enterprise groups in much the same way that establishments form part of enterprises and, so, enterprise based measures have the same shortcomings. But the argument can be stretched too far, resulting in a definition that links back to ultimate owners. For example one entrepreneur, say, might own many heterogeneous enterprise groups that own in turn a number of heterogeneous enterprises. But the rationale cannot be based on ultimate ownership as the ultimate owners for most companies and certainly listed corporations are shareholders. What matters most is the level at which decisions are made, such as those that affect expansion and innovation, and where operational control resides. Policy makers are interested in understanding what makes a successful business. The factors and business characteristics that determine this are inextricably linked to operational control.

Measures based on enterprises come closest to these criteria, as the degree of innovation, decision making etc within a business is likely to be closely related to the organisational and management structures that exist at the enterprise level. Research and development, product design and product advertising for example will usually be developed centrally within an enterprise with establishments benefiting from spill-overs; indeed, even innovative ideas generated at the establishment level are likely to permeate throughout the enterprise as upward spill-overs.

Of course, not all innovation is generated, decisions made, control resides etc at the enterprise level, particularly where enterprises are foreign-owned, or, where the enterprise controls foreign subsidiaries that generate innovative ideas say. But formulating definitions on this basis would not be useful for domestic policy makers nor for international comparisons, in much the same way that local or regional policy makers would not find enterprise (only) information based at the national level particularly useful. That is not to say however that this information (foreign-ownership and multi-national) is not important, far from it. Policy makers and analysts are interested in understanding how any of the characteristics of businesses help provide competitive advantages, whether that be related to the numbers of PhDs employed or foreign ownership.

Ownership is a particularly important characteristic. In many countries a large source of innovation, for example, emanates from abroad. Many studies have demonstrated that foreign owned enterprises are often more profitable than similar domestically owned enterprises.[8] This often reflects higher investment made by the foreign parent company but it is also, at least partly, to do with the management and organisational structures and practices in place. Identifying who the owners are is, therefore, of interest in fully understanding the factors of innovation. However, this information can be difficult to acquire for all businesses. Many business registers, for example, the most widely used source for the derivation of business demography statistics, do not contain this information. Moreover, the country in which a company finds its headquarters is not necessarily the source of innovation. Companies place their headquarters in countries for a number of reasons; some may be related to entrepreneurship and innovation, for example, access to capital or favourable tax regimes but others may not be. The difficulty in tracing the source of innovation therefore is non-trivial. Consider for example Mittal steel, the world's largest steel

---

[8] See, also the OECD Handbook on Economic Globalisation Indicators and The Measurement of Scientific and Technological Activities Oslo Manual: Guidelines for Collecting and Interpreting Innovation Data, 3rd Edition.

maker. It has steel making facilities in 14 countries, is listed on the New York and Amsterdam exchanges, has its headquarters in Amsterdam, and is owned by an Indian living in London. In other words, although it is of interest to identify foreign ownership, some care is needed in interpretation.

That said it's important to put the differences between establishment and enterprise based indicators into context. The vast majority of enterprises have only one establishment; and this is especially the case for small and medium enterprises (SMEs), where there is considerable policy interest. Large new business are typically opened by a larger enterprise group, whether that be foreign or domestically owned and, so, statistics that compare levels of small business entries are likely to be comparable across countries even if the business definitions differ.

Estimates of total business entries and exits are less comparable if different business definitions are used across countries but this can be at least partly mitigated where rates are concerned. Typically, entry (and exit) rates are calculated as the ratio of entries (exits) to the total business population active in the year in question. Comparisons of entries and exits across countries based on different business definitions can be made more comparable when rates are compared as biases work in the same direction in both the numerator and the denominator—for example establishment entries will be higher than enterprise entries but so too will be the population of establishments compared to the population of enterprises.

7.3.3 Enterprise Exits and Entries - Large and Small Economies

Although the Enterprise definition for businesses is to be preferred to other concepts it is by no means perfect where international comparisons are concerned. When an enterprise with headquarters in one EU country for example sets up a new production unit in another a new enterprise is recognised. However, when an enterprise with its headquarters in one US state say sets up a new production unit in another US state this will generally be recorded as the creation of a new establishment. Seen another way, this means that estimates of the size and number of enterprises between two economic blocs, equal in every way, except that one is a nation state and the other a collection of nation states, will differ, even if exactly the same national concepts are applied. In fact, all other things being equal, comparisons will show that enterprises in the nation state, although fewer, are larger and grow more in periods of expansion (and contract more during recessions) than enterprises in an equivalently sized economic-bloc of nation states. The same cannot be said however of birth and death rates. Jarmin et al. 2003 compared enterprise births in the US, on a national and state basis, and showed that churn (birth+death) rates were very similar.[9] They also showed that the average size of new establishments entering a state market for the first time was, on average, larger than the average size of a new enterprise

---

[9] Although a comparison of turnover rates of establishments versus enterprises revealed that turnover rates in establishments were approximately 11% lower than enterprise turnover rates.

(13.7 employees versus 12.7), reflecting the fact that expanding enterprises do so with a tried and trusted business recipe and so less risk of subsequent failure. As such, when these firms open new establishments (or expand into new markets), they can be less risk-averse and recruit more employees than may have been the case when the business was first set-up. The same study also showed that 1/3 of total enterprise growth up to 1997 experienced by surviving firms born in 1977 reflected the expansion of enterprises into neighbouring states. These biases could help to explain, at least partly, why a number of studies (e.g. Bartlesman et al 2003) have shown that US business entries were on average smaller and grew faster[10] than businesses in many EU countries; where the expansion of businesses into neighbouring markets was not picked-up up as growth but as new entries. One way of improving comparability in these cases is to separately identify foreign and domestically owned entries, although for small economies, for example Luxembourg and New Zealand, foreign owned entries may reflect a significant proportion of total entries.

This is not to say that business demography statistics, using enterprises as the business unit, cannot be compared, across unevenly sized economies. The point is that one cannot look at the statistics in isolation and care is needed in drawing conclusions, particularly those that are likely to impact on policy. In fact, as shown later, comparisons of domestically owned entries and exits are not impaired by variations in economic size.

7.3.4 Recommended Business Definition

In summary this framework recommends the adoption of the enterprise as the statistical unit for businesses where the definition of an enterprise follows that of the International Standard Industrial Classification of All Economic Activities (ISIC, Rev.3) described as *"An enterprise is an institutional (legal) unit or the smallest combination of institutional units that encloses and directly or indirectly controls all necessary functions to carry out its production activities. An enterprise may be a corporation, a quasi-corporation, a non-profit institution, or an unincorporated enterprise. The requirements of an enterprise are that it has one ownership or control. It can however be heterogeneous with regards to its economic activity as well as its location."*

For practical purposes, this definition is equivalent to that used by Eurostat ("the smallest combination of legal units that is an organisational unit producing goods or services, which benefits from a certain degree of autonomy in decision-making, especially for the allocation of its current resources. An enterprise carries out one

---

[10] During recessions the converse might be expected, namely lower average growth in US firms. But much depends on the biases of the cohort of firms selected. Many studies implicitly select a cohort of successful firms, as only firms surviving between two periods of time are selected. Moreover, shrinking firms are also less likely to be included the greater the period between the reference years as they are most likely to go out of business and, so, be excluded from the sample.

or more activities at one or more locations. An enterprise may be a sole legal unit")
and is the definition applied in the 1993 System of National Accounts (SNA 93).

That is not to say however that indicators based on other definitions of businesses units are not useful. Establishments in North America, for example, are
sufficiently similar to local units in Europe to consider the possibility of a site-
level start-up indicator. Ideally this would have two components, new sites due to
births, and new sites created by existing enterprises. Both are of interest for studying
employment dynamics and the impact of entrepreneurship at the regional and local
levels. Although not stated it is implicit in the recommendations that follow that
supplementary indicators based on site-level definitions for business units should be
produced if possible.

7.4 Defining births

7.4.1 Births versus Entries

In the previous section the term 'entry' was used, although not defined, to describe
the arrival or creation of a new enterprise in the economy. But new enterprises can
appear in a number of ways reflecting many demographic events, such as mergers and take-overs. Many of these entries are not therefore directly relevant to the
study of entrepreneurship or creative destruction. That is not to say that they are not
important but their economic impact differs, certainly their impact on employment
will differ; mergers for example often lead to reductions in overall employment,
whereas completely new creations will generate employment, even if they result
in employment losses in other businesses through competitive pressures related to
creative destruction.

Moreover, entries are not and never likely to be comparable across countries. In
practice, entries are derived from registrations with administrative sources but the
legal and administrative requirements that determine how and when businesses register with national administrative sources vary considerably from country to country,
and are likely to continue to do so. This section attempts to differentiate between
entries, which include any demographic events that lead to the creation of new
enterprises even if they previously existed in different forms, and *births*; the term
used in this framework to describe the creation of a combination of new production
factors, such as organisation, location, employment and fixed assets, and which, in
theory, at least are comparable across countries.

It is often relatively easy to measure business entries, i.e. those businesses that
are present in a given period but were not present in the previous period. It is more
difficult however to identify births (sometimes referred to as creations *ex nihilo*).
In other words, to identify entries due to re-registrations, reactivations, take-overs
and other demographic events, that is, those entries that are merely continuations of
enterprises that previously existed but where no, or a limited number, of production
factors have changed. In order to be able to proceed, therefore, it is first important

to identify all of the demographic events that lead to business entries and to create simple rules establishing which demographic events, and under which conditions, lead to births. These are set out in the following section.

A clarification is needed before moving on however. This framework concerns itself with the measurement of business demography data on an annual basis. Reference periods are therefore taken as calendar years. That is not to say however that the deliberations and conclusions below cannot also be applied to longer or shorter reference periods, in most cases they can. For simplicity however the framework recommendations should be taken to apply to calendar year data.

7.4.2 Demographic Events

Perhaps one of the most important and contentious considerations in defining births is 'timing', that is, when births occur. There are many ways in which an enterprise's birth date can be identified and defined; as the birth of any business reflects a number of stages (Baldwin et al. 2002). Typically it starts as the idea of an entrepreneur. This idea may then be acted upon and be evolved in a number of ways. It might be incorporated as a business which appears in official business registers immediately or it may remain unincorporated, registering on administrative (e.g. VAT, income or employment) registers once activity is of a sufficient size. Clearly, viewed in this context, the point at which a birth should be defined is non-trivial. This issue of timing is dealt with in the following section. This section only considers types of demographic events.

7.4.3 Entries

Entries reflect the appearance of a new enterprise within the economy, whatever the demographic event, be that a merger, renaming, split-off etc. Other demographic events can create entries within sub-sectors of the economy such as relocations and reclassifications from one industrial or institutional sector to another. Entries can also appear as the result of a birth.

7.4.4 Changes in Controlling Legal Unit, Activity and Locations

The general definition of a birth reflects a new enterprise and its corresponding creation of a combination of production factors such as site, labour, organisational structures, plant and machinery etc with the restriction that no other enterprises are involved in the event. Births exclude, therefore, entries into the population due to mergers, break-ups, split-offs, or restructuring of enterprises, since these do not reflect the creation of a combination of new production factors.

A challenging issue for births, therefore, concerns the treatment of a business that preserves some production factors or characteristics related to production factors (such as the main economic activity) but creates some new ones as it moves from one sub-population to another. Many characteristics exist but only a few are practically measurable or interpretable in this context (see below for why labour and capital are excluded)—controlling legal unit, activity and location. How many of these need to change before a birth can be recorded is ultimately an arbitrary decision. Therefore, it is sensible to adopt, at least partially, the Eurostat continuity rules;[11] which, with one exception, record a birth if two of the three factors change. The exception adopted by Eurostat concerns the case where an unincorporated business simultaneously moves to a new location and changes its legal form to become incorporated (i.e. the controlling legal unit changes from a natural person to a legal person to limit liability). The Eurostat convention is that this does not reflect a birth.

However, the definition for births adopted in this framework[12] is based on enterprises with employees, as discussed below, and so differs from the Eurostat definition. As such, all unincorporated businesses with no employees that become incorporated are treated as births, irrespective of any other changes, although unincorporated businesses with employees that change location and legal form are not. Like Eurostat however, all enterprises that move location and change activity (and have employees in their new manifestation) are treated as births. These rules are summarised in the table below.

Arguably continuity of employees, including management and fixed assets should also be included with the three factors listed above, since these are clearly factors of production. But establishing the continuity of employees and fixed assets is very difficult to achieve in practice, particularly for smaller enterprises; especially because these factors can be expected to change over time for reasons not related to births (e.g. staff turnover, depreciation etc). As such, they are excluded from the two-out-of-three rule described above.

Some countries have been able to link employers and employees over time and have used these links to help determine births. This method has been tested in New Zealand where an entry is not a birth if at least 70% of employees move from an old registration to a new one. Similar work in Canada is reported in Baldwin et al. (2002). However these are generally exceptions rather than the rule. That all said, location and activity are likely to be closely related to employees and, so, the two-out-of-three rule is likely to proxy births that might be identified using employee-employer links.

The two-out-of-three rule applies to businesses that have not gone through a period of dormancy beforehand. Where dormancy does occur, births can occur for some reactivations, see Table 7.2.

---

[11] See chapter 14 of the Eurostat Business Registers Recommendations Manual.

[12] Although it is premature to invoke the definition for births before the reader has a chance to become familiar with the deliberations that lead to the definition recommended below it is convenient, for ease of exposition, to do so in the discussion of this demographic event.

Table 7.2 Changes in Controlling Legal Unit, Activity and Location that lead to Births[I]

Enterprise	Change in			New entry is a birth
	Activity	Location	Legal Form (Unincorporated versus Incorporated)	
Unincorporated	Y	Y	Y	Y
with Employees	Y	Y		Y
	Y		Y	Y
Incorporated (III)	Y	Y	Y (II)	Y (II)
	Y	Y		Y
	Y		Y (II)	Y (II)
		Y	Y (II)	Y (II)
Unincorporated	Y	Y	Y	Y
without Employ-ees		Y	Y	Y
	Y		Y	Y
			Y	Y

(I) For simplicity it is assumed that listed demographic events aside, all other things are equal; particularly employment which is assumed to be the same before and after the demographic event(s).
(II) Except where the 'newly created' unincorporated enterprise has no employees; in which case the original incorporated enterprise is recorded as having died, see Section 5.
(III) All incorporated enterprises are assumed to have employees. In some countries, albeit in very few and exceptional circumstances, some incorporated enterprises have no employees but for simplicity this framework ignores these.

7.4.5 Mergers

Mergers involve a consolidation of the production factors of two or more enterprises into one new enterprise, such that the previous enterprises are no longer recognisable. The new enterprise is not a birth; unless the merged enterprise has employees and the original enterprises had none.

7.4.6 Renamings

Clearly, all other things equal, renamed enterprises are not births; indeed even including them in entries is best avoided.

7.4.7 Break-ups

This event involves a splitting of the production factors of an enterprise into two or more new enterprises in such a way that the previous enterprise is no longer recognisable. All other things equal the new enterprises are not considered to be births.

7.4.8 Split-offs

This event is similar to a break-up but, in this case, the original enterprise survives in a recognisable form and one or more new enterprises are created. All other things equal, the new enterprises are not considered to be births.

7.4.9 Changes of Ownership (one-to-one take-over)

This event simply involves a change in the controlling legal unit. All other things equal, this should not be considered to be a birth.

7.4.10 Joint Ventures

Joint ventures should be considered as births if they involve the creation of new factors of production, including operational control of its activities. Eurostat determines that new factors have been created if less than half of the total employment of the joint venture enterprise is transferred from the participating enterprises. This is likely to be difficult to measure with any accuracy so Eurostat recommends the rule: If employment of new (joint venture) enterprise > 2 x (total employment of participating enterprises before creation of the joint venture minus total employment of participating enterprises after creation of the joint venture), then the joint venture is a birth. This is a fairly restrictive determining rule, since it ignores other factors of production such as assets, location, activity, organisational factors etc. The preference in this framework is that joint-ventures should be treated as births if a new location is created and the activity of the joint-venture differs from the controlling Enterprise Groups. However, the difference between this preference and the Eurostat approach is likely to be negligible in practice and, so, this framework's recommendation is for countries to use the approach that is simplest to achieve in their case. European economies that have already begun to produce statistics for the Eurostat Business Demography database, are, of course, encouraged to continue with the Eurostat approach.

7.4.11 Re-structuring Within an Enterprise Group and Enterprise Groups

This event reflects a combination of break-ups, split-offs and mergers. All other things equal it does not result in any births.

7.4.12 Ancillary Activities

Creations of enterprises by an Enterprise Group, solely for the purpose of consolidating an ancillary activity of the Enterprise Group should not be treated as births. Ancillary activities typically relate to activities such as personnel management but many other activities can be viewed as ancillary. A Eurostat Task Force on Statistical Units concluded that the following activities could be considered as ancillary if the resulting goods or services are only provided within an Enterprise Group.

NACE Rev 1.1 code - Activity
28.62   Manufacture of tools
28.74   Manufacture of fasteners, screw machine products, chain and springs
45.50   Renting of construction or demolition equipment with operator
50.10   Sale of motor vehicles
50.20   Maintenance and repair of motor vehicles
50.30   Sale of motor vehicle parts and accessories
50.40   Sale, maintenance and repair of motorcycles and related parts and accessories
51   Wholesale trade and commission trade, except of motor vehicles and motorcycles
52.7   Repair of personal and household goods
60.24   Freight transport by road
63.1   Cargo handling and storage
63.2   Other supporting transport activities
63.4   Activities of other transport agencies
65.21   Financial leasing
70   Real estate activities
71.1   Renting of automobiles
71.21   Renting of other land transport equipment
71.22   Renting of water transport equipment
71.23   Renting of air transport equipment
71.31   Renting of agricultural machinery and equipment
71.32   Renting of construction and civil engineering machinery and equipment
71.33   Renting of office machinery and equipment, including computers
71.34   Renting of other machinery and equipment n.e.c.
71.4   Renting of personal and household goods n.e.c.
72   Computer and related activities
73.1   Research and experimental development on natural sciences and engineering
73.2   Research and experimental development on social sciences and humanities
74.11   Legal activities
74.12   Accounting, book-keeping and auditing activities; tax consultancy
74.13   Market research and public opinion polling
74.14   Business and management consultancy activities
74.15   Management activities of holding companies
74.2   Architectural and engineering activities and related technical consultancy
74.3   Technical testing and analysis
74.4   Advertising
74.5   Labour recruitment and provision of personnel
74.6   Investigation and security activities
74.70   Industrial cleaning
74.81   Photographic activities
74.82   Packaging activities

74.85   Secretarial and translation activities
74.86   Call centre activities
74.87   Other business activities n.e.c

The list may not be exhaustive and there may be other activities that could also be considered as ancillary.

7.4.13 Relocations

Certainly if an enterprise relocates to a different country this should be recorded as a birth, even if the production factors, (except land and buildings of course) were also transferred. Where the relocation occurs within the same economy[13] however, the same does not hold. Indeed, even if the relocated company were to acquire new production factors such as labour and capital the event should still not be considered as a birth unless the relocation coincides with a change in activity or a change in controlling legal unit (except if the legal form changes from unincorporated with employees to incorporated with employees).

7.4.14 Reclassifications

On its own a reclassification from one industrial or institutional sector into another does not result in a birth, even though the enterprise may appear for the first time in a particular sub-population. If the reclassification coincides with a change in location or controlling legal unit the reclassification should be recorded as a birth.

7.4.15 Reactivations

Reactivations are difficult to deal with conceptually. A business that is dormant for a few months (possibly due to seasonal activities) before eventually re-starting would not be considered to be a birth. However, if the period of dormancy was ten years or more, it would be harder to argue that the reactivation could be treated as a continuation of the previous activity. Ultimately the choice of the threshold after which reactivations should be treated as births needs to be defined by convention. Eurostat currently set this at two full calendar years. In other words, enterprises that exist in period t but that were previously inactive in t-1 should not be viewed as births if the same enterprise was active in period t-2 (with one exception described in more detail in the birth definition below); where the periods reflect calendar years. In these circumstances the enterprise is considered to have been dormant in period t-1.

---

[13] However if the interest was at the sub-national level, relocations from the region to another would be considered new births.

If however the firm was also inactive in period t-2 but active in period t-3 the firm should be treated as if it had exited in t-3 and so, a birth occurs in t. In the US Census Bureau longitudinal database no reactivations are recorded as births, irrespective of the period of 'dormancy'.

This framework prefers the Eurostat convention, partly because it is easier to implement (the US approach implies, at least in theory, that information on dormant enterprises is stored indefinitely and complicates the measurement of exits) but also because the convention sits more comfortably with the ethos that underpins creative destruction. Most businesses that become dormant for periods of longer than two calendar years are likely to do so because of competitive market conditions rather than by design. Some businesses may of course fall into this 'design' camp, for example those that trade according to long-run cycles, such as 'El Nino fishermen' or specialised manufacturers that respond to very sporadic demand, but these are likely to be very limited and so can be safely ignored.

7.4.16 Comparing Entries and Births

Clearly estimating births is a lot more complicated than entries. It is legitimate to question therefore whether the effort involved in moving from entries to births makes any significant empirical difference. The simple answer is yes. Fig. 7.3 below uses data for France from the Agence Pour la Création d'Entreprises (APCE) to illustrate this. It shows that around one third of all entries are not births. Similar results were obtained in studies for New Zealand (Mead 2005) and Canada (Baldwin et al. 2002) both of which showed that at least 20% of entries were not births.

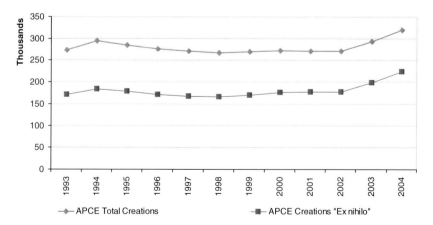

Fig. 7.3 Births and Entries in France

7.4.17 Timing

Thus far we have managed to identify the demographic events that lead to births and those that don't but perhaps the most important definition concerns the time at which a birth occurs. There are many ways in which an enterprise's birth date can be identified and defined. In extremis one might define it as the date at which the initial idea was formed but this is clearly an impractical definition; partly because of the difficulty in defining this date (which may be many years before any activity ever occurs) partly because many ideas never see the light of day but especially because it will be literally impossible to measure this concept in a harmonised way, if at all, within, let alone across, countries.

The approach typically used by statistical offices is to take the date when the enterprise first appeared on an administrative or statistical business register as a business entry, removing (to varying degrees) entries not deemed to be births. This is a pragmatic approach but it does not lend itself well to a harmonised definition across countries as it requires, first, harmonised rules for registration; which is unlikely to ever happen. Moreover it does not necessarily follow that just because a business registers for administrative purposes it will engage in market activity, as the entity may remain inactive or dormant indefinitely.

The concept itself needs to be defined in such a way that, in theory at least, it is replicable across countries, meaning that it should not be conditional, in theory, on legal and administrative arrangements. The only practical way to do this is to record a birth at the point that some tangible and measurable activity occurs. In practice this leaves only a few criteria that can be used, separately, or in combination, to define the creation date of a birth on the basis of: turnover indicators; employment indicators; production indicators (including own-account production of fixed assets), even if first sales occur at a later date; and a certain time (years, months, etc) after a business has been economically active; whether activity is measured via turnover, employment or production.

7.4.18 Timing Criteria

Each of these criteria is considered in turn below.

7.4.19 Turnover

This lends itself well to a definition for birth-dates as it is measurable and demonstrates that the birth has gone beyond the raw idea stage to income generation. It does not necessarily imply that any production of goods and services occurs however because receipts can be received in advance of any production occurring; not that this represents a reason to eliminate it as an option.

Where the concept may provide problems is in the fact that, in theory at least, it includes births with sales as little as 1 cent. The risk therefore is that the measure could lead to estimates of births that were swamped by economically insignificant births, including many that have little long term growth or survival prospects; although the impact of this could be mitigated by weighting births by turnover. A variant therefore is to retain the concept but with a size threshold; determined by a level of turnover that measures only economically significant business entries as births. There are two major problems with this variant. The first is that an economically significant threshold is a subjective measure that will, moreover, differ across countries depending on the size of their economies and their per capita income. The second is that, even assuming that a unique threshold for all countries and industries could be determined at some point in time in a common currency, it would change in national currencies in line with exchange rate movements and over time would need to change in line with some to-be-determined measure of inflation (that would need to reflect inflationary pressures in all countries and the product prices of all industries). These are insurmountable conceptual and practical (measurement) problems that mean that if turnover is to be used as (one of) the criterion for births it needs to be based on any turnover over zero.

It should be recognised, however, that the use of such a threshold (any turnover greater than zero) will mean that the time spent by a business in its development period will be considered as gestation. Businesses that start-up and fold before any revenue is realised will therefore not be included. This is not of course perfect since some of these businesses would have invested heavily in people and capital before folding but to draw the line elsewhere would be possibly a case of throwing out the baby with the bathwater since many other businesses would also come into scope, unless, for example, thresholds governing employment and investment were used in isolation, which can cause further complications.

7.4.20 Employment

Employment based measures present more formidable challenges than turnover based statistics as employment statistics include all forms of employment whether the workers are paid employees or not. But statistics in this latter component of employment are difficult to collect. Many small, typically unincorporated, businesses, for example, will employ unpaid family workers who may each participate to the enterprise in different ways; some will work full-time some part-time.

Clearly there are similarities between employment and turnover based measures in so far that thresholds will exclude some entries but that is not to say that the conclusions are necessarily the same. Employment based measures are not affected by exchange rate movements or inflation but they are extremely sensitive to practical measurement issues. Does a new enterprise with a sole-proprietor working one day a week or one day a year, for example, constitute a birth, even if it is not economically significant, and do the drivers behind the creation, which can be very varied, matter.

Another possible factor that could be used to define enterprise births therefore relates to the motivating factors of entrepreneurs. New businesses can be created for many different reasons, reflecting varying degrees of innovation and different types of (Schumpeterian) entrepreneurial change. For example they may be formed through 'push' or 'pull' factors. 'Push' entrepreneurs reflect those, dissatisfied with their current positions, who, for reasons unrelated to their entrepreneurial characteristics, are pushed into starting a new business. 'Pull' entrepreneurs on the other hand are those who are have a desire to grasp the new opportunities and higher rewards (financial or otherwise) presented by a business opportunity.

The numbers of 'push' entrepreneurs in any particular economy may have little to do with the pervasiveness of an entrepreneurship-culture within that economy. For example, other things equal, economies with little or no social safety nets might have higher numbers of 'push' entrepreneurs than those with generous social security systems but it would be over-simplistic to ascribe this to a difference in intrinsic entrepreneurship levels in the populations at large. Moreover, although it is clear that policy measures designed to increase entrepreneurship in either country will have some similarities, for example ensuring that barriers to entry are not prohibitive, important differences will also exist between 'push' and 'pull' creations, meaning that considerable caution is needed in comparing the numbers of births across countries; particularly those at different stages of economic development. Many, usually informal, businesses in developing economies for example, provide employment to their owners only, and, because they tend to be subsistence-motivated, have very limited growth potential.

'Pull' entrepreneurs have a different motivator. Their businesses are usually innovative, exploiting opportunities presented by new technologies, business processes, expertise, knowledge, and, so, are more likely than 'push' businesses to grow and to improve productivity, profitability and competition within an economy.

Both sets of entrepreneurs are important but in different ways and governments need to ensure that their policies adequately reflect both. However, separately estimating the levels of the two sets of entrepreneurs (without the use of dedicated surveys) is not likely to be practicable in any country, which is partly why demography statistics published by NSOs rarely, if ever, split businesses this way. However the lack of a breakdown is arguably not that important when considering business demography birth, death and survivability statistics. Policy makers are, in the main, interested in identifying the factors that lead to successful businesses, one of these factors will almost certainly be motivation but there will be many others—access to capital, tax policy, start-up costs, foreign/domestic ownership etc. Identifying the contribution of these factors to successful and failing firms is clearly of import and this can be done using more focused surveys targeting successful or failed firms.

A further consideration with employment based measures, is that, used on their own, they are not necessarily correlated with turnover based notions of economic activity. A sole-proprietor for example will typically invest considerable time in developing a business plan, searching for premises, marketing, research etc before any market activity occurs. Indeed the business may never move to the sales or production stage. Clearly, therefore, employment based measures that embrace employment in its most general sense need to be coupled with some measurable characteristics of activity such as turnover or production.

But this still leaves open the question of how much employment is needed to record a birth. The Eurostat definition for Business Demography is to include all business entries, satisfying the criterion for births, that appear on the statistical register regardless of employment size; although this is qualified with a requirement that business registers should include all businesses with a labour input of at least one person half-time and smaller businesses if possible.

It will never be possible for any business register or statistical source to capture all businesses or business activities such as car-boot sales and bartering for example, which are, at least theoretically, in scope, or to differentiate between push and pull creations. So, the definition for births must rely on some notion of economic significance. The Eurostat suggested and optional threshold described in its Business Register regulations implies that this significance can be established, in practice, when half a full-time equivalent is employed (although it should be noted that the Business Demography recommendations manual makes no explicit reference). This is not always easy to measure.

Additionally, comparisons of births based on employment measures are likely to be affected by the levels of informality or underground production that occurs within each economy, as 'informal' enterprises are typically small with no or very few employees. All other things equal therefore, countries with high levels of informality are more likely to have lower levels of births than countries with low levels of informality; although if a concerted effort was made to bring informal businesses into the formal economy the opposite is likely to be the case.

An alternative approach therefore is to restrict the definition of employment to employees only, such that only entries that have employees can be considered as being in scope for births. This has some attractions over total employment based measures as, typically, employees are easier to measure and, secondly it provides a more meaningful measure of economic significance; certainly a measure based on employees is likely to limit the numbers of 'push' enterprises as these are less likely to have employees than 'pull' enterprises. Cross country comparisons based on the employee approach will still be affected by the differing levels of informality across economies but, because informal enterprises are disproportionately those with no employees, the impact is likely to be smaller than for employment based measures. One important aspect to realise in this approach is that births are not exclusively drawn from entries, as an enterprise active in period t-1 but with no employees will be recorded as a birth in t if employees are taken on in period t.

The key interest for policy-makers after-all, in the context of business demography statistics, is in the understanding of which businesses are likely to grow and create employment. Many sole-proprietor enterprises will never get to the 'employing' stage and, so, birth statistics that include all of these businesses may be difficult to interpret. That is not to say that these businesses are not important, merely that including them in birth statistics may not provide a clear picture of future growth prospects and innovation.

Moreover, business entries are particularly sensitive to changes in the status of individuals which, in turn, are often driven by legal and tax considerations. Business entries also include therefore "pseudo-enterprises", sometimes also referred to as "false self-employed", where a person acts as an employee of an enterprise, in that they effectively work for that enterprise every day over a long period of time but for legal or tax purposes are technically self-employed. Changes in tax legislation therefore that make it beneficial for employees to switch from employee to self-employed status are likely to see business entries increase without any direct change in overall employment (see also Vale and Powell 2002, Brandt 2004). That said, employee based measures can also be affected by differences in the propensity to incorporate across countries and over time—since sole-proprietors that become incorporated also become employees.

By extension it is worth considering whether the threshold to establish economic significance could be extended above the one-employee level to higher levels. Although it is worth noting that using high thresholds can create biases across countries even after birth levels have been normalised to create birth-rates, using the total population of enterprises, human population or GDP say. Small economies for example, with small (human) populations, will inevitably have less potential to create large new enterprises than economies with much larger populations. That said, two, three, four, five employee thresholds, say, are worth considering although, as shown in the section on Deaths, these alternatives create problems in defining deaths and births in a consistent and meaningful way.

7.4.21 Production

Although turnover and production are largely coincidental they are not the same and for some business entries there may be a considerable lag between the two. For example, production (e.g. production of factories and development of software systems) commonly occurs some time before turnover. However this type of production is mainly related to capital acquisition rather than the production of goods and services for sale; which are closely linked to turnover and of more direct interest to identifying successful firms. As such, turnover is arguably a better indicator to use than production, particularly because own-account production does not necessarily imply that any market activity ever occurs. Moreover, identifying when own-account production occurs, particularly in very small enterprises, is likely to be too difficult to implement and measure in a consistent way for all enterprises and is relatively subjective. Budding entrepreneurs and inventors, for example, might spend some time developing ideas and inventions within their garages well before, if ever, a marketable product or productive asset emerges.

7.4.22 Years of Economic Activity

An alternative definition, based more closely on a measure of economic significance, is to define births as those business entries that have remained active for a certain period of time. Such an approach could lead to the removal of very short-lived enterprises, for example those that survive for less than one-year. This approach is not considered further here however, as it is more closely linked to indicators of survival which are discussed later and is also discussed in the context of point-in-time versus live-during-period estimates below.

7.4.23 Data Sources: Censuses, Surveys, Statistical and Administrative Business Registers and Thresholds

Thus far considerations have focused on the theoretical aspects of births and birth dates but the key aim of this framework is to propose a set of indicators that can be produced by all OECD statistical offices and, so, practical considerations of data availability cannot be ignored.

In practice, the level of births within an economy can only be measured using statistical or administrative business registers. This information varies across countries, although within Europe they have moved much closer together as a result of regulations concerning Business Registers.

That all said, it is important for producers and users of enterprise demography statistics to recognise their potential limitations in the context of international comparability - the main one being that the appearance of a business on administrative or business registers does not necessarily coincide with the date at which the business first became active. In some countries for example, businesses may be required to register, or voluntarily register, before any turnover is recorded or production occurs. Indeed it does not necessarily follow that all of these businesses will ever be involved in production; instead they may remain permanently inactive. In yet other countries the administrative registers capture businesses after they have already been active for a while; usually because businesses need to exceed some threshold (commonly turnover or employment based) before registration. In practice this may mean that many small and micro enterprises will be excluded.

The existence of thresholds in business registers is perhaps the most important factor that can cause differences in business demography statistics, as illustrated in Section 2. Although they attempt to be as exhaustive as possible, business registers will, in practice, use one threshold or another that excludes some businesses. Commonly, as described above, the thresholds are based on monetary values, using turnover as the indicator for example, or they are based on employment levels. However the thresholds may be based on other criteria reflecting the institutional make-up of businesses, for example they may exclude some industrial sectors, like agriculture, or all unincorporated firms say. Finally the registers, in all countries, will exclude firms operating exclusively in the 'black' or underground economy.[14] Although the economic importance of missing firms is generally not significant, when set against total economic activity, their importance in the context

---

[14] Additionally, it is important to recognise that registers with information on firm employment and turnover may also be affected by underground production.

of entrepreneurship, and in particular with regards to Small and Medium Enterprise (SME) policy, is greater, and such shortcomings in business register information need to be recognised in the context of business demography statistics.

Survey based approaches to the measurement of births are also possible but these will typically be of lower quality than information derived from registers, which, in theory, cover all businesses above a certain threshold; although it may be easier to derive estimates of births from surveys since respondents will be able to describe precisely how their businesses were created: takeovers, births etc. Moreover, survey based approaches may also capture the creation of informal enterprises. Survey data have been used by some countries, most notably in the DOSME[15] project for countries of Central and Eastern Europe. This approach can be useful when registers are not sufficiently developed and has the advantage of being able to collect more information on entrepreneurship than is available from other sources but it also suffers from the usual constraints of survey errors and sample size limitations when detailed data breakdowns are required.

In theory, census data can be at least as good, and sometimes better than register based information, if they have less scope restrictions, but the cost of running a census of businesses every year makes this approach unrealistic for most countries. Data from less frequent censuses may still be of interest but, as discussed in the section on periodicity below, they raise major comparability issues.

This framework does not specify a unique data source for calculating estimates of births. The Eurostat Business Demography database is based on information within business registers but many countries outside the EU do not currently have adequate statistical or administrative business registers, indeed, even within the EU the comprehensiveness of these registers varies across countries and time.

This framework does however express a preference for register based approaches on the grounds that all OECD countries have them and so information on births can be derived without any increase in administrative burdens for businesses and because, despite the incomparability of business registers in practice, it is possible to derive business demography statistics based on registers that are less affected by these differences; as shown below. Moreover, in calculating birth-rates, using births as a percent of the total population of enterprises, the conceptual consistency between the denominator and numerator populations can only realistically be maintained using the same source information. Survey based approaches may also be used to measure the total population of enterprises but they are complicated by issues of multiple-counting of enterprises and require survey respondents to differentiate between statistical business units. If business registers do exist, but a survey based approach is still used to estimate births, there is a risk that inconsistencies between the numerator and denominator arise, for example at the industrial sector level or because the numerator includes births of informal enterprises not included in the business register population.

---

[15] Demography Of Small and Medium-sized Enterprise.
See: http://forum.europa.eu.int/irc/dsis/dosme/info/data/en/index.htm

If business registers are used as the basis for measurement it follows that the higher the (common) activity (turnover and employment) thresholds for births the more comparable the indicators across countries are likely to be, as, typically, differences in coverage of business registers occur at the very small enterprise level. However, improved ease of comparability has to be balanced against the loss of information relating to small enterprises; an area of considerable policy interest. This is particularly so for small countries where biases may be inadvertently introduced. However, as shown below, it is possible to use a definition for births using thresholds that maintain the economic relevance of the concept whilst, at the same time, improving the potential for international comparability.

7.4.24 Point-In-Time versus Live-During-Period-Births

An issue that is of particular relevance in the context of business register approaches is when the population of businesses is measured. There are two approaches. The first, point-in-time, takes a snapshot of businesses in consecutive periods, preferably, at the end or beginning of calendar years for which estimates are required (assuming that the time-period of attention is annual births) and, so, is analogous to a 'stocks' approach. The second approach, live-during-period, measures the population of enterprises during the course of the calendar year, and, so, can be seen as a 'flows' approach. This latter approach lends itself well to the estimation of short-lived births, that is, those that enter and exit the population of enterprises during a calendar year. The former approach may not however fully capture these births, depending on the supplementary information available in each country. Moreover, it may introduce biases across countries and industries. Many of the businesses that are active for less than a year will be excluded altogether, but those that, by chance, are active on the day the snap-shot is taken will be included. Therefore, if a reference date such as 31 December/1 January is used, short-lived businesses with activities related to the Christmas period are likely to be included but businesses with different seasonal patterns of activity such as tourism or agriculture-related activities could be under-represented; which may be particularly relevant in the context of Northern versus Southern hemisphere comparisons.

The required supplementary information to correct for any differences between point-in-time and live-during-period approaches may not be available in all countries and so it will not always be possible to record these short-lived births; which can be significant: Eurostat "live during period" enterprise survival data covering 48 observations for 18 countries over 4 years show that on average just over 87% of births in a given year are also active in the following year; indicating that the number of short-lived births that are born and die within the same calendar year is not insignificant. Removing these short-lived births from any definition of births would, of course, remove this issue of incomparability but, at the same time, as mentioned above, it could introduce others, namely those related to seasonal activities that occur within the snap-shots. It seems preferable therefore for countries to record these short-lived births separately. This issue is discussed in more detail in Vale (2006) and in the section on birth rates below.

7.4.25 Periodicity

This issue concerns whether the source data are sub-annual, annual, or less frequent. The majority of the sources identified in Section 2 concern annual data, though quarterly and monthly data sets are available for some countries. Indeed, in a few cases, data availability is linked to economic censuses at intervals of five years.

For data with a periodicity of greater than one year it is difficult to construct estimates of births that can be compared to annual data, as the proportion of short-lived births that will be missed increases considerably. In Japan, annualised average rates are calculated for the years between censuses (Takahashi 2000), but these mask the natural year on year variability usually observed in business entry and birth data.

If sub-annual data include counts of births they can simply be added to produce annual totals, though these totals will be higher than those based on annual snap-shots and for which no supplementary information is available; due to better coverage of businesses that survive for less than one year.

Work to convert quarterly establishment start-up data from the Business Employment Dynamics series produced by the US Bureau of Labor Statistics to an annual basis has resulted in differences of over 40% between annualised 'births' and the sum of 'births' for the four separate quarters. This is a result of both the removal of short-lived businesses, and improvements to the purity of the birth estimates by better linkage of establishments over time, and is documented in Pinkston and Spletzer (2004).

7.4.26 Birth Definition

In concluding from the above, it follows that a definition for births should be based on a combination of turnover and employment measures, where the turnover component reflects any turnover above zero. The employment based component can be based on total employment or employee indicators; the latter being, arguably, the more relevant in the context of business dynamics, entrepreneurship, innovation and growth and certainly more relevant in the context of employment creation. Moreover, employee based measures are clearly easier to record than employment based measures, which are complicated by the subjectivity of determining when employment actually occurs. Combining employment based measures with turnover can remove this subjectivity but the issues of measurement and economic significance remain. Perhaps the most important of these is measurement. Not all countries are able to compile statistics on this basis, as shown in Section 2. In fact no country will ever be able to record all small unincorporated enterprises unless every market enterprise, no matter how large, is required to register; which would constitute a disproportionately costly administrative burden. Moreover, and as described above, employment based measures are very sensitive to changes in tax legislation, particularly in the context of employees moving to 'false' self-employed. It is theoretically possible to remove these new enterprises from the population of entries and, so, from births but this is not likely to be simple to do in practice.

Ultimately an employment threshold is needed; one that can only be determined by convention, taking into account a range of factors: interpretability, ease of calculation, data availability, and comparability. The recommendation made in this framework is to record the birth of an enterprise as when it takes on board its first employee and records some turnover; subject to the removal of any 'false' births from the population of entries that are created as a result of other demographic events, such as take-overs, described above.

That is not to say that this measure will not be affected by institutional factors that may treat entries, with little real economic difference, differently. Sole-proprietors, for example, that become incorporated will be treated as a birth if an employee threshold of one is used, and in this context it is important to note that the propensity of incorporating businesses differs across countries, and often, over time. One way to ameliorate this is to also record births of enterprises using higher employee thresholds, such as two, three etc, up to ten say, as complementary indicators, since, the higher the threshold, the lower the probability of a birth occurring as the result of an unincorporated enterprise with no employees becoming incorporated. Indeed, at the two employee threshold, only unincorporated partnerships that become incorporated are likely to distort birth levels, and these are likely to be negligible when compared to total births.

As such this framework also recommends that complementary birth statistics are also calculated on the basis of a two-employee threshold, following the same additional rules that apply for births, using the one-employee definition; these births are referred to in this framework as *economic births*. The comparability of this measure is certainly less likely to be adversely affected by policy measures, such as income tax and corporation tax differentials which provide incentives and disincentives for self employed unincorporated enterprises to incorporate, and, moreover, it can be produced by most OECD countries.

These measures differ from the Eurostat definition, which takes employment rather than employees as a threshold and which is a broader definition for births. The difference in this convention is mainly driven by the fact that statistical business registers in OECD countries are more varied than in Eurostat countries, where regulations that have improved convergence exist, but also partly reflects an attempt to produce economically meaningful indicators that can be easily constructed and which are less affected by the differing levels of exhaustiveness in national business registers, at least where very small enterprises are concerned.

In summary therefore the point at which a birth of an enterprise occurs is when employees and turnover are both greater than zero for the first time[16] and no other

---

[16] In practice, many countries impute employees from turnover, or vice-versa, if one of these variables is missing (as recommended by Eurostat), thus, in practice, the only cases where a value

enterprises are involved in the event. This does mean therefore that births in year t are not always sourced from entries in year t; for example, enterprises that existed and were active in calendar year t-1, with no employees, that became enterprises with employees in t would be births in calendar t.

The recommendation of this framework therefore is that births should be recorded on a calendar year basis, recording any births that occur on and within 1 January and 31 December. For some OECD countries, particularly those that compile business register data using snap-shots and financial years, this may not be so easy. For strict comparisons on a calendar year basis, such data sets would need to be apportioned between years, though in practice this may not be necessary if births rates are fairly stable over time.

The type of data source used to estimate births is important and business registers are preferable to survey or census based measures. However, because some countries use live-during-period approaches to updating their registers, countries are encouraged to separately identify short-lived enterprises (those that are born and die within the same calendar year); partly to improve the comparability with countries that use point-in-time approaches to register updating and partly because these enterprises are of different economic significance and policy relevance to enterprises that survive for longer periods. That said this framework advocates a general preference for live-during-period based estimates of births.

Another issue that affects comparability in an unintentional way is the statistical unit used to define businesses, and described in Section 3; which demonstrated that a large economy will have lower enterprise births than an equally sized group of countries even if the numbers of new establishments are the same; as a result of the creation of new enterprises in each country by foreign owned multinationals. As such, and because the distinction is of policy interest in its own right, this framework recommends that estimates of births should separately identify whether enterprise births are foreign or domestically owned. Births can be defined as follows: A birth amounts to the creation of a combination of production factors with the restriction that no other enterprises are involved in the event. Only enterprises with employees and turnover can be considered in scope for births. A birth of an enterprise occurs when employees and turnover are both greater than zero for the first time. Births do not include entries into the population due to mergers, break-ups, split-offs, or restructuring of enterprises. Births do not include entries into a sub-population resulting only from a change of activity, controlling legal unit or location but do include entries if two of these three factors change, excluding entries that arise from an unincorporated business with employees simultaneously moving to a new location and changing its legal form to become incorporated with employees (and therefore limit liability). Births in calendar year t do not include enterprises active in calendar year t, following inactivity in t-1 and that had both employees and turnover in t-2, which are viewed as reactivations, but do include enterprises reactivated after

---

will be zero are those where positive confirmation of this has been received from a survey or administrative source.

periods of inactivity spanning two or more calendar years. Births in period t also include enterprises that were active in t-1 but that had no employees. Births in calendar year t include enterprises active in calendar year t following inactivity in t-1 and active in t-2 but with no employees.

A secondary, measure but of equal importance, referred to here as 'economic births' relates to a two-employee threshold and is also recommended by this framework. Economic Births occur when the second employee is recruited or turnover first occurs, whichever of the two occurs latest. Economic births do not include entries into the population due to mergers, break-ups, split-offs, or restructuring of enterprises. Economic births do not include entries into a sub-population resulting only from a change of activity, controlling legal unit or location but do include entries if two of these three factors change, excluding entries that arise from an unincorporated business with employees simultaneously moving to a new location and changing its legal form to become incorporated with employees (and therefore limit liability). Economic births in calendar year t do not include enterprises active in calendar year t, following inactivity in t-1 and that had both employees and turnover in t-2, which are viewed as reactivations, but do include enterprises reactivated after periods of inactivity spanning two or more calendar years. Economic births in period t also include enterprises that were active in t-1 but that had one or less employees. Economic births in calendar year t do include enterprises active in calendar year t following inactivity in t-1 and active in t-2 but with no employees.

Ideally births (and economic births) should be split by activity (2 3 and 4 digit ISIC level if possible), legal form (limited liability companies, sole proprietors, partnerships, public corporations and non-profit institutions serving households), employment size, turnover and ownership (foreign and domestic), and should separately identify those births that are born and die within the same calendar year. However, in recognition that this level of breakdown may be difficult to achieve in practice, particularly when one considers the disclosure issues it raises, births (and economic births) at the 2-digit level, broken down by employment size, ownership and/or turnover, provide an acceptable information set. Additionally, with this option, births (and economic births) can be shown broken down by employee size-bands, preferably, 1, 2-4, 5-10, 10-20, and 20+ (although, of course, the 1 employee size band is redundant for economic births). Table 7.3, below summarises the definition for births ignoring for simplicity more complex demographic events such as mergers and takeovers.

It is important to note that those countries that use employee and/or turnover thresholds in their business registers above the one-employee and greater-than-zero-turnover thresholds recommended in this framework will have lower levels of births than in equivalently sized countries that have business registers with no thresholds. Moreover, where these thresholds are driven by legal and/or fiscal requirements further distortions may arise. For example, countries that use VAT registers as the primary source for their statistical business register may record fewer businesses than might be expected just above this threshold; as businesses operating marginally above the threshold might be inclined to declare revenue to the authorities just below to avoid any increased burdens that might come with being VAT registered. National

Table 7.3 Defining Births by Turnover and Employees

Enterprise had Employees and/or Turnover in

T-2		T-1		T	
Employees	Turnover	Employees	Turnover	Employees	Turnover
N	N	N	N	Y	Y
N	Y	N	Y	Y	Y
N	N	N	Y	Y	Y
Y	Y	N	N	Y	Y
Y	Y	N	Y	Y	Y
Y	N	Y	N	Y	Y
N	Y	N	N	Y	Y

Statistical Offices are encouraged therefore to develop their business registers to ensure that all enterprises with one or more employee and any turnover are recorded.

A couple of cautionary notes merit mention here. The first concerns comparisons of Eurostat defined birth rates, based partly on employment, and those recommended in this framework, based partly on employees. The Eurostat statistics provide information showing separately the births of zero-employee enterprises. Removing these births from the Eurostat total figures will not result in statistics that are comparable with the definition for births given in this framework, as the net result will not include within births any enterprise that moves from a zero-employee size class to a one or more employee size class; which are included as births in this framework. The same is true where estimates of economic births are concerned, since Eurostat figures for births excluding one-employee and zero employee births, will not include any births that occur when enterprises of this size move into the two-employee category.

The second cautionary note concerns changes to the coverage of business registers. In some countries business registers cover only a sub-set of the entire population of market enterprises. Any increase in the coverage of the register should not, by default, be included as births even it is not possible to differentiate between those enterprises in the newly covered sub-population that were active at time t and earlier and those that were born in time t.

7.5 Defining deaths

7.5.1 Deaths and Exits

Like Births, defining deaths and when they occur is also non-trivial. Businesses may, for example, remain registered on business registers, an important source of information for business demography statistics, even though they no longer exist. Equally, like births, the process of firm death can also be arbitrary. Many businesses, for example, experience a process of decline or dying before they are finally wound-up. And some businesses enter receivership before being wound-up, continuing some administrative functions even if normal activity is permanently ceased.

Moreover there is a difference between business closures and business failures. The former reflects a withdrawal from the market that may have been anticipated at the outset of the businesses creation. Differentiating between these businesses and the point at which businesses begin their decline is also of policy interest.

These difficulties notwithstanding however, the corollary to the definition for births is that the death of an enterprise should reflect, in a general sense, the destruction of a combination of production factors. By extension this excludes exits that occur through other demographic events such as mergers, take-overs, break-ups, name changes, or restructuring of a set of enterprises. Equally, where the focus is on a particular sector, deaths do not include enterprises that are reclassified out of the sector of interest if no other demographic event is coincident with the reclassification, namely a change in the legal form of the enterprise or location.

Recalling the measures recommended for estimating births, it follows that businesses with more than one employee in calendar year t that have less than one employee in calendar years t+1 and t+2 can be considered to have died in calendar year t.

This is not a perfect definition since the business could have remained active in calendar years t+1 and t+2, albeit with no employees, and, so, differs from the more general description of business exits; which are normally considered to be those that cease to be active, in other words, go out of business altogether. Businesses that experience a decline in employment size below a set employee threshold do not necessarily cease activity. These declines may, for example, reflect cyclical troughs in activity or periods of restructuring and downsizing that result in increased probability of survival or profitability over the longer term.

However, using a more general definition for deaths based on activity criteria alone would result in an inconsistency with the definition used for births that could lead to interpretative difficulties. For example, if all new creations of enterprises in an economy are below the one employee threshold recommended for births, and none grow to be an employing firm, it is possible, at least in theory, that measures of births and deaths in this economy would show, incongruously, persistently high levels of deaths but never any births. As such, it is important to distinguish between deaths and the more common definition for business exits and to refer to deaths as the statistical corollary of the definition used for births.

Although imperfect, because the definition for deaths does not measure all business exits in the sense that the enterprises have ceased to be active, the definition does reflect the exit of firms that cease to be businesses with employees, and, so, is readily interpretable in an economically meaningful way. Like births however the definition is affected by the propensity of businesses to incorporate, since the higher the population of businesses with one employee or more, the higher the likelihood of more deaths. Additionally, using the definition proposed for deaths in this framework, the levels of deaths can also be affected by the propensity of incorporated businesses to become unincorporated; as incorporated businesses with one employee that become unincorporated with no employees would result in a death.

It is possible to use other definitions for deaths but these would be inconsistent with the definition for births and, in any case, many of these alternative definitions also present challenges for comparability across countries and over time. For example, one might consider legal failures, based on bankruptcy say, as a measure. But bankruptcy laws differ across countries. In some countries, for example, enterprises can declare themselves as bankrupt but are able to continue trading with receivers in operational control. Often this results in the winding-up of the enterprise as it goes into liquidation[17] but sometimes the enterprise is able to continue operating, albeit with more restrictive operations and under new management. This means that some enterprises on business registers, say, may be active but also bankrupt, making it very difficult to use a concept of deaths based on bankruptcy, particularly as some nominally bankrupt companies may recover.

Other possibilities exist for a definition of deaths, the most obvious being when businesses cease trading altogether. But, as demonstrated above, this concept presents practical difficulties when compared to the definition of births.

7.5.2 Demographic Events

Exits

Exits reflect the failure and closure of enterprises within the economy, whatever the demographic event be that a merger, renaming, split-offs etc. Other demographic events can create exits within sub-sectors of the economy such as relocations, and reclassifications from one industrial or institutional sector to another. Exits also occur because of deaths.

7.5.3 Changes in Controlling Legal Unit, Activity and Locations

Using the definition for births as a reference point, it follows that under certain circumstances deaths can occur in conjunction with changes in the controlling legal

---

[17] The question whether units in liquidation should be treated as active or not was discussed in the Eurostat Business Demography Working Group meeting of April 2004. More precisely, the question had arisen whether a dying enterprise should be considered active even if its remaining activities are related only to its liquidation e.g. selling production factors or managing administrative procedures. Several Member States reported on their practice in a written consultation by e-mail during the summer of 2004. The clear tendency was to consider these units active as long as they have either turnover or employment regardless of the type of the activity. This position is in line with the principle in the Eurostat Business Demography methodology that a change of activity alone during the lifetime of an enterprise is ignored. A few member states reported that a further distinction was needed. If there is information available on a court decision on bankruptcy, the business should no longer be considered as active, whilst a unit awaiting the decision on bankruptcy is still regarded as active. This is not proposed in this framework, which, in any case, adopts a different definition of deaths to that used by Eurostat. The Eurostat definition, consistent with its definition on births, records a death only when all employment and turnover has ceased for more than two calendar years; which differs from the definition used in this framework that records a death when the enterprise ceases to have employees or turnover for more than two calendar years.

unit, activity or location. Indeed, all births resulting from a change in two or more of the controlling legal unit, activity and location also result in a death; unless the original enterprise that exited had no employees to start with. These circumstances are summarised below. When an enterprise experiences a change in one or more of the controlling legal unit, activity and location, such that an exit and entry occurs in the business population the exit is viewed as a death in the following circumstances shown in the Table 7.4:

7.5.4 Mergers

Mergers involve a consolidation of the production factors of two or more enterprises into one new enterprise, such that the previous enterprises are no longer recognisable. The new enterprise is not a birth and the enterprises that existed before the merger are not viewed as deaths; unless the merger coincides with a change in employment such that no employees exist in the merged entity but existed in the original enterprises.

7.5.5 Renamings

Clearly the renaming of an enterprise does not, on its own, result in a death of the original enterprise.

Table 7.4 Changes in Controlling Legal Unit, Activity and Location that lead to Deaths[I]

Enterprise	Change in			Exit is a death
	Activity	Location	Legal Form (Unincorporated versus Incorporated)	
Unincorporated	Y	Y	Y	Y
with Employees	Y	Y		Y
	Y		Y	Y
Incorporated (III)	Y	Y	Y	Y
	Y	Y		Y
	Y		Y	Y
		Y	Y	Y
			Y	Y(III)

(I) For simplicity it is assumed that listed demographic events aside, all other things are equal; particularly employment which is assumed to be the same before and after the demographic event(s).
(II) Except where the 'newly created' unincorporated enterprise has no employees; in which case the original incorporated enterprise is recorded as having died, see Section 5.
(III) Only if the newly created unincorporated enterprise has no employees.

7.5.6 Break-ups

This event involves a splitting of the production factors of an enterprise into two or more new enterprises, in such a way that the previous enterprise is no longer recognisable. The new enterprises are not considered to be births and the enterprise that existed before the break-up is not considered to have died.

7.5.7 Changes of Ownership (one-to-one take-over)

This event simply involves a change in the controlling legal unit. All other things equal, no death occurs unless the enterprise moves from incorporated to unincorporated with no employees.

7.5.8 Joint Ventures

Cessations of joint ventures should be considered as deaths only if they were originally introduced as births.

7.5.9 Re-structuring Within an Enterprise Group and Enterprise Groups

This event reflects a combination of break-ups, split-offs and mergers. All other things equal it does not result in any deaths.

7.5.10 Deaths: Failures and Closures

Another issue of interest in the context of deaths is the difference between deaths that have occurred because of a failure and those that occur through closure, where closures reflect a withdrawal from the market anticipated at the outset of the businesses creation (Brian Headd 2003). Differentiating between these two types of exits is clearly of policy interest, since the former reflects the failure of some business model whereas the latter often reflects a successful business model. However, the information on whether enterprises become inactive through failure or closure is not readily available. Moreover the distinction between deaths because of failures or closure is not always clear. For example a consultant of an enterprise, of which he or she is the sole employee and owner, might choose to become an employee of another enterprise if the remuneration offered was greater, resulting in the death of his/her business, but it is not clear whether this represents a failure or a closure. As stated above, the reasons for deaths are clearly of importance to policy makers, but, like many other statistics relating to factors of success and failure, these reasons can generally only be established via dedicated surveys that target known deaths.

7.5.11 Death Definition

Deaths can be defined as follows: A death amounts to the economic destruction of a combination of production factors with the restriction that no other enterprises are involved in the event.

An enterprise death in calendar year t occurs when an enterprise with one or more employees and some turnover in calendar year t records zero employees or zero turnover in calendar years t+1 and t+2. Deaths do not include exits from the population due to mergers, take-overs, break-ups, or restructuring of enterprises. Deaths do not include exits from a sub-population resulting only from a change of activity, controlling legal unit or location but do include exits if two of these three factors change, excluding exits that arise from an unincorporated business with employees simultaneously moving to a new location and changing its legal form to become incorporated with employees (and therefore limit liability).

Ideally deaths should be split by activity (2 3 and 4 digit ISIC level if possible), legal form (limited liability companies, sole proprietors, partnerships, public corporations and non-profit institutions serving households), employment size, turnover and ownership (foreign and domestic), *and should separately identify those deaths that are born and die within the same calendar year.* However, in recognition, that this level of breakdown may be difficult to achieve in practice, particularly when one considers the disclosure issues it raises, deaths at the 2-digit level, broken down by employment size, ownership and/or turnover, provide an acceptable information set; additionally, with this option, deaths can be shown broken down by employment size-bands, preferably, 1, 2-4, 5-10, 10-20, and 20+.

In theory, estimates of total deaths in an economy should include all market enterprises that satisfy the definition set out above. In practice however business demography statistics are largely based on the information available in business registers, which may only cover a sub-set of the entire population of market enterprises. If changes are made to the coverage of the business register it is necessary to ensure that deaths are correctly measured. Decreases in the numbers of enterprises resulting from reductions in the coverage of registers (for example by increasing say the employment or turnover thresholds in the business register) should not, by default, be included as deaths. On occasions it may not be possible to identify those enterprises no longer on the register that actually died. Where this occurs these enterprises should not be arbitrarily included as deaths.

The definition for deaths used above is the corollary of births given earlier. In the same way one might consider whether a definition of economic deaths would be useful as a complement to economic births. This has not been included in this framework because it is not clear that the notion of an economic death has quite the same analytical use as an economic birth; although there is no reason in principle or practice why this indicator could not be developed.

7.5.12 Practical Issues

The definition of deaths means that a death cannot be established until two full calendar years after it occurred. This affects timeliness. It means that estimates of deaths in calendar year t will not be available until calendar year t+3. One way of providing provisional estimates of deaths in calendar year t, early in calendar year t+2, is to make projections regarding the number of enterprises inactive in calendar year t+1 that are likely to remain inactive in calendar year t+2, based on historical average ratios.

7.5.13 Point-In-Time versus Live-During-Period-Deaths

Like Births, point-in-time estimates of Deaths, are likely to provide lower estimates than live-during period estimates.

7.6 Birth and Death Rates

7.6.1 Populations

Thus far the framework has focused on providing the conceptual underpinning of definitions for births and deaths. However, total estimates of births and deaths, although of interest, cannot be compared across economies unless they are normalised in some way for the differences in sizes of each economy. This process of normalisation produces estimates of birth and death rates that can be used to compare the levels of creative destruction and entrepreneurship across economies. A number of different denominators can be used to achieve this. Typically, statistical offices use the population of enterprises active in the reference year of interest but other measures can also be used—for example the working-age population or even GDP. Each measure has some advantages and disadvantages over the others and each is considered in turn below.

7.6.2 Populations of Enterprises

Although the definitions for births and deaths proposed in this framework are based on a one-employee threshold it does not necessarily follow that the population of enterprises must also reflect the same threshold; that is, active enterprises with one employee or more.

However, not doing so can lead to very severe restrictions on international comparability of birth and death rates. The coverage of the known population of all enterprises, with and without employees, will differ, in practice, across countries; depending on the legal requirements of enterprises to register. In many countries only businesses above a certain size threshold are required to register, and these thresholds vary across countries. Typically this means that the coverage of very small, micro, enterprises varies significantly across countries, and, as such, invalidates the use of the entire measurable and observable population of enterprises as a denominator.

This is not however the case if coverage of the population of enterprises is defined in a consistent way with the coverage of births and deaths. In other words, if the population of enterprises is to be used as a denominator it must include only the population of active enterprises with one or more employee.

Consistency in the enterprises covered by births, deaths and the enterprise population is typically the practice used by all countries that produce birth and death rates, irrespective of the definitions used for births and deaths since these countries will usually record births and deaths on the same basis as the observable population of enterprises.

Despite its widespread use however, the measure is not without some disadvantages. Economies in transition for example, particularly those moving from centrally planned to market economies, will generally have fewer market enterprises than in equivalently sized market economies. Under these circumstances these economies will display higher birth and death rates than in a similarly sized market economy even if the levels of births and deaths are the same in both.

Moreover the population of enterprises will be affected by the varying levels of enterprise consolidation that occurs across countries. As described earlier demographic events such as mergers and break-ups, for example, do not impact on births but they do impact on the population of enterprises. As such the business population in any country will fall, all other things equal, as a result of industry consolidation via mergers and acquisitions for example, but birth rates will rise even if the level of births over time is unchanged. Of course this example over-exaggerates the potential impact of such events. In most OECD economies the number of enterprises is at least in the hundreds of thousands and, so, typically, demographic events that change the size of the denominator (the enterprise population) will have a minimal impact on the overall birth and death rates.

However, care is needed when interpreting rates across countries with very different levels of industry consolidation or de-regulation. Consider for example two identical economies, except one has a number of near-monopoly or state controlled sectors and the other a more competitive market. Even if the levels of births were the same in both countries, counter-intuitively perhaps (as one might expect higher rates in more competitive economies) the rates would be higher in the monopoly market. The example is of course imperfect since one might also expect births to be lower in the near-monopoly market but the point is to illustrate an arithmetical fact that can hamper the interpretability of rates. One might consider attempting to alleviate this particular problem by focusing only on specific sectors (and so showing birth and death rates in specific industrial sub-sectors using only the population of enterprises in the same sub-sectors). However, this is not advisable since the smaller the sub-population the greater the potential impact of demographic events and importance of the starting position; an issue of particular relevance where new (hi-tech) industries are concerned.

This latter point illustrates what is in part a philosophical conundrum. Although the population of enterprises provides a population from which deaths are sourced it is not so obvious that the same holds for births; since these are sourced, at least for domestically owned births, from the population of budding entrepreneurs; in other words the working-age human population.

7.6.3 Human (Working-Age) Population

The working-age population is arguably a better denominator than the population of enterprises since it is not affected by any of the disadvantages described above. However, there are a number of practical difficulties that complicate the use of this measure. The first concerns the working-age definition which will differ across countries, as will the age at which individuals are legally permitted to create new enterprises. The second relates to the size of the informal, or underground, economy. Countries with a large number of underground enterprises will have lower birth rates than countries with smaller informal economies even if the total births of formal and informal enterprises are the same. This problem is likely to be lessened however if business populations are used.

For some specific purposes other sub-sets of the human population may be used, an example of this is the use of the population of unemployed persons for analyses designed to illustrate the extent to which unemployment encourages entrepreneurship. Great care is needed to accurately interpret data using such sub-populations, as, in practice, only a proportion of new businesses are actually started by people who were previously unemployed

7.6.4 GDP

GDP is the least desirable of the three indicators described here that can be used as a denominator and is not recommended. GDP at current prices should definitely not be used as the basis of the denominator as GDP estimates need to be converted into a common currency which means that, all other things equal, birth rates in countries will change if exchange rates change. Moreover, in periods of very high inflation year-on-year birth rates will show systematic declines even if the levels of births are unchanged. GDP in constant prices provides a better measure although birth rates will be affected by differences in purchasing power parities across countries and the choice of the reference period in which estimates are converted to a common currency.

7.6.5 Recommended Population Measure

In concluding, the choice for the population definition boils down to one of 'the population of enterprises' or 'the working-age population'. This framework recommends the former, although, in recognition of some of the possible interpretative difficulties embodied in this measure, when used to calculate birth rates, and, in recognition of the diagnostic possibilities offered by the latter measure, it also recommends that a complementary indicator for birth and death rates be based using the working-age population as a numerator.

7.6.6 Point-In-Time versus Live-During-Period-Populations

If the denominator is based on the human population, point in time estimates are generally used, i.e. the number of people on a specific date. Where it is based on a business population, two main approaches exist. The traditional approach, followed in most of the data sets used by NSOs, is to use point in time business population data. This is consistent with human demography and allows a "stocks and flows" approach to business demography.

An alternative approach is to use the population of businesses that were considered to be in scope at any point during a given reference period. This approach is favoured by Eurostat in their business demography data collections, partly because it ties in with the approach used to collect financial variables (e.g. turnover for a given period), and partly because it was thought at the time to be easier for countries that did not have accurate birth dates for units in their business registers. This is still Eurostat's view although anecdotal evidence suggests a review could be worthwhile.

It is clear that a live during period population will be larger than one on a point in time basis. The extent of the difference will depend on various factors, but mainly on the length of the period, and the degree of churn (i.e. joiners and leavers) in the business population. As a result, data compiled using a point in time population will not be directly comparable with those based on a live during period approach.

There is a danger with the point in time approach that short-lived businesses that start and close in the period between two reference points may not be included in the business population, or indeed births. This risk is theoretically removed using the live during period approach but, in practice, is only really solved for either approach by having accurate information on birth and death dates or very frequent (daily) observations of the whole population.

However it is important to note that live-during-period estimates do present other complications that need to be corrected for. Like exits and entries, live-during-period measures are affected by other demographic events. For example mergers may result in the appearance of a new enterprise registration and, so, live-during-period population estimates will record a larger population of enterprises than point-in-time estimates. The following example provides an illustration of this. At the beginning of a given year, country A's telecoms sector is dominated by a former state monopoly. Shortly after the start of the year, however, it is taken over by a foreign telecoms business, with all activity transferred to a new subsidary of the foreign business. Later in the year the subsidiary merges with a utility company, and forms another new enterprise. Thus the original enterprise would be counted three times by the live during-period approach. In theory however it is possible to overcome these difficulties by adjusting the population of enterprises for mergers, take-overs etc in the same way (and using the same information set) that exits and entries are transformed into births and deaths, although it would still be necessary to know the beginning of period point-in-time estimate.

It is however possible to estimate a live during period population by adding the total number of business entries during a period (and that survive into the next period) to the point in time estimate for the start of that period; if it is assumed that the numbers of short-lived births (those that are born and die within the same period) are negligible. Similarly a point in time population can also be estimated from live during period data. (Vale 2006) shows that for most OECD member countries, birth rates based on live during period business populations are between 1% and 2% lower than those based on point in time populations).

However live-during-period based estimates present other complications that are not so easy to overcome. Policy makers and analysts are equally interested in estimates of birth and death rates that provide some measure of employment creation as a percentage of total employment (see below). But the nature of employment makes this very difficult to do as enterprise employment levels will vary during the reference period. Moreover, further complications arise when an enterprise purchases an establishment belonging to another enterprise; giving rise to the possibility that live-during-period employment estimates for the total economy are less than the sum of live-during-period estimates of industrial sectors. For estimates of births and deaths weighted by employment it is clear that point-in-time estimates provide the only practical basis for measurement and, for consistency (and not only because they are simpler to calculate), it follows that birth and death rates should also be calculated on this basis.

7.6.7 Birth, Economic Birth and Death Rate Definition

Birth and death rates are based on a denominator and a numerator. The numerators for birth and death rates follow the definitions for births and deaths respectively, given earlier in this framework. The denominator for both birth and death rates is the population of enterprises with one employee or more and active (turnover greater than zero) at a reference point-in-time in the reference period.

A supplementary indicator for both birth and death rates is also recommended using the working-age population as a denominator.

In line with the recommendation given for birth rates it follows that a similar definition is needed for economic birth rates, where economic births are as defined earlier in the report. By extension, for economic birth rates, the population of enterprises used as a denominator should include only those enterprises with two or more employees and are active at a reference point-in-time during the reference period.

Ideally birth, death and economic birth rates should be split by activity (2 3 and 4 digit ISIC level if possible), legal form (limited liability companies, sole proprietors, partnerships, public corporations, non-profit institutions serving households), employment size, turnover and ownership (foreign and domestic), *and should separately identify those births and deaths that are born and die within the same calendar year.* However, in recognition, that this level of breakdown may be difficult to achieve in practice, particularly when one considers the disclosure issues it raises, birth, death and economic birth rates at the 2-digit level, broken down by employment size, ownership and/or turnover, provide an acceptable information set; additionally, with this option, birth, death and economic birth rates can be shown broken down by employee size-bands, preferably, 1, 2-4, 5-10, 10-20, and 20+ (although, of course, the 1 employee size band is redundant for economic births).

7.6.8 Weighted Births and Deaths

Although nominal birth and death rates are of considerable interest, they do not paint a complete picture of the economic contribution of births and deaths. Analysts and policy makers, for example, are particularly interested in their contribution to employment. Turnover is also often of interest, but less so, and, moreover, more difficult to estimate in practice and, so, is not mentioned further here. This interest, is two-fold, the first concerns the direct employment gained or lost when a birth or death occurs as a percentage of total employment, and the second concerns the longer term employment growth prospects of births, which is discussed in Section 8. This section focuses on the former area of interest.

7.6.9 Percentage (Direct) Contribution of Births to Employment

The direct contribution births make to employment, as a percentage of total employment, can be shown by simply taking the total number of employee jobs created in each birth and dividing this total by the total number of employees in the economy.

The reference to 'direct' in the paragraph above is deliberate and is included to highlight the fact that the indicator measures only employment creation related to the birth of an enterprise at its birth. It does not therefore measure any employment that may subsequently occur in years to come.

In theory it would be better to record these jobs on a full time equivalent basis but it is recognised that this is usually difficult to achieve in practice, since it would require specific treatment for seasonal activities where information is seldom available. As such it is preferable to record merely the head-count figures and not full-time equivalents.

7.6.10 Percentage (Direct) Contribution of Births to Employment-Definition

Birth Rates should be supplemented by indicators showing the number of employee jobs created by enterprises when they are born as a percentage of total employees in the relevant reference period, where the total population of employees should be calculated using a point-in-time approach.

7.6.11 Percentage (Direct) Contribution of Deaths to Employment

The death of an enterprise is generally thought to follow a period of decline, which often lasts more than one calendar year.[18] Arguably, therefore, indicators showing the (negative) contribution made by deaths to employment should be able to fully account for the process of dying, in other words, attribute jobs lost during the enterprise's demise to the time of death. Empirically, however, this is easier said than done; as it would require the identification of the point in time in which each enterprise began its decline and subsequent death. If this were based say, on the point at which employment was at a maximum, the negative contribution of deaths would also include any job losses that were driven by productivity and/or technological advances say; meaning that the estimates would be biased upwards.

An alternative approach would be to define the point at which an enterprise began to die as the point at which both turnover and employment began to decline. However even this approach is imperfect. Some enterprises for example may consciously decide to reduce turnover and employment in response to market conditions, for example, reductions in the pool of skilled and affordable workers or the desire to protect the brand by reducing supply. Additionally employment and turnover falls could coincide with productivity increases and falls in the prices of raw inputs.

Equally, not adjusting for the process of decline that many dying enterprises undergo introduces potential biases in statistics that show the relative proportion of deaths by size class, with upward biases for smaller businesses. The approach adopted by Eurostat to overcome this potential bias is to define the size class of the enterprise by the average employment over the period during which the enterprise was active. However this is not a perfect panacea, especially if the period between birth and death is long,

Ultimately some convention is needed. One pragmatic approach is to take the maximum employee levels, averaged over the year and on a full time equivalent (FTE) basis, in the two calendar years before an enterprise's death to calculate the negative contribution made to employee levels. However evidence from two European countries suggests that, in practice, employment for the period in which death occurs is not significantly different to that of previous periods.

---

[18] That said, initial research in two EU Member States has shown that employment for the period in which death occurs is not significantly different to that of previous periods.

Moreover, attempting to create indicators for employee weighted deaths that reflect the whole process of dying introduces an asymmetry between employee weighted births and deaths; since the indicator for employee weighted births measures only the direct and immediate relative contribution of births to employment. Taking employment losses at the point of death is, therefore, arguably the most pragmatic approach; certainly it is by far the simplest and provides estimates of jobs lost through deaths, as a percentage of total employees, which are immediately interpretable and consistent with the concept used for births.

7.6.12 Percentage (Direct) Contribution of Deaths to Employment- Definition

Death Rates should be supplemented by indicators showing the number of employee jobs lost by deaths as a percentage of total employees, where the total population of employees should be calculated using a point-in-time approach.

7.7 Survival rates

7.7.1 Survival Rates

Indicators of birth and death rates can provide an important insight into creative destruction and form invaluable inputs into the analyses of productivity growth at the enterprise level. But this is not the whole story. Of particular interest in the context of business demography analysis and entrepreneurship policy development is the survivability of newly formed enterprises. Two countries for example might have very similar birth and death rates, consistent over time but if one has births that all die within the first year and the other has births that all die after twenty years, say, the levels of creative destruction, innovation and growth potential in the latter economy are almost certainly higher. Focusing on birth and death rates alone therefore can be misleading. Policy makers need to know that their policies are not only encouraging the creation of new enterprises but the creation of successful enterprises that increase the long-term productive capacity and wealth of the economy.

Survival rates show the probability of an enterprise still being in business 'x' years after the enterprise birth. How these rates are calculated depends a great deal on the treatment of other demographic changes which do not result in an enterprise death such as reactivations, mergers, break-ups etc but, put simply, an enterprise has survived if it has not died.[19]

---

[19] This definition of survival differs from that used by Eurostat which defines survival to exclude cases where enterprises merge, break-up or are taken over by an existing enterprise. In these cases Eurostat view the enterprise as not having survived based on the view that a non-survival is not necessarily a death. The view of this framework is that this sits uncomfortably with the definition

Survival rates can be shown at many different levels, for example they can describe the survivability of all births in the economy over a number of years, or they can describe specific sub-sectors, for example a particular cohort of enterprise births in a particular reference year with the same activity and legal form and size class say.

A key question for policy makers concerns the characteristics of enterprise births that have relatively high and low probabilities of survival over time, and how these businesses evolve. Enterprise creation and destruction are part of a process of experimentation, where new firms first make their initial investments unsure of their potential success. Because of this initial uncertainty firms do not start out positioning themselves at a unique optimal size but they may decide to grow once they have learned more about their chances to be profitable. Traditional models of firm learning under uncertainty suggest that while many enterprise births may not survive for long those that do should grow very fast to reach the average incumbent size. As they approach the minimum efficient scale, gain experience and accumulate assets, survivors increase their chances of staying in the market over time. As the enterprise matures (and grows) and the environment becomes less uncertain, the conditional probability of surviving should be expected to decrease. This evolution is important and, as such, estimates of survival rates for any given cohort of enterprises, with defined characteristics, such as legal form, need to continue to track this cohort even if the characteristics of any of the enterprises changes over time.

In this way, and ignoring events such as mergers, break-ups etc, for simplicity, the probability that births at time t with legal form i, industrial sector, j, and size class, k[20] at time t are still active in calendar year $t+\tau$, referred to as the *year-t τ survival rate* for enterprises born at time t, can be defined as:

$$ {}^{\tau}s_t^{i,j,k} = {}^{\tau}S_t^{i,j,k} \Big/ B_t^{i,j,k} \tag{7.1} $$

Where ${}^{\tau}s_t^{i,j,k}$ is equal to the number of enterprise births in calendar year t that survive into t+τ and $B_t^{i,j,k}$ is equal to the number of births in calendar year t. Note that the definition includes the possibility that enterprises can die in the same calendar year of their birth. In other words the *year-t τ survival rate* reflects the probability of births being active in at least t consecutive calendar years, but not necessarily $\tau*12$ months. It is important to note that, although the characteristics of an enterprise, such as size class, sector, or legal form say, may change over time, survival rates group all births on the basis of their characteristics prevailing at the time of birth. Indicators of survival rates of births born in year t are of interest if there is some

---

used for deaths both in this framework and in the Eurostat definition. In theory the Eurostat definition for survivals provides for the possibility of declining survival rates even if no deaths occur. That said, in practice, the difference in treatment of these demographic events is not, on its own, expected to significantly distort comparisons between the two frameworks.

[20] Note that other enterprise characteristics can be shown, for example ownership.

intrinsic relationship between the year of an enterprise's birth and its subsequent probability of survival, facilitating, for example, investigations into the evolution of survival rates for different birth-year cohorts over time; which might be related to changes in economic conditions, such as consumption patterns, competitiveness, competition policy or other policy measures. An alternative measure is to show the probability of all births in a particular cohort, with different birth years, surviving a certain number of years, τ, after their birth. These rates are referred to here as the *average τ-year survival rate,* $^{\tau}s^{i,j,k}$, where

$$\tau s^{i,j,k} = \sum_{t=t1}^{t=t2-\tau} {}^{\tau}S_t^{i,j,k} \Bigg/ \sum_{t=t1}^{t=t2-\tau} B_t^{i,j,k} \tag{7.2}$$

Where t1 and t2 represent the start and end years over which average rates are calculated and τ is less than or equal to (t2-t1), and, as before, the 'cohort' reflects enterprises with the same characteristics i ,j and k, irrespective of their birth year.

A key issue for both *average τ-year survival rate*s and *year-t τ survival rates* concerns the maximum value of τ for which they should be calculated and after which their analytical value is negligible. For example it is theoretically possible to calculate the probability of an enterprise survival 100 years after its birth but this is unlikely to be of much use for policy purposes even if were possible to estimate these probabilities in practice. Ultimately the period of time for which survival rates should be calculated has to be selected by convention. Clearly the larger the value of τ the less relevant the survival measure and the harder it is to measure.

Anecdotal evidence, see Fig. 7.4 below for example, suggests, as would be expected, that it is in the initial years of a birth where a great degree of uncertainty abounds; related to the, often innovative and untested, business plans of births. [21]

This initial period typically lasts about 5 years after which the uncertainty is gradually lessened, as enterprises business move closer to the average incumbent size, and the conditional probability of survival is likely to increase (the hazard rate, see below, is likely to decrease). The recommendation of this manual therefore is that *average τ-year survival rate*s and *year-t τ survival rates* should be calculated for $\tau = 0$ to 5.

The chart above, for New Zealand, shows that even for small enterprises, the year-on-year difference in survival rates levels off after three years.

Figure 7.5 above, showing the conditional probability of enterprises born in 1995 surviving at least one extra year[22], illustrates this point better and shows that 5 years

---

[21] Evidence suggests that these survival statistics are under-estimates. The statistics are calculated on the basis that if a business ceases to exist under exactly the same legal status or structure then it is assumed to have collapsed, presumably due to financial difficulties. These "deaths" can signify other events, such as those described in section 5.

[22] This conditional probability corresponds to 1-the hazard rate. $h_{t,\tau}^{i,j,k}$, the hazard rate, $= 1 - {}^{\tau+1}S_t^{i,j,k} / {}^{\tau}S_t^{i,j,k} = 1 - {}^{\tau+1}S_t^{i,j,k} / {}^{\tau}S_t^{i,j,k}$

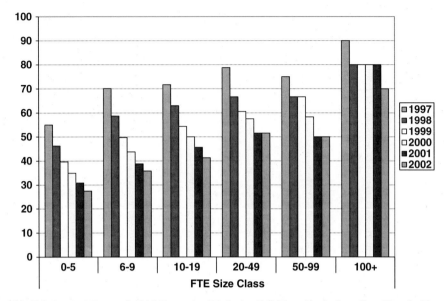

Fig. 7.4 Survival Rates of 1995 Enterprise Births by Full Time Equivalent Size Class in New Zealand
Source: New Zealand, Ministry of Economic Development

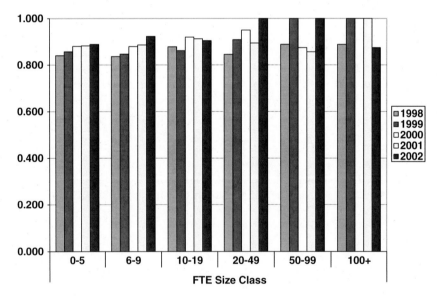

Fig. 7.5 One-Year Conditional Probability of Survival of 1995 Enterprise Births in New Zealand

after birth the conditional probability of survival stabilises; and, so, one can conclude that they have the same conditional probability of survival as older enterprises. A related issue concerns the period of time over which average t-year survival rates should be calculated. Clearly t1 and t2 should not be too far apart otherwise the average will combine probabilities of survival over what might be incomparable periods; a gap of, say, 50 years between t1 and t2 say might be interesting for historians, for example, but would be of limited use for policy makers interested in the impact of current policies and market conditions on survival rates. That said, the average period should ideally embody one complete economic cycle, to avoid the introduction of potential biases related to points in the economic cycle.

7.7.2 Survival Rate(s) Definition

This framework recommends that two measures of survival are developed by NSOs. The first is the *year-t τ survival rate,* which shows enterprise births in year *t* that have not died τ years later as a per cent of all enterprise births in year *t*.

The second is *average τ-year survival rates* which shows all births in period t1 to t2-τ that have not died *t* years after their birth, as a per cent of all enterprise births in years t1 to t2-τ. This corresponds approximately to the un-weighted average *year-t τ survival rate* over periods t1 to t2-τ. The periods t1 and t2 should correspond to one economic cycle.

Rates should be calculated for τ = 0 to 5. Ideally both measures should be split by activity (2 3 and 4 digit ISIC level if possible), legal form (limited liability companies, sole proprietors, partnerships, and public corporations), employment size, turnover and ownership (foreign and domestic). However, in recognition, that this level of breakdown may be difficult to achieve in practice survival rates at the 2-digit level, broken down by employment size, ownership and/or turnover, provide an acceptable information set; additionally, with this option, survival rates can be shown broken down by employment size-bands, preferably, 1, 2-4, 5-10, 10-20, and 20+.

7.7.3 Survival Rates—measurement issues

Survival rates in countries that only record enterprises above the thresholds recommended in this framework for births are likely to show an upward bias as their births are more likely to have already survived their formative and turbulent start-up years, when the likelihood of failure is higher.

7.8 High growth enterprises and gazelles

7.8.1 Defining Growth by Enterprise Characteristics

One of the key interests in business demography statistics relates to the growth potential of births as well as the growth potential of existing enterprises. Indeed, an important catalyst for the development of business demography statistics was the innovative database developed by David Birch in 1979.

Birch suggested that conventional methods used at the time for determining the contribution of different sized enterprises to employment growth produced misleading results. Prior to Birch's work much of the analyses on firm growth assumed little if any inter-class movement of firms (and in so doing implicitly reduced the ability to identify creative destruction). Many of these analyses produced estimates of the contribution large enterprises made to growth in calendar year t by generally assuming that the same enterprises were large in years t and $t-1$. Because these enterprises were defined as large on the basis of their size in calendar year t however, Birch contended that these analyses produced biased results of employment growth: high estimates for large enterprises and low for small enterprises.

Birch instead defined enterprises by their size class in the base year of his study (the year from which growth rates were determined). On this basis, he argued that small enterprises were considerably larger employment creators than had previously been thought, and that they contributed the majority of employment growth (82%) in the US during the 1970s.

However Birch's approach is not without contention, since it is one of two main views that dominate the study of the allocations of businesses to size classes when studying growth.

The main alternative to Birch's approach defines an enterprise's size on the basis of its average size in line with the underlying theory that the pattern of employment in enterprises fluctuates randomly, depending on variations in demand and other transitory factors, around a trend, and so that in equilibrium each enterprise has some typical size. Birch's approach (see also Kirzner 1997) reflects a more turbulent system, where the business environment sees continuous changes in tastes and technologies say, and where enterprises continuously adapt to exploit opportunities; adjusting employment in the process. This view assumes that there is no equilibrium path towards which businesses converge.

This framework does not provide a view on which of the two economic theories are the most plausible, both have their merits, and can be useful as long as their derivation is clear.

7.8.2 High Growth Enterprises

For obvious reasons, one of the most important indicators used in studying entrepreneurship is an indicator of high growth enterprises. At the same time however there is very little unanimity on how this indicator should be defined in an international context. Typically national statistical institutions, analysts and policy makers will adopt an approach based on convention. For example, the International Consortium on Dynamic Benchmarking of Entrepreneurship, led by FORA, a research and analysis division under the Danish Ministry for Economic and Business Affairs, defines high growth enterprises as all enterprises, less than five years old, with more than 15 employees at the start of the observation period and that had either 60% more employees and/or turnover at the end of the observation period.

Part of the rationale behind the 15 employee threshold is to avoid introducing biases that overstress the importance of small enterprises. To illustrate, if the number of employees is taken as the determinant for growth, an increase of one employee in an enterprise that starts with one employee will reflect 100% growth, whereas an enterprise with 100 employees that takes on an extra 50 has lower growth. To focus on the former enterprise as being of greater policy and analytical interest than the latter is likely to be misguided. On the other hand, focusing merely on the absolute size of employment gains biases towards large firms.

Birch (1987) and Schreyer (2000), attempted to reduce the size of these biases by weighting growth by absolute employment gains. High growth enterprises were then defined as the 10% of enterprises who scored highest on this measure. Although useful in interpreting business dynamics within economies, for example the measure provides information on the most successful enterprises and their characteristics, such as size and sector, it is much harder to interpret these measures across countries, and so this approach is not considered further here.

Ultimately, for simple cross-country comparisons of high growth enterprises, a Danish approach is necessary; where the definition is established by convention. However some qualifications are necessary. Clearly the study of turnover growth is important but there are a number of factors which complicate cross-country and inter-temporal comparisons when turnover thresholds are used. Inflation is the first; which introduces potential biases between high and low inflation countries, between high and low inflation periods, and between high and low inflation products and, so, industries; especially commodity industries. The second reflects the relationship between turnover and income (profits, value-added) across industrial sectors. A retail enterprise for example that shifts its sales from low value products to the same quantity of higher value products will not necessarily increase profits nor employment, particularly if the shift is dictated by changes in consumer tastes. As such this framework will not adopt a measure that is based, even in part, on turnover.

Other qualifications are necessary however. Even though the Danish approach introduces a size threshold of 15 to avoid introducing biases that overstress the importance of small enterprises, biases still exist. Very large enterprises for example will be much less likely to increase their size by 60% but ignoring large enterprises with significant growth, albeit below 60%, would be arguably negligent of policy makers, since their ultimate objective is to increase well-being, whether that be via encouraging increased employment in large or small firms; both of which can be entrepreneurial and innovative; although, because the Danish measure focuses on young firms the threshold is not likely to create a significant distortion since very few new enterprises start, or grow very quickly to become, very large. At the same time the use of a threshold also complicates cross-country comparisons, very small countries for example are more likely to have proportionally fewer enterprises with more than 15 employees than much larger countries for example.

Clearly supplementary indicators for high growth firms with less than 10 employees and high growth firms with hundreds of employees could help to address these issues, where the growth threshold for smaller firms is higher than 60% and for large firms lower than 60%, but the framework avoids making firm recommendations in this area as these supplementary indicators are best developed on a country by country basis.

7.8.3 High Growth Definition

The approach advocated in this framework is to provide information on employment growth broken down by size class and employee growth bands. All enterprises with more than one employee are considered in scope, irrespective of their age. Many studies focus only on young firms but these often assume that older firms are not entrepreneurial or are of little interest in its study. This framework takes a different view; namely it does not exclude the possibility that older firms can be innovative and entrepreneurial.

The recommended size-class bands are 10-19, 20-49, 50-249 and 250-499, and 500+, and the recommended growth bands are 0-10, 10-20, 20-30, 30-40, 40-50 and 50+ average annualised growth over the observation period, where the observation period should be no more than, and preferably, three years; this is partly because the longer the observation period the greater the difficulty in ensuring that businesses are not affected by other demographic events. In this way high growth enterprises, broken down by size classes, can be defined by users in line with the growth bands. It is possible to consider smaller size bands but it is not clear what benefit these would provide. Enterprises with less than 10 employees are not included as to do so would create an indicator of high growth enterprises that would potentially be swamped by small enterprises. An enterprise with 1 employee, for example, that increases employment by one every year would show 300% growth over three years. That is not to say that these enterprises are not of interest but clearly some threshold is needed.

Ideally, for each size class, the breakdown by size band should show the percentage of enterprises in each growth band, as a percentage of all enterprises with 10 or more employees and the total working age human population. Further breakdowns of enterprises by characteristics, such as legal form and industry are also recommended. The breakdown by industry is particularly important because in many sectors, for example pharmaceuticals, potential growth of small enterprises is restricted by development and R&D costs say.

The definition for growth should define enterprises on the basis of their size class at the beginning of the observation period and growth must exclude any changes due to other demographic events such as mergers, take-overs and break-ups. In recognition that this level of breakdown may present disclosure problems, a high growth definition, given below, should be attempted as a minimum.

All enterprises with average annualised growth in employees greater than 20% per annum, over a three year period, and with more than 10 employees in the beginning of the observation period, should be considered as high growth enterprises. These enterprises should be broken down by as detailed a size class band as possible, legal form and ISIC industry, and shown as a percentage of all enterprises with more than 10 employees at the start of the observation period and as a percentage of the human working age population.

Understanding the mechanisms that lead to enterprises contracting is also of considerable policy interest. The study of enterprise failure has long been of interest but is complicated by the difficulty in obtaining information from entrepreneurs about the factors that caused failure, since commonly the information concerning the entrepreneur, such as address, is related to the enterprise, and so the entrepreneur is difficult to track. It may be easier however to track 'failing' enterprises. As such national statistics institutes should be encouraged to additionally record those enterprises, and their characteristics, that reduce employment by more than 15% per annum on average over a two year period.

The charts below, using simulated data illustrates the type of information that can be provided using this definition, and the importance of the size class breakdown. Figure 7.6 shows that no large enterprises, with more than 500 employees, grow by more than 10%, but at the same time, as shown in Fig. 7.7, the growing firms in this cohort contribute over 25% of total employment growth.

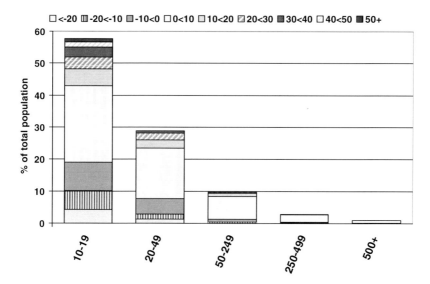

Fig. 7.6 Distribution of Enterprises by Size Class and Growth Band

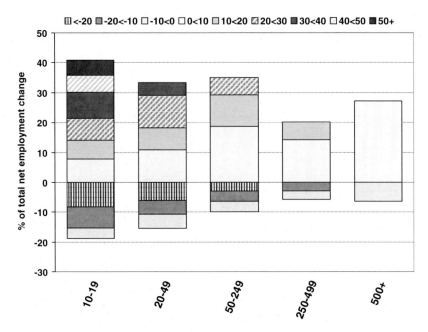

Fig. 7.7 Distribution of Employment Change by Enterprise Size Class and Growth Band

7.8.4 Gazelles

In practice, high growth businesses will be typically young; this is partly a function of the learning and expansion process that young businesses typically undergo—grow, to reach some optimal size or die—but it also partly reflects the correlation (bias) between size (small) and growth (high) potential. Young high growth businesses are typically referred to as gazelles in the literature.

This framework defines 'gazelles' as high growth businesses of less than 5 years old. Information on gazelles should include estimates of employment growth broken down by size class and employee growth bands. The recommended size-class bands are 10-19, 20-49, 50-249 and 250-499, and 500+, and the recommended growth bands are 0-10, 10-20, 20-30, 30-40, 40-50 and 50+ average annualised growth over the observation period, where the observation period should be no more than, and preferably, three years (in practice very few gazelles will appear in the higher size class bands, as young firms are typically small. Ideally, for each size class, the breakdown by size band should show the percentage of enterprises in each growth band, as a percentage of all enterprises with 10 or more employees and as a percentage of the working age human population. Further breakdowns of enterprises by characteristics, such as legal form and industry are also recommended.

The definition for growth should follow the principles outlined above, namely that enterprises are defined on the basis of their size class at the beginning of the observation period and growth must exclude any changes due to other demographic events such as mergers, take-overs and break-ups. In recognition that this level of breakdown may present disclosure problems, a high growth definition, given below, should be attempted as a minimum.

All enterprises less than 5 years old with average annualised growth in employees greater than 20% per annum, over a three year period, and with more than 10 employees in the beginning of the observation period, should be considered as gazelles. These enterprises should be broken down by as detailed a size class band as possible, legal form and ISIC industry, and shown as a percentage of all enterprises, with more than 10 employees at the start of the observation period and as a percentage of the human working age population.

Acknowledgments The views expressed in this paper are those of the author and do not necessarily reflect the views of the OECD or its member countries.

References

ABS (2004) Business Entries and Exits, A Conceptual Framework. Paper produced by the Australian Bureau of Statistics, October 2004

Ahmad N, Vale S (2005) Moving Towards Comparable Business Demography Statistics. Paper presented at the OECD Structural Business Statistics Expert Meeting, Paris, November 2005

Baldwin JR, Beckstead D, Girard A (2002) The Importance of Entry to Canadian Manufacturing with an Appendix on Measurement Issues. Statistics Canada Research Paper

Barnes M, Haskel J, Maliranta M (2002) The Sources of Productivity Growth: Micro-Level Evidence for the OECD

Bartelsman EJ, Scarpetta S, Schivardi F (2003) Comparative Analysis of Firm Demo-graphics And Survival: Micro-Level Evidence For The OECD Countries. OECD Economics Dept Working Paper 2002

Bartelsman E, Haltiwanger J, Scarpetta S (2004) Microeconomic Evidence of Creative Destruction in Industrial and Developing Countries. World Bank Policy Research Working Paper

Bartelsman E, Haltiwanger J, Scarpetta S (2005) Measuring and Analyzing Cross-country Differences in Firm Dynamics. Paper presented to the 2nd EUKLEMS Consortium Meeting, June 2005, Helsinki

Birch D (1987) Job Creation in America: how our smallest companies put the most people to work. Free Press, New York

Brandt N (2004) Business Dynamics in Europe. OECD Science, Technology and Industry Working Paper

Cella P, Viviano C (2004) Register Entries / Exits and Demographic Flows: Some Comparisons for Statistical Aggregates. Paper presented to the 18th International Roundtable on Business Survey Frames, October 2004, Beijing

Choi B, Ward D (2004) Analysis of Statistical Units Delineated by OECD Member Countries. Paper presented to the 18th International Roundtable on Business Survey Frames, October 2004, Beijing

Davis SJ, Haltiwanger J, Jarmin R, Krizan CJ, Miranda J, Nucci A, Sandusky K (2005) Measuring the Dynamics of Young and Small Businesses: Integrating the Employer and Nonemployer Universes. Preliminary paper presented to the US National Bureau of Economic Research Conference on Research in Income and Wealth, April 2005, Bethesda

Davis T (2006) International Entrepreneurship Statistics Programme: Report on the OECD Entrepreneurship Indicators Project and Proposed Action Plan. CFE/SME (2006)7, OECD, Paris

Eurostat (2003) Eurostat Manual of Recommendations for Business Registers. Eurostat

GEM (2004) Global Entrepreneurship Monitor 2004.Global Report

Headd B (2003) Redefining Business Success: Distinguishing Between Closure and Failure. Small Business Economics 21:51–61

Herczog A, van Hooff H, Willeboordse A (1998) The Impact of Diverging Interpretations of the Enterprise Concept. Prepared for Eurostat by Statistics Netherlands

Jarmin R, Miranda J, Sandusky K (2003) Alternative Measures of Business Entry and Exit. Paper presented at the OECD Workshop on Improving statistics on SMEs and Entrepreneurship, 2003: COM/STD/NAES/DSTI/EAS(2003)12

Kirzner I (1997) Entrepreneurial Discovery and the Competitive Market Process: An Austrian Approach. Journal of Economic Literature 35(1):60–85

Klapper L, Laeven L, Raghuram R (2004) Business Environment and Firm Entry: Evidence from International Data. US National Bureau of Economic Research Working Paper

Mead G (2005) Statistics New Zealand Business Frame Strategy and Developments Related to Statistics on SMEs and the Support of Longitudinal Business Statistics. Paper presented at the OECD Structural Business Statistics Expert Meeting, November 2005, Paris

Mills D, Timmins J (2004) Firm Dynamics in New Zealand: Comparative Analysis with OECD Countries. Paper presented to the 2004 conference of the New Zealand Association of Economists

Pinkston JC, Spletzer JR (2004) Annual Measures of Gross Job Gains and Gross Job Losses. US Bureau of Labor Statistics, Monthly Labor Review, November 2004

Schreyer P (2000) High Growth Firms and Employment. OECD DSTI working paper, DSTI/DOC(2000)3

Takahashi M (2000) Business Demography and the Japanese Business Survey Frame. Paper presented to the 14th International Roundtable on Business Survey Frames, November 2000, Auckland

Vale S (2006) The International Comparability of Businesses Start-Up Rates. Forthcoming

Vale S, Powell C (2002) Estimating Under-coverage of Very Small Enterprises. Paper presented to the 16th International Roundtable on Business Survey Frames, October 2002, Lisbon

Vale S, Powell C (2003) Developments in Business Demography - Reconciling Conflicting Demands. Paper presented to the Comparative Analysis of Enterprise (micro) Data Conference, September 2003, London

Volfinger Z (2004) Coverage of the Hungarian Business Register. Paper presented to the 18th International Roundtable on Business Survey Frames, October 2004, Beijing

Chapter 8
Entrepreneurship Performance and Framework Conditions: A General Framework

Morten Larsen

Abstract This chapter presents a benchmark methodology developed by FORA, the Research and Analysis Division of the Ministry of Economic and Business Affairs, the National Agency for Enterprise and Construction in Denmark and the OECD. First the general methodology is presented. Next the methodology is exemplified by illustrating how the method can be used to provide policy makers with an overview of the policy areas which areas are key in a country's overall strategy to promote entrepreneurship.

8.1 Methodology

In 2001 OECD Ministerial report, *The New Economy: Beyond the Hype*, concluded that entrepreneurship, Knowledge building and knowledge sharing, information and communications technology (ICT), and human capital were key elements for enhancing productivity and growth performance in knowledge-based economies (OECD, 2001). Since 2001 Denmark has worked with the OECD on developing a benchmark methodology which can be used to assess a country's performance and framework conditions on the four drivers of growth (see National Agency for Enterprise and Construction, 2005, OECD, 2005). The method goes beyond traditional benchmark analyses in looking at both framework conditions and performances, as well as testing the correlation between the two. The benchmark methodology adopted has seven main steps.

In the first step, the driver of growth, for example entrepreneurship is defined and performance indicators are selected to measure the growth driver, for example level of entrepreneurship.

In the second step the best performing countries are selected as benchmark countries based on the normalised performance indicators.

In the third step indicators of the relevant business environment is collected and normalised. The quality of the business environment in each country is then

Morten Larsen
FORA, Ministry of Economics and Business Affairs, Division for Research and Analysis, Denmark
mrl@ebst.dk

analysed. There is no prior information about the relative importance of the indicators, and some aspects of performance and business environment are hard to quantify. To compensate test for robustness is carried out. The test assigns different weights to the indicators, performance and business environment respectively, to check if the changing of weights influences the ranking of the countries.[1]

In the fourth step a test for correlation between performance and business environment is carried out. A strong correlation is assumed to indicate a connection between a good business environment and good performance.

In the fifth step weak points in the business environment are identified comparing the countries of interest with the best performing countries.

However not all areas are equally important for performance and critical areas of the business environment are identified in the sixth step. This is done by looking at both the areas of the business environment which have been given high priority by the best performing countries and the correlation between areas of the business environment and performance.

Finally possible improvements of weak points in business environment are identified using peer reviews to learn from policies in best performing countries. Peer reviews are based on a qualitative approach and do not rely on quantitative indicators. The method used to assess policies can be compared to the case study method, as it focuses on how a few countries succeed. A policy implemented in a benchmarking country is not necessarily an effective policy in another country. The analysis highlights the main challenges for each policy area and then lists effective policy responses in the top-performing countries and emphasise national evaluation of policies and other quantitative and qualitative evidence of the effectiveness of the policies.

The methodology presented here thereby allows policy makers to compare their business environment to that of the best-performing countries. It also highlights the potentially most important policy areas for productivity growth and helps policy makers to prioritise policy actions. Finally, the micro-policies identified can point to policy actions to remedy identified deficiencies in important parts of the business environment.

---

[1] There is no direct solution for selecting weights. A new sensitivity technique has been developed for this type of analysis, which assigns weights randomly to each of the normalised indicators. In this study the calculation was repeated 10 000 times and the weights were drawn from a uniform distribution (from 0 to 1) for each of the indicators. This gives a distribution of possible rankings for each country. The probability of being among the top three, top five or top ten performing countries can be calculated based on that distribution. The figures in this chapter are based on these probability calculations.

8.2 Entrepreneurial Performance and Business Environment in Denmark

The benchmark methodology is applied to construct the Entrepreneurship Index. The Entrepreneurship Index is a yearly report comparing Danish entrepreneurship activity and the Danish entrepreneurial framework conditions with other OECD countries.

As mentioned the rationale behind the benchmark approach is that differences in country entrepreneurship performance may be explained by differences in the quality of country framework conditions. While the benchmark approach fails to identify any causal connection, it does, however, allow for identifying best-practice policies. If the top-performing countries have particularly effective framework conditions in specific policy areas it is assumed that those framework conditions are very important to entrepreneurial activity. Thus the Entrepreneurship Index allows for carving out particularly important framework conditions and identifying countries that may serve as role-models for Denmark's entrepreneurial efforts.

The 2005 Entrepreneurship Index has been compiled by the National Agency for Enterprise and Construction and FORA. An international consortium of internationally renowned entrepreneurship experts and government representatives have made valuable contributions in discussing the overall model, and have provided valuable input into the link between entrepreneurship activity and framework conditions.

8.3 Objectives of the Entrepreneurship Index

The main objective of the Entrepreneurship Index is to measure the status and development of entrepreneurship activity and framework conditions in Denmark compared to other OECD countries.

Entrepreneurship is high on the agenda in Denmark and the Government has set two ambitious goals: in 2010 Denmark should be part of the European entrepreneurial elite, and by 2015 Denmark should have the worlds' highest share of high-growth start-ups.

The latter is the most ambitious and form the starting point for most analysis carried out in the 2005 index. The analysis is based on the assumption that there is a time lag in terms of performance improvements; it takes 3 to 5 years before any improvements in framework conditions will materialise in a better country performance. If this indeed is the case by 2010 Denmark should be among the countries with the best framework conditions.

Following this it is the sub-goals of the index to answer the following three questions:

- Are Denmark's framework conditions and the level of entrepreneurial activity moving in the right direction vis-à-vis the top entrepreneurship countries as well as other European countries? Is Denmark currently on track to meet the goals set by the Danish Government

- Which framework conditions should Denmark address to catch up with the leading entrepreneurial countries?
- Which tangible efforts should be carried out before 2010 to catch up with the best?

To answer the last question the method must be complemented by other types of analyses. While the model provides a comprehensive view of Denmark's entrepreneurship activity and the quality of Danish framework conditions as well identifying areas that new improvement, it does, however, fail to provide input for drafting specific initiatives to improve Denmark's entrepreneurial record. The model may point to countries from which Denmark can draw inspiration. However, a simple cut-and-paste approach may be detrimental to Denmark's entrepreneurship efforts.

8.4 International Comparisons

Framework conditions conducive to entrepreneurship cover a wide range of areas; the presence of efficient markets, unlimited access to capital, the presence of skills required to launch and subsequently grow an enterprise and the presence of a proper incentive structure that provide tangible benefits for enterprising individuals. Finally, the entrepreneurial culture should motivate people to become entrepreneurs, reward entrepreneurial efforts and accept if things do not go according to plan.

What are the practical implications of this? How much capital is needed? What should the incentive structure be like? How are the necessary entrepreneurial skills nurtured? What is the impact of liberalisations on entrepreneurial entry barriers? The questions pertaining to framework conditions are endless.

No optimal method exists in answering these or related questions. However, international comparisons of entrepreneurship activity levels and framework conditions may provide answers to some or all of the questions. By comparing Danish entrepreneurship activity and the Danish entrepreneurial framework conditions with other OECD countries the 2005 Entrepreneurship Index makes it possible to assess Denmark's strength and weaknesses.

The 2005 Entrepreneurship Index uses 57 indicators to measure framework conditions and 4 indicators to measure entrepreneurship activity. Significant effort has been placed on a quality assessment of the applied indicators.[2] The indicators have been assessed by applying a quality manual built on the UN and the OECD's quality manual.

---

[2] http://www.foranet.dk/Publikationer/Rapporter/Data/Indicator%20Manual.aspx for a detailed report pertaining to this issue

8.5 Entrepreneurial Activity

Entrepreneurial activity can be measured in a myriad of ways. Depending on the purpose of the analysis, various definitions may be applied. The entrepreneurship index applies a composite measure for entrepreneurial activity that combines data on start-up activity and new-firm growth as these are highly correlated with productivity growth.

New-firm start up rates is comprised of two separate indicators:

- Actual start-up rates, measures the number of new enterprises as a share of the total stock of enterprises. Start-up rates are compiled by Eurostat, The Statistical Office of the European Union and are derived from new-firm registrations.
- The so-called Total Entrepreneurial Activity (TEA) index, which measures the share of the population that are involved in the start up of an enterprise, and the number of people running a start-up enterprise (no more than $3 1/2$ years old). The TEA index is compiled by the Global Entrepreneurship Monitor (GEM) consortium, a multi-national research program that supply yearly evaluations of entrepreneurship activity. 34 countries participated in the GEM in 2004.

New-firm growth is comprised of two separate indicators:

- The share of new enterprises with 2001 to 2003 revenue growth above 60 percent. The indicator is based on data for new enterprises launched from 1997 through 2001, with at least 15 year's work for one person in 2001 and which was still in business in 2003.
- The share of new enterprises with 2001 to 2003 employee growth above 60 percent from 2001 to 2003. The indicator is based on data for new enterprises launched from 1997 through 2001, with at least 15 year's work for one person in 2001 and which was still in business in 2003.

In terms of start-up rates Denmark performs well, especially when measuring actual start-up rates (the share of newly-registered enterprises as a share of the total stock of enterprises). Denmark has a mediocre ranking on GEM's TEA index, which measures the share of the adult population engaged in an enterprise start-up and the number of people running a start-up enterprise (no more than $3 1/2$ years old). With regards to new-firm growth Denmark is ranked in the bottom part of the index (Table 8.1).

8.6 Selecting the Top-Performing Countries

Differences found in individual country rankings imply that the selection of top-performing countries in terms of entrepreneurial activity will depend substantially on the choice of weights for each of the four indicators.

Table 8.1 Denmark's ranking on the indicators for entrepreneurship activity

Actual start-up rates – 2001 and 2002

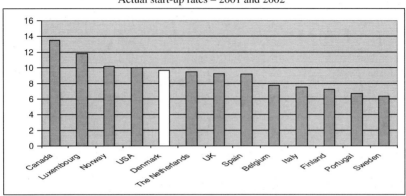

TEA index –
2004

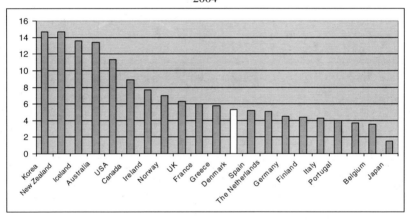

Number of entrepreneurs
with + 60 percent revenue growth – 2001-2003

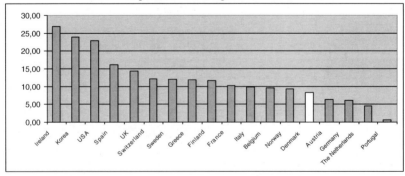

Sources: Eurostat, GEM (2004), Schtt (2005A), Bureau van Dijk, Statistics Canada, US Census,
US, Small Business Administration and author's calculations.

Various decompositions of growth show both start-up rates and new firm growth to be vital. This implies that these indicators are important, yet, the contributions of each individual indicator may vary across countries. When drafting a composite index for entrepreneurial activity, it remains unclear how individual indicators should be weighed. To overcome this obstacle, a robustness analysis is carried out. The robustness analysis shows the frequency with which countries are ranked in the Top-3, Top-5 and Top-10, respectively, regardless of weights applied.

The robustness analysis shows that Korea, Canada and the United States rank in the Top-3 in all but a few of the calculations. Ireland claims Top-3 rankings in approximately 20 percent of the calculations. The UK and Spain claim Top-5 rankings in 80 and 20 percent of the outcomes, respectively. Consequently, we see a significant gap between the Top-3 and the European elite (Fig. 8.1).

In light of this analysis, Korea, Canada and the United States are selected as the top-performing countries in terms of entrepreneurial activity. Consequently, they are the standards of reference throughout this analysis. The robustness analysis shows that Denmark ranks in the bottom part of the index alongside Germany, Austria, Portugal and the Netherlands. Denmark claims only a limited number of Top-10 rankings, and no Top-3 or Top-5 rankings.

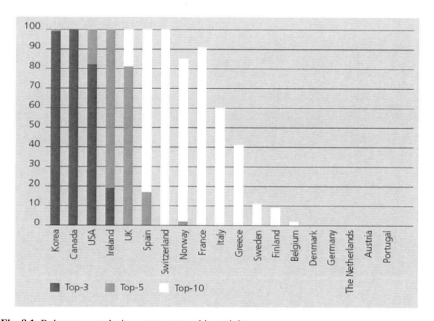

Fig. 8.1 Robustness analysis—entrepreneurship activity
Note: The robustness analysis shows the frequency with which countries are ranked in the Top-3, Top-5 and Top-10, respectively, using different weights. A total of 100 000 weights have been applied, which resulted in 100 000 different rankings. Iceland has not been included in the calculations since only one indicator is available for Iceland. Therefore, Iceland's ranking is independent of the weights applied.

8.7 Entrepreneurship Framework Conditions

The number of policy areas that affect entrepreneurial activity is exhaustive. A careful examination of concepts and instruments combined with a theoretical run-down of the correlation between policy and entrepreneurship has materialised into 23 policy areas (Hoffmann and Gabr, 2005). The list is thought to be exhaustive but not final. The emergence of new indicators may allow for a more detailed analysis. Correspondingly new knowledge will continuously expand our understanding, which in turn may lead to the inclusion of new policy areas (Fig. 8.2).

A multi-faceted and adequate picture of each of the policy areas requires a large number of indicators. Presently 18 of the 23 policy areas are covered by internationally comparable indicators. Denmark has taken the initiative to further building and refining of internationally comparable indicators. In the short term the areas of entrepreneurship education, bankruptcy legislation, restarting possibilities and entrepreneurship infrastructure will be further developed.

A total of 57 indicators are applied in measuring country framework conditions. Country data coverage for indicators related to framework conditions is significantly higher as compared to data coverage for country performance indicators.

To measure the quality of country framework conditions, individual policy areas must be weighted together. No universal method exists in assigning individual weights. Consequently, a robustness analysis is carried out to determine the frequency with which countries are ranked in the Top-3, Top-5 and Top-10, respectively, regardless of the weights assigned.

The rankings are shown to be robust. Regardless of weights applied, the United States, Canada and Korea claim the majority of Top-3 rankings. A second group of

Total measure for entrepreneurship framework conditions					
Factors affecting entrepreneurship performance	Market Access	Capital	Ability	Incentives	Culture/Motivation
	Access to foreign markets	Capital Taxes	Trad. Business education	Income tax	Entrepreneurial motivation
	Entry-barriers	Wealth and bequest tax	Entrepreneurship infrastructure (private)	Bankruptcy legislation	Incentives towards specific groups
Policies areas affecting entrepreneurial performance	Technology transfers	Loans	Entrepreneurship education	Business tax and fiscal incentives	Communication about heroes
	Procurement regulation	Venture capital	Restart possibilities	Labour market regulation	
		Stock markets	Entrepreneurship infrastructure (public)	Administrative burdens	
		Business Angels		Social Security discrimination	

Fig. 8.2 Policy areas applied in measuring entrepreneurship framework conditions
Note: Indicators marked in light green is covered by at least one quality-approved indicator that allows for international comparisons. Red policy areas are not covered by internationally comparable or quality-approved indicators (please refer to http://www.foranet.dk/Publikationer/ Rapporter/Data/Indicator%20Manual.aspx for an in-depth evaluation of the quality of individual indicators)

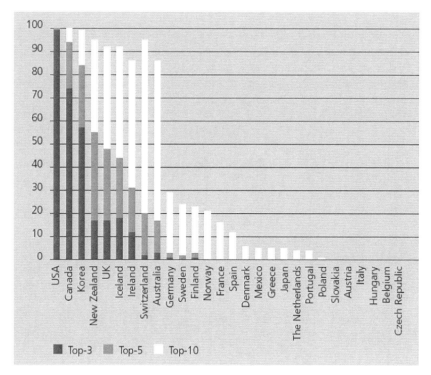

Fig. 8.3 Robustness analysis—entrepreneurial framework conditions

Note: Figure robustness analysis shows the frequency with which countries are ranked in the Top-3, Top-5 and Top-10, respectively, using different weights. A total of 100 000 weights have been applied which results in 100 000 different rankings

countries, including New Zealand, the United Kingdom, Iceland, Switzerland and Australia make the Top-10 in all but a few of the outcomes and make the Top-5 ranking regularly. A third group covers 13 countries that occasionally post Top-10 rankings, but rarely claim the Top-5 rankings. A fourth group show sporadic Top-10 rankings.

Denmark belongs to the third group alongside Finland, Sweden, Norway, Spain, Japan and Poland. Denmark rarely posts Top-10 rankings and only very seldom Top-5 rankings. The robustness analysis shows results to be robust to changes in weights. Hence, in the following section equal weights are applied in plotting Denmark's framework conditions against those of the Top-3 countries (Fig. 8.3).

8.8 Correlation Between Entrepreneurial Activity and Framework Conditions

The Entrepreneurship Index is built on the assumption that differences in country performances can be explained by differences in the country's framework conditions.

Hence, one should be able to detect a positive correlation between entrepreneurial policies and entrepreneurial activity levels. Improved framework conditions will materialise into better performance, but there is a time lag (3 to 5 years) before such improvements can be registered in a country's performance.

The lack of time series for several indicators makes it impossible to show a causal connection between high-quality framework conditions and a high level of entrepreneurial activity.

However, the assumption is supported by a range of company-level policy area studies.

The 2004 Index highlighted the correlation between framework conditions and entrepreneurship performance. However, the results were somewhat fragile as the correlation was based on data from 14 countries.

Furthermore, the data on new-enterprise growth was based on only few observations for some of the countries. Korea, in particular, scored significantly higher in entrepreneurship performance than the quality of the country's framework conditions would indicate.

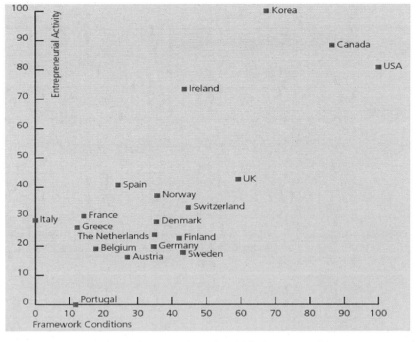

Fig. 8.4 Correlation between entrepreneurial activity and framework conditions
Note: The graph shows the correlation between country performance and framework condition rankings. Values have been normalised on a scale from 0 to 100. Y-axis = entrepreneurial activity, X-axis = framework conditions. R2 is.58, which means that the chosen framework condition indicators explain close to 60 percent of the variation in performance among the OECD countries.

This year has seen a significant improvement in the Korean growth data, and more countries have been added to the analysis. The new data reconfirms the positive correlation between framework conditions and performance (Figure 8.4).

As shown in the 2004 Index, there appears to be a correlation between high-quality framework conditions and a high level of entrepreneurial activity.

However, the correlation is still fragile. Compared to the group of European countries, Korea, the United States and Canada have significantly better framework conditions and distinctively higher activity levels. Korea's activity levels are significantly higher than dictated by the quality of the country's framework conditions.

8.9 Denmark's Framework Conditions vis-à-vis the Top-3

Denmark still faces some obstacles to matching the framework conditions of the Top-3. The overall distance between Denmark and the Top-3 is determined by the individual gaps detected for each of the 18 quantifiable policy areas. For the majority of the 18 policy areas, Denmark trails the Top-3. This is particularly evident in the areas of personal income tax, entrepreneurship education, bankruptcy legislation (including restart possibilities) and, to some extent, financing (Fig. 8.5).

This figure conceived to illustrate the gaps between Denmark and the Top-3 performing countries. The figure shows the contributions of individual policy areas to the total gap (Fig. 8.5).

8.10 How Should Resources Be Prioritised?

A simple conclusion as to the prioritisation of resources would be to highlight policy areas where Denmark trails the top-3. However it is possible to refine the analysis. Not all of the selected policy areas are equally important to entrepreneurship performances. A range of methods have been developed to show the relative importance of a given policy areas. Methods are still being developed, and any meaningful break down of policy areas should be supplemented by qualitative assessments and the inclusion of various entrepreneurship studies.

The applied method divides policy areas into four separate boxes. A high correlation between policy area indicators and entrepreneurship activity implies that the policy in question is highly important to entrepreneurship activity. If the top-performing countries have particularly strong framework conditions in specific policy areas is taken as an indications that the policy area(s) in questions are highly important.

A framework that combines the aforementioned methods is presented below. The model uses the colours green, yellow and red to illustrate Denmark's position vis-à-vis the Top-3. Six areas, entrepreneurship education, restart possibilities, personal income taxes, venture capital, labour market regulation and access to foreign markets, are high-priority areas and are highly correlated. This leads us to conclude that the six areas are particularly important to entrepreneurial activity.

Denmark is far behind the Top-3 in the areas of entrepreneurship education, restart possibilities, and income taxes, and is somewhat lagging on venture capital. Denmark is at the same level with the Top-3 in labour market regulation and access to foreign markets (Fig. 8.5).

The Top-3 countries have given high priority to corporate tax and bankruptcy legislation, which are other areas where Denmark trails the top performing countries considerably. However, these policy areas are not highly correlated with

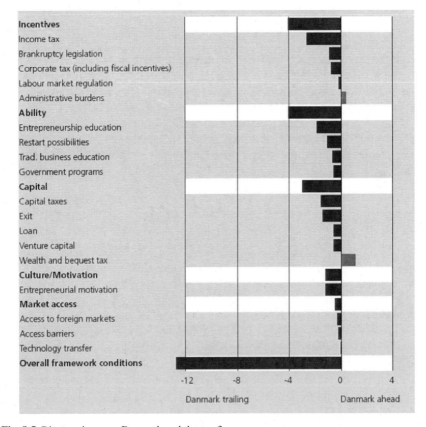

Fig. 8.5 Distance between Denmark and the top 3
Note: The light green bars show Denmark ahead of the Top-3, red bars indicate that Denmark is trailing. Individual policy areas are normalised on a scale from 0 to 100. The 18 policy areas are assigned identical weights (1/18). The value for individual policy areas is the difference between the Top-3 and Denmark x 1/18. This allows for the combination of individual policy areas, providing a picture of individual policy area contributions to the overall gap. Please refer to www.foranet.dk for a detailed description of how differences between Denmark and the Top-3 are calculated.

entrepreneurial activity. Culture/motivation is highly correlated with entrepreneurial activity, but is considered less important among the Top-3 countries.

This implies that Denmark should pay particular attention to the following areas: entrepreneurship education, restart possibilities, personal income taxes, and, to some extent, venture capital.

It is also possible to detect if the four chosen policy areas are correlated with indicators for start-up and new-firm growth. This approach should be treated with some caution. Only two indicators are available for start-up activity and new-firm growth, respectively, and country data coverage is far from exhaustive.

Entrepreneurship education, personal income taxes and restart possibilities are all significantly correlated with the indicators for start-up activity. Venture capital is somewhat correlated with start-up indicators, but not significantly.

Entrepreneurship education, personal income taxes and venture capital are significantly correlated with indicators for growth. The correlation for restart possibilities is somewhat lower, but is not significant.

The policy areas that are correlated with the composite indicator of performance differ only slightly from the policy areas that are correlated with start-up and new-firm growth indicators. At the same time, there is an element of uncertainty in this latter approach. However, the results do not give rise to any revision of the conclusion that the four areas are important to entrepreneurial activity.

Table 8.2 Selecting important policy areas

	Low Correlation with Performance	Significantly Correlated with Performance
High Priority among Top-3	• Corporate tax • Bankruptcy legislation • Wealth and bequest tax • Administrative burdens	• Entrepreneurship education • Restart possibilities • Personal income tax • Venture capital • Labour market regulation • Access to foreign markets
Low Priority among Top-3	• Exit • Capital taxes • Government programmes • Trad. business education • Loan capital • Technology transfer	• Culture/motivation • Entry barriers

Note: The policy areas are ranked by applying two criteria: i) the boxes on the right hand side are all significantly correlated with performance indicators at a 5 percent level, ii) the top hand boxes are highly prioritised among the Top-3 countries, i.e. the average value for the Top-3 is higher than the average for all framework conditions among the Top-3 countries.

The selection of the four policy areas hinges on three factors that may influence results—the quality of the underlying indicators, the weights applied, and the group of reference countries.

A quality assessment of the chosen indicators highlights restart possibilities, personal income taxes and venture capital as high-quality indicators, while the two indicators covering the area of entrepreneurship education are of somewhat lower quality. However, Denmark's poor ranking in the latter area has been confirmed by several studies (National Agency for Enterprise and Construction, 2004A). An assessment of the quality of the underlying indicators does not give rise to any revision of the selection of policy areas in which Denmark should intensify its efforts.

Throughout the analysis, indicators area assigned equal weights. A comprehensive sensitivity analysis identifies the areas of entrepreneurship education, restart possibilities and personal income taxes as particularly important in more than 95 percent of the outcomes. Venture capital is more sensitive to weights, but is shown to be very important in 75 percent of the calculations and is a high-priority area among the Top-3 countries regardless of the weights applied. Consequently, weights are not believed to play a significant role in the conclusions reached in this study.

The gap between Denmark and the Top-3 countries is greater than 20 percent in the areas of entrepreneurship education, restart possibilities and personal income taxes for all combinations of weights assigned to the indicators. The venture capital gap is more susceptible to various combinations of weights due to the relative size of the Danish seed capital market as compared to Korea and the United States. Consequently, the area of venture capital is assigned the colour yellow, while the remaining three policy areas are marked in red.

Compared to Denmark, the United States, Korea and Canada have different social, cultural and economic structures. When comparing Denmark to the European elite—the United Kingdom, Ireland and Iceland—Denmark performs well against the European Top-3 in the areas of venture capital and restarting possibilities. Here, Denmark is at the same level with the European elite. For the remaining policy areas, the conclusions are similar to those found when comparing Denmark to the United States, Korea and Canada (Please refer to www.foranet.dk for a comparison between Denmark and the European Top-3).

References

Hoffmann A. Hoffmann A, Hoffmann G, Hesham M (2005) A General Policy Framework for Entrepreneurship. FORA, Copenhagen

Hoffmann A. National Agency for Enterprise and Construction (2004) Entrepreneurship Education at Universities—a benchmark study, EBST, Copenhagen

Hoffmann A. OECD (2001) The New Economy: Beyond the Hype. The OECD Growth Project, OECD, Paris

Part III
The Current Applied Research
on Entrepreneurship

Chapter 9
Self-Employment and Unemployment in Spanish Regions in the Period 1979–2001

Antonio Aníbal Golpe and André van Stel

Abstract This chapter investigates the relation between changes in self-employment and changes in unemployment at the regional level in Spain in the period 1979-2001. We estimate a vector autoregression model as proposed by Audretsch, Carree, van Stel and Thurik (2005) using a data base for Spanish regions. By estimating the model we are able to empirically distinguish between two directions of causality. On the one hand increases in self-employment may contribute to lower unemployment rates (the 'entrepreneurial' effect). On the other hand, higher unemployment rates may push individuals into self-employment, thereby contributing to higher self-employment rates (the 'refugee' effect). In our analysis of these two effects we distinguish between higher and lower income regions within Spain. We find empirical support for the 'entrepreneurial' effect to exist, both in higher income and in lower income regions. As regards the 'refugee' effect, the evidence is mixed. We find empirical support for this effect for higher income regions. Remarkably, we do not find evidence for a 'refugee' effect in lower income regions of Spain, even though unemployment rates are on average higher in these regions. We argue that this may be partly related to a lack of incentives for unemployed individuals in these regions to find paid employment.

JEL-code: E24, L11, M13, O10, O52

Keywords: entrepreneurship, self-employment, unemployment, economic growth, Spain

André van Stel
EIM Business and Policy Research, Zoetermeer, Netherlands
Cranfield University School of Management, UK
ast@eim.nl

9.1 Introduction

Recently the relation between self-employment and unemployment has been the topic of many scientific investigations. The relation is of considerable policy importance as self-employment is seen as a route to escape unemployment. Not only do unemployed individuals who turn self-employed contribute to bringing down unemployment by providing a job for themselves, but they may also hire employees who would otherwise not find a job. The relation is quite complex however as there are two directions of causality involved. On the one hand self-employment may lead to a decrease in unemployment, and on the other hand unemployment may lead to an increase in self-employment (Audretsch et al. 2005). The first effect may be labeled the 'entrepreneurial' effect. A higher number of entrepreneurs in an economy contributes to higher levels of competition which, in the longer run, may lead to higher productivity levels and lower levels of unemployment (Geroski 1989). The second effect may be labeled the 'refugee' effect. When unemployment levels are high, an unemployed individual may find it hard to find a wage-job as a paid employee, and may found a new firm in order to escape from unemployment.[1]

As the 'entrepreneurial' and 'refugee' effects are in opposite directions, it is important to disentangle these two effects in empirical work. Also, it is important to use long times series as there may be considerable lags involved in the relation (Fritsch and Mueller 2004). Using a data base for 23 OECD countries in the period 1974-2002, Audretsch et al. (2005) estimate a two-equation model where the two effects are estimated in separate equations. These authors find evidence for both effects to exist, but the 'entrepreneurial' effect is found to be stronger. However, as the estimation results of Audretsch et al. (2005) are based on 23 countries, it is imaginable that the relation is different for individual countries. For instance, the 'refugee' effect may be stronger in countries with relatively high unemployment levels such as Spain.

The present chapter focuses on the relation between self-employment and unemployment in Spain. The relation may be particularly interesting for Spain as unemployment levels are historically very high. Our approach is inspired by that of Verheul et al. (2006). These authors also focus on the relationship for Spain, by investigating the specific residuals for Spain from the Audretsch et al. (2005) estimations. Their analysis suggests that not only the quantity but also the increased quality of self-employment may have contributed to recent decreases in the Spanish unemployment rate. However, their research method is indirect as the coefficients on which the studied residuals are based, are established for the whole sample of 23 OECD countries. In the present paper we propose a more direct method to investigate the relation for Spain by estimating the Audretsch et al. (2005) model using data on self-employment and unemployment rates for 17 Spanish regions in the period 1979-2001. In addition, as there are quite severe differences in income levels between different parts of Spain, we also investigate whether the relation

---

[1] For a more elaborate description of these effects we refer to Audretsch et al. (2005).

differs between higher income regions and lower income regions within Spain. For instance, we may expect the 'refugee' effect in lower income regions (where unemployment levels are higher) to be stronger compared to higher income regions.[2] The aim of our exercises is to throw more light on the nature of the relation between self-employment and unemployment for Spain.

The chapter is organised as follows. In Section 2 we will present our data base on self-employment and unemployment rates for Spanish regions. In Section 3 we will describe the empirical model. In Section 4 we will present and interpret the estimation results while the final section concludes.

9.2 Self-employment and Unemployment Rates in Spanish Regions

Our data base consists of annual data for 17 Spanish regions (NUTS-II spatial aggregation level) and the sample period spans from 1979 to 2001. We use two variables: the self-employment rate and the unemployment rate. The self-employment rate is defined as the number of self-employed individuals including own account workers and employers, divided by total labour force. The unemployment rate is defined as the number of unemployed divided by total labour force. Both variables have been gathered from Encuesta de Poblacion Activa (EPA) provided by the Statistical Spanish Institute (INE). The data relate to the whole private sector, i.e. including all sectors of the regional economies.

As an illustration Table 9.1 shows the self-employment rates for each region for the years 1979, 1989 and 2001. There are great differences across regions. For example, Galician self-employment rates are on average twice as high as Basque Country (País Vasco) self-employment rate. As we can see, self-employment rates are decreasing during the last years. The predominant trend is downward with the exception of País Vasco. Statistics on international labour (e.g. *OECD Labour Force Statistics*) show that the downward trend in self-employment is mainly due to agriculture where the number of self-employed decreases drastically over the last few decades.

Table 9.2 reports data on the unemployment rate for the same years in our sample. As we can observe, during the 1980s, the unemployment rate was, on average, increasing and in the 1990s, this rate was decreasing again. The increasing unemployment rate during the 1980s was in part related to economic reforms following the switch from the Franco dictatorship to democracy in the 1970s. The decrease in unemployment during the 1990s was in part related to the large amounts of EU structural funds being channelled to the Spanish economy following EU-entry

---

[2] Alba-Ramírez (1994) shows that the duration of unemployment significantly increases the probability of becoming self-employed for Spain and the United States.

Table 9.1 Self-employment rates in Spanish regions over the period 1979-20011

Region	1979	1989	2001
Andalucía	18.43	14.24	13.34
Asturias	21.89	18.85	20.09
Canarias	16.58	12.70	12.07
Cantabria	23.70	19.43	16.60
Castilla la Mancha	26.66	22.61	19.77
Castilla León	27.15	24.38	21.43
Extremadura	25.17	20.06	20.16
Galicia	33.03	28.57	22.51
Murcia	19.61	14.18	14.06
Comunidad Valenciana	17.23	17.19	15.20
Average of lower income regions	22.95	19.22	17.52
Aragón	22.94	22.55	18.90
Baleares	20.95	17.68	14.82
Cataluña	15.11	14.46	14.54
Madrid	10.04	9.58	9.64
Navarra	19.92	18.23	18.55
País Vasco	11.89	13.59	14.70
La Rioja	29.33	24.16	25.34
Average of higher income regions	18.60	17.18	16.64

Source: INE (EPA). Self-employed workers include both own account workers and employers. Self-employment rates relate to the whole economy (i.e. including agriculture)

Table 9.2 Unemployment rates in Spanish regions over the period 1979-2001

Region	1979	1989	2001
Andalucía	13.85	27.00	18.67
Asturias	7.34	18.01	7.74
Canarias	10.63	21.25	10.75
Cantabria	5.50	17.65	8.69
Castilla la Mancha	7.67	14.19	9.49
Castilla León	6.73	16.58	10.05
Extremadura	13.49	26.63	14.51
Galicia	3.40	12.32	11.02
Murcia	7.96	16.43	10.66
Cdad. Valenciana	6.64	15.46	9.44
Average of lower income regions	8.32	18.55	11.10
Aragón	6.48	12.16	4.99
Baleares	4.83	10.76	5.95
Cataluña	7.99	14.16	8.63
Madrid	10.38	13.00	7.57
Navarra	8.42	12.60	4.85
País Vasco	9.36	19.28	9.79
La Rioja	4.14	9.91	4.52
Average of higher income regions	7.37	13.12	6.61

Source: INE (EPA).

in 1986.[3] Besides the heavy *fluctuations* in the unemployment rates we also note that the *level* of unemployment is structurally high, in particular in the low-income regions.[4] Verheul et al. (2006) argue that this may be related to the relatively generous unemployment benefits in Spain and a relatively low level of labour market flexibility.

In the present chapter we will investigate whether increases in self-employment lead to subsequent decreases in unemployment (the 'entrepreneurial' effect) and whether increases in unemployment lead to subsequent increases in self-employment (the 'refugee' effect). We also investigate whether there are differences in these hypothesized effects between higher income regions and lower income regions. For instance, from Table 9.2 we see that unemployment is considerably higher in lower income regions hence we may expect the 'refugee' effect in these regions to be stronger compared to higher income regions. Concerning the 'entrepreneurial' effect, it could be that human capital levels differ between higher and lower income regions and hence that the impact of self-employment on unemployment differs as well (van Stel et al. 2005).

9.3 Model and Methods[5]

As we have seen the relationship between unemployment and entrepreneurship is complex. It is generally assumed that there is a two-way causation between changes in the level of entrepreneurship and that of unemployment: an *entrepreneurial* effect of entrepreneurship reducing unemployment and a *refugee* effect of unemployment stimulating entrepreneurship. Audretsch et al. (2005) try to reconcile the ambiguities found in the relationship between unemployment and entrepreneurship and estimate a vector auto-regression (VAR) model. In a VAR model a vector of dependent variables is explained by one or more lags of the vector of dependent variables, i.e., each dependent variable is explained by one or more lags of itself and of the other dependent variables. Audretsch et al. (2005) estimate a two-equation VAR model with the change in unemployment and the change in entrepreneurial activity as dependent variables. While these authors use a data base on self-employment at the country level (this is the so-called COMPENDIA data base, described in detail elsewhere in

---

[3] For a more elaborate description of developments in the Spanish economy during the 1970s, 1980s and 1990s we refer to Verheul et al. (2006).

[4] In order to split our sample in higher and lower income regions, we use the regional per capita income levels. The lower income regions (regional per capita income is lower than Spanish per capita income) are Andalucía, Asturias, Canarias, Cantabria, Castilla La Mancha, Castilla León, Extremadura, Galicia, Murcia and Comunidad Valenciana. The other group (per capita income is higher than Spanish per capita income) is formed by Aragón, Islas Baleares, Cataluña, La Rioja, Madrid, Navarra and País Vasco.

[5] This section is based on Verheul et al. (2006).

this book), in the present chapter we will estimate the VAR model using data at the
regional level for Spain (see Section 2). The model reads as follows:

$$U_{it} - U_{i,t-L} = \alpha + \sum_{j=1}^{J} \beta_j (E_{i,t-jL} - E_{i,t-(j+1)L}) + \sum_{j=1}^{J} \gamma_j (U_{i,t-jL} - U_{i,t-(j+1)L}) + \varepsilon_{1it}$$

(9.1)

$$E_{it} - E_{i,t-L} = \kappa + \sum_{j=1}^{J} \lambda_j (U_{i,t-jL} - U_{i,t-(j+1)L}) + \sum_{j=1}^{J} \mu_j (E_{i,t-jL} - E_{i,t-(j+1)L}) + \varepsilon_{2it}$$

(9.2)

where U is unemployment, E is entrepreneurial activity (self-employment), i is a
region-index, L is the time span in number of years, and J is the number of time lags
included. The expected sign of the joint impact of the β-coefficients is negative and
the expected sign of the joint impact of the γ-coefficients is positive. The inclusion
of lagged dependent variables on the right hand side in the VAR model allows for a
test for the direction of causality (Granger 1969).

Equations (1) and (2) are estimated using ordinary least squares.[6] We consider
changes in self-employment and unemployment over periods of two years, i.e., L
equals 2. Furthermore, following Audretsch et al. (2005) we test for different time
lags, in order to gain insight in the lag structure between unemployment and self-
employment. Inclusion of more lags seems more compelling because the employment impact of entrepreneurship is not instantaneous. Rather it requires a number
of years for the firm to grow (Fritsch and Mueller 2004). Rather than imposing a
lag structure for the impact of the lagged variables in Equations (1) and (2), we test
for the statistically superior lag structure by using likelihood ratio tests. We start by
including only one lag, and then, one lag at a time, we include further lags until
the LR test rejects inclusion of further lags. In terms of Equations (1) and (2), this
procedure determines the value of J.

9.4 Results

We estimate the VAR model using data for Spanish NUTS-II regions over the period
1979-2001. As we use bi-annual data, and the maximum lag is four years (given the
inclusion of a lagged dependent variable), the number of years included is ten (1983,
1985,..., 2001). Hence in the one-lag model the number of observations is 170 (as
there are 17 regions). In the two- and three-lag models we lose one or two years of
observations hence the number of observations for these models equals 153 and 136,
respectively. As mentioned in the Introduction, we also split the sample in higher
and lower income regions to see whether estimation results differ between the two
groups. Estimation results are presented in Tables 9.3 to 9.5.

---

[6] We also applied weighted least squares. The results were similar to those presented in Section 4.

Table 9.3 Estimation results for whole sample

	Model Ia 1 lag	Model Ib 1 lag	Model IIa 2 lags	Model IIb 2 lags	Model III 3 lags
Equation (1):dependent variable $U_t - U_{t-2}$					
Constant	−0.944	−0.992	−1.133	−1.446	−1.139
	(−3.289)	(−3.092)	(−3.281)	(−4.494)	(−3.281)
$E_{t-2} - E_{t-4}$	−0.938	−0.440	−0.467	−0.362	−0.355
	(−3.234)	(−1.348)	(−1.474)	(−1.181)	(−1.188)
$E_{t-4} - E_{t-6}$			−1.240	−1.052	−0.931
			(−3.899)	(−3.493)	(−3.134)
$E_{t-6} - E_{t-8}$					−0.357
					(−1.122)
$U_{t-2} - U_{t-4}$	0.442	0.354	0.368	0.311	0.213
	(6.464)	(4.438)	(4.568)	(4.146)	(2.673)
$U_{t-4} - U_{t-6}$			−0.245	−0.410	−0.351
			(−2.934)	(−5.048)	(−4.299)
$U_{t-6} - U_{t-8}$					−0.274
					(−3.414)
Loglikehood	−1701.268	−1541.124	−1530.420	−1346.324	−1340.352
R^2	0.232	0.143	0.254	0.298	0.365
P-value Granger causality	0.001	0.202	0.001	0.002	0.012
N	170	153	153	136	136
Equation (2):dependent variable $E_t - E_{t-2}$					
Constant	−0.325	−0.305	0.226	−0.229	−0.112
	(−4.208)	(−3.820)	-(−2.500)	(−2.473)	(−1.103)
$U_{t-2} - U_{t-4}$	0.009	0.015	0.026	0.024	0.018
	(0.517)	(0.779)	(1.222)	(1.101)	(0.768)
$U_{t-4} - U_{t-6}$			−0.003	−0.007	0.010
			(−0.153)	(−0.302)	(0.437)
$U_{t-6} - U_{t-8}$					−0.049
					(−2.076)
$E_{t-2} - E_{t-4}$	−0.168	−0.144	−0.110	−0.137	−0.159
	(−2.157)	(−1.769)	(−1.324)	(−1.559)	(−1.823)
$E_{t-4} - E_{t-6}$			0.183	0.172	0.218
			(2.192)	(1.984)	(2.511)
$E_{t-6} - E_{t-8}$					0.104
					(1.116)
Loglikehood	−1474.348	−1326.982	−1324.480	−1176.838	−1173.354
R^2	0.022	0.020	0.052	0.064	0.113
P-value Granger causality	0.624	0.437	0.462	0.546	0.088
N	170	153	153	136	136

Note: T-values are between brackets. 'Preferred' models are indicated in italics.

Table 9.4 Estimation results for higher income regions

	Model Ia 1 lag	Model Ib 1 lag	Model IIa 2 lags	Model IIb 2 lags	Model III 3 lags
Equation (1):dependent variable $U_t - U_{t-2}$					
Constant	−0.795	−1.083	−0.746	−1.189	−0.914
	(−1.837)	(−2.334)	(−1.780)	(−3.051)	(−2.473)
$E_{t-2} - E_{t-4}$	−0.105	−0.043	−0.082	0.505	0.419
	(−0.234)	(−0.092)	(−0.175)	(1.052)	(0.951)
$E_{t-4} - E_{t-6}$			−1.471	−1.201	−0.894
			(−3.076)	(−2.740)	(−1.975)
$E_{t-6} - E_{t-8}$					−0.320
					(−0.711)
$U_{t-2} - U_{t-4}$	0.398	0.289	0.389	0.297	0.112
	(3.891)	(2.480)	(3.564)	(2.944)	(1.007)
$U_{t-4} - U_{t-6}$			−0.384	−0.602	−0.449
			(−3.296)	(−5.081)	(−3.849)
$U_{t-6} - U_{t-8}$					−0.371
					(−3.488)
Loglikehood	−699.9941	−631.0241	−620.4896	−544.8206	−538.5164
R^2	0.192	0.120	0.375	0.493	0.585
P-value Granger causality	0.812	0.927	0.006	0.003	0.074
N	70	63	63	56	56
Equation (2):dependent variable E Constant $E_t - E_{t-2}$					
Constant	−0.097	−0.023	−0.023	−0.007	0.052
	(−0.953)	(−0.231)	(−0.203)	(−0.062)	(0.435)
$U_{t-2} - U_{t-4}$	0.063	0.091	0.091	0.095	0.093
	(2.614)	(3.606)	(3.259)	(3.162)	(2.580)
$U_{t-4} - U_{t-6}$			−0.004	0.008	0.027
			(−0.130)	(0.240)	(0.728)
$U_{t-6} - U_{t-8}$					−0.045
					(−1.310)
$E_{t-2} - E_{t-4}$	−0.459	−0.433	−0.447	−0.504	−0.492
	(−4.350)	(−4.268)	(−3.698)	(−3.523)	(−3.471)
$E_{t-4} - E_{t-6}$			−0.052	−0.072	0.052
			(−0.424)	(−0.554)	(0.354)
$E_{t-6} - E_{t-8}$					0.175
					(1.210)
Loglikehood	−597.8075	−534.6414	−534.1511	−476.9339	−475.0365
R^2	0.267	0.328	0.331	0.326	0.367
P-value Granger causality	0.009	0.000	0.004	0.007	0.002
N	70	63	63	56	56

Note: T-values are between brackets. 'Preferred' models are indicated in italics.

Table 9.5 Estimation results for lower income regions

	Model Ia 1 lag	Model Ib 1 lag	Model IIa 2 lags	Model IIb 2 lags	Model III 3 lags
Equation (1):dependent variable $U_t - U_{t-2}$					
Constant	−0.987	−1.069	−1.490	−1.567	−1.760
	(−2.261)	(−2.301)	(−2.652)	(−3.418)	(−2.560)
$E_{t-2} - E_{t-4}$					
	−0.721	−0.718	−0.806	−0.895	−0.822
	(−1.624)	(−1.491)	(−1.6869)	(−1.973)	(−1.799)
$E_{t-4} - E_{t-6}$					
			−1.020	−0.746	−0.715
			(−2.127)	(−1.666)	(−1.578)
$E_{t-6} - E_{t-8}$					−0.351
					(−0.736)
$U_{t-2} - U_{t-4}$	0.404	0.381	0.360	0.306	0.259
	(3.989)	(3.400)	(3.105)	(2.881)	(2.337)
$U_{t-4} - U_{t-6}$			−0.136	−0.317	−0.307
			(−1.123)	(−2.756)	(−2.635)
$U_{t-6} - U_{t-8}$					−0.181
					(−1.525)
Loglikehood	−1004.800	−908.0787	−905.4444	−796.0758	−794.7470
	0.200	0.165	0.213	0.258	0.283
P-value Granger causality	0.108	0.139	0.041	0.052	0.121
N	100	90	90	80	80
Equation (2):dependent variable $E_t - E_{t-2}$					
Constant	−0.434	−0.426	−0.355	−0.337	−0.267
	(−4.083)	(−3.896)	(−2.632)	(−2.488)	(−1.641)
$U_{t-2} - U_{t-4}$					
	−0.019	−0.023	−0.019	−0.016	−0.022
	(−0.754)	(−0.885)	(−0.683)	(−0.588)	(−0.751)
$U_{t-4} - U_{t-6}$					
			0.016	0.018	0.023
			(0.557)	(0.603)	(0.723)
$U_{t-6} - U_{t-8}$					−0.033
					(−1.035)
$E_{t-2} - E_{t-4}$					
	−0.075	−0.039	−0.024	−0.069	−0.063
	(−0.691)	(−0.341)	(−0.205)	(−0.576)	(−0.521)
$E_{t-4} - E_{t-6}$					
			0.156	0.181	0.195
			(1.353)	(1.535)	(1.625)
$E_{t-6} - E_{t-8}$					−0.003
					(−0.020)
Loglikehood	−863.5121	−777.9787	−776.9628	−689.2842	−688.6701
	0.012	0.012	0.034	0.061	0.075
P-value Granger causality	0.453	0.379	0.727	0.740	0.647
N	100	90	90	80	80

Note: T-values are between brackets. 'Preferred' models are indicated in italics.

Determining the 'Preferred' Models

First, we determine the optimal number of lags. Looking at the upper part of Table 9.3, comparing Model Ib to IIa,[7] we can establish that the LR test statistic equals $2 \times (1541.124\text{-}1530.420) = 21.408$. As the χ^2 critical value at 5% level equals 5.99 (there are two restrictions here), Model Ib is rejected in favour of Model IIa. Indeed, we can see that the additional self-employment term $(E_{t-4}\text{-}E_{t-6})$, is highly significant.

Similarly, based on the LR test, Model IIb is rejected in favour of Model III. However, in this case the value of the LR test statistic is much lower (11.944). Furthermore, the rejection is established primarily because of the additional lagged dependent variable, which is highly significant (t-value -3.414). The additional self-employment term is not significant though (t-value -1.122). Because in Equation (1) we are mainly interested in the lag of the self-employment variable (indicating the 'entrepreneurial' effect), we will base our interpretations of the results on the two lag model (Model IIa), despite the rejection of the two lag model in the LR test.

When looking at the lower part of Table 9.3, comparing Model Ib to IIa, the LR test statistic equals 5.004 which is not significant at the 5% level. Therefore we consider Model Ia the statistically optimal model.[8] In a similar line of reasoning, we consider Models IIa (upper part of the table) and Ia (lower part of the table) the optimal models for the higher income regions estimations in Table 9.4 Looking at the upper part of Table 9.5 (lower income regions), comparing Model Ib to IIa, the LR test statistic equals 5.269 which is not significant at the 5% level. However, because the additional self-employment variable is significant (t-value -2.127), and the test statistic is close to the critical value (5.99), we consider Model IIa a better model than Model Ib. A third lag does not add to the explanatory power of the model though. From the lower part of Table 9.5 it is clear that Model Ia is the preferred model.

To summarize, in all three tables the two-lag model is the preferred model for the 'entrepreneurial' effect, while for the 'refugee' effect the one-lag model is to be preferred. Apparently, it takes more time for entrepreneurship to contribute to economic development, than it takes unemployed individuals to start new businesses. The preferred models will be the basis for our interpretations and are indicated in the tables in italics.

---

[7] Note that the estimation sample has to be identical before the likelihood ratio test may be applied. For this purpose Model Ia was re-estimated using 153 observations, resulting in Model Ib.

[8] We note that in Model III there is a significantly negative estimate for the third lag of unemployment. However, as there is no single significantly negative estimate for the unemployment variables in the lower parts of Tables 4 and 5 (where the sample is split into higher and lower income regions), we consider this a non-representative result.

Interpreting the Estimation Results

From Model IIa in Table 9.3 we conclude that there is a clear 'entrepreneurial' effect. Both lagged self-employment rates have a negative sign, and the second lag is highly significant. The empirical support for the 'entrepreneurial' effect is confirmed by the significance of the Granger causality test (p-value 0.001). The value of this test statistic indicates that self-employment contributes significantly to bringing down regional unemployment, even when lagged dependent variables are included as control variables. The same patterns can be found for the 'entrepreneurial' effect in Tables 9.4 and 9.5. Comparing the values of the coefficients across the three tables, we see that the magnitude of the effect is approximately the same. Hence we conclude that there is clear evidence for an 'entrepreneurial' effect, both in higher income regions and in lower income regions in Spain. These results are in line with research by Congregado et al. (2005). Using a micro-econometric approach these authors show that particularly *higher educated* entrepreneurs are likely to grow their businesses. Either they hire employees directly at the start of business operations or they expand their business after having worked some time as an own-account worker. Congregado et al. (2005) also show that the share of higher educated self-employed individuals in total self-employment in Spain has increased considerably from the early 1990s onwards. Hence the negative effect of self-employment on unemployment found in Tables 9.3-9.3 is not surprising.

Considering the 'refugee' effect, we find mixed results. In Table 9.4 (higher income regions) there is a significantly positive effect of changes in unemployment on subsequent changes in self-employment, confirming the 'refugee' hypothesis. The Granger causality test is also passed. However, for the lower income regions (Table 9.5) the effect of unemployment on self-employment is not significant.[9] Indeed, in this case the Granger causality test is not passed. Apparently, in the complete sample regressions the lower-income regions result dominates as there is also no significant effect in Table 9.3 The absence of a 'refugee' effect in the lower income regions may seem surprising, in particular when considering the relatively high unemployment rates. We might have expected a positive impact, in particular because wage employment is likely to be even harder to find in regions with high unemployment rates (see Table 9.2). What then might explain the non-significant result? There may be several explanations. *First*, it could be that unemployed individuals lack the skills to set up and maintain a firm. *Second*, the demand conditions in high unemployment regions may be unfavourable for the start-up of new firms. In particular this second reason might in part explain the different results for the higher and lower income regions samples.

However, we believe a *third* reason may also play a role. This is related to a possible lack of incentives for young unemployed individuals in Spain to find employment (either wage- or self-employment). Some studies show that unemployment

---

[9] The effect is even estimated to be negative. This may indicate that in regions with high unemployment the (demand) conditions are not favourable for starting a business. Note however that the t-value is below unity.

among high-educated and young individuals in Spain is relatively high (e.g. Bento-lila and Jimeno 2003). For instance, university students in Spain have a lower probability of finding employment than students in other OECD countries: the unemployment rate among university students in the age category of 25 to 34 years old in Spain is 11.5 percent, compared to a European average of 6.2 percent (OECD 2005; European Commission 2005). Although the first-mentioned argument (lack of skills to start a business) may explain why lower-educated unemployed do not start businesses, this explanation does not seem valid for these higher-educated unemployed. Instead it may be that there are not enough incentives to find employment. This may be related to the relatively high replacement rate (the percentage of the last-earned income that an unemployed individual receives) in Spain, compared to other countries (OECD 2004). Also, cultural attitudes may play a role. In particular in the South of Spain[10] (which overlaps greatly with the lower income regions, see Tables 9.1 and 9.2) people appear to accept unemployment as a part of everyday life. Unemployment is perceived of as an opportunity to increase the quality of life – having more flexibility in time use and more leisure time available – rather than as a problem. Ahn et al. (2004) show that, for a sample of unemployed individuals in Spain, maintaining social relations (with neighbours, friends or relatives) has a significantly positive influence on individual satisfaction levels in the domains of leisure time and health. This observation is in line with the observation that in Spain most young people stay home with their parents until they get married (and sometimes even after marriage). As a result the economic consequences of being unemployed are not that harsh (Garcia-Rubiales 2004).

9.5 Conclusions

In this chapter we investigated the relation between changes in self-employment and unemployment at the regional level in Spain in the period 1979-2001. We estimated a vector autoregression model using a data base for Spanish regions. We found empirical support for the 'entrepreneurial' effect (i.e. a negative effect of self-employment on subsequent unemployment) to exist, both in higher income and in lower income regions. As regards the 'refugee' effect (i.e. a positive effect of unemployment on subsequent self-employment), the evidence was mixed. We found empirical support for this effect for higher income regions but we did not find evidence for a 'refugee' effect in lower income regions of Spain.

Our chapter has several policy implications. *First*, the empirical support for the 'entrepreneurial effect' found in this chapter suggests that entrepreneurship is a promising route to combat unemployment. Research by Congregado et al. (2005) shows that particularly the high-educated self-employed are likely to contribute to bringing down unemployment. Hence it may be good policy to invest in (higher)

---

[10] For information on regional disparities in unemployment see: López-Bazo et al. (2002), Villaverde and Maza (2002), Bande et al. (2004), Garcia-Rubiales (2004).

education levels of the population in general and in entrepreneurship education in particular. *Second*, concerning the lack of a 'refugee' effect in the lower income regions, we argued that high unemployment benefits and a cultural component of preferring leisure time over labour time (and the associated higher income), might be explanatory factors. This suggests that the government might at least think about reforming parts of the social security system.[11] Considering the mentioned cultural component, this may be harder to influence by policy, but at least an attempt could be made to change the attitude towards unemployment (for instance by pointing at the positive influence on self-esteem levels of earning your own money). See also Verheul et al. (2006) for a discussion of possible policy measures to be taken in Spain. Finally we want to mention some limitations of our work. *First*, our self-employment measure is not ideal in the sense that it includes the self-employed in the agricultural sector. Due to problems related with sampling design, it is not possible to split the data into sectors at the Spanish regional level. As the number of self-employed in agriculture is relatively large, and because this sector is different from other sectors in the economy, we need to be careful with our interpretations. Future research may study the impact of agriculture on the results when data availability has improved. *Second*, we realise that there may be other factors that determine changes in unemployment and self-employment at the regional level. Future research may concentrate on including additional independent variables like the regional wage level.

Acknowledgments The current chapter builds on Audretsch, Carree, van Stel and Thurik (2005) and on Verheul, van Stel, Thurik and Urbano (2006).

References

Ahn N, García JR, Jimeno JF (2004) Well-being consequences of unemployment in Europe. Working Paper 2004–11 FEDEA

Alba-Ramirez A (1994) Self-Employment in the Midst of Unemployment: The Case of Spain and the United States. Applied Economics 26:189–204

Audretsch DB, Carree MA, Stel AJ van, Thurik AR (2005) Does Self-Employment Reduce Unemployment? Papers on Entrepreneurship, Growth and Public Policy #07/2005, Jena, Germany: Max Planck Institute of Economics

Bande R, Fernández M, Montuenga V (2004) Regional Unemployment in Spain: Disparities, Business Cycle and Wage Setting. Paper presented at XIX National Conference on Labour Economics, Modena, September 2004

Bentolila S, Jimeno JF (2003) Spanish unemployment: the end of the wild ride? FEDEA (Fundación de Estudios de Economía Aplicada), Documento de Trabajo 2003–10, April 2003

Congregado E, Golpe A, Millán JM (2005) Determinantes de la oferta de empresarios. In: García J, Pérez J (eds) Cuestiones Clave de la Economía Española, Perspectivas actuales 2004. Ed. Comares, pp 165–187

European Commission (2005) Key data on education in Europe. See: www.eurydice.org

---

[11] Using Spanish micro data, Congregado et al. (2005) find that those unemployed individuals who receive higher unemployment benefits have a smaller probability to enter self-employment.

Fritsch M, Mueller P (2004) The effects of new business formation on regional development over time. Regional Studies 38:961–975

Garcia-Rubiales V (2004) Unemployment in Spain: An analysis of labor mobility and young adult unemployment. Stanford University Department of Economics, Honor thesis 2004

Geroski PA (1989) Entry, innovation and productivity growth. Review of Economics and Statistics 71(4):572–578

Granger CWJ (1969) Investigating causal relations by econometric models and cross-spectral methods. Econometrica 37:424–438

López-Bazo E, Del Barrio T, Artis M (2002) The regional distribution of Spanish unemployment. A spatial analysis. ERSA conference papers, European Regional Science Association

OECD (2004) OECD Employment Outlook 2004. Reassessing the OECD Jobs Strategy, OECD, Paris

OECD (2005) Education at a Glance: OECD Indicators, OECD, Paris

Stel AJ van, Carree MA, Thurik AR (2005) The Effect of Entrepreneurial Activity on National Economic Growth. Small Business Economics 24(3):311–321

Verheul I, Stel AJ van, Thurik AR, Urbano D (2006) The Relationship between Business Ownership and Unemployment in Spain: A Matter of Quantity or Quality? Estudios de Economía Aplicada 24(2):435–457

Villaverde J, Maza A (2002) Salarios y desempleo en las regiones españolas. Papeles de Economía Española 93:182–194

Chapter 10
Tax Incentives and Entrepreneurship: Measurement and Data Considerations

Herbert J Schuetze

Abstract Governments and economic actors around the world have instituted a vast array of programs to help foster entrepreneurship. Perhaps the most commonly utilized and complex policy tool available is the income-tax system. The interplay between tax policy and entrepreneurial activity has received a great deal of attention in the economics literature. While this literature has provided a great deal of knowledge regarding the effects of tax policy on entrepreneurship the work is far from complete. A number of the shortcomings in the literature result because of a lack of quality data focused on self-employment outcomes. The purpose of this chapter is to illustrate the current state of knowledge regarding the impacts of taxation on entrepreneurship, to identify areas in which additional research is particularly warranted and the data requirements necessary to fill in these gaps in the literature.

JEL classification: H24, H25, J23, H26

Keywords: taxations, entrepreneurship, compliance

10.1 Introduction

Citing the potential benefits of a more entrepreneurial labour market, economic actors around the world have established a number of programs and policies aimed at developing entrepreneurial activity. Broad-based institutions such as the European Parliament, OECD and the European Commission actively encourage countries under their influence to pursue policies to "foster entrepreneurship".[1] Likely as a result, most OECD countries have public policy programs designed to assist new business development. The policy tools utilized vary significantly across countries

---

Herbert J Schuetze
Department of Economics, University of Victoria, PO Box 1700 STN CSC, BC V8W
hschuetz@uvic.ca

[1] See, for example, European Commission (1998) and OECD (1998).

E. Congregado, *Measuring Entrepreneurship.*
© Springer 2008

and include the provision of start-up financial capital,[2] aid in the development of human capital or business skills, reductions in administrative burdens associated with starting and running a business, and self-employment training programs that target the unemployed in the hope of returning these workers to the ranks of the employed.[3]

Perhaps the most commonly utilized and complex policy tool available is the income tax system. Tax policies can affect the decision to become self-employed in various ways. In general, the tax system can make self-employment more or less attractive than wage and salary work—either pulling potential entrepreneurs into self-employment or pushing workers out of wage and salary jobs and into self-employment. Every tax system, including those that attempt to treat the self and wage-employed equally, influences the choice of employment sector. Thus, because all governments tax, it can be said that every government's policy port-folio influences the entrepreneurial decision. This fact highlights the importance of understanding the relationship between tax systems and entrepreneurship.

Given the important role of taxation it is not surprising that the interplay between tax policy and entrepreneurial activity has received a great deal of attention in the economics literature. While this literature has provided a great deal of knowledge regarding the effects of tax policy on entrepreneurship the work is far from com-plete. A number of the shortcomings in the literature are simply the result of the complexity of the issues. However, many of the gaps result because of a lack of quality data focused on entrepreneurial outcomes. The purpose of this chapter is to illustrate the current state of knowledge regarding the impacts of taxation on entrepreneurship, to identify areas in which additional research is particularly war-ranted and the data requirements necessary to fill in these gaps in the literature.

To this end, Section 2 of the chapter provides a survey of the theoretical literature. The focus is on identifying the likely impacts of the key elements of income tax policy (as indicated by economic theory) on the entrepreneurial decision. Section 3 provides a discussion of the empirical literature related to the impacts of tax pol-icy on self-employment. Section 4 includes an examination of the literature on the impacts of income tax non-compliance on self-employment rates and the factors that influence this type of "self-employment". A discussion of the key gaps in the empirical literature resulting from a lack of quality data and the data requirements necessary to overcome these closes the paper in Section 5.

An underlying issue which I will return to throughout the chapter is the distinc-tion between the terms "entrepreneurship" and "self-employment". Thus, before beginning I will attempt to define these terms and discuss their use in the context

---

[2] Given the critical need for such funds it is not surprising that most developed countries have small business financing programs. For example, the US Small Business Administration invests billions of dollars annually to help new firms get started and SME policies in Europe typically include financing for small business.

[3] Such programs are offered across OECD countries. For a general discussion of these programs among OECD countries, see OECD (1998), and for an exhaustive review of this and similar pro-grams in the US, see Vroman (1997).

of the impacts of income-tax incentives. Entrepreneurship, despite its importance, is an elusive concept. Often definitions refer to the creation of a new, usually small, business. The emphasis appears to be on individuals who are enterprising or innovative in their approach and who assume some degree of risk in their business venture. Indeed, it is likely that these are some of the attributes that policy-makers seek out when they advocate the development of a more entrepreneurial economy. The "self-employed", in comparison, are individuals who simply work for themselves. This is the measure used in most of the empirical studies in the literature.

Because the group of workers defined as self-employed includes individuals engaged in widely varying activities, it likely mis-measures the amount of entrepreneurial activity. For example, included in this group are individuals who operate chain stores. Chain store operators may encounter some degree of risk but we might not think of these workers as innovative given that they typically follow a stylized approach that is common across all establishments in the chain. More directly pertinent to the current study, this measure also includes individuals who "contract out" their wage employment jobs by establishing businesses (which is often undertaken, as is discussed below, to avoid taxation). While this type of re-labeling might expose the worker to greater risk of layoff, because the worker is doing the same job the activity carried out in the business would not be characterized as innovative. For reasons such as these the self-employment measure likely overstates the amount of entrepreneurial activity. On the other hand, this measure leaves out individuals engaged in enterprising or innovative behaviour in more established firms. This mismatch between the activity which policy makers aim to encourage, "entrepreneurship", and the activity which is measured in most empirical studies, "self-employment", highlights the importance of the distinguishing between these two activities. Given the potential impacts of the tax system on self-employment for the purpose of tax avoidance this distinction is perhaps of the utmost importance in the current discussion. I will return to this issue throughout the chapter.

10.2 Theory: Taxation and Entrepreneurship

This section provides a survey of the theoretical literature that investigates the relationship between income tax policy and entrepreneurship.[4] Two separate strains of the literature are highlighted. The first examines how tax policy affects the choice between wage employment and self-employment. The focus in this literature (as I will show) has been on how the tax system affects the relatively higher risk associated with entrepreneurship and, therefore, the relative attractiveness of self-employment vis-à-vis wage employment. Given the distinction in definitional terms highlighted above and this focus on risk, one might argue that this literature

---

[4] The literature surveys in this and subsequent sections are adopted from Bruce and Schuetze (2004). Here, however, the discussion is focused on the many data and measurement issues that arise in the literature.

relates more closely to the "entrepreneurial" than the "self-employment" decision. The second strain of the literature examined in this section looks at the issue of income tax noncompliance and how the relative ease of noncompliance in self-employment affects sector choice. This literature likely relates more closely to the "self-employment" decision given that these individuals enter the self-employment sector for the purposes of hiding income and not because they are innovative.

10.2.1 Impacts of Taxation on Choice of Sector

It is relatively straightforward to show that a system of differential taxation across sectors can make the choice to become an entrepreneur more or less attractive. Indeed, in most countries business income is taxed differently from wage earnings on a paid job. Income from incorporated businesses is typically taxed under an altogether different tax system than income from wage employment and the operation of an unincorporated business. However, even when taxed under the same system businesses are taxed differently. Various business expenses are typically tax deductible and often include the costs of items such as vehicles and housing that provide non-business consumption benefits. That differential taxation can influence the decision to invest in self-employment is not at all surprising. Less intuitive are the results that emerge from models which recognize that entrepreneurship, more so than wage employment, offers an uncertain return.

Underlying many models of entrepreneurship choice is the notion that entrepreneurship offers an uncertain return. In particular, it is argued that workers allocate their fixed amount of labour between the safer wage sector and the relatively risky self-employment sector to maximize the return on their labour portfolios. In this setting taxation can be shown to have somewhat counterintuitive impacts on entrepreneurship. For example, Domar and Musgrave (1944) are among the first to show that the taxation of risky investments such as entrepreneurship (with liberal loss offsets) can increase investment in these risky assets. The intuition behind Domar and Musgrave's argument proceeds as follows. The imposition of a proportional income tax system with full loss offsets[5] has two effects on investment in risky assets. First, the tax reduces the expected yield of the investment and this will discourage investment (implicitly assuming constant relative risk aversion). Second, the tax is such that the government will share in the risk—collecting more tax revenue if the venture is successful and refunding revenue to the risk-bearer if it fails. They show that the net effect is such that private investment in the risky asset (that of the entrepreneur in this context) may decrease but that total investment (that born by the entrepreneur and the government) will increase.

It is important to emphasize that this result relies on the strong assumption that losses can be fully offset. Under conditions of partial loss deduction, Domar and

---

[5] Full loss offset is a tax clause that allows entrepreneurs with operating losses to apply these losses against income subject to taxation from other sources.

Musgrave (1944) show that the two opposing effects described above continue to operate and the impact on investment in risky ventures is uncertain. One's ability to reduce income tax liabilities by deducting net business losses from other taxable income depends on tax law and the individual's income situation. Even when full loss offsets are permitted by tax law, an individual's ability to take advantage of the law may be limited by the amount of taxable income from other sources. Tax laws that allow individuals to carry losses forward over a number of years are more likely to result in full loss offsets in practice. Thus, tax rules relating to losses likely influence the level of entrepreneurial activity.

Indeed, Gentry and Hubbard (2000) suggest that tax systems do not typically offer full loss offsets for entrepreneurs. Thus, they argue, greater progressivity of the tax schedule (aside from decreasing average returns) reduces the returns of those who succeed disproportionately to those who do not. In a model without the risk reducing benefits of full loss offsets they show that increasing convexity of the tax schedule discourages entrepreneurial activity even among workers who are risk neutral.

The result that taxation can lead to increased investment in risky assets such as self-employment, under certain conditions, is later confirmed in more general settings by Mossin (1968), Stiglitz (1969), Ahsan (1974)[6] and Kanbur (1981). Mossin (1968) and Stiglitz (1969) confirm this result using expected utility models, which place fewer and more realistic restrictions on individual utility. These models suggest that a third effect of taxation on risky investment must also be considered. They argue that, because increases in taxes reduce wealth, the effects of these changes in wealth on ones preferences for accepting risk must also be taken into consideration. As a result, the set of conditions under which taxes increase entrepreneurship (risk-taking) are greater. Ahsan (1974) also uses an expected utility model but extends the model to examine how the impacts of progressive taxes on risk-taking differ from proportional taxation. He shows that, holding tax revenue constant, risk-taking is greater under progressive taxation than under proportional taxation. The intuition is that increased progressiveness of the tax system helps to smooth income when faced with uncertain returns. Finally, Kanbur (1981) notes that the literature on portfolio allocations made at the margin between risky and safe investments does not capture the discrete nature of the choice between entrepreneurship and wage employment. Thus, he adapts the model to a general equilibrium framework which allows for an accounting of the discrete nature of the entrepreneurial choice. Due, in part, to the interactions between occupation sectors in the general equilibrium setting, he finds the effect of progressive taxation on the equilibrium number of entrepreneurs to be ambiguous under all conditions.[7]

---

[6] In a more recent paper, Ahsan (1990) examined the impact of broad based taxes (income and consumption) in an intertemporal context. He found that, in such a setting, broad based taxes either decrease or leave unchanged the amount of risk taken.

[7] For a review of further refinements to these basic results see Parker (2004).

In practice, income tax systems are complex and interactions between different elements of the tax code can generate unanticipated outcomes. For example, Feldstein and Slemrod (1980), Gordon (1998) and Cullen and Gordon (2002) point to the fact that the US tax system is such that, above some threshold, taxable income is taxed at a lower rate under the corporate tax system than under the personal tax system. Given that entrepreneurs have the option to incorporate, this element of the tax code effectively allows them to reduce the progressivity of the income tax system. Thus, it is argued that this option, which is not available to wage workers, creates an incentive to become an entrepreneur. In addition, Cullen and Gordon (2002) argue that this endogeneity of choice in incorporation status can result in greater than full loss offsets when the personal tax rate is higher than the corporate rate.

In summary, the theoretical literature shows that, even for the simplest tax system, the effect of taxation on the equilibrium number of entrepreneurs is far from clear-cut. This is primarily because of the risk sharing that is introduced through the income tax system. When coupled with the fact that entrepreneurs' risk preferences are likely heterogeneous, this risk sharing role of the tax system leads to ambiguous results. The results become even less clear when consideration is given to the general equilibrium effects of taxation on occupational choice and the complex nature of interactions between various elements of the typical tax code. To add one more layer of complexity to the issue, one need also to consider the very real possibility that legislated taxes differ from those that are paid by entrepreneurs. This is the topic of the next sub-section.

10.2.2 Noncompliance and Choice of Sector

To this point I have discussed the theoretical impacts of taxation on entrepreneurship under the implicit assumption that individuals comply with the tax code. However, among business owners numerous opportunities exist to reorganize income to avoid taxation or to simply evade taxes altogether. Unlike wage workers, no third party exists to withhold taxes on behalf of entrepreneurs. Thus, the taxes paid by entrepreneurs can differ greatly from those legislated by the tax code.

A number of researchers model the endogenous choice of occupation between a sector in which tax evasion possibilities exist (entrepreneurship) and one where there are no such opportunities (wage sector) in order to identify the impact of evasion on sectoral choice and optimal tax policy (Watson 1985, Kesselman 1989, Pestieau and Possen 1991, 1992, and Jung et al. 1994). All of the models which include audits conclude, not surprisingly, that greater auditing intensity results in less evasion and, therefore, participation in the "evadable" sector. Most argue that a rise in the level of personal taxation, ceteris paribus, will result in an increase in entrepreneurial activity. This is simply because the benefit of tax avoidance increases with the level of taxation. However, there are a number of offsetting factors which may not allow such a clear cut conclusion.

For example, Jung et al. (1994) argue that tax evasion introduces uncertainty about whether or not the illegal behavior will be identified by the tax authority. Because taxes reduce wealth, this may change one's willingness to accept risk. Thus, under decreasing relative risk aversion an increase in the tax rate increases the individual's risk aversion and entrepreneurship becomes less attractive. Watson (1985) points out the possibility for general equilibrium feedback, which may offset the self-employment inducing effects of taxes in this setting. In particular, he notes that an increase in supply to the entrepreneurial sector will result in a decrease in profits in that sector, which will make entrepreneurship less attractive. Thus, he argues, the net impact of an increase in taxation is indeterminate.

10.3 Empirical Research Investigating the Effects of Taxation on Self-Employment

As the previous section suggests, the theory is ambiguous as to the relationship between tax policy and the level of entrepreneurship in a jurisdiction. Thus, it is left to empirical research to determine the nature of this association. Aided by the availability of longitudinal databases containing multiple years of information for large samples of current and potential entrepreneurs, research on this topic has flourished in recent years. Despite improvements in the quality of data and research methodologies, however, no consensus has been reached in the empirical literature.

An inherent empirical challenge to overcome in identifying the relationship between the tax rate faced by an individual and the likelihood that she/he becomes self-employed is the issue of tax rate endogeneity. The problem is that an individual's marginal tax rate is endogenous to the entrepreneurship decision because the tax rate is a function of whether or not one is self-employed. Modern statistical techniques and the ability to track individuals over time using newly developed panel data has allowed researchers to deal with this problem. However, a number of significant obstacles remain, which may account for the ambiguity in results across studies.

Almost all of the empirical studies measure the extent of entrepreneurial activity as the fraction of the employed population reporting that they work for themselves. According to my definitions above this is the fraction that is "self-employed". Placed in the context of the current discussion, this implies that all of the income tax factors discussed above, including those related to risk sharing and noncompliance, have an influence on the variable of interest in these studies. Given the multitude of avenues by which taxes effect "self-employment" and (as we shall see) the widely varying settings in which the empirical studies have been carried out, it is perhaps not all that surprising that the literature has not reached a consensus. Refinements in the data that allow researchers to sort "entrepreneurs" from the "self-employed" would no doubt help in attempts to distinguish between the various ways in which the income tax system affects these various forms of self-employment behavior. I will revisit this issue later in the chapter.

This section provides a review of the empirical literature that investigates the link between taxes and self-employment outcomes. This literature can be divided into three broad categories: time series studies, cross-section studies, and individual-level panel data studies. Each of these categories is summarized below paying particular attention to the type of data and the measure of self-employment activity utilized. For the reader's convenience Table 10.1 provides a summary of the studies discussed by the type of data employed.

Table 10.1 Summary of Empirical Findings on the Effects of Taxation on Self-Employment

Approach	Author(s)	Tax Effect	Tax Measure(s)	Period	Country
Time Series					
	Long (1982a)	+	marginal - hypothetical couple	1963–77	US
	Blau (1987)	+/–	marginal - 2 points in distribution	1948–82	US
2nd Generation					
	Parker (1996)	+/+	marginal - 2 points in distribution	1959–91	UK
	Robson (1998)	0/+	marginal/average	1968Q3–93Q4	UK
	Robson &Wren (1998)	–/+	marginal/average	1978–92	15 OECD
	Briscoe et. al (2000)	–	marginal	1979–96	UK
	Bruce & Mohsin (2003)	+	corporate, capital gains, estate	1950–99	US
Cross-Section					
	Long (1982a)	+	average marginal	1970	US
	Long (1982b)	+	expected liability wage employment	1970	US
	Moore (1983)	+	individual and payroll	1978	US
	Parker (2003)	0	conditional SE tax liability	1994	UK
Individual Panel					
	Schuetze (2000)	+	state/provincial tax "climate"	1983–94	Canada/US
	Bruce (2000)	+/–	expected marginal/average	1970–92	US
	Gentry & Hubbard (2000)	- convexity	marginal tax "spread"	1979–92	US
	Bruce (2002)	- exits	expected marginal/average	1970–91	US
	Cullen and Gordon (2002)	+	aggregate average	1964–93	US

Adopted from Bruce and Schuetze (2004)

10.3.1 Time Series Studies

Early time-series studies on taxes and self-employment generally conclude that higher federal tax rates are associated with higher rates of self-employment (Long 1982a, Blau 1987). The explanation typically given for this result is that high tax rates drive workers out of paid employment, or wage jobs, into entrepreneurial ventures where they can more easily avoid or evade taxes. However, the results of more recent, "second generation", time-series studies, which typically use more sophisticated time series econometric tools to account for cointegration,[8] are more mixed (Parker 1996, Robson 1998, Robson and Wren 1998, Briscoe et al. 2000, Bruce and Mohsin 2003).

Long's (1982a) finding is based on a short (1963-1977) time series regression, where the number of U.S. individual income tax returns with business income as a share of all individual income tax returns is regressed on a proxy variable capturing the tax environment in any given year. The tax proxy used is a hypothetical marginal income tax rate facing the typical married working couple and is included to overcome the issue of endogeneity. Blau (1987) follows Long's (1982a) method but uses a longer time series of U.S. data (1948-1982) and a survey-based measure of the self-employment rate. His tax variables consist of two marginal tax rates at different points in the income distribution. While his findings at the higher marginal tax rate support Long's, Blau finds that increases in lower-bracket marginal tax rates actually reduce the self-employment rate. This empirical puzzle is not explained by Blau, but foreshadowed the importance of tax progressivity that is addressed by later researchers.

While early "second generation" time series studies also find a positive relationship between taxes and self-employment, more recent studies do not. Parker (1996) is the first to address cointegration using a 1959 to 1991 time series of United Kingdom data. Similar to Blau (1987) he uses two marginal tax rates associated with two different levels of income. Unlike Blau, however, Parker finds a positive relationship between both tax rates and the rate of self-employment. Studies by Robson (1998) and Robson and Wren (1998) also find support for the view that individuals turn to self-employment in order to avoid taxes.

What is unique about these two studies is that they are the first to consider the difference between the impacts of marginal and average tax rates. Robson and Wren (1998) provide a theoretical model that predicts that higher marginal tax rates reduce self-employment while higher average tax rates increase self-employment. They argue that, while higher average tax rates increase the incentives to evade taxes (and enter self-employment), marginal tax rates reduce the return to effort in entrepreneurship and, therefore, the level of entrepreneurial activity. Both Robson (1998) and Robson and Wren (1998) find a positive relationship between

---

[8] The case where two or more series exhibit a common trend but might not necessarily be closely linked.

self-employment and the average tax rate and Robson and Wren confirm the negative effect of marginal tax rates in their regressions.[9]

Unlike these early "second generation" time series studies, more recent studies using similar methods have failed to find a positive link between tax rates and self-employment. Briscoe, Dainty, and Millett (2000), who examine a 1979-1996 time series of self-employment in the British construction industry, find evidence to suggest that higher overall tax rates might lead to lower self-employment in this narrow focus.[10] In addition to the usual personal income and payroll taxes, Bruce and Mohsin (2003) consider corporate income taxes, capital gains taxes, and estate taxes in a long (1950–1999) time series of U.S. data. Results generally indicate that taxes have statistically significant but very small and scattered effects on entrepreneurship rates. In terms of other tax policy variables, only the top corporate income tax rate and payroll tax rates on wage and self-employment income are found to be particularly important.

10.3.2 Cross-Section Studies

The finding that higher tax rates lead to more self-employment as measured by aggregate time series is interesting, however, the time series studies described above are unable to address individual-level decisions to enter or remain in self-employment. A better understanding of this relationship is only possible through the analysis of cross-section or panel data.

The evidence from early cross-section studies generally supports the early findings in the literature of a positive relationship between tax rates and self-employment. Long (1982a) investigates the effects of income tax rates on the ratio of self-employment to total employment within a metropolitan area. Using 1970 U.S. Census data, he finds that increases in the average marginal and average income tax rates in a metropolitan area are associated with increases in the self-employment rate in that area. Long (1982b) finds similar results examining the impact of an increase in an individuals expected wage-and-salary tax liability. Expanding on Long's research, Moore (1983) focuses instead on the role of payroll taxes. Using 1978 U.S. CPS data, Moore finds the impacts of changes in the payroll tax to be larger than those of the expected wage-and-salary income tax.

The most recent cross-sectional study of taxes and self-employment casts doubt on the importance of tax policy in the self-employment decision. Parker (2003) examines two 1994 cross sections of UK data and, after multitude of specification and robustness tests, finds no evidence that the decision to be self-employed is

---

[9] The coefficients on the marginal tax rates in Robson (1998) are not statistically significant.

[10] Briscoe et al. (2000) focused more on changes over time in the relative enforcement of tax liabilities among self-employed construction workers. Their data reveal the possibility that self-employment rates within this single industry are highly sensitive to tax policies other than tax rates.

sensitive to taxes or opportunities for evasion. He points to earlier studies' omission of relative incomes between self-employment and wage employment as a reason for their finding of significant tax effects. However, an important shortcoming of Parker (2003), and indeed all of the cross-section studies above that use individual tax information, is that the issue of potential tax rate endogeneity is not addressed. A number of panel data studies use various means to overcome the possible endogeneity of individual-specific tax rates.

10.3.3 Individual-Level Panel Data Studies

Partly due to the availability of richly detailed pseudo-panel and longitudinal data at the individual level, empirical research on taxes and self-employment has been able to tackle the issue of tax rate endogeneity. The use of repeated cross-sections and panel data allow the researcher to identify exogenous changes in tax rules through time. Thus, instrumental variables and other such techniques can be used to overcome the endogeneity issue. As I outline below, this approach and others have been utilized in a number of recent studies that utilize the many benefits of panel data.

Schuetze (2000) is one of the first studies to address tax rate endogeneity. This is achieved by using asynchronous variation in the aggregate "tax climate" across tax jurisdictions (states and provinces) in the United States and Canada. Using repeated cross-sections for the two countries covering the period 1983 through 1994, he finds that increases in average income tax rates have large and positive effects on the rate of male self-employment.

Bruce (2000, 2002) uses U.S. data from the Panel Study of Income Dynamics and, unlike previous studies, focuses on differential tax treatment of the self-employed and its impact on both the entry and exit decisions. Both of these studies involve the use of exogenous changes in tax rules to generate instrumental variables for addressing the possible endogeneity of individual-specific tax rates. He finds somewhat counter-intuitive results which suggest that increasing an individual's expected marginal tax rate on self-employment income (holding the wage tax rate constant) increases the probability of entry, while a similar increase in the average self-employment income tax rate decreases this probability. Similarly, he finds that higher tax rates on self-employment income reduce the probability of exit from self-employment. He explains his results by arguing that changes in differential tax treatment not only alter net returns to labour, but also affect the incentives to capture relevant tax preferences (or to evade or avoid taxation altogether).

Gentry and Hubbard (2000) use the same data as Bruce (2000) but focus instead on tax progressivity. They argue that full-loss offsets are unlikely and under such conditions progressive rate schedules act as a tax on success in self-employment. In such a setting, they argue, the rewards to successful firms are reduced more than the support given to unsuccessful firms. Consistent with this hypothesis, they find that the probability of entry into self-employment increases as tax rates become less progressive.

Contrary to Gentry and Hubbard (2002), Cullen and Gordon (2002) argue that the interplay between the individual and corporate tax structures in the U.S. allows for greater than full-loss offsets. Because of this and the Domar and Musgrave (1944) risk-sharing argument, they suggest that raising personal tax rates likely increases the extent of entrepreneurial activity. Using repeated cross sections of U.S. tax return data from 1964 through 1993, their results support this hypothesis. It should be noted, however, that their focus was on a much more limited definition of self-employment than those found in most other analyses.[11] Like some of the more recent studies, they also use aggregate (averaged) tax measures to avoid concerns of tax rate endogeneity.

Summing up, while there is little consensus in the empirical literature regarding the nature of the relationship between tax policy and self-employment, the results of these studies do suggest that taxation is likely an important determinant in the self-employment decision. The ambiguity in conclusions across studies may result from the fact that the measure of self-employment activity used in most of these studies captures both "entrepreneurial" and "self-employment" activity. Indeed, there is evidence contained in the empirical results presented above that bare this out. The results in Gentry and Hubbard which suggest that (controlling for the level of taxation) progressivity of the tax system has an impact, may imply that individuals respond to changes in risk which is most likely to be associated with "entrepreneurial" activity. On the other hand, the numerous results in the literature which suggest that individuals become self-employed to avoid taxation imply a response in terms of "self-employment" activity.

The ability to identify individuals engaged in "entrepreneurial" activity, separately from those engaged in "self-employment" would no doubt help to explain the ambiguity in the empirical literature and allow for a better understanding of the tax affects. Distinguishing which activity is affected by changes in the tax code is important because the appropriate policy response depends critically on whether entrepreneurship or self-employment is influenced. While this distinction is important for the broader entrepreneurship literature it is of particular concern in the income tax setting because of the possibility for tax non-compliance. Unfortunately, data that is currently available does not allow researchers to measure the two activities separately.

While this data limitation hampers researchers' ability to draw distinctions between the impacts of taxes on entrepreneurship and self-employment, another strain of literature can help to shed some light on this issue. In the context of taxation, a key issue in making this distinction is whether or not the self-employment activity conducted is associated with a desire to avoid taxation. There is a significant and growing literature devoted to identifying the nature of tax non-compliance among the self-employed. Clearly, an understanding of noncompliance by the

---

[11] Cullen and Gordon (2002) focus on entrepreneurship as indicated by the presence of a non-corporate loss from a proprietorship, partnership, or subchapter S corporation that was larger than 10 percent of reported wage and salary income. They further restricted the analysis to tax returns filed by single individuals.

self-employed and the factors that influence this decision will help to identify this type of "self-employment". Thus, in the next section I provide an overview of this literature.

10.4 Entrepreneurship and Tax Non-Compliance

In this section I examine two parts of the literature that investigates tax non-compliance by the self-employed. First, in order to provide an indication of how big the issue of non-compliance is, I review the relatively few[12] papers in the literature that estimate the magnitude of non-compliance by self-employed individuals. While my primary objective is to highlight the amount of under-reporting by the self-employed, I also discuss some of the data limitations that hamper this research. Second, I examine the evidence regarding the factors that influence the degree of non-compliance among the self-employed. Identification of these factors can help to distinguish responses to tax policy for tax avoidance purposes from those with a more entrepreneurial intent.

10.4.1 The Magnitude of Tax Non-Compliance by the Self-Employed

There are two primary sources of microdata that are utilized to investigate non-compliance by the self-employed. These are tax audit data and household expenditure data. Only two countries, to my knowledge, collect and have made available data from tax audits; the United States and New Zealand. Under the Taxpayer Compliance Measurement Program (TCMP) a stratified random sample of individual and corporate income tax returns are subjected to intensive audits. The US Internal Revenue Service uses the results of these audits to publish estimates of the difference between federal tax liabilities reported and assessed liabilities owed by individuals and corporations (the so-called "tax gap"). Similar data (the "ORACLE" database) is also collected by the New Zealand Inland Revenue Department.

As an example of the estimated magnitude of noncompliance by the self-employed, the US General Accounting Office (1990) suggests that corporations and the self-employed accounted for $45 billion of the estimated $85 billion tax gap in 1987. Further, focusing on unreported income by individuals in the same year, the GAO estimates that self-employed filers account for 63% of the $48 billion in unreported income in 1987. Thus, it appears that non-compliance among the self-employed in the US is non-trivial.

---

[12] While there are many papers in the literature that attempt to estimate underground activity at the aggregate level, these studies do not identify the non-compliance activities of the self-employed. For a comprehensive review of these approaches in an international context see Schneider and Enste 2000.

While quite revealing, the use of this type of audit data to identify non-compliance among the self-employed has a number of shortcomings. First, estimates of non-compliance based on audits are not very reliable. Such estimates rely heavily on the auditors' ability to identify under-reporting and interpret the tax laws as they pertain to tax deductions and tax credits. It is highly unlikely that income-tax auditors are able to identify all income that is concealed from the tax authorities. Second, such audit data are not widely available.

An alternative approach to estimate non-compliance by the self-employed, developed by Pissarides and Weber (1989), uses household expenditure micro-survey data, which is more widely available than audit data. The Pissarides and Weber (1989) approach can be summarized in terms of two stages. In the first stage, a prediction regarding the relationship between household food consumption and after-tax income, controlling for household characteristics is obtained. In order to obtain an undistorted estimate of the marginal propensity to consume food, the data is restricted to households obtaining all of their income from wage and salary employment. These households are assumed to have very few opportunities to conceal income. In the second stage, this estimated relationship between food consumption and after-tax income is used to impute estimates of "true" income for self-employed households. The difference between imputed income and reported income provides an estimate of non-compliance.

Pissarides and Weber apply this approach using expenditure data from the UK for 1982 and find that, on average, true self-employment income is one and a half times that of reported self-employment income. They conclude that their estimate implies that non-compliance among the self-employed accounted for 5.5 percent of GDP in that year. Baker (1993) replicates their analysis using the same expenditure series from the UK for the years 1978 to 1991 and finds results that are similar to Pissarides and Weber.[13] This approach is also applied using data from Canada (Mirus and Smith 1996, Schuetze 2002) and Sweden (Apel 1994). The estimates using Canadian data, while still significant in magnitude, are much lower than those using UK data. For example, Schuetze (2002) examines several years of expenditure data from Canada between 1969 and 1992 and finds that self-employed households concealed, on average, between 11 and 23 percent of total income over this period.[14] Apel (1994) applied the approach using data from the 1988 Swedish Hushallens utgifter (HUT) family expenditure survey and found results that fell

---

[13] More recently, Lyssiotou et al. (2002) extended the Pissarides and Weber (1989) approach by estimating a system of consumer demands and allowing for a more appropriate specification of the Engel curve. Their results suggest that the Pissarides and Weber approach likely understates the amount of under-reporting by the self-employed.

[14] Mirus and Smith's (1996) estimate of under-reporting using 1990 data from Canada was somewhat smaller than the estimate from Schuetze (2002) using the same data. Schuetze attributes this difference to the fact that Mirus and Smith included part-time workers in their sample while his sample was restricted to full-time workers.

somewhere between those for the UK and Canada. Apel estimated that Swedish self-employed concealed around 35 percent of income in 1988. However, because of the relatively low rate of self-employment in Sweden in that year, he concludes that non-compliance among the self-employed accounted for 1 percent of GDP.

Both the expenditure-based estimates of non-compliance among the self-employed and those utilizing tax audit data suggest that the amount of income tax under-reporting by the self-employed is significant. The fact that the estimates vary significantly across countries suggests that country specific factors, such as tax policy and other institutions, may be important determinants of non-compliance by the self-employed. The next section, which summarizes the research literature on the determinants of non-compliance, bares this observation out.

10.4.2 The Factors that Influence Tax Non-Compliance by the Self-Employed

While a number of studies examine the determinants of non-compliance in a broader context (see, for example, Andreoni et al. 1998, Slemrod 1992), only a few examine non-compliance by the self-employed. These studies, which are summarized in this sub-section, suggest that a number of the determinants of non-compliance are subject to manipulation through tax policy while others are an inherent part of a country's economic characteristics.

Studies using TCMP audit data suggest that higher marginal tax rates and lower audit rates (both of which are chosen by policy makers) are associated with increased under-reporting. Clotfelter (1983) utilizes a single year of TCMP audit data and examines the impact marginal tax rates have on under-reported income among individuals operating non-farm businesses in the US. In a regression setting using variation in the marginal tax rates (corrected for under-reporting) faced across individuals for identification, he finds that marginal tax rates have a positive effect on under-reporting among the self-employed. Joulfaian and Rider (1998) take a slightly different approach and use variation in the US tax code across types of business and time[15] to identify the impact of marginal tax rates on the income gap. In particular, they note that tax liabilities on sole proprietorship income were higher than other self-employment income sources in the US throughout the 1980's. Utilizing pooled TCMP data from 1985 to 1988, they find that, controlling for the audit rate, an increase in the marginal tax rate is associated with a larger income gap. In addition, using variation in audit rates over time they find (not surprisingly) that higher audit rates are associated with reductions in the amount of income under-reporting.

Giles (2000) uses data from the 1993 to 1995 New Zealand ORACLE firm audit database to examine the impact of various firm characteristics on compliance. In a series of limited dependent choice model regressions he examines the roles of

---

[15] The period examined straddles major changes to the US tax code which occurred in 1986.

firm size and industrial sector, among other factors, on the probability that a firm is engaged in avoidance or evasion. He finds that smaller firms are less likely to comply with the tax rules. He argues that this result may be due to the fact that larger firms typically have more options to avoid taxation without evading, have greater resources (such as access to tax specialists and lawyers) to avoid violations of the tax code and are in complex tax situations that make detection difficult. In addition, he finds significant differences in the probability of compliance across industrial sector.

Disaggregated estimates of non-compliance, using the expenditure approach described above, suggest that industrial sector is not only an important factor in determining the probability of non-compliance, as in Giles (2000), but also influences the amount of income that goes unreported by the self-employed. Baker (1993) and Schuetze (2002) utilize family expenditure data from the UK and Canada, respectively, to provide industry level estimates of under-reporting among the self-employed. Both find significant variation in the fraction of income under-reported by the self-employed across industries. This general finding is also confirmed using the US TCMP audit data (US General Accounting Office 1990). Schuetze (2002) suggests that his results are likely explained by variation across industries in the opportunity to conceal income. He finds greater under-reporting in Canada in industries typically thought to provide services through informal arrangements and that frequently involve cash transactions.

Finally, Schuetze (2006) provides evidence that the choice of taxation unit (individual versus household) likely influences the extent of non-compliance by the self-employed. He argues that, in a progress tax system, individual taxation creates an incentive to redistribute income among household members. Because, unlike the wage sector, there is no third party reporting income in the self-employment sector, the opportunity to redistribute income in this manner is likely feasible only for the self-employed. Most forms of this "income splitting" among the self-employed are illegal in Canada. Utilizing exogenous variation in the tax codes across Canada and the US (the tax unit is primarily the individual in Canada and the household in the US), he estimates the extent of income splitting in Canada for a number of years between 1988 and 1998. He finds evidence that a significant number of Canadian self-employed households engage in illegal income-splitting.

The research summarized in this sub-section suggests that tax jurisdiction specific factors and firm characteristics are important determinants of income-tax non-compliance. Thus, whether observed responses to changes in tax policy are by business owners whose intent is "entrepreneurial" or those whose intent is to avoid taxation likely varies with the tax policies under which the sample is ruled and the firm characteristics of the sample. In particular, the research suggest that the overall level of taxation, audit probability, the unit of taxation and the industrial composition of the sample being analyzed all influence whether the researcher is likely to observe changes in the number of "entrepreneurs" versus the number "self-employed" in response to adjustments to tax policy.

10.5 Outstanding Research Questions and Data Requirements

It is clear from the discussion above that researchers have made a good deal of progress and have added to our understanding of the sometimes intricate interactions between tax policy and self-employment outcomes. However, much more research is needed to enable policy makers to design effective and efficient tax policy towards entrepreneurship that avoids the pitfalls associated with non-compliance. Many of the shortcomings in the literature are simply the result of the complexity of the issues but some of the gaps result because of a lack of quality data focused on self-employment outcomes. This section outlines the more pressing issues for research on the impacts of taxes on entrepreneurship outcomes that result because of a lack of data and identifies the characteristics of the data required for their investigation.

As is indicated by the above literature review, one of the key obstacles in attempting to measure the impacts of tax incentives on entrepreneurship is the inability of researchers to disentangle the effect of tax incentives on entrepreneurs from their effects on other self-employed individuals. The problem stems from the fact that the measure of entrepreneurship available in most data sets is far too broad to capture business owners who embody the characteristics typically associated with "entrepreneurs". This issue, which is common to all research focused on entrepreneurship, is particularly troublesome for the tax literature on entrepreneurship because of the potentially large number of individuals who enter self-employment to avoid taxation. As troubling as this problem is, it is likely that better quality data would go a long way in solving it.

One solution pertaining to survey data would be to adopt survey questions that capture the degree to which the activity carried out by the business owner is "entrepreneurial". As discussed in the introduction to this chapter most definitions of an entrepreneur include individuals who are innovative and take risks in developing a business. Questions such as "Is the business a franchise?", "How many other businesses operate in the same industry?", "Was the business purchased from a previous owner?", and "How many other businesses in the industry apply the same business plan?" would help to elicit whether the individual is innovative. To identify the degree to which the individual is adopting risk, questions such as "How much new capital is invested in the business?" and "How much of the owner's own capital is invested in the firm?" could be asked of respondents. Identification of "entrepreneurs" as distinct from other self-employed, including would be tax avoiders, would allow researchers to examine directly the impacts of tax policy on entrepreneurship.

In fact, this approach allows for an even richer examination of the relationship between tax policy and entrepreneurship. Identification of the separate elements that make up an entrepreneur (innovation and risk) allows one to identify on which dimension(s) a given tax policy change impacts entrepreneurial activity. The ability to examine how tax policy influences risk taking directly would be useful to test the conclusions of the theoretical literature, which (as outlined above) has focused on the role of risk in the entrepreneurship decision. This would also potentially allow researchers to examine how important each of the entrepreneurial dimensions is as a determinant for success and to develop tax policies that target these characteristics.

This is an important point in light of recent proposals to measure entrepreneurship by identifying firms that increases employment substantially over a given time period (see for example, Ahmad OECD Chapter 7, and Hessels Chapter 13 of this book). In other words, these identify entrepreneurial firms as those that succeed in terms of employment growth. While such measures would allow researchers to identify how policies affect this desirable outcome, they would not provide enough information to determine the mechanisms by which entrepreneurs become successful. In some sense these measures capture entrepreneurship through an ex-post evaluation of the entrepreneur as opposed to identifying the ex-ante dimensions of the entrepreneur's ability.

A second approach to tackling the problem is to develop data that allows the researcher to better identify individuals who enter self-employed to avoid taxation. This would allow one to pull out tax evaders from the group of self-employed but wouldn't allow for further disentanglement of the other self-employed from entrepreneurs. Thus, while not providing direct evidence on entrepreneurial outcomes, this approach would allow researchers to identify, for example, how the tax code impacts noncompliance among the self-employed; a key component of the overall impacts of taxation. There are a number of possible approaches aimed at identifying this activity (outlined above), each with its own pros and cons.

Direct measures, such as tax audit data, provide very rich information on the amount and form of tax avoidance by the self-employed. However, audit data are very expensive to collect and, therefore, are an unlikely to provide a solution to the identification problem. The data required to generate indirect measures of noncompliance, such as those proposed by Pissarides and Weber (1989), are much less expensive to collect but provide less than perfect information on the form and extent of non-compliance. Nonetheless, there is some scope to improve the data used in identifying the noncompliant through such indirect measures.

Given the links between income and tax outcomes of individuals within a family, household data is likely to be preferred to identify non-compliance. Because this approach relies on information regarding household expenditure, detailed information on individual expenditure items is required. Information on individual household members' income is also necessary and should, if possible, be directly linked to administrative data reported on income tax returns. The data currently used for this approach relies on survey responses from family members, which may differ from what is reported to tax authorities. This can lead to biased results if individuals report their income correctly in response to the survey but under-report income for tax purposes. In general, improvements in the estimates would be brought about by more detailed questioning of the financial situations of both self-employed and wage employed workers in such surveys.

These suggestions are intended as a starting point in what is hoped will be an ongoing discussion regarding current data deficiencies related to the measurement of entrepreneurship. In order to better aid policy makers around the world in their attempts to encourage "entrepreneurship" researchers require better identification of the activities and outcomes targeted by their policies. It is only by disentangling "entrepreneurship" from other "self-employment" activities that the complex links between tax policy and self-employment can be explored.

Acknowledgments This paper was prepared for the Workshop on Entrepreneurship Statistics, February 7th—8th 2006, Huelva, Spain (organized by the Andalusian Statistics Institute and the University of Huelva). I am solely responsible for any omissions or errors. Address: Department of Economics; University of Victoria; PO Box 1700 STN CSC; Victoria, BC V8W 2Y2. (250)721-8541 (tel).(250)721-6214 (fax). E-mail: hschuetz@uvic.ca.

References

Ahsan, SM (1974) Progression and Risk-Taking. Oxford Economic Papers 26:318–328

Ahsan SM (1990) Risk-Taking, Savings, and Taxation a Re-Examination of Theory and Policy. The Canadian Journal of Economics 23(2):408–433

Andreoni J, Erard B, Feinstein J (1998) Tax Compliance. Journal of Economic Literature 36: 818–60

Apel M (1994) An Expenditure-Based Estimate of Tax Evasion in Sweden. Department of Economics Uppsala University Working paper 1994

Baker P (1993) Taxpayer Compliance of the Self-Employed: Estimates from Household Spending Data. Institute for Fiscal Studies Working paper No. W93/14

Blau DM (1987) A Time-Series Analysis of Self-Employment in the United States. Journal of Political Economy 95(3):445–467

Briscoe G, Dainty A, Millett S (2000) The Impact of the Tax System on Self-Employment in the British Construction Industry. International Journal of Manpower 21(8):596–613

Bruce D (2002) Taxes and Entrepreneurial Endurance: Evidence from the Self-Employed. National Tax Journal 55(1):5–24

Bruce D (2000) Effects of the United States Tax System on Transitions Into Self-Employment. Labour Economics 7(5):545–574

Bruce D, Mohsin M (2003) Tax Policy and Entrepreneurship: New Time Series Evidence. Working Paper University of Tennessee

Bruce D, Schuetze HJ (2004) Tax Policy and Entrepreneurship. Swedish Economic Policy Review 2(11):233–265

Clotfelter CW (1983) Tax Evasion and Tax Rates: An Analysis of Individual Returns. Review of Economics and Statistics 65(3):363–73

Congregado E, Golpe A, Millán JM (2003) Some Empirical Aspects of Self-Employment in Spain during the nineties. Seminario de Análisis Económico, Universidad de Huelva, SAE WP 20

Cullen JB, Gordon RH (2002) Taxes and Entrepreneurial Activity: Theory and Evidence for the U.S. NBER Working Paper No. 9015

Domar ED, Musgrave RA (1944) Proportional Income Taxation and Risk-Taking. Quarterly Journal of Economics 58:388–422

Erard B (1992) The Influence of Tax Auditing on Reporting Behavior. In: Slemrod J, Arbor A (eds) Why People Pay Taxes. University of Michigan Press, Michigan

European Commission (1998) Fostering Entrepreneurship in Europe: Priorities for the Future. Communication for the Commission to the Council, COM (98) 222 final

Fairlie RW, Meyer BD (2000) Trends in Self-Employment Among White and Black Men: 1910–1990. Journal of Human Resources 35(4):643–669

Feldstein M, Slemrod J (1980) Personal Taxation, Portfolio Choice, and the Effect of the Corporate Income Tax. Journal of Political Economy 88:854–66

Gentry WM, Hubbard RG (2000) Tax Policy and Entrepreneurial Entry. American Economic Review 90:283–287

Giles D (2000) Modelling the Tax Compliance Profiles of New Zealand Firms. In: Scully G, Caragata P (eds) Taxation and the Limits of Government. Boston: Kluwer Academic Publishers, Boston

Gordon R (1998) Can High Personal Tax Rates Encourage Entrepreneurial Activity? IMF Staff Papers 45(1):49–60

Joulfaian D, Rider M (1998) Differential Taxation and Tax Evasion by Small Business. National Tax Journal 51(4):675–687

Jung YH, Snow A, Trandel GA (1993) Tax Evasion and the Size of the Underground Economy. Journal of Public Economics 54:391–402

Kanbur SM (1989) Risk Taking and Taxation: An Alternative Perspective. Journal of Public Economics 15:163–184

Kesselman JR (1989) Income Tax Evasion: An Intersectoral Analysis. Journal of Public Economics 38:137–182

Long JE (1982a) Income Taxation and the Allocation of Market Labor. Journal of Labor Research 3(3):259–76

Long JE (1982b) The Income Tax and Self-Employment. National Tax Journal 35:31–42

Lyssiotou P, Pashardes P, Stengos T (2002) Estimates of the Black Economy based on Consumer Demand Approaches. University of Guelph Working Paper

Mirus R, Smith RS (1996) Self-Employment, Tax Evasion and the Underground Economy: Micro-Based Estimates for Canada. Working Paper No 1002 Cambridge MA: International Tax Program, Harvard Law School

Moore RL (1983) Self-Employment and the Incidence of the Payroll Tax. National Tax Journal 36:491–501

Mossin J (1968) Taxation and Risk-Taking: An Expected Utility Approach. Economica 35:74–82

OECD (1998) Fostering Entrepreneurship: The OECD Jobs Strategy. OECD, Paris

Parker SC (1996) A Time Series Model of Self-employment under Uncertainty. Economica 63:459–75

Parker SC (2003) Does Tax Evasion Affect Occupational Choice? Oxford Bulletin of Economics and Statistics 65(3):379–394

Parker SC (2004) The Economics of Self-Employment and Entrepreneurship. Cambridge University Press, Cambridge

Pestieau P, Possen UM (1991) Tax Evasion and Occupational Choice. Journal of Public Economics 45:107–125

Pestieau P, Possen UM (1992) How Do Taxes Affect Occupational Choice. Public Finance 47(1):108–119

Pissarides CA, Weber G (1989) An Expenditure Based Estimate of Britain's Black Economy. Journal of Public Economics 39(1):17–32

Robson MT (1998) The Rise in Self-Employment Amongst UK Males. Small Business Economics 10:199–212

Robson MT, Wren C (1999) Marginal and Average Tax Rates and the Incentive for Self-Employment. Southern Economic Journal 65(4):757–773

Schneider F, Enste D (2000) Shadow Economies: Size, Causes, and Consequences. Journal of Economic Literature 38(March):77–114

Schuetze HJ (2000) Taxes, Economic Conditions and Recent Trends in Male Self-Employment: A Canada-U.S. Comparison. Labour Economics 7(5):507–544

Schuetze HJ (2002) Profiles of Tax Non-Compliance Among the Self-Employed in Canada: 1969–1992. Canadian Public Policy 28(2):219–238

Schuetze HJ (2006) Income Splitting Among the Self-Employed in Canada and the Optimal Unit of Taxation. Canadian Journal of Economics (Forthcoming)

Slemrod J, Arbor A (1992). Why People Pay Taxes: Tax Compliance and Enforcement. University of Michigan Press, Michigan

Stiglitz JE (1969) The Effects of Income, Wealth, and Capital Gains Taxation on Risk-Taking. The Quarterly Journal of Economics 83(2):263–283

US General Accounting Office (1990) Tax Administration: Profiles of Major Elements of the Tax Gap. Document GGD-90-53BR. Washington, DC: GAO.

Vroman W (1997) Self-Employment Assistance: Revised Report. The Urban Institute, Washington

Wasylenko M (1997) Taxation and Economic Development: The State of the Economic Literature. New England Economic Review March/April: 37–52

Watson H (1985) Tax Evasion and Labor Markets. Journal of Public Economics 27:231–46

Chapter 11
Using Survival Models with Individual Data

Juan Antonio Máñez, María Engracia Rochina and Juan Antonio Sanchis

Abstract Since there exists in this literature a common interest to unravel the sources of both permanence in the self-employment status and firm survival, the present chapter is devoted to provide guidelines to applied researchers about which methods are suitable for any particular application related to self-employment and firm survival. Further, it should be noted that the econometric analysis of survival (duration) is a very wide field, and that the modest aim of the following sections in this chapter is to introduce the reader to such kind of econometric analysis.

11.1 Introduction

On theoretical grounds it is quite difficult to agree with a unique and exhaustive definition of entrepreneurship and entrepreneur. The recognition of the multidimensional nature of the entrepreneur and entrepreneurship related activities, contributes to the lack of consensus about what entrepreneurship is exactly about. As stated in Parker (2004) "entrepreneurship has only recently come to be regarded as a subject". On empirical grounds, however, the entrepreneur and entrepreneurship concepts are much more delimited. The reason for this diversion between applied and theoretical developments is clear and mainly related to the availability of data. Thus, entrepreneurship studies have focused their attention mainly in two different aspects in this topic. On the one side, "many applied labour economists have equated self-employment with entrepreneurship" (Parker 2004). We can find many references in the applied economic literature on self-employment (see, among others, Congregado et al. 2005, García-Mainar and Montuenga-Gómez 2005, Martínez-Granado 2002, Carrasco 1999). According to this approach, the theoretical concepts of entrepreneur and entrepreneurship have been substituted by self-employed and self-employment in empirical studies. On the other side, although less popular because of the lack of suitable data availability, we find the assimilation of the entrepreneurship and

JA Máñez
Universitat de València
juan.a.manez@uv.es

entrepreneur terms with small firms and small firms runners, respectively. According to this approach empirical entrepreneurship studies are mainly focussed on the market entry and exit rates of small firms in the economy. The main interest is related to the question about what makes small firms survive, succeed, grow and increase its efficiency against failure and exit from the market in general (Mata and Portugal 1994; Audretsch and Mahmood 1994; Mata et al. 1995; Esteve et al. 2004, Esteve and Máñez 2004) or from international markets in particular (Esteve et al. 2006). In this task of uncovering the determinants of firm success the innovative capacity of firms and the link between innovation and survival prospects at the firm level plays an important role (this stands behind the Schumpeterian entrepreneur concept).

Since there exists in this literature a common interest to unravel the sources of both permanence in the self-employment status and firm survival, the present chapter is devoted to provide guidelines to applied researchers about which methods are suitable for any particular application related to self-employment and firm survival. Further, it should be noted that the econometric analysis of survival (duration) is a very wide field, and that the modest aim of the following sections in this chapter is to introduce the reader to such kind of econometric analysis.

The chapter is divided into 8 sections. The second is devoted to explain what survival analysis is about. In the third and fourth sections we outline some particular characteristics of survival data and why these characteristics preclude the use of standard methods such as Ordinary Least Squares. Section five introduces some basic concepts of survival analysis. Section six describes empirical issues and estimation. Some possible extensions of the methods presented are covered in section seven. Finally, section eight briefly summarises the data requirements to undertake survival analysis.

11.2 What Is Survival Analysis About?

Econometric survival models analyse the length of time that an individual spends in a relevant state before experiencing the transition to another state. Some examples for survival analysis are: in entrepreneurship analysis, the study of self-employment duration; in relation to firms dynamics, the analysis of the determinants of lifetime duration (from the entry to the exit of the market); in exports, the analysis of the period of time for which a firm uninterruptedly exports; and when studying R&D activities, the analysis of the period of time for which a firm uninterruptedly performs R&D activities.

It is important to define some relevant concepts related to survival data. Following Cameron and Trivedi (2005): (i) a state is a classification of an individual or firm at a point of time (being this classification exclusive); (ii) a transition is a change from one specific state to another; (iii) a spell is each one of the episodes in which the individuals remain in the relevant state; and, (iv) a spell duration is the length of time that the individual spends in the relevant state.

The analysis of survival with actual data may be complicated for a number of reasons (Cameron and Trivedi 2005). First, there are several related distributional functions to model durations. Secondly, there are many sampling schemes (inflow sampling, outflow sampling, stock sampling or population sampling). Thirdly, the data on spell duration can be censored or truncated (this is the major reason for modelling transitions rather than mean duration). Fourthly, in survival data one may observe multiple spells for an individual (repeated spells), e.g., an individual can be first self-employed, then work as a paid-employee, and eventually became self-employed again. For this individual, we observe two self-employment spells that probably are not independent. Fifthly, one can observe more than a unique possible transition out of the relevant state (multiple state transitions). Following with the self-employment example, when an individual exits from the self-employment pool, the only possibility is not only the transition to a paid-employment job; she could also be retiring or becoming inactive.

In this chapter we will mainly focus on the case of a single spell per subject and a unique possible transition out of the relevant state. This is the most standard case for survival analysis and statistical and microeconometric packages implement the survival methods presented in this chapter for this chapter.

As stated in Jenkins (2004) many of the models designed to analyze survival times are distinctive because the need to take into account some special features of these data: in relation both to the characteristics of the dependent variable used for the analysis (survival time itself) and to the explanatory variables used in the models. In the next section we consider and define these particular features.

11.3 Some Particular Characteristics of Survival Data

11.3.1 Censoring and Truncation of Survival Time Data

To introduce the concepts of censoring and truncation we make use of Fig. 11.1. In this figure, we assume that our observation window (period of time for which we follow the individuals) starts in t_0 and ends up in T.

Censoring refers to whether we observe or not the dates of starting and ending of a specific spell. This means that if there is censoring we do not know the exact length of the spell. There are two types of censoring:

- Right censoring: at the observation windows the spell end date is not observed. If we suppose that entry occurred in survival time $t_0 + k$ and the spell is still going on at time T, we only know that the complete spell would terminate some time later than T (end of the observation window).
- Left censoring: in this case we do not know the exact length of the spell because the start of the spell date is not observed (i.e., the spell started before t_0).

Truncation refers to whether or not we observe a spell in our data, and the sample selection effect depends on survival time itself:

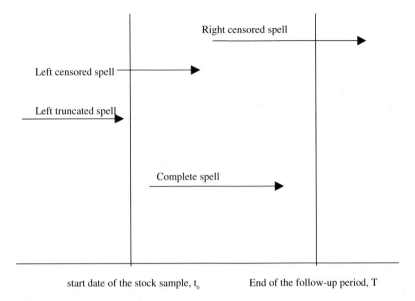

Fig. 11.1 Censoring and truncation

- Left truncation: this is the case when we only observe in the sample those observations (individuals or firms) that have survived more than a minimum amount of time. This case is also known by economists as *stock sampling with follow*-up (Jenkins 2004). Ignoring left truncation leads to overestimate duration.
- Right truncation: this is the case when only those individuals with a transition by a particular date are included in the sample, and so only "relatively" long survival times are excluded from the sample. An example of right truncation can be drawn from an outflow sample from the unemployment registry. Suppose that we only observe those individuals that have left unemployment by the end of 2005 and not those that are still unemployed. Ignoring right truncation leads to underestimate duration.

Finally, if both entry and exit dates are observed we have a complete spell.

11.3.2 Fixed versus Time Varying Covariates

It is important to distinguish between fixed and time-varying covariates as it has important implications for the analytical methods. As put forward by Jenkins (2004) if one has only fixed explanatory variables the analytical methods and the empirical estimation are easier. However, with time-varying covariates some model interpretations no longer hold and data have to be reorganized ("episode splitting") to account for time variation of the explanatory variables and to estimate survival models.

Fixed covariates are those that do not vary over time. There are two possibilities for fixed explanatory variables: either variables that are intrinsically fixed, like activity classification for firms or gender when analyzing self-employment spells; or those cases in which we only observe the characteristics of the subjects in the moment they enter the sample. Having only fixed covariates implies to carry out a cross section analysis.

Time varying covariates are those that vary over time. We can distinguish between time-varying covariates that vary with calendar time (for example, the growth rate of unemployment as an indicator of the business cycle in entrepreneurship analysis) and those that vary with survival time (like tax benefits enjoyed by new entrepreneurs that decrease with survival time and finish after a few years).

11.3.3 Continuous versus Discrete Time Data

In general, it is assumed that the transition out from one state may occur at any particular instant in time, thus the stochastic process generating survival data occurs in *continuous* time. However, as pointed out by Jenkins (2004), survival time is not necessarily a continuous variable. There are some cases in which survival times are grouped, banded or interval censored in discrete intervals of time and others in which the underlying transition process is an intrinsically discrete one.

Thus, in continuous data it is assumed that time is continuous and that the transition out of the current state can occur at any instant in time. An example of continuous time data in entrepreneurship analysis would be to use a social security registry to measure self-employment spells. Using this data we know the exact date in which the transition in or out of self-employment happens. With intrinsically discrete data transition out of the current state is something that can occur only in terms of discrete points. For example, one can consider the duration of a washing machine. When modeling how long it takes for the washing machine to break down, it would be natural to model failure times in terms of the number of the discrete washes that the washing machine was in operation and not in terms of months or years. Finally, if survival times have been grouped or banded into discrete intervals (like weeks, months or years), not at exact times, we have interval censored data. For example, in the European Community Household Panel the data is recorded yearly. Therefore, we do not know the exact date in which an individual enters or exits the self-employment pool, at most we know the year of entry and the year of exit.

11.4 Drawbacks of Standard Econometric Methods Applied to Survival Data

One of the characteristics of survival time is that this is a positive variable. Thus, one could be tempted to estimate a model of log survival times on the corresponding regressors by ordinary least squares (OLS, hereafter). However, OLS cannot handle some problems related to survival time data: (1) censoring (and truncation) of spell duration data; (2) time-varying covariates; (3) grouped, banded, or interval data; and (4) behavioural modelling.

11.4.1 OLS and Right-censored Data

Let us assume we have a sample of survival times where we observe T_i in place of T_i^* for some of the observations. Being T_i^* the true survival times, $T_i < T_i^*$ the observed durations for right-censored spells, and $T_i = T_i^*$ the observed durations for completed spells. Given that the true survival time is not observed for right-censored spells we could, for instance, run an OLS regression of $\log(T_i)$ on the vector of explanatory variables X_i (for simplicity, but without lack of generality, assume that this vector only contains a unique explanatory variable X), fitting the following model

$$\log(T_i) = \alpha + \beta X_i + \varepsilon_i \qquad (11.1)$$

Let us assume that in the true relationship between X_i and T_i^* a lower X is associated to a longer T. That means the true $\beta < 0$. Further, assume that the incidence of the right-censoring problem is higher for longer durations. Therefore, for lower values of X, which are associated to longer true survival times, we only observe $T_i < T_i^*$. All this will force the estimated relationship in (1) to be $\beta < 0$ but biased because of $|\beta'| < |\beta|$. The observed and estimated slope would be less negative than the one that would be obtained if we were able to fit the model with the true T_i^*'s for right-censored observations. Overestimation of the slope will also happen if we would exclude all the censored spells in the OLS estimation.

Measuring spell duration not as its actual duration but as the observed duration leads to a measurement error problem in T_i that, given our assumptions, is especially serious at longer durations. Excluding censored spells altogether supposes a sample selection type problem in which we end up estimating with a non-random subsample of the population.

11.4.2 OLS and Time-varying Covariates

A second problem with OLS regression is that it cannot handle time-varying covariates as for a single dependent variable value T there are multiple values for the covariates X_t. Notice that for survival data, individuals may be observed at several stages during the spell and covariates may take different values over the spell. If one were to choose one value of the time-varying covariates associated to each spell duration T, which one should be chosen and which are the consequences of that choice? If we choose, for instance, the values just at the time before spell completion (transition time) we will face a problem of inconsistency as completed survival times vary across spells. An additional problem with this approach would be how to handle censored observations for which by definition we do not observe the occurrence of the event under consideration. Another option is choosing the value of the covariate at the start of the spell. Although this is a consistent definition for all spells, we will be wasting all the information provided by time-varying covariates since we will be treating them as fixed.

11.4.3 OLS and Grouped, Banded, or Interval Data

As above introduced, survival time can be a continuous or a discrete variable. When dealing with grouped, banded, or interval data, survival time is not observed as continuous, therefore using OLS is incorrect as this technique assumes that the dependent variable is continuous.

11.4.4 OLS and Behavioural Modelling

Most behavioural models are framed in terms of decisions about whether or not to do something (in the entrepreneurship literature an example of such a decision could be whether or not to become self-employed) and not in terms of spell duration that is the dependent variable for OLS estimation. That means we are mainly interested in modelling directly transitions or the risk of a given event happening in a point of time rather than durations themselves. The focal point of both econometric duration models and underlying theoretical economic models is analysing this risk. As stated in Van den Berg (2001) "In general, theories that aim at explaining durations focus on the rate at which the subject leaves the state at duration t given that has not done so yet. In particular, they explain the hazard at t in terms of external conditions at t as well as the underlying economic behavior of the subjects that are still in the state at t. Theoretical predictions about a duration distribution thus run by way of the hazard of that distribution". Therefore, to cope with behavioural models we should be able to directly model transition probabilities taking into account the number of periods already in a given state.

To sum up, we need methods: (i) with the ability of dealing with censored (and truncated) spells; (ii) recognizing the longitudinal and sequential (passage of time) nature of the spell data, what requires to be able to exploit the extra-information provided by time-varying covariates (varying either with calendar or mainly with survival time); (iii) allowing the direct estimation of transition probabilities (the risk of transition out of the state given that this has not yet happened); and (iv) allowing time to be treated either continuous or discretely. As pointed out in Jenkins (2005) "The solution is to model survival times indirectly, via the so-called 'hazard rate', which is a concept related to chances of making a transition out of the current state at each instant (or time period) conditional on survival up to that point". Estimation methods based on the maximum likelihood or sometimes the partial likelihood principles are the solution to the problems of using OLS regression.

11.5 A Key Statistical Concept in Survival Analysis: The Hazard Function

11.5.1 Definition of the Hazard Function

The definition of the hazard function depends on the continuous or discrete nature of survival time. Starting by the continuous case, the hazard function is the instantaneous probability of leaving a state conditional on survival up to time t. Using an example within the entrepreneurship literature, we can define it as the probability that an individual leaves self-employment in t given that she has already been self-employed up to t. It is mathematically defined as

$$\theta(t) = \lim_{\Delta t \to \infty} \frac{\Pr[t \leq T < t + \Delta t \,|\, T \geq t]}{\Delta t} \tag{11.2}$$

The discrete-time hazard function is the probability of transition at discrete time t_j, $j = 1,2,...$, given survival up to time t_j:

$$\theta_j = \Pr\left[T = t_j \,\middle|\, T \geq t_j\right] \tag{11.3}$$

In this chapter we concentrate in survival models in the class of proportional hazard models (PHM, hereafter). The reason for this is twofold. On the one hand, they are the most widely used formulation in survival analysis in general, and in Economics in particular. On the other hand, they allow for a nice interpretation of the coefficients in the hazard function. To ease notation, unless other thing stated, in this section we assume continuous time from now onwards.

Under a proportional hazard specification the hazard function can be written as

$$\theta(t \,|\, X) = \theta_0(t) \exp(X'\beta) \tag{11.4}$$

where $\theta_0(t)$ is the baseline hazard function that depends only on t and $\exp(X'\beta)$ is the hazard component which incorporates the covariates and is not a function of t.

Hazard functions of the form (4) are proportional to the baseline hazard, with scale factor $\exp(X'\beta)$. If a covariate X_k suffers a one unit increase holding the values for other covariates constant, the new hazard is $\exp(\beta_k)$ time the original hazard

$$\theta(t \,|\, X_{new}) = \theta_0(t) \exp(X'\beta + \beta_k) = \exp(\beta_k)\theta(t \,|\, X) \tag{11.5}$$

or, equivalently, the change in the hazard is β_k times the original hazard

$$\partial\theta(t \,|\, X)/\partial X_k = \theta_0(t) \exp(X'\beta)\beta_k = \beta_k\theta(t \,|\, X) \tag{11.6}$$

Therefore, in PHMs β should be interpreted as a proportional change in the hazard caused by a unit change in the relevant covariate. A change in a covariate has the effect of a multiplicative change in the hazard function. Therefore, a positive coefficient produces an increase in the hazard if the corresponding covariate increases and, thus, a decrease in the expected duration.

The PHM can be further extended to incorporate time-varying covariates. Up to here we have not explicitly considered that covariates may change during the spell. For example, during a self-employment spell the fiscal treatment for self-employees may change. The requirement for this type of covariates is to be weakly exogenous. With time-varying covariates the hazard function in (4) is now

$$\theta\left(t \,|\, X_t\right) = \theta_0\left(t\right)\exp\left(X_t'\beta\right) \tag{11.7}$$

A further generalization of the PHM incorporates the existence of individual unobserved heterogeneity into the model. The common solution to incorporate it is to specify multiplicative unobserved heterogeneity uncorrelated with regressors. This individual unobserved heterogeneity component is known in the survival analysis literature as 'frailty'. The reason to introduce it multiplicatively is because in this way it measures a proportional increase or decrease in the hazard rate of a given individual relative to that of an average individual. After the inclusion of this final component the generated type of models are called mixed proportional hazard models (MPHM, hereafter). Using the PHM in (7) unobserved heterogeneity is accounted for by inclusion of the multiplicative term v_i. That is,

$$\theta\left(t \,|\, X_{it}\right) = \theta_0\left(t\right)\exp\left(X_{it}'\beta\right)v_i \tag{11.8}$$

From now onwards we are going to work with this general specification of the conditional hazard function.

11.5.2 Hazard Function Components

The Baseline Hazard ($\theta_0\left(t\right)$)

The baseline hazard is the hazard that, after controlling for the covariates and the unobserved heterogeneity component, can be attributed to the passage of survival time in the spell. This hazard is common to all the individuals/spells and summarizes how the hazard varies with survival times. The shape of the baseline hazard determines the patterns of duration dependence:

$$\frac{d\theta_0\left(t\right)}{dt} \begin{cases} > 0 \rightarrow \text{Positive duration dependence} \\ < 0 \rightarrow \text{Negative duration dependence} \\ = 0 \rightarrow \text{No duration dependence} \end{cases} \tag{11.9}$$

We find two different approaches to specify the baseline hazard. On the one hand, a parametric specification in which it is assumed that $\theta_0\left(t\right)$ follows a given functional form. The more common functional forms are time-invariant (exponential specification, with a constant baseline hazard, too restrictive in practice); monotonically increasing, decreasing or constant with time (Weibull specification, containing as a particular case the exponential, widely used in econometrics); or more flexible functional forms through the incorporation of polynomials in t (polynomial baseline hazards, allowing for a U-shaped baseline hazard function). On the other hand, there are non-parametric (semi-parametric) approaches in which one leaves the data to determine the shape of the baseline hazard (the piece-wise constant hazard specification, or the Cox model, 1972, 1975, very much used empirically).

Unobserved Heterogeneity or Frailty (v_i)

The frailty term is the hazard that, after controlling for the covariates and the duration dependence component, can be attributed to unobserved individual heterogeneity. We can distinguish two different approaches for the specification of this term. First, a parametric specification in which it is assumed that v_i is generated according to a parametric distribution function. Common generating distribution functions are the Gamma function, the inverse Gaussian, and the log-normal. Since assuming a Gamma distribution for the frailty component is quite flexible and has many attractive properties, usually v is assumed to be Gamma distributed with unit mean and variance σ^2 to be estimated from the data (Meyer 1990). The null hypothesis of variance equal to zero can be tested. Under the null, unobserved heterogeneity is not relevant and the adequate model will be the model without individual unobserved heterogeneity. Rejection of the null implies that unobserved heterogeneity is important to explain duration. Secondly, unobserved heterogeneity can be treated non-parametrically. Heckman and Singer (1984) allowed for an arbitrary distribution for the individual heterogeneity term. They proceeded by assuming that there is a number of different types of individuals (or "mass points" in the distribution of individual heterogeneity) so that individuals can only be assigned to different types according to probabilities. This is reflected in the hazard function incorporating an extra term allowing for different intercepts, one for each different type. For instance, if one assumes a model with two types (type = 1, 2), then the hazard becomes

$$\theta_{type}(t \mid X_{it}) = \theta_0(t) \exp\left(m_{type} + \beta_0 + x_{it}'\beta\right) \tag{11.10}$$

where the term $X_{it}'\beta$ in (8) is split into the common intercept β_0 and slope terms $(x_{it}'\beta)$, and the unobserved heterogeneity term v_i is redefined as $\exp\left(m_{type} + \beta_0\right)$. Thus, m_{type} characterises the non-parametric distribution of the individual heterogeneity component. The intercept for type-1 individuals is β_0 and for type-2 individuals is equal to $m_{type2} + \beta_0$ (the mass-point for type-1 is normalized to zero). To check for the existence of unobserved heterogeneity we test if m_2 is different from zero.

The lack of control for unobserved individual heterogeneity may cause some problems. First, the degree of negative (positive) duration dependence in the hazard is over-estimated (under-estimated). This is the result of a selection process. For instance, with negative duration dependence, high v-value individuals finish the spell more rapidly. Then, as time goes by a higher proportion of individuals with low values of v remains alive, which implies a lower hazard. Secondly, positive (negative) β parameters are under-estimated (over-estimated). Finally, estimated coefficients cannot longer be interpreted as the proportionate response of the hazard to a change in a given covariate.

11.6 Empirical Issues and Estimation

In this section, we use as an example to illustrate the empirical questions related to survival, the analysis of duration of exporting spells in Esteve *et al.* (2006), since among our works on survival is the one that most closely resembles a survival analysis of new entrepreneurs. In the corresponding dataset survival time is observed as discrete (interval-censored data).[1]

The steps to follow in such a survival analysis are the following: first, reorganization of the data; secondly, descriptive analysis including univariate tests; and thirdly, estimation.

11.6.1 Re-organization of the Data or 'Episode Splitting'

In order to incorporate time-varying covariates, we have to re-organize the data into spell-period format (we need to have as many rows per spell as periods lasts the spell). Further, we have to create a binary dependent variable, y_{ik}, taking the value of one the last period of the spell (period of the transition out of the state) and zero elsewhere.

We illustrate this in Table 11.1 by means of an individual that completes its exporting spell in period 3. Since transition out of the relevant exporting status takes place in period 3, the censoring indicator takes value zero in periods 1 and 2, and one in period 3.

Table 11.1 Episode splitting example

Individual's identifier	Within spell interval identifier(k)	Created binary dependent variable (new censoring variable y_{ik})
1	1	0
1	2	0
1	3	1

---

[1] Notice that survival data in economic applications are often interval-censored. For example, self-employment durations may be grouped into weeks or months. A person who is self-employed at the end of moth two but not at the end of month three has a spell in the range of two to three months.

11.6.2 Descriptive Analysis

Non-parametric Estimation of Survival Functions: The Kaplan-Meier Estimator

The survival function, $S(t) = \Pr[T > t]$, is the probability that the duration or spell length is higher than t. In the continuous time case, the survival function is monotonically declining from one to zero, and it is related to the hazard according to $\theta(t) = -d \ln(S(t))/dt$, where the hazard is the change in the log-survival function. However, the discrete-time survival function is obtained recursively from the hazard as $S(t) = \Pr[T \geq t] = \prod_{j|t_j \leq t} (1 - \theta_j)$, $j = 1, 2, \ldots$, where the survival function is a decreasing step function with steps at t_j. For a descriptive purpose, it can be interesting to know the shape of the survival function before considering any regressor.

The Kaplan-Meier estimator of the survival function is the sample analogue $\hat{S}(t) = \prod_{j|t_j \leq t} (1 - \hat{\theta}_j) = \prod_{j|t_j \leq t} (r_j - d_j)/r_j$, where d_j is the number of spells ending (failures) at time t_j and r_j the number of spells at risk of failure. This is a decreasing step function with a jump at each discrete failure time.

Consider the data set of firms that has been used by Esteve et al. (2006). The variable of interest is the duration of exporting spells of Spanish manufacturing firms, measured in numbers of years. Figure 11.2 shows the Kaplan-Meier estimator of the empirical survival function: survival time is represented in the horizontal axis and in the vertical axis we represent the proportion of exporting spells started that are still in progress after a given number of years.

As expected, the estimated survival function declines rapidly at the beginning and slowly at the end. Whereas almost 25% of the firms complete their exporting spells the first year, after four years 62.5% of the exporting spells are still going on,

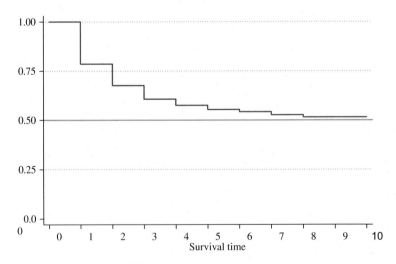

Fig. 11.2 Kaplan-Meier Survival Estimate

and after 8 years this figure more than 50%. In any case, it should be noted that the observed pattern of the empirical survival function is not completely attributable to time (duration dependence). To be able to isolate the effect of time on the hazard one has to take into account both observable (covariates) and unobservable individual characteristics (unobserved heterogeneity component).

Non-parametric Univariate Tests

A previous step to estimation is to carry out non-parametric univariate tests to get a first flavour of the isolated effect of each one of the relevant covariates on duration. These non-parametric tests check for the equality of survival functions across the r groups in which the explanatory variables classify the spells (Log-rank, Wilcoxon, etc.). These tests are extensions of non-parametric rank tests to compare two or more distributions for censored data. Under the null hypothesis, there is no difference in the survival rate of each of the r groups at any of the exit times (Cleves et al. 2004).

For example, Table 11.2 presents the results for the log-rank and Wilcoxon tests for the variable size that classifies firms in two size groups: small and large firms. The results point out the existence of remarkable differences in the survival prospects across the two size groups. This jointly with the information about mean durations allows concluding that large firms (size=1) have longer survival prospects in exporting. In a self-employment context it may be interesting to perform this testing procedure with variables such as gender or a categorical variable summarising educational background.

11.6.3 Estimation

As above mentioned, the use of maximum likelihood estimation permits to overcome all the problems imposed by the particular nature of the survival data. To build up the likelihood function, we should take into account that not all duration spells contribute equally to the likelihood function. For instance, the contribution of completed spells is different to the contribution of right-censored spells, and this is different to the contribution of a left-truncated spell.

When building up the maximum likelihood function to estimate a PHM, it is necessary to carry out some checks and to take some relevant decisions. First, we have to check whether the survival time variable is continuous or discrete. Secondly, whether we use a parametric or non-parametric specification for the baseline hazard.

Table 11.2 Non-parametric tests

Non-parametric tests of equality of survival functions and mean duration by explanatory variables.[1,2]				
	Log-rank	Wilcoxon	Mean Duration	
Size group	8.68	9.67	Size=0	6.05
	(0.003)	(0.002)	Size=1	8.04

Notes: 1) 1414 observations, 407 firms, and 167 exits
         2) p-value in parenthesis

Thirdly, we have to decide whether to choose a parametric specification or mass-points approach to model the unobserved heterogeneity component. Figure 11.3 summarises the steps to follow to choose the model that best suits the characteristics of our data and our decisions.

Regardless of the continuos/discrete survival time, as it is possible to observe in Fig. 11.3, the first decision in the estimation of PHMs is to choose a parametric or non-parametric specification for the baseline hazard function. As for the continuous time models, the two more common parametric specifications are assuming that the baseline hazard follows either an exponential or Weibull distribution. Among the non-parametric (semi-parametric specifications) the most widely used are the piecewise constant hazard model (especially used in applications to unemployment duration) and the Cox PHM (CPHM). The piecewise constant hazard model divides in segments with constant hazard rates the baseline hazard function. In the semi-parametric CPHM the functional form of the baseline hazard is left unspecified and it is not required for the estimation of the coefficients.

The discrete time representation of an underlying continuous time PHM is a complementary log-log model (*cloglog*, hereafter) including a baseline hazard to take into account the passage of survival time. Again the first decision to take is the functional form of the baseline hazard. The more common specifications are to assume that the risk is monotonically increasing, constant or decreasing with time (equivalent to the Weibull model in continuous time) or to allow for a separate intercept for each survival time period along the spell duration.

The third decision is whether to model the unobserved individual heterogeneity parametrically or non-parametrically. As for the parametric treatment, different distributional assumptions for the unobserved heterogeneity component lead to dif-

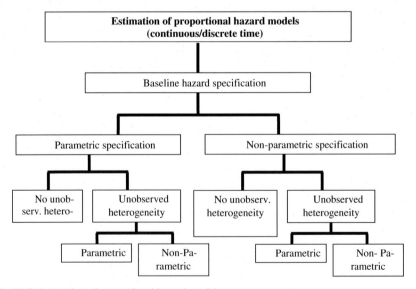

Fig. 11.3 Estimation of proportional hazard models

ferent MPHMs. One widely used combination in the continuous time models is the Weibull-Gamma mixture that includes the exponential-gamma mixture. In discrete-time PHMs it is also common the use of the Gamma heterogeneity distribution (Han and Hausman 1990, Meyer 1990). Both for the continuous or the discrete time cases one may alternatively choose a discrete distribution for unobserved heterogeneity (the non-parametric method proposed by Heckman and Singer 1984). In all cases, it should be taken into account that whether to consider or not unobserved heterogeneity is not a choice. We must include an individual heterogeneity term and test its relevance to explain duration.

11.6.4 Estimation Results

Table 11.3 shows estimation results for the discrete time PH *cloglog* model estimated by Esteve et al. (2006). We have just selected, for illustration, the coefficient estimate for the variable size and the parameters controlling for duration dependence. Results are sequentially presented for a *cloglog* model without taking into account any potential unobserved individual heterogeneity (model 1), for a *cloglog* model assuming a Gamma distribution for an included individual heterogeneity term (model 2) and for a *cloglog* model treating unobserved individual heterogeneity non-parametrically (model 3). The three estimates also treat the baseline hazard non-parametrically by creating 10 interval-specific dummy variables (one for each spell-period at risk), given that the longest observed spell in the data set is 10 periods. However, we can only estimate the first 8 dummies because we observe no spell completion in years 9 and 10.

The three reported estimates give quite similar results as we do not find evidence of unobserved heterogeneity either in model 2 or in model 3. In model 2 we cannot reject the null that the unobserved heterogeneity variance component (σ^2) is equal to zero, and in model 3 we cannot reject that the mass-point for type 2 is statistically no different to the mass-point for type 1, meaning that there is not unobserved individual heterogeneity. These results suggest that model 1 is the appropriate one. Hence, hereafter comments and prediction results are based on this model.

The coefficients of the duration interval dummies (that inform us about the shape of the baseline hazard) show in general a decreasing pattern, suggesting that the risk of exit from export markets decreases with survival time. However, to better know the shape of the baseline hazard, we carry out pairwise comparisons to test whether the differences between the baseline hazard coefficients are significant. From this testing procedure we can conclude that: first, differences in hazard rates from survival years 1 to 3 are statistically non-significant; secondly, differences in hazard rates from survival years 4 to 8 are also statistically non-significant; and finally, the constant hazard rate for years 1 to 3 is statistically higher than the constant hazard rate for years 4 to 8. Therefore, we detect negative duration dependence and the existence of non-linearities in the pattern of negative duration dependence.

In relation to a firm characteristic such as size, we find that duration in export markets is longer for large than for small firms (the hazard rate for large firms is 54.5% lower than that for small firms, the reference category).

Table 11.3 Maximum likelihood estimates for the discrete time proportional hazard models

	Model 1 cloglog without individual unobserved heterogeneity		Model 2 cloglog with Gamma individual unobserved heterogeneity		Model 3 cloglog with non-parametric individual unobserved heterogeneity (2-mass points)	
	Hazard rate	p-value	Hazard rate	p-value	Hazard rate	p-value
Firm characteristics						
Size group	0.455	0.025	0.454	0.021	0.455	0.020
Duration dependence						
d1	0.077	0.000	0.077	0.000	0.076	0.058
d2	0.059	0.000	0.060	0.000	0.058	0.033
d3	0.054	0.000	0.054	0.000	0.053	0.026
d4	0.029	0.000	0.029	0.000	0.028	0.007
d5	0.021	0.000	0.021	0.000	0.020	0.004
d6	0.015	0.000	0.015	0.000	0.015	0.004
d7	0.021	0.000	0.021	0.000	0.021	0.008
d8	0.018	0.000	0.019	0.001	0.018	0.014
Log likelihood	−398.896		−398.896		−398.897	
N. of observations	1365		1365		1365	
N. of spells	407		407		407	
Test for unobserved individual heterogeneity			LR test of Gamma variance = 0 Chibar2(01) = 0.001 p-value = 0.487		Mass point 1 = 0 Mass point 2 = 0.071 p-value = 0.989	

11.6.5 Post-estimation Results

Once one has the model estimates, it is possible to draw the predicted hazard function and the predicted survival function for different values of the covariates.

Figures 11.4 and 11.5 show the predicted hazard and survival functions that correspond to small and large firms when all other covariates except those catching duration dependence have been set at their sample means. In Fig. 11.4, we observe that the predicted discrete hazard rate, that shows the evolution of firm failure risk over time, for large firms is below that of small firms, i.e. the hazard rate for small firms is higher than that of large ones. As a consequence, in Fig. 11.5 the survival function of large firms is above that of small firms[2].

---

[2] Hazard contributions for survival years 9 and 10 are set equal to 0 because there is no spell completion for this survival periods.

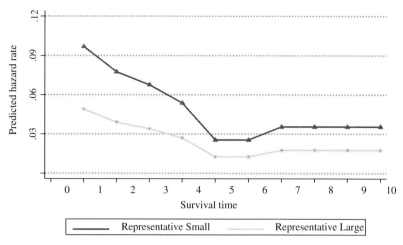

Fig. 11.4 Predicted hazard rate by size

11.7 Extensions

There are more complex survival models which include multiple spells, and multiple destinations. For instance, there can be models with several states, such as unemployment, part-time employment, full-time employment, self-employment, and out-of the labour force. Furthermore, there can also be data in which for a given individual there are multiple spells in a given state. When considering these extensions econometric analysis become rather complex.

In what follows, we introduce the basis of two specific extensions: the competing risks models and multiple or repeated spell models.

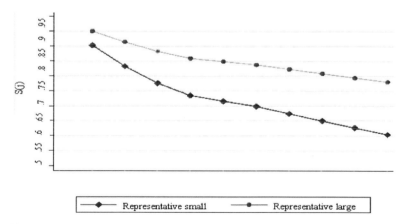

Fig. 11.5 Survival function by size

11.7.1 Competing Risks Models

These are models with multiple destinations from the current state. As an example, in an analysis of self-employment duration, we may want to know about not only time until exit by whatever route, but also about time to exit to unemployment compared to time to exit to paid-employee status.

The simplest case for competing risks models is the independent competing risks model (for continuous time). Consider the existence of two destinations (A, B) with independence of destination hazard risks $(\theta_A(t, X_{it}); \theta_B(t, X_{it}))$. The important implication from the independence assumption is that we end up estimating standard single risks models for each single risk. The only requirement is defining for each destination new censoring variables that consider as censored survival times both the original right censored survival times and the ones corresponding to survival times ending in a different destination. For discrete time, things are much more complex because, among other things, we cannot any longer assume independence of destination hazard risks.

11.7.2 Multiple or Repeated Spell Models

These are models in which the same individual experiments more than one spell. As an example of these models consider the case of an individual who was self-employed in t, paid-employee in $t+k$ and self-employed again in $t+k+d$, so she would have two self-employment spells. Assuming full independence of spells we only have to pool the spells and then use the standard single risks models. However, allowing for spells dependence things quickly get rather harder in terms of more data requirements and/or more complex and non-standard estimation methods (see the theoretical papers by Allison 1984, Van den Berg 2001). Spells dependence may either come from: (i) correlation in unobserved heterogeneity components across different spells from the same individual (the more complex and non-standard estimation methods are required); or (ii) current spells dependence on previous number and spell durations. For this latter case, more data are required, such as information about the number and the duration of previous spells in the state. Because of data availability, the use of this information is very much exploited by studies about employment/unemployment spells.

11.8 Data Requirements for Survival Analysis of Entrepreneurship

When interested in survival analysis the ideal characteristics of the dataset would be as follows:

- First, longitudinal (panel) data allowing exploiting to the full the richness of these methods. For the design of surveys this implies to interview and follow individuals repeatedly on consecutive time periods.

- Secondly, the inclusion of retrospective questions allowing solving left-censoring problems and also contributing to the treatment of repeated spells. Consider, for instance, the case of an individual already self-employed in the moment of the stock sampling. If we do not know the moment in which this individual became self-employed, this spell is left-censored and it cannot be used in estimation with the subsequent information loss (likely affecting not only efficiency but also generating bias).

- Finally, if the transition out of the relevant state can be due to multiple causes, it would be interesting to know the actual one to be able to carry out competing risks analysis. For instance, when an individual leaves the self-employment state it could be because she becomes paid-employee, she retires, etc.

Acknowledgments We are grateful to participants at the Workshop on Entrepreneurship Statistics (held at Punta Umbría, Huelva, Spain) for helpful comments. We also thank the organisers (from University of Huelva) and the sponsor (Instituto de Estadística de Andalucía) of this workshop for inviting us to participate. Usual disclaimers apply. Financial support from the Spanish Ministry of Science and Technology (Project number SEJ2005-05966), and from the Generalitat Valenciana (Project number GV05/183) is gratefully acknowledged.

References

Audretsch DB, Mahmood, T (1994) The rate of hazard confronting new firms and plants in US manufacturing. Review of Industrial Organization 9:41–56

Allison PD (1984) Event history analysis: Regression for longitudinal data. Newbury Parca, Sage, CA

Cameron AC, Trivedi PK (2005) Microeconometrics: Methods and Applications. Cambridge University Press, Cambridge

Carrasco R (1999) Transitions to and From Self-employment in Spain: An Empirical Analysis. Oxford Bulletin of Economics and Statistics 61:291–450

Cleves MA, Gould WW, Gutierrez RG (2004) An introduction to survival analysis using Stata, Stata Corporation, College Station, Texas

Congregado E, Golpe AA, Millán JM, Román C (2006) Survival within entrepreneurs: Which Europeans are the best job-creators? Universidad de Huelva, mimeo

Parker SC (2004) The economics of self-employment. Cambridge University Press, Cambridge

Cox DR (1972) Regression models and life tables. Journal of the Royal Statistical Society 34:187–220

Cox DR (1975) Partial likelihood. Biometrika 62:269–76

Esteve S, Máñez JA (2004) Life Duration of Manufacturing firms. LINEEX Working Paper 06/04

Esteve S, Sanchis A, Sanchis JA (2004) The determinants of survival of Spanish manufacturing firms. Review of Industrial Organization 25:251–73

Esteve S, Máñez JA, Rochina ME, Sanchis JA (2007) A survival analysis of manufacturing firms in export markets. In: Arauzo J, Manjón M (eds) Firm Demography and Industrial Location. Edward Elgar (Forthcoming)

Garcia-Mainar I, Montuenga-Gómez VM (2005) Education returns of wage earners and self-employed workers: Portugal vs. Spain. Economics of Education Review 24:161–70

Han A, Hausman J (1990) Flexible Parametric Estimation of Duration and Competing Risk Models. Journal of Applied Econometrics 5:325–53

Heckman JJ, Singer B (1984) A method for minimizing the impact of distributional assumptions in econometric models for duration data. Econometrica 52(2):271–320

Jenkins SP (2004) Survival Analysis. Unpublished manuscript, Institute for Social and Economic Research, University of Essex, Colchester, UK

Martinez-Granado M (2002) Self-Employment and Labour Market Transitions: A Multiple State Model. Discussion paper 3661 CEPR

Mata J, Portugal P (1994) Life duration of new firms. Journal of Industrial Economics 42:227–45

Mata J, Portugal P, Guimaraes P (1995) The survival of new plants: start-up conditions and post-entry evolution. International Journal of Industrial Organization 13:459–81

Meyer R (1990) Unemployment insurance and unemployment spells. Econometrica 58:757–82

Van den Berg G (2001) Duration Models: Specification, Identification and Multiple Durations. In: Heckman J, Leamer E (eds) Handbook of Econometrics. North-Holland, Vol 5, Ch. 55

Chapter 12
Entrepreneurial Human Capital: Essays of Measurement and Empirical Evidence

Emilio Congregado, Mónica Carmona and Concepción Román

Abstract The aim of this paper is to survey the evidence on the relationship between self-employment and human capital from two fields in particular, economics of self-employment and empirical research on growth, emphasising in the sensibility of results to proxies used to capture education. Although, the emphasis is very much on education, rather than on any broader concept of human capital -due to the difficulties to capture other mechanisms of human capital accumulation- other concepts are also considered.

12.1 Introduction

The aim of this chapter is to study the evidence on the relationship between self-employment and entrepreneurial human capital from two perspectives. In particular, signalling the main mechanisms when the accumulation of a specific kind of human capital –entrepreneurial human capital- occurs, and from an economics of self-employment perspective, emphasizing on the sensibility of the results obtained for different proxies used to capture the stock and its accumulation processes. Although the emphasis is very much on education, rather than on any broader concept of human capital -due to the difficulties to capture other mechanisms of human capital accumulation-, other mechanisms are also considered.

A priori, it seems that individuals with higher knowledge on consumer's preferences, markets, production sets, and even on business administration techniques, have an advantage, a higher capacity to identify profit opportunities, to reduce inefficiencies, to face up to incertitude and to innovate.[1] Thus, a potential entrepreneur will combine different types of knowledge in order to form a good

Emilio Congregado
University of Huelva
congregado@uhu.es

[1] There is a large theoretical literature studying the allocation of individuals and their effort among productive and unproductive entrepreneurial activities. Murphy et al. (1991, 1993) show empirical evidence for the hypothesis that talented individuals are more important for growth if they are engineers rather than lawyers. Similarly, Baumol (1990) uses historical evidence to support the idea that growth increases if society manages to direct more entrepreneurial talent to productive

or service that satisfies the preferences not captured yet, or will introduce some changes in order to use the resources in a more efficient way. This set of specific knowledge may be called entrepreneurial human capital. Hence, the possession of a large entrepreneurial human capital stock will operate in two senses: first, from an individual level, individuals with a higher stock will detect a higher set of profit opportunities, and probably those opportunities with the highest returns. In addition, a higher entrepreneurial human capital stock will be related to a higher decision making ability addressed to enhance the economy efficiency. Second, and from an aggregate perspective, the crucial question could be if individuals that belong to countries or regions more "entrepreneurial" and with high productivity match with countries or regions that are endowed with the highest entrepreneurial human capital stocks at the present.

As we can imagine, the origin of this type of knowledge can be diverse. Several individuals could have some innate abilities that favour their dedication to entrepreneurial activities, while others could acquire this kind of knowledge through experience, or through their participation in formal education processes. Even, and according to this view, a denser entrepreneurial network can generate a positive externality effect on entrepreneurial human capital accumulation. This same situation happens in economies that give great importance to formal education in entrepreneurship.

Hence, the key questions are how we can measure the stock of this specific kind of human capital, and how we can identify the sort of knowledge that must be fostered in order to enhance entrepreneurial human capital. Once this question is solved and their role as determinant for the decision to become entrepreneur and on the success is demonstrated, we must wonder about the most effective methods to accumulate this capital, including the role of the experience and the intergenerational transfers in this process.

The opportunity of this analysis is given by the role given to foster entrepreneurial skills by European authorities as one of the main strategic areas to boost entrepreneurship. However, *The Action Plan*,[2] is unbalanced towards measurements aimed to foster entrepreneurial attitudes (risk) regarding to the relatively scarce tools designed to foster entrepreneurial skills (entrepreneurial human capital).[3]

Focusing on this, we can have serious doubts about the level of effectiveness of some of these measurements on education policies designed to plan the offer

---

activities rather to rent-seeking activities. In an analogous way, Holmes and Schmitz (2001) focus on the role of the "steady of trade" on the extent of unproductive entrepreneurship.

[2] Action Plan: "The European Agenda for Entrepreneurship" (COM (2004), Brussels, 11.02.2004). In Europe, and after the debate opened by the Green Paper on Entrepreneurship, the Commission developed an Action Plan, in which a general framework to foster entrepreneurship has been established. The general diagnosis used as basis for government intervention is that the EU is not fully exploiting its entrepreneurial potential. The Action Plan outlines a series of key actions related to five strategic areas, being one of them the promotion of learning about entrepreneurship in the European education system.

[3] Some exceptions are given by: i) the introduction of entrepreneurship education in universities for students and researchers for all fields, specially in technical universities; ii) the integration of entrepreneurship education into all schools' curricula.

favouring some specific kinds of studies, a policy close to the idea of the "allocation of talent" between productive and unproductive activities. However, the only way to solve this debate is given by the propositions and empirical results derived from the economics of self-employment.

In any case, it seems a priori that education must have a crucial role, at least, in order to: i) encourage more people to become entrepreneurs, increasing required knowledge to search profit opportunities; ii) increase the probability of success (measured in terms of the permanence in self-employment); and, iii) foster economy growth, because the positive correlation between human capital and economic growth is a well-demonstrated effect in literature.

To help us to understand the way in which entrepreneurial human capital operates, we have divided this chapter in three parts clearly differentiated. The first part introduces a selective review of the literature with the aim to set the entrepreneurial human capital concept, and to describe the different ways the entrepreneurial human capital process can operate. The second part focuses on the microeconometric results obtained in the analysis of the occupational choice decision effect of education and their private returns, reviewing the theoretical essays on the connection between education and self-employment. This part also shows a detailed review of the evidence, focusing on the pertinence of proxies used to capture education. Additionally, the effect of education on entrepreneurial success is also considered.

On the other hand, the last part is devoted to provide some additional empirical evidence on the entrepreneurial human capital effects using a set of alternative available proxies to capture some mechanisms through the entrepreneurial human capital accumulation process in order to explore the sensitivity of the results for the proxy used.

12.2 Entrepreneurial Human Capital and Essays of Measurement

As for any other productive factor, the analysis of the offer determinants and of the economic agent willingness to perform their entrepreneurial role will provide us with some keys to understand the entrepreneurial human capital role at the time of deciding to become an entrepreneur.

At first sight, any agent has the chance to offer his effort time to perform the entrepreneurial role. To do so, each agent is endowed with certain capacities derived from abilities and knowledge, either innate or acquired. This knowledge will allow him to evaluate a set of profit opportunities, wider or more limited, depending on the stock owned.

To some extent, the entrepreneurial role is similar to a chemist labour when mixing substances, either to obtain a new compound or to modify an already existing one. Thus, to generate a new productive composition or to improve an already existing one, the entrepreneurial factor will need to use all the knowledge about goods and services demand, factor markets, available technology and entrepreneurial management techniques, to be able to estimate the profit opportunities latent in the market, to generate productive combinations to capture such opportunities, to improve the efficiency of already established activities, or even to innovate.

We will agree that, to perform any of those tasks, to own specific knowledge related to them is crucial. We will refer from now on to this type of specific human capital which contributes directly to improve the way of carrying out any of the vectors playing a role in the performance of the entrepreneurial function, as entrepreneurial human capital.

As the reader will have probably noticed, mechanisms for the accumulation of this type of human capital may be diverse. On the one hand, part of this knowledge will be derived from inherent abilities, from the experience acquired through this participation in the productive process, the one obtained from formal education, that one obtained through intergenerational transfers, or even the experience derived from certain positive externalities, that is, through an informal diffusion of the entrepreneurial culture.

This knowledge arrangement may even become a requirement to become entrepreneur. As a society is becoming more developed in a technological sense, it is possible that the level of entrepreneurial human capital requested to capture profit opportunities increase, becoming, occasionally, a real obstacle preventing the access to the performance of the entrepreneurial role.

In the same way, the complexity of certain entrepreneurial organizations may cause, even during the design stage of a productive combination or a business idea, the necessity of creating work teams, whose members have a specialized human capital able to carry out the different functions of entrepreneurial role.

Thus, if we want to capture the entrepreneurial human capital in only one person, economy or sector, we should try to capture, somehow, both the stock of entrepreneurial knowledge and their processes of accumulation, bearing on mind the existence of several mechanisms, from which this knowledge may be generated.

12.2.1 Education in Entrepreneurship: How to Measure the Stock?

Several studies report that workers with higher levels of education are more likely to be self-employed -Evans and Leighton (1989) or Borjas and Bronars (1989)-. The key question is how can we approach the measurement of this stock?

When we try to measure this stock, we face to the same difficulties, which traditionally human capital measurement has coped with. Consequently, the most intuitive and common way of approaching the human capital stock measurement, in an extra level, is to operationalize entrepreneurship concept through self-employed people, and to quantify human capital stock through the academic level obtained by self-employed people.

Limitations for this way of proceeding are well known: i) the attainment level obtained is an imperfect proxy of the actual level of knowledge, because the knowledge acquired by people of the same level and sort of studies may be different, not only among individuals, but also in territories; ii) not all kinds of studies have the same effect over the productive activities,[4] iii) the formal educative processes are not the only mechanism through which human capital may be acquired; iv) they do not capture entrepreneurial human capital of an economy or sector, but the human capital of those who have already decided to choose this occupation.

The indicators commonly used to measure this stock, usually derives from the exploitation of levels and types of studies in human population surveys, in which the occupation and professional situation of the individuals are known. Using the Labour Force Survey, it is possible to make exchanges between the employed people and the levels and types of studies, or between the different types of employed people, bearing in mind the professional situation or occupation and the levels or the types of studies. Any of these exchanges, provided that the design of the survey allows it according to sampling errors, let us capture the stock of knowledge only to a certain extent. The less accurate approach would be to measure the level of studies of the self-employed people, comparing it with that of the employees, calculating the percentage of employees or self-employed people with medium level or higher level studies. Obviously, following this procedure, we would not be capturing the set of entrepreneurial knowledge of the individuals of an economy, but *expost* verifying if those that have decided to become entrepreneurs have a higher or lower level of studies than those that have decided to become paid-employees.

A different approach, maybe more accurate, (though taking as starting point a priori elements and with some constraints of international comparison) would be to decide, according to the different types of study, the levels and types of study whose contents contribute more directly to the accumulation of entrepreneurial knowledge, and once established those ones, analysing the percentage of the population that has these types of studies with regard to those with a knowledge, whose contents are more distant from the entrepreneurial role performance.

In any case, and leaving aside comparison problems related to curricula differences among the countries, and even in the same type of studies in different educative institutions within the same country, the maximum we could capture using this indicator would be the added result of the accumulation of entrepreneurial human capital through the voluntary participation in formal educational processes, and this implies to consider that acquired capacities are the same among individuals for the same level and type of study.

But even in its role as indicator of the entrepreneurial human capital stock, focusing on the type of study would not allow us to reflect neither inherent entrepreneurial capacities or those acquired through other non-formal processes nor the differences among individuals which have reached the same level and type of study.

---

[4] This problem may be solved by analysing self-employed people by type of study, defining those with more proximate contents to those required for the entrepreneurial role performance.

The use of entrepreneurial abilities *tests* performed among individuals coming from different educational systems with the same level of studies (analogous to those performed to verify the knowledge acquired in different educational systems) could be a good solution to find more accurate indicators.[5]

If we make reference to literature, we will notice that it shows a wide variety of principles at the time of evaluating the effect that education has over the entrepreneurial network.[6] Studies such as those of Evans and Leighton (1989a, 1989b), Blanchflower and Meyer (1994) and Schuetze (2000), among others, conclude that there is a positive relationship between the educational level obtained and the probability of carrying out an enterprising activity.

In relation to this, Ucbasaran et al. (2006) analyse how the general human capital (both educational and labour experience) and the entrepreneurial human capital (experience as company owner, managing abilities and technical capabilities) have an effect on the searching and identification of business opportunities. They find that those entrepreneurs with a higher level of human capital identify and pursue a higher number of business opportunities. Also, the entrepreneurial human capital appears more strongly related to both variables than the general human capital.

Parker and Van Praag (2006) distinguish between the way of accessing to the entrepreneurial network and the decision of accessing itself. They consider two different ways to access to the entrepreneurial network: starting a new business or continuing an already existing one. This distinction is quite interesting, since policies have to be different if we want to foster the expansion of the entrepreneurial network or to keep the already existing one. They study the specific features which favour one or the other way of accessing and conclude that those people with a higher educational level and richness choose to access to entrepreneurial network through the first mechanism, that is, to start a new business, whereas based on the previous experience in managing roles, the necessary requirements to restart a business and the risk, they choose to continue with an already established business.

There are also studies in which earnings functions are analysed and conclude that formal education and qualifications increase the incomes. Van der Sluis et al. (2006)

---

[5] Recently, Van der Sluis and Van Praag (2006) have observed a positive influence of the general intelligence on the incomes obtained, and argue that such an influence in the labour activity performance is due mainly to the effect of intelligence on the acquisition of knowledge applicable in the working centre and in the reaction in complex situations. With regard to the specific abilities and capacities, they observed that both technical capability and managing capability have a deep, positive effect on the entrepreneurial results, whereas the effect of social capabilities is positively significant, but smaller.

[6] Reader will have notice the conscious omission of the impact of education on the entrepreneurial spirit. We think it is advisable to distinguish between the possession of knowledge about entrepreneurial techniques and abilities from the transfer, through formal education, of a social image of the entrepreneurial activity as positive model encouraging this way the enterprising spirit. We are interested in capturing, among other things, the role played by the educational system on the acquisition of abilities and capacities that allow to capture profit opportunities, not as a mechanism through which modifying attitudes towards risk. This last guideline is explicitly included in the Action Plan of the European Union.

study the human capital performance, particularly formal education influence, both for entrepreneurs and employees. They find the education performance is higher for entrepreneurs than for employees. This could be due to the smaller number of organizational limitations which the entrepreneurs face to when optimising the more profitable use of their education with regard to those of the employees. Firms provide with better chances of optimising the education of the individuals and their corresponding performance, so those entrepreneurs with higher educational levels are related to better entrepreneurial results in terms of benefits, incomes, growth and survival.

On the other hand, Bhattacharjee et al. (2006) show that the impact of education in the survival of new businesses is greater for firms created by individuals which have had a previous labour experience on their preferred activity branch, whereas it is limited for others. To constitute a firm may constitute a way of continuing working in the preferred activity sector, avoiding in this way the depreciation of human capital, which can be observed on those who are unemployed or working in a different sector not related to their abilities.

12.2.2 Other Entrepreneurial Human Capital Acquisition Mechanisms

If we have already stated that it is difficult to create indicators to measure the output of entrepreneurial human capital resulting from the investment process on education, it is even more complex to find indicators to capture other ways of acquisition. Thus, to measure the accumulation of entrepreneurial human capital not resulting from a voluntary decision, such as the one resulting from the learning by doing[7] or from intergenerational transfers of entrepreneurial knowledge, we will have to use different proxies derived from population surveys exploitations, where with different accuracy we can use data related to labour history of the individuals or even to indicators elaborated from the analysis of social and labour features of the ancestors. In this sense, the previous experience in the activity sector by the individuals changing to self-employment or the fact of having had previous experiences in this field are commonly used indicators trying to capture the concept of "learning by doing", whereas the data related to educational levels or professional situation of the ancestors or relatives have been used as proxies for the entrepreneurial human capital acquired through intergenerational transfers.

In this sense, experience, for instance, has been used to be proxied by a variable constructed as current age minus school-leaving age. This is an imperfect measurement since it takes no account of breaks from labor force participation in individuals' work histories. On the other hand, the previous experiences to self-employment,

---

[7] Perhaps we could also include here the concept of "learning by exporting" coined by Grossman and Helpman (1991).

or the experience of ancestors and relatives in self-employment have also been used to capture, to some extent, this type of mechanisms.

To act systematically, a good strategy to approach to the dimensions and aspects being measured and also to the essays of measurement of this type of human capital, may be through the review of the essays of measurement of entrepreneurial human capital and their accumulation processes, in the empirical analysis of self-employment.

12.3 Measurement Approaches and Results

As we have stated, the main problem this empirical literature faces to is how to approximate to different human capital variables with the available information. We have discussed, as starting point, about the concept and the dimensions considered in order to maintain (from different perspectives and depending on its origin) the entrepreneurial human capital stock and its sources, using the available statistical sources and indicators

The primary statistical sources to extract indicators on entrepreneurial human capital endowments are Human Population Surveys. In fact, Labour Force Surveys or households panels usually include some variables about educational attainment, the type of studies completed and the labour history of the individuals and their parents.

Making an abstraction of the precision of this type of indicators in our attempt to measure the entrepreneurial human capital, these indicators have been used to analyse the role of education from four types of studies: these indicators has been used to analyse the role of education in the decision to change to self-employment, in the analysis of the duration into self-employment, and in the study of education returns in self-employment. Although, more relatively poor, there are some essays devoted to the analysis of the contribution of entrepreneurship education to economy growth, from a macroeconometric approach, using aggregate data.

Our goal is to study in depth the exact role played by the entrepreneurial human capital, using the available indicators, both in the decision to change to self-employment and in its role for success, using alternative proxies to detect the accuracy of the results in relation to the proxies used.

To undertake this task, and from a microeconometric approach, using microdata from population surveys, we present some new evidences about the role of the formal education, the experience (training or learning by doing, proxied through previous experience or even by the duration in employment), and the role of inter-generational transfers of entrepreneurial abilities on the probability to change to self-employment and on the probability of survival in self-employment.

These exercises are designed with a double aim: first of all, as an optimum presentation strategy of the common problems which have to be faced to by this type of estimations due to the use of the proxies already mentioned to capture the human capital and to have an idea of the accuracy of the results in relation to the proxy used.

Specifically, we are interested in knowing the effect of the selection bias (abilities: innate or acquired), in discussing about the relevancy of the variables, which try to capture the entrepreneurial human capital, at least in four directions: i) first of all, because in the best case, the use of these proxies would allow us to capture the formal education effects; ii) knowing if all acquired knowledge is equally effective to develop the entrepreneurial function; iii) what is the role of study sector interacting with educational level?, and finally; iv) if educational levels cross country are comparables.

In previous literature, the effect of entrepreneurial human capital has been tested at least from four perspectives or approaches. First, there are studies that explore the effects of different human capital proxies (age, experience, level or type of education, or parental status as proxy of the intergenerational transfer of entrepreneurial abilities) on the probability of being or becoming self-employed. These are self-employment selection models. Second, there are papers that are also interested in the effects of those human capital variables in the duration on the self-employment. Other studies are focused on the returns of these variables. These are works on self-employment earnings functions. Finally, there are a more scarce literature exploring the relationship between economy growth and different mechanisms of the entrepreneurial human capital accumulation process. Taking into account our main aim, we will be focused on the first two approaches.

As we have mentioned above, the main problem this empirical literature faces to is how to approximate the different human capital variables with the available information. In this sense, experience, for instance, is used to be proxied by a variable constructed as current age minus school-leaving age. This is an imperfect measurement, since it takes no account for breaks from labour force participation in individuals' labour histories. Education is usually measured either as years of education completed or as a set of dummy variables for specific qualifications. Neither of these proxies is perfect.

Using different proxies and different econometric specifications, as well as different data sources may explain the divergent results in this empirical literature. In this section, we review the main results obtained, and we present some new evidences, designed in order to prove some difficulties associated to the proxy or even to the sample used. We start with the effects of age, experience and education in self-employment selection and duration models, and finally we review the intergenerational transfer effects.

12.3.1 Entrepreneurial Human Capital as Necessary Condition to Become Entrepreneur: The Role of Formal Education

It is a common feature for first empirical jobs, in which the determinants of the transition to self-employment are analysed, the attempt to check the hypothesis that sets that older workers or those with greater previous experience have accumulated entrepreneurial abilities and business relationships and, therefore, the age or experience should increase the probability of becoming an entrepreneur. The essays of Evans and Leighton (1989a), Blanchflower and Meyer (1994), Schuetze (2000), Clark and Drinkwater (1998), Rees and Shah (1986), Fujii and Hawley (1991), Robinson and Sexton (1994), Bates (1995), Boden (1996), Blanchflower (2000), Flota and Mora (2001), Lofstrom (2002), Clark, Drinkwater and Leslie (1998), and Moore and Mueller (2002), among others, find evidences that show the existence of a positive relation between the age and the probability of being an entrepreneur, though we will have to admit that the proximity between the indicator and the dimension to be measured is not too satisfactory.

Evans and Leighton (1989a) performed a logit analysis for USA using separate estimations for white men and white women. In both cases, the effect of age (measured as age, age squared and age cube in the men estimation, and as a set of dummy variables for each of eight age categories in the women case) on the probability of being self-employed is significant and positive, so age is considered a strong determinant of the self-employment rate. Also in both cases, the frequency of self-employment increases with the amount of education, measured as the proportion of each age cohort which had attained the following educational levels: less than high-school, high-school, less than college, college and graduate school. The results of this essay fit with those expected. Since it might be the case that older workers have accumulated entrepreneurial abilities, savings and business links making them more likely to be self-employed, it might be expected that older and more experienced people become entrepreneurs. Also it may be expected that higher levels of education promote entrepreneurship because people with higher education are better informed about business opportunities. In that sense, there are several essays that report the same findings. Also for USA, Blanchflower and Meyer (1994), using the US Survey of Income and Program Participation conducted by the US Bureau of the Census of the period 1983-1986, and with education proxied by years of schooling and Scheutze (2000), making use of US Current Population Surveys for the period 1983-1994, obtain the same results. The first essay also analyses duration and they found that older entrepreneurs are significantly more likely to succeed. The same results for UK are reported by Clark and Drinkwater (1998) with data from the General Household Survey from 1973 to 1995 and from the 1991 Census Sample of Anonymised Records.[8]

Despite these results being reasonable and expected, there are studies in which the results are different from those. There are works that report no significant age effects, but positive educational effects on the probability of being self-employed. This is the case of Evans and Leighton (1989b), who performed an analysis for USA with data of the National Longitudinal Survey for 1966-1981 and the Current Population Surveys for 1968-1987. They found that the probability to change to self- employment is roughly independent of age; that the years of wage experience

---

[8] Rees and Shah (1986), Fujii and Hawley (1991), Robison and Sexton (1994), Bates (1995), Boden (1996), Blanchflower (2000), Flota and Mora (2001), Lofstrom (2002), and Moore and Mueller (2002) are other essays with similar results.

are neither statistically nor substantively significant, but the probability of access is higher for individuals who have had prior self-employment experience; and that the relationship between educational attainment (years of education) and the probability of being or becoming self-employed is positive. Finally, they found that the probability of leaving self-employment decreases with duration in self-employment.

However, essays with the opposite results are more frequent. Blanchflower and Meyer (1994) use Australian Longitudinal Survey of 1985–1988 and report no education effects and non linear relationship between age and the probability of self-employment. In relation to duration, they found that unlike for the USA, in Australia, the probability of moving out of self-employment is not higher the younger the individual is. Those with lower levels of education and some of the most qualified were especially likely to leave self-employment. Taylor (1996) for UK uses the first wave of a large scale British panel data set, the British Household Panel Study and reports a clear relationship between age (age and age squared) and the probability of being self-employed, whereas education (degree, other higher qualification, A levels, O levels, other qualifications) plays a little role. Schuetze (2000) with data from the Canadian Surveys of Consumer Finances for 1983–1994 explains significant and positive relationship of age and self-employment and unlike what is typically found, the higher education had almost no effect on the probability of being self-employment for Canadian men. For UK, Clark and Drinkwater (2002) using the Fourth National Survey of Ethnic Minorities (199–1994), and the 1991 Census Sample of Anonymous Records obtain that for men and women, self-employment tendency increases with age, but a diminishing rate: But education (degree, vocational qualification, A levels, O levels, apprenticeship and no stated qualifications) is not a strong determinant of self-employment status. In this essay, education level is a much stronger predictor of whether an individual is in paid-employment versus unemployment, with those with higher qualifications more likely to be employed.[9]

And also, there are studies with positive age effects and negative education effects. Clark, Drinkwater and Leslie (1998) used pooled years of the General Household Survey over the period 1973–1995 to study human capital earnings functions for the self-employed people. They found that regardless the ethnicity, older people and those without formal qualifications are more likely to be found in self-employment. Blanchflower, Oswald and Stutzer (2001) used International Social Survey Program data set for 1997–1998 for 23 nations, and reported that the probability of being self-employed is strongly increasing in age, whereas this probability is lower among high education educated workers.

All the above analysis has a common starting point. In all of them, and not taking into account the proxy used, the estimation strategy goes through the specification of discrete choice models, in which the probability of changing to self-employment -regardless the initial state considered- depends on a set of individual and economic environment characteristics, whose relationships derive from the traditional problem

---

[9] Other studies with the same type of results are Schiller and Crewson (1997) for USA and Maxim (1992) for Canada.

of occupation choice. However, in most of the referenced works, and in many cases due to the limitations imposed by the data base used, these models are estimated without bearing on mind that the factors, and even the way these determine the decision of changing to self-employment, may vary according to the initial state. In the same way, most of these essays do not consider the existence of variants between the different types of self-employment.

Focusing on the effects this estimation strategy could have on the significance, and even the sign of the proxies used to measure the effect of education on the decision of becoming an entrepreneur, in the table below we can see the result of estimations of the probability to change from paid-employment to the different types of self-employment using the 8 waves of the PHOGHE for the 15 countries of the EU in 1994–2001, showing some of the proxies traditionally used to capture the effect of the entrepreneurial human capital on the probability to change to self-employment. In this Table 12.1, from which we have excluded (to be clear enough) those explicative non-educational variables, we have evidences supporting the idea that there is a greater probability to change, whatever the type of self-employment considered as final state, among those who own a higher education. This probability is measured based on the level of the studies completed.

On the other hand, Table 12.2 above shows the effects of these same variables, but focusing now on the change from unemployment. As in the previous case, we find evidences about the existence of a strong positive effect of the education level on the change to self-employment.

However, the results obtained are conditioned by at least the following elements: i) we have to add the difficulties implied by the characteristics of our sample, including individuals from 15 countries with different educational systems, to the elements which limit the accuracy of the level of studies completed as a proxy of the stock of entrepreneurial human capital; ii) the results seem to indicate that the consideration of a single final state may affect the significance and magnitude of the effects.

Table 12.1 Effects of Education on the Change from Paid-employment to Self-employment

Final State	Self-employed	Employer	Own-account worker
Transition	Prob [SE t | PW t-1]	Prob [EMP t | PW t-1]	Prob [OA t | PW t-1]
Number of transfers	2931	1778	1153
	–8,0571	–9,8283	–7,3464
Constant	(–20,52)	(–19,22)	(–12,29)
Self-employed	0,4909	0,4909	0,3569
relatives	(8,89)	(8,36)	(3,94)
Secondary educa-	0,1054	0,1451	0,0692
tion (2)	(2,1)	(2,27)	(0,88)
University studies	0,4508	0,586	0,2704
(2)	(8,07)	(8,08)	(3,22)

Reference categories: (1) Non-cohabiting individuals, (2) No education or primary education, (3) Public sector, (4) Industrial sector, (5) Large or very large firm (>49 employees), (6) Non-indefinite contract, (7) Spain

Table 12.2 Effects of Education on the Change from Unemployment to Self-employment

Final State	Self-employed	Employer	Own-account worker
Transition	Prob [SE t | PW t-1]	Prob [EMP t | PW t-1]	Prob [OA t | PW t-1]
Number of transfers	836	342	494
Constant	–4,5783	–4,9024	–5,6494
	(–6,51)	(–4,42)	(–6,48)
Age	0,0957	0,0345	0,1391
	(2,99)	(0,72)	(3,43)
Age*Age	–0,0016	–0,001	–0,0021
	(–3,93)	(–1,62)	(–3,96)
Self-employed relatives	0,6983	0,6216	0,7528
	(6,93)	(4,1)	(6,11)
Secondary education (2)	0,4824	0,5365	0,4558
	(5,37)	(3,99)	(4,01)
University studies (2)	0,9613	1,1924	0,8373
	(8,57)	(6,92)	(6,07)

(1) Non-cohabiting individuals, (2) No education or primary education, (3) Spain

12.3.2 The Type of Study and the Intergenerational Transfer of Entrepreneurial Human Capital

It is an accepted stylised fact that workers who have self-employed parents are more likely to be self-employed than those who do not.[10] From this finding, they conclude that the transfer of human capital is the important channel to explain the intergenerational correlation of self-employment status.

Dunn and Holtz-Eakin (2000) undertake a study for USA with National Longitudinal Surveys of Labour Market Experience. They report no significant effects of age on self-employment, and also, no significant effects of education (considered as various educational levels: less than high school, high school, some college, college graduate and post college) in self-employment. Nevertheless, they found strong correlation (positive effect) of self-employment experience of the parents and the probability of being self-employed. Parents' self-employment experience has a very large and significant effect, just about doubling the probability of the son accessing to self-employment. Fathers have a strong influence and mothers have a weak and insignificant influence on son's self-employment. Having two self-employed parents have the strongest effect. The mother's effect is strongest for daughters,

---

[10] Some studies follow the same line. Thus, among the participants in the Eurobarometer, the children of the own-account workers were more prone to work by their own account than those of the employees, whereas the Global Monitoring Entrepreneurship reveals that those individuals trusting on their competencies and experience have a probability of creating a new company or manage it, which is two to seven times higher and, in the case of those who know someone who have created an enterprise recently, the probability is approx. three to four times higher. The British Household Survey shows a higher probability of seriously consider the creation of a business among those people who have been previously in contact with the entrepreneurial initiative (through friends, family or education).

although father's effect and the "both" effect are also strong and significant. The interpretation might be that entrepreneurial tastes or abilities are also transferred more strongly from parents to children of the same gender. They also report that the sons of more successful entrepreneurs are more likely to access self-employment than sons of less successful entrepreneurs.[11]

Although in the estimation presented for transfers to self-employment in Europe, and using the existence of self-employed relatives as a proxy of this mechanism of human capital accumulation, we have showed evidences of a strong and positive effect on the probability to change to the self-employment, we can try to search the use of more accurate proxies using an alternative sample.

Thus, Table 12.3 shows the results of the estimation of a probit, in which the probability to become an entrepreneur depends on a set of individual features and on a series of economic environment variables. The exercise, undertaken with the microdata of the second quarter in 2000 of the Spanish Labour Force Survey, will allow us to try a series of alternative proxies[12], since for interviewed people it is possible to know a set of additional socio-educational characteristics and, at the same time, to count with information about educational levels and professional status of the parents, regardless they are in the sample or not.

Although the use of this sample have the inconveniences of not allowing us the use of income proxies, of not observing transfers, but self-employed individuals and in spite of being limited to people between 16 and 35 years old, the estimation with this sample allow us to test other proxies and, at the same time, to check once

Table 12.3 Participation probit (EPA, II/2000)

Final State	Self-employment		Employer		.Own-account	
Human capital proxy	Coef.	p-value	Coef.	p-value	Coef.	p-value
Age	0,1916	0,000	0,1910	0,000	0,2006	0,000
Age2	–0,0020	0,000	–0,0020	0,000	–0,0018	0,012
Experience	0,0121	0,000	0,0110	0,000	0,0170	0,084
Experience2	0,0000	0,000	–0,0000	0,000	–0,0000	0,000
Secondary School	0,0092	0,922	–0,0493	0,626	0,2703	0,195
Higher School	–0,5568	0,000	–0,5432	0,000	–0,6436	0,029
Engineers and Busines-sAdministration	0,2869	0,164	0,1761	0,457	0,6095	0,000
Lawyer, architects	–1,4160	0,012	–1,227	0,003	–22,50	0,118
Parents Higher School	0,1727	0,002	0,0503	0,564	0,6940	0,001
Father self-employed	0,1419	0,039	0,1963	0,009	–0,1054	0,500
Mother self-employed	0,1163	0,012	0,0215	0,797	0,5185	0,000

---

[11] Also, Laband and Lentz (1983) and Evans and Leighton (1989b) for USA, and Taylor (1996) for UK report positive and significant effects of having a self-employed parent on the probability of being self-employed.

[12] The choice of this period is due to the fact that in this period, together with the variables considered in each period, an additional module is added, consisting of all those individuals that in the referenced period left their studies for the first time. They are individuals with ages between 16 and 35 years old, who have leaved or interrupted their studies during more than one year.

more the effects of experience and level of studies on the probability to become self-employed.

The backward elements used in our estimation of a probit of participation in the self-employment involve variables included in the Spanish Force Survey about the level of studies completed and the type of studies and, at the same time, we incorporate both dummies to collect the effect of education and the type of occupation of the parents on the children's occupation choice.

From the results obtained, and together with the positive effect of the previous experience, it seems a bit surprising the lack of significance of the dummy of secondary education and the negative effect of the completion of a higher education. It seems that, among those who access for the first time to the labour market upon completing their studies, the level of studies allow them to issue a signal, which makes easier the receipt of paid-employment offers and decreases the choice of self-employment as occupation.

The second hypothesis we would like to check is if those types of studies more related to the learning of entrepreneurial abilities (mainly technical studies and business administration studies) foster the choice of self-employment as occupation among those who abandon studies for the first time. Although the result is not significant for all self-employed people, it seems to be a clearly positive effect of the bachelors in Engineering and those in Business Administration on the chance of becoming employer with employees, being this an effect not observed neither for lawyers nor architects. However, this last type of study seems to be positively related to the chance of becoming an own-account worker.

Finally, and according to the analysis of the mechanisms of knowledge intergenerational transfers, the educational level of the parents, and specially those having parents who are self-employed, seems to have a positive effect on the probability to become also self-employed.

12.3.3 Entrepreneurial Human Capital in Duration Models

However, most empirical studies have focused on the decision to access to self-employment. These essays contribute to detect and explain the variables, which make an individual to make the decision of accessing to self-employment, but not necessarily the variables which make an individual to be successful in self-employment. One clear trend in the literature analyses the determinants of firm's survival (see, for example, Segarra and Callejón (1999), Esteve, Sanchis and Sanchis (2004a, 2004b), Esteve and Máñez (2004) Esteve et al. (2005) for Spain, and Jorgensen (2005), for Denmark).

However, to the best of our knowledge, just a few exceptions have been working in order to explore the determinants of the individual success within self-employment measured in terms of survival on this state. The essays of Evans and Leighton (1989), Bates (1990), Holtz-Eakin et al. (1994), Holmes and Schmitz (1996), Taylor (1999), for the UK, Carrasco (1999), for Spain, Johansson (2000), for Finland, or Falter (2002), for Switzerland, or Reize (2004), for Germany, can be considered as examples in which the duration in self-employment can be considered as an indicator to measure success.

The starting point of this type of works is the analysis of the duration in self-employment. Let T, the number of years the individual is self-employed. The distribution of this variable can be characterized by means of the following hazard function or exit rate:

$$\varphi(t) = P(T = t \setminus T \geq t) \tag{12.1}$$

where, $\varphi(t)$ is the probability of being self-employed, for exactly t years relative to the group of individuals who have been self-employed for at least t years (given survival up until time t).

In this line, by using a panel data sample from the European Community Household Panel (ECHP, EU-15) for the period 1994–2001, we estimate some single and competing risk duration models, to study the underlying determinants of self-employment success, measured in terms of survival on this state. In general our results support the fact that formal education is positively associated with the probability to survive in self-employment. We interpret this result as an indicative of how education enhances an individual's human capital and enable the discovery and exploitation of more efficiently business opportunities. The probability to survive in self-employment, *conditional on not having left self-employment before 1994* increases with duration in self-employment (decreasing hazard rate), for employers (vs. own-account workers, perhaps due to the existence of higher exit costs), for individuals endowed with higher education levels (vs. medium, basic and no education), and with previous experience in self-employment.

12.4 Conclusions

To summarize, we can observe that empirical literature on entrepreneurial human capital has different results, either in models of self-employment choice and duration or in earnings functions models. That is, the results are highly weak and sensitive to changes in the proxies used to approximate the different variables, in the econometric specifications and in the samples used.

The use of different proxies and different econometric specifications, as well as the different data sources, may explain the divergent results in this empirical literature.

Perhaps, inverse results are conditioned by problems associated to samples. Estimations include only transfers within a small period and we consider only new entrepreneurs characteristics.

In any case, we can infer from our study that it is required studying in depth the development of proxies, which allow to capture the entrepreneurial human capital and its accumulation processes. In this sense, import and adaptation of the measurement methods of the human capital reveal as an appropriate strategy. Thus, the problems which measurement of human capital must face to are shared by the measurement of this specific type of human capital. The use of self-employment data, by education level, by sector of study, or by experience, can be a first strategic approach to the entrepreneurial human capital measurement. However, in order to move forward in the international analysis and comparisons, we must to progress in the development of international quality Education Surveys, emphasizing on entrepreneurial abilities, and on the field of comparable international series.

We have also to progress in the definition of those types of studies and abilities which we consider specifically related to the performance of the entrepreneurial role and also in how to measure the entrepreneurial capital, not only for self-employed, but for any individual.

Finally, once this measurement is achieved, we would need to focus on the analysis of the matching between the entrepreneurial human capital and professional human capital, that is, between the adequacy of the type of human capital requested to employees by the entrepreneurial network of a specific sector.

References

Alba-Ramírez A (1994) Self-employment in the midst of unemployment: The case of Spain and the United States. Applied Economics 26:189-204

Baumol WJ (1968) Entrepreneurship in Economic Theory. American Economic Review Papers and Proceedings 58:64-71

Baumol WJ (1990) Entrepreneurship: Productive, Unproductive and Destructive. Journal of Political Economy 98:893-921

Blanchflower DG (2000) Self-employment in OECD countries. Labour Economics 7:471-505

Blanchflower DG, Meyer BD (1994) A longitudinal analysis of the young self-employed in Australia ands the United States. Small Business Economics 6:1-19

Blanchflower DG, Oswald A, Stutzer A (2001) Latent Entrepreneurship across nations. European Economic Review 45:680-91

Clark K, Drinkwater S (1998) Ethnicity and self-employment in Britain. Oxford Bulletin of Economics and Statistics 60:383-407

Clark K, Drinkwater S (2002) Enclaves neighbourhood effects and employment outcomes: ethnic minorities in England and Wales. Labour Economics 7:603-28

Commission of The European Communities (2004) Action Plan: The European agenda for Entrepreneurship, Brussels 11022004 COM(2004) 70 final

Commission of The European Communities (2005) Progress report on the implementation of Phase I key actions of the Action Plan: The European Agenda for Entrepreneurship.Commission Staff Working Paper Brussels 06062005 SEC(2005) 768

Dunn T, Holtz-Eakin D (2000) Financial capital human capital and the transition to self-employment: evidence from intergenerational links. Journal of Labour Economics 18:282-305

Evans DS, Leighton LS (1989a) The determinants of changes in US self-employment 1968-1987. Small Business Economics 1:111-19

Evans DS, Leighton LS (1989b) Some empirical aspects of entrepreneurship. American Economic Review 79:519-35

Fairlie RW, Meyer BD (1996) Ethnic and racial self-employment differences and possible explanations. Journal of Human Resources 31:757-93

Flota C, Mora MT (2001) The earnings of self-employed Mexican-Americans along the US-Mexico border. Annals of Regional Science 35:483-99

Fujii ET, Hawley CB (1991) Empirical aspects of self-employment. Economic Letters 36:323-29

García-Mainar I, Montuenga-Gómez VM (2005) Education returns of wage earners and self-employed workers: Portugal vs Spain. Economics of Education Review 24:161-70

Hamilton BH (2000) Does entrepreneurship pay? An empirical analysis of the returns to self-employment. Journal of Political Economy 108:604-31

Holmes TJ, Schmitz JA (2001) A gain from trade: From unproductive to productive entrepreneurship. Journal of Monetary Economics 47:417-46

Kawaguchi D (2002) Human Capital accumulation of salaried and self-employed workers. Labour Economics 10:55-71

Laband DN, Lentz BF (1983) Like father like son: toward an economic theory of occupational following. Southern Economic Journal 50:474-93

Lofstrom M (2002) Labour market assimilation and the self-employment decision of immigrant entrepreneurs. Journal of Population Economics 15:83-114

Maxim PS (1992) Immigrants visible minorities and self-employment. Demography 29:181-98

Moore CS, Mueller RE (2002) The transition from paid to self-employment in Canada: the importance of push factors. Applied Economics 34:791-801

Murphy KM, Shleifer A, Vishny R (1991) The Alloaction of Talent: Implications for Growth. The Quaterly Journal of Economics 106(2):503-30

Parker SC (2004) The economics of self-employment and entrepreneurship. Cambridge University Press, Cambridge

Rees H , Shah A (1986) An empirical analysis of self-employment in the UK. Journal of Applied Econometrics 1:95-108

Robison PB, Sexton EA (1994) The effect of education and experience on self-employment success. Journal of Business Venturing 9:141-56

Schuetze HJ (2000) Taxes economic conditions and recent trends in male self-employment: a Canada-US comparison. Labour Economics 7:507-44

Schultz TW (1975) The Value of the Ability to Deal with Disequilibria. Journal of Economic Literature 13(3):827-46

Schiller BR, Crewson PE (1997) Entrepreneurial origins: a longitudinal inquiry. Economic Inquiry 35:523-31

Spence M (1973) Job market signalling. Quarterly Journal of Economics 87:355-74

Taylor MP (1996) Earnings independence or unemployment: Why become self-employed? Oxford Bulletin of Economics and Statistics 58:253-66

Chapter 13
Global Entrepreneurship Monitor and Entrepreneurs' Export Orientation

Jolanda Hessels and André van Stel

Abstract The Global Entrepreneurship Monitor (GEM) presents an annual assessment of the national level of 'early-stage' entrepreneurial activity and the institutional conditions to which it is subject in a large number of countries. Within the framework of GEM a TEA (Total early-stage Entrepreneurial Activity) index has been developed to measure (early-stage) entrepreneurial activity. Next to this TEA index, the GEM also provides an indicator for the prevalence of *export-oriented* entrepreneurs within countries. This chapter presents an example of an empirical analysis using macro-level GEM data for 36 countries. More specifically, this chapter investigates whether the presence of export-oriented entrepreneurs is a more important determinant of economic growth than entrepreneurial activity in general. Our results suggest that export-oriented entrepreneurship is indeed more important for achieving high economic growth rates than entrepreneurial activity in general.

JEL-classification: F23, L25, L26, O47, O57

Keywords: Global Entrepreneurship Monitor, entrepreneurship, export, economic growth

13.1 Introduction

The Global Entrepreneurship Monitor (GEM), a worldwide research project, presents an annual assessment of the national level of early-stage entrepreneurial activity and the institutional conditions to which it is subjected in a large number of countries. A TEA (Total early-stage Entrepreneurial Activity) index has been developed to be able to measure early-stage entrepreneurial activity within countries. This index is a combination of nascent entrepreneurs (those currently involved in

Jolanda Hessels
EIM Business and Policy Research, Zoetermeer, The Netherlands
joh@eim.nl

concrete activities to set up a new business) and owners of young businesses (those currently owning a business that is less than 42 months old). Furthermore, within the framework of GEM also an indicator has been developed for export activity among new or early-stage entrepreneurs. An important focus of the GEM project involves the exploration of the role of entrepreneurship in national economic growth.

Entrepreneurship is considered an important mechanism of economic development (Schumpeter 1934; Baumol 2002) and for developing competitive economies (Hawkins, 1993). For example, entrepreneurs may contribute to economic growth because they are important for introducing or generating innovations (Autio, 1994; Acs and Audretsch, 2003). In particular, entrepreneurs contribute to a process of variety and selection where many individual entrepreneurs pursue an observed market opportunity and try to economically exploit a new idea. However, due to an increased uncertainty in the global knowledge economy, it is not clear a priori which of these different new ideas are economically viable (Audretsch and Thurik, 2000). Only after setting up a new business, entrepreneurs find out what consumers prefer and hence, whether their new ideas are economically viable. Most of these new ideas will not be economically viable but some of them will be. The successful ideas often turn into innovations. When there are more entrepreneurs pursuing new ideas, the level of competition is higher and the process of variety (i.e. a large number of different new ideas being pursued) and selection will be more intense. From an economy-wide point of view this higher intensity increases the probability of actual innovations taking place (i.e. of economically viable ideas being 'selected' through the market). Several studies confirm a positive impact of entrepreneurship on national economic growth for developed countries (see e.g. van Stel, 2006).

There is increased attention for firms that are involved in international activity from inception or shortly thereafter. Such firms are commonly referred to as 'born globals' (Rennie, 1993; Knight & Cavusgil, 1996), or 'international new ventures' (Oviatt & McDougall, 1994). There is evidence that the number of born globals or international new ventures is increasing (Oviatt & McDougall, 1994). Born global firms are thought to be of importance in terms of innovation and employment (Moen, 2002). However, only a few empirical studies have investigated the effect of export on business performance among new ventures (Bloodgood et al., 1996; McDougall & Oviatt, 1996; Zahra et al. 2000). Furthermore, whereas it is generally acknowledged that internationally oriented new ventures are important in terms of economic growth (Moen, 2002) to our knowledge, this link has not been investigated empirically. We aim to extend the literature on new venture export activity and growth by focusing on the country level. In particular the present chapter builds on the assumption that exporting entrepreneurs develop specific skills (including innovative skills) through their export activity and, consequently, a high number of exporting entrepreneurs may be even more conducive to the process of variety and selection described above, compared to high numbers of domestically operating entrepreneurs. In other words, high numbers of exporting entrepreneurs may have a particularly strong impact on competition, innovation and economic growth.

To summarize, in studying the relationship between entrepreneurial activity and growth we expect that in particular export-oriented entrepreneurship will make an important contribution to economic growth. Therefore, we will investigate in this chapter whether the presence of export-oriented entrepreneurship makes a more important contribution to national economic growth than entrepreneurial activity in general. This issue is of specific interest to policy-makers since governments in many countries have developed programs that focus on the promotion of export activity.

The chapter is structured as follows. Section 2 presents an overview of the GEM project and some of its main indices. Subsequently, in Section 3, an example is provided of how GEM data may be used for empirical analysis. In this section we present the data and research method. In Section 4 we present the results of our empirical analysis of the association of the presence of export-oriented entrepreneurs and national economic growth. Finally, in Section 5 we discuss the outcomes and conclusions.

13.2 Global Entrepreneurship Monitor: Entrepreneurial Activity, Export Orientation and Economic Growth

13.2.1 GEM Project: Objectives, Methods and Measures

The Global Entrepreneurship Monitor (GEM) project was initiated in 1999 with ten participating countries, expanded rapidly in its early years to 21 countries in the year 2000, 29 countries in 2001 and to 37 countries in 2002. In 2006 there were 42 national teams. The GEM research program provides an annual assessment of the national level of entrepreneurial activity within countries. The research program is based on a harmonized assessment of the level of national entrepreneurial activity for all participating countries. It also involves the exploration of the role of entrepreneurship in national economic growth. There are systematic differences between countries. Some countries that reflect low economic growth have a high level of entrepreneurial activity. The GEM program is a major effort aimed at describing and analyzing entrepreneurial processes within a wide range of countries.

The GEM program focuses on the following main objectives:

- to measure differences in the level of entrepreneurial activity between countries; various measures for entrepreneurial activity, according to various stages of the business cycle.
- to uncover factors that lead to appropriate levels of entrepreneurship, and
- to suggest policies that may enhance the national level of entrepreneurial activity; The GEM results may provide useful suggestions for policy makers. For example, the GEM results shows that the share of informal investors in the adult population is low in the Netherlands from an international perspective. Results from GEM have also indicated that informal investment is an important source of start-up capital for new and starting firms. This may call for policies to enhance the number of informal investors/stimulate more people to invest in other people businesses by creating adequate mechanisms.

As part of the GEM research different types of data are collected:

- Adult Population Survey (APS): This is a representative population survey of adults that is held every year in each participating country. In each country at least 2,000 adults take part in a telephone interview. One part of the questionnaire consists of items related to participation in entrepreneurial activities. These activities refer to starting a new firm, owning and managing a new firm and informally investing in another's new firm (informal investors). The other part of the questionnaire aims to assess attitudes and perceptions towards entrepreneurship and knowledge of the entrepreneurial climate.
- Standardized questionnaires completed by experts in each country. This questionnaire contains a series of statements concerning entrepreneurial framework conditions in a country, such as financial support, government policies and programs (e.g. aimed at stimulating female entrepreneurship, high growth firms), education and training, attitudes, cultural and social norms, innovation & technology transfer etc.
- The GEM co-ordination team collects standardized cross-national data on a variety of national characteristics and attributes (e.g. GDP, growth in GDP, exports) from a wide range of harmonized international sources.
- Every year an executive global report is published, see e.g. Acs et al. (2005). Also, most national teams publish their own national reports. Furthermore, GEM data is used by researchers for scientific purposes (see for example Reynolds et al., 2005).
- The principal objective of the GEM project is to measure early-stage entrepreneurial activity for each country, and to do this in such a harmonized way that comparisons between countries can be made. To this end the so-called Total early-stage Entrepreneurial Activity or TEA-index is calculated. The TEA index is a combination of identifying:
- nascent entrepreneurs: people currently involved in concrete activities to set up a new business; Nascent entrepreneneurs are those individuals between the ages of 18 and 64 years, who have taken some action toward creating a new business in the past year. To qualify for this category, these individuals must also expect to own a share of the business they are starting and the business must not have paid any wages or salaries for more than three months.
- owner/managers of young businesses: people currently owing a business that is less than 42 months old. The entrepreneurs report that they are active as owner/managers of new firms that have paid wages or salaries for more than three months, but less than 42 months.

The sum of these two measurements allows GEM to calculate the prevalence rates of early-stage entrepreneurial activity in each country. The people that qualify for early-stage entrepreneurial activity are identified by means of randomly telephoning at least 2,000 adults per country. The TEA index/prevalence rate of Early-stage Entrepreneurial Activity is the number of entrepreneurially active individuals in the two categories above, per 100 (people) in the adult population 18–64 years of age (based on the adult population surveys).

13.2.2 Entrepreneurship and Export Orientation

It is important to look at export when studying entrepreneurship. First, export may be one of the means for realising growth of a business. As a result of increased economic integration firms, even small and new firms are increasingly involved in foreign markets. Traditionally, research on export used to be focused on large (multinational) enterprises. Currently there is more attention for internationalisation of small and new firms as it is acknowledged that SMEs are increasingly involved in international markets (Reynolds 1997). The increasing commitment of small and new firms in the international market place is rooted in for example technological changes (especially in the field of information and communication technology and transport) and the liberalisation of international trade (European Commission 2004). The dominant view in the literature with regard to the process of internationalisation is the stage theory of internationalisation (Johanson and Vahlne 1977; Eriksson et al. 1997). According to this view the internationalisation process of a firm evolves in a sequential and developmental way leading from low to high commitment in foreign markets. This means that firms are likely to start their internationalisation with activities that involve less risk, such as export, before they will be involved in a more substantial commitment in foreign markets such as producing abroad. As enterprises have more experience with internationalisation and foreign markets they are more likely to increase commitment in foreign markets.

The stage theory has been challenged by empirical studies that point to the existence and growth of the number of young enterprises that are involved in international activities from inception. These enterprises are commonly marked as international new ventures (McDougall et al. 1994) or born globals (Knight and Cavusgil 1996). However, the stage theory and the born globals perspective do not necessarily contradict, as internationalisation may also be gradual for born globals, even though it follows a compact, rapid progress (European Commission 2004). Also, the existence of born global does not seem to be representative for SMEs in general as they are typically found in global niche markets.

Empirical research in the field of internationalisation of small and new firms tends to focus on single countries using micro-data. There is a lack of empirical studies using cross-country data. This is related to the fact that international export statistics do not make a distinction according to size-class. This is where the GEM project can contribute, because it provides cross-country data on involvement in exports of new and starting firms. In particular, GEM provides a mechanism for measuring export orientation of early-stage firms. Export orientation is measured as the average percentage of customers that live outside a country's borders as assessed across a random sample of a country's early-stage entrepreneurs.

The degree to which new businesses expect to export their goods and services provides an indication of their capacity to increase national wealth through international trade. Exports may be important for national economic growth but also for firms because it widen's a company's customer base, to increases sales revenues. Furthermore, geographic market diversity may help to offset slums in domestic markets and it can lengthen the life-cycle of products or services that are already matured in the home market.

13.2.3 Entrepreneurship, Export Orientation and Economic Growth

Some previous empirical studies have found evidence of an impact of entrepreneurship on economic growth (e.g. van Stel 2006). We expect that in particular export-oriented entrepreneurship makes a significant contribution to national economic growth. This is related to (assumed) higher skill levels of exporting entrepreneurs, thereby contributing to more intense levels of competition in the economy and increasing the innovative capacity of economies. Export activity may not only generate financial benefits for new ventures, but is likely to result in increased knowledge and higher human capital levels, also for small and new firms (Lu and Beamish 2001). For example, in case of entry into foreign markets firms often have to develop new resources and capabilities since the knowledge and capabilities that the firm has developed for the local or national market are often not suitable to operations abroad (Lu and Beamish 2001). Export may also result in the accumulation of knowledge of foreign markets and in the development of new organizational capabilities through the accumulation of experience abroad (Johanson and Vahlne 1977). Also, when many new firms engage in export activity, the chance that the knowledge gained through this activity spills over to other firms may be considered relatively high. The reason for this is that small and new firms have a lot of business contacts with other firms (for instance through cooperation or through buyer-supplier relations) which may lead to exchange of knowledge. Via these so-called spillovers knowledge may accumulate not only at the firm level (i.e. the exporting firm) but also at the aggregate level (i.e. the firm population in general).

In combining the potential benefits of export activity for new ventures (e.g. in terms of financial gains or competence development) and the potential for knowledge spillovers to the rest of the economy, we hypothesize that export activity among new ventures is more positively related to national economic growth than entrepreneurial activity in general. Furthermore, we expect that the relationship between export orientation among new ventures and economic growth may differ for different groups of countries along their level of economic development. Therefore, we will investigate in the next sections whether the presence of export-oriented entrepreneurship is a more important determinant of national economic growth than entrepreneurial activity in general, taking into account a country's level of economic development. This will be explained further in the next section.

13.3 Method

13.3.1 Data and Sample

Data on entrepreneurial activity and export-oriented entrepreneurship are taken from the Global Entrepreneurship Monitor (GEM). We use a sample of 36 countries participating in GEM in 2002.

Whereas a large number of organization publish international comparative export data such as the WTO, OECD, UN (Commodity Trade Statistics Database-COMTRADE) and Eurostat, there are no official international comparative export statistics relating to exports by small and new firms. In this respect the GEM initiative fills an important gap by providing a harmonized measure for export orientation of entrepreneurs across countries.

In the current study we investigate whether the presence of export-oriented entrepreneurs is a more important determinant of national economic growth than entrepreneurial activity in general. Our empirical analysis builds on a previous article by van Stel et al. (2005) in which it is investigated whether Total early-stage Entrepreneurial Activity (TEA) -as defined below- influences GDP growth for a sample of 36 countries. The authors find that the TEA indeed affects economic growth but that the influence depends on the level of economic development. In particular the contribution to economic growth is found to be stronger for more highly developed countries, as compared to developing countries. The authors argue that this may be related to higher human capital levels of entrepreneurs in higher developed countries.

In the current chapter we will perform a similar regression analysis but next to the general TEA, we will also use the TEA export rate as independent variable and compare its impact on economic growth with the impact of the general TEA index. The data and model used in this study are described below.

Next to data on early-stage entrepreneurial activity (TEA) and early-stage export activity (TEA export) from the GEM we also use data from secondary sources on GDP growth, per capita income, and the growth competitiveness index (GCI). The sources and definitions of all variables we use are described below.

13.3.2 Measures

Total Early-Stage Entrepreneurial Activity (TEA)

TEA is defined as the percentage of adult population that is either actively involved in starting a new venture or is the owner/manager of a business that is less than 42 months old. Data on total early-stage entrepreneurial activity are taken from the GEM Adult Population Survey for 2002.

Total Early-Stage Export Activity (TEA Export)

The TEA export rate is defined as the percentage of adult population that is either actively involved in starting a new venture or is the owner/manager of a business that is less than 42 months old, and has customers abroad. Data on early-stage export activity are also taken from the GEM Adult Population Survey 2002.

Growth of GDP (ΔGDP)

Real GDP growth rates are taken from the IMF World Economic Outlook database of the International Monetary Fund, version September 2005.

Per Capita Income (GNIC)

Gross national income per capita 2001 is expressed in (thousands of) purchasing power parities per US$, and these data are taken from the 2002 World Development Indicators database of the World Bank.

Growth Competitiveness Index (GCI)

Data on the GCI 2001 are taken from page 32 of The Global Competitiveness Report 2001–2002. The GCI is constituted of the following three main factors assessing a country's potential for economic growth: the quality of the macro-economic environment, the state of the public institutions and the level of technology. For further details about this index we refer to McArthur and Sachs (2002).

Analysis

We investigate whether export-oriented entrepreneurship may be considered a determinant of economic growth, next to technology, public institutions and the macroeconomic environment (which are captured in a combined way by the GCI). As both entrepreneurship and the factors underlying the GCI are assumed to be structural characteristics of an economy, we do not want to explain short term economic growth but rather growth in the medium term. Therefore we choose average annual real GDP growth over a period of four years (2002–2005) as the dependent variable in this study. Following van Stel et al. (2005) we use (the log of) initial income level of countries, to correct for catch-up effects, and lagged growth of GDP, to correct for reversed causality effects, as additional control variables. Following van Stel et al. (2005), we allow for the possibility of different effects of highly developed and developing countries. In addition we also test whether the effect of TEA is different for transition countries.[1] TEA rates may reflect different types of entrepreneurs in countries with different development levels. In particular human capital levels may differ between higher and lower developed countries, implying different impacts on economic growth. This is tested by defining separate TEA variables for different

---

[1] The 36 countries in our sample are: Argentina[D], Australia, Belgium, Brazil[D], Canada, Chile[D], China[T], Taiwan, Denmark, Finland, France, Germany, Hong Kong, Hungary[T], Iceland, India[D], Ireland, Israel, Italy, Japan, Korea, Mexico[D], Netherlands, New Zealand, Norway, Poland[T], Russia[T], Singapore, Slovenia[T], South Africa[D], Spain, Sweden, Switzerland, Thailand[D], United Kingdom and United States. Mark [D] indicates developing country while mark [T] indicates a transition country. In the categorisation rich versus poor, eleven of the twelve countries marked as [D] or [T] are classified as (relatively) poor, the exception being Slovenia.

Table 13.1 Entrepreneurial activity rates (2002) for 36 countries

	TEA rate	TEA export rate		TEA rate	TEA export rate
Argentina	14.15	1.82	Japan	1.81	0.36
Australia	8.68	4.06	Korea	14.52	7.23
Belgium	2.99	2.21	Mexico	12.40	3.50
Brazil	13.53	0.77	Netherlands	4.62	2.24
Canada	8.82	6.09	New Zealand	14.01	8.92
Chile	15.68	7.81	Norway	8.69	4.87
China	12.34	4.30	Poland	4.44	1.20
Denmark	6.53	2.95	Russia	2.52	0.46
Finland	4.56	3.52	Singapore	5.91	3.56
France	3.20	2.35	Slovenia	4.63	2.91
Germany	5.16	4.56	South Africa	6.54	1.98
Hong Kong	3.44	2.34	Spain	4.59	2.29
Hungary	6.64	1.76	Sweden	4.00	1.74
Iceland	11.32	7.35	Switzerland	7.13	4.95
India	17.88	0.25	Taiwan	4.27	1.61
Ireland	9.14	6.57	Thailand	18.90	6.09
Israel	7.06	3.07	United Kingdom	5.37	2.50
Italy	5.90	2.17	United States	10.51	2.15
Mean	8.11	3.40			
Standard deviation	4.59	2.24			

groups of countries (rich versus poor; highly developed versus transition versus developing). Our model is represented by Equations (1) and (2). These equations are estimated separately by OLS. The hypothesis of a more positive effect for rich countries corresponds to coefficient b_1 (b_2) being larger than coefficient c_1 (c_2). Furthermore, the hypothesis that export-oriented entrepreneurs contribute more to national economic growth than entrepreneurs in general corresponds to b_2 (c_2) being larger than b_1 (c_1).

$$\Delta GDP_{it} = a + b_1 TEA^{rich}_{i,t-1} + c_1 TEA^{poor}_{i,t-1} + d \log(GNIC_{i,t-1})$$
$$+ eGCI_{i,t-1} + f \Delta GDP_{i,t-1} + \varepsilon_{it} \qquad (13.1)$$

$$\Delta GDP_{it} = a + b_2 TEA\_export^{rich}_{i,t-1} + c_2 TEA\_export^{poor}_{i,t-1}$$
$$+ d \log(GNIC_{i,t-1}) + eGCI_{i,t-1} + f \Delta GDP_{i,t-1} + \varepsilon_{it} \qquad (13.2)$$

13.4 Results

The results of our empirical exercises are in Tables 13.2 and 13.3. In Table 13.2 the regression results of the impact of the general TEA index are presented (see Equation 1), while Table 13.3 shows the results using the TEA export rate (see Equation 2).

Table 13.2 Explaining economic growth from TEA rate; N=36

	Model 1	Model 2	Model 3
Constant	19.6 **	26.1 **	22.2 **
	(4.2)	(3.0)	(2.5)
TEA	.047		
	(0.8)		
TEA rich	.087		
	*(1.8)		
TEA poor	−.005		
	(0.1)		
TEA highly developed		.11 **	
		(2.2)	
TEA transition		.19	
		(1.4)	
TEA developing		.023	
		(0.2)	
log (GNIC)	−2.2 **	−2.8 **	−2.4 **
	(2.8)	(2.7)	(2.6)
GCI	.62	.64	.63
	(0.7)	(0.8)	(0.7)
lagged gdp growth	.37 **	.30 **	.22
	(2.9)	(2.1)	(1.2)
R^2	0.626	0.636	0.662
adjusted R^2	0.577	0.576	0.592

Absolute heteroskedasticity-consistent t-values are between brackets. Dependent variable is average annual growth of GDP over the period 2002-2005. TEA is Total Entrepreneurial Activity rate (*Global Entrepreneurship Monitor*); GCI is growth competitiveness index 2001 (*Growth Competitiveness Report*); GNIC is per capita income of 2001; Lagged GDP growth is average annual growth of GDP over the period 1998-2001.
* Significant at a 0.10 level.
** Significant at a 0.05 level

Tables 13.2 and 13.3 reveal, as hypothesized, that the presence of export-oriented entrepreneurs indeed seems to be more important for achieving GDP growth than entrepreneurship in general. Comparing the coefficients of the various TEA rates across the tables, we see that in each of the three model variants the impact of TEA Export is higher compared to the impact of TEA in general. For instance, the TEA rate has a coefficient of 0.047 (Table 13.2), while the coefficient of the TEA export rate is 0.13 (Table 13.3).

As indicated before, an important element in our analysis is to distinguish between different groups of countries. Table 13.2 confirms, in accordance with earlier findings of van Stel et al. (2005), that it is important to distinguish between different groups of countries along their level of economic development in investigating the relationship between entrepreneurship and economic growth. In particular, the table reveals that for rich countries the impact of entrepreneurial activity is significantly positive, whereas the impact for poor countries is effectively zero (Model 2). Looking at the results for our export variable (Table 13.3) a first finding is that having more entrepreneurs with export orientation seems to be important in

Table 13.3 Explaining economic growth from TEA export rate (1–100% of customers from abroad); N = 36

TEA export	Model 1	Model 2	Model 3
Constant	22.3 **	22.1 **	22.3 **
	(6.2)	(4.4)	(6.0)
TEA_export	.13 *		
	(1.8)		
TEA_export rich	.13		
	(1.6)		
TEA_export poor	.14		
	(1.0)		
TEA_export highly developed		.16 *	
		(1.9)	
TEA_export Transition		.47 **	
		(2.1)	
TEA_export Developing		.10	
		(0.9)	
log (GNIC)	–2.4 **	–2.4 **	–2.4 **
	(3.5)	(3.0)	(3.6)
GCI	.54	.54	.66
	(0.6)	(0.6)	(0.7)
lagged gdp growth	.33 **	.33 **	.24
	(2.6)	(2.4)	(1.3)
R^2	0.639	0.639	0.658
adjusted R^2	0.592	0.578	0.587

Absolute heteroskedasticity-consistent t-values are between brackets. Dependent variable is average annual growth of GDP over the period 2002-2005. TEA is Total Entrepreneurial Activity rate (*Global Entrepreneurship Monitor*); GCI is growth competitiveness index 2001 (*Growth Competitiveness Report*); GNIC is per capita income of 2001; Lagged GDP growth is average annual growth of GDP over the period 1998-2001.
* Significant at a 0.10 level.
** Significant at a 0.05 level

highly developed as well as in transition countries (Model 3). The effect is strongest for transition economies. We find no evidence of an impact of new ventures export activity on GDP growth in developing countries. Van Stel et al. (2005) find no impact of entrepreneurship in general on economic growth in developing economies. For these economies we also find no evidence that *export-oriented* entrepreneurship contributes to economic growth. It may be that human capital levels of entrepreneurs in these countries are too low.

13.5 Conclusion and Discussion

This chapter presents an introduction to the GEM project and describes its objectives, methods and a number of its measures for entrepreneurial activity. Whereas GEM is well known for its index for early-stage entrepreneurial activity (TEA), its data also provide an indicator for export orientation among early-stage ventures. This is important since official international comparative export statistics on exports do not provide a distinction according to size-class or age of firms. This chapter presents an empirical analysis using this indicator for early-stage export activity. More specifically, this chapter investigates whether the presence of export-oriented entrepreneurs is a more important determinant of national economic growth than entrepreneurial activity in general. We also compare the extent of influence of export-oriented entrepreneurship on GDP growth for three groups of countries: highly developed economies, transition economies and developing economies. The distinction between these three groups of countries relates to the shift from the managed to the entrepreneurial economy (Audretsch and Thurik 2000). In particular, the nature of entrepreneurship is likely to be different for higher and lower developed countries hence the impact on economic growth may also differ (van Stel et al. 2005).

For the groups of highly developed countries and transition countries we find that export-oriented entrepreneurship contributes more strongly to macro-economic growth than entrepreneurial activity in general. The effect is particularly strong for transition economies. The results of our study do not provide evidence of a relationship between new ventures' export orientation and economic growth for developing countries.

The findings of this study suggest that in developed countries export orientation among new ventures contributes to economic growth. In developed countries, technologies are in general more widely available than in less developed countries and enterprises increasingly specialize in knowledge-based activities. Therefore, new ventures' foreign operations may be based on the presence of specific technological knowledge, skills and valuable resources that are available within the firm. For these ventures international expansion is viable and sometimes even necessary for survival, and they are likely to display high international involvement. Furthermore, these ventures are likely to develop specific skills (including innovative skills) through their export activity, and may, therefore, have a particularly strong impact on economic growth.

In our study we find a particular strong impact of export-oriented entrepreneurship on economic growth for transition economies. Transition economies have a highly educated labor force, a relatively low level of GDP, and a highly turbulent economy. One explanation for the relatively strong positive impact we find may be that especially the high degree of environmental dynamism in these countries positively affects the international orientation of new firms and the development of competences. Research suggests that environmental dynamism and the ensuing turbulence can stimulate or even push new ventures to internationalize their sales and to intensify their export activities (McDougall et al. 1994; Oviatt and McDougall 1994). Our results suggest that in the kind of turbulent environment that is characteristic for transition economies exporting entrepreneurs may have a particularly strong impact on competition, innovation and consequently economic growth.

The results of our study reveal that export-oriented new ventures do not seem to make a significant contribution to economic growth in developing countries. Because of the relatively high rates of necessity entrepreneurship associated with the low level of economic development in these countries, new entrepreneurs—including export-oriented entrepreneurs—will tend to have low levels of human capital and will mainly be active in low-technology and low value added economic activities, such as agriculture. This may result in a low level of benefits and development of skills and competences at the firm level (Zahra et al. 2000) and may consequently explain that these firms do not so much contribute to macro-economic growth. Our results underline the suggestions made by Wennekers et al. (2005) that, because of their stage of development, low-income countries should not have a strong focus on the promotion of new business creation and that it may be more beneficial for these countries to foster the exploitation of scale economies, e.g. through foreign direct investment.

Limitations of this study include the small sample size and the focus on export orientation only and not on other modes of internationalization. Future research could benefit greatly from longitudinal data and from including other modes of internationalization.

References

Acs ZJ, Arenius P, Hay M, Minniti M (2005) Global Entrepreneurship Monitor, 2004. Executive Report, London Business School, London, UK and Babson College, Wellesley, MA

Acs ZJ, Audretsch DB (2003) Innovation and Technological Change. In: Acs ZJ, Audretsch DB (eds) Handbook of Entrepreneurship Research. Kluwer Academic Publishers, Boston, MA, pp 55–79

Audretsch DB, Thurik AR (2000) Capitalism and democracy in the 21st century: from the managed to the entrepreneurial economy. Journal of Evolutionary Economics 10 (1):17–34

Autio E (1994) New technology-based firms as agents of R&D and innovation. Technovation 14(4):259–273

Baumol W (2002) The Free-Market Innovation Machine: Analyzing the Growth Miracle of Capitalism. Princeton University Press, Princeton

Bloodgood JM, Sapienza HJ, Almeida JG (1996) The Internationalization of New High-Potential U.S. Ventures: Antecedents and Outcomes. Entrepreneurship Theory and Practice 20(4): 61–76

Eriksson K, Johanson J, Majkgård A, Sharma DD (1997) Experiential Knowledge and Cost in the Internationalization Process. Journal of International Business Studies 28 (2):337–60

European Commission (2004) Internationalisation of SMEs. Observatory of European SMEs; Report 2003 No. 4, Report submitted to the Enterprise Directorate General by KPMG Special Services, EIM Business & Policy Research, and ENSR, Brussels

Hawkins DI (1993) New Business Entrepreneurship in the Japanese Economy. Journal of Business Venturing 8:137–50

Johanson J, Vahlne JE (1977) The internationalization process of the firm: A model of knowledge development and increasing foreign market commitments. Journal of International Business Studies 8(1):23–32

Knight GA, Cavusgil ST (1996) The born global firm: a challenge to traditional internationalisation theory. Advances in International Marketing 8:11–26

Lu JW, Beamish PW (2001) The internationalization and performance of SMEs. Strategic Management Journal 22(6-7):565–86

McArthur JW, Sachs JD (2002) The Growth Competitiveness Index: Measuring Technological Advancement and the Stages of Development. In: Porter ME, Sachs JD, Cornelius PK, McArthur JW, Schwab K (eds) The Global Competitiveness Report 2001–2002. Oxford University Press, New York, pp 28–51

McDougall P, Covin J, Robinson R, Herron L (1994) The effects of industry growth and strategic breadth on new venture performance and strategy content. Strategic Management Journal 15(7):537–553

McDougall PP, Oviatt BM (1996) New venture internationalization, strategic change, and performance: a follow-up study. Journal of Business Venturing 11:23–40

Moen O (2002) The Born Globals. A new generation of small european exporters. International Marketing Review 19(2):156–175

Oviatt BM, McDougall PP (1994) Toward a theory of international new ventures. Journal of International Business Studies 25(1):45–64

Rennie MW (1993) Global competitiveness: born global. The McKinsey Quarterly 4:45–52

Reynolds P, Bosma N, Autio E, Hunt S, De Bono N, Servais I, Lopez-Garcia P, Chin N (2005) Global Entrepreneurship Monitor: Data Collection Design and Implementation 1998–2003. Small Business Economics 24(3):205–231

Reynolds PD (1997) New and Small Firms in Expanding Markets. Small Business Economics 9(1):79–84

Schumpeter JA (1934) The Theory of Economic Development. Harvard University Press, Cambridge, MA

Stel A van, Carree M, Thurik AR (2005) The Effect of Entrepreneurial Activity on National Economic Growth. Small Business Economics 24:311–321

Stel A van (2006) Empirical Analysis of Entrepreneurship and Economic Growth. Springer Science, New York

Wennekers S, Van Stel A, Thurik R, Reynolds P (2005) Nascent Entrepreneurship and the Level of Economic Development. Small Business Economics 24(3):293–309

Zahra SA, Duane Ireland R, Hitt MA (2000) International expansion by new venture firms: international diversity, mode of market entry, technological learning, and performance. Academy of Management Journal 43(5):925–950

Chapter 14
Labour Market Institutions and Entrepreneurship

Antonio Aníbal Golpe, José María Millán and Concepción Román

Abstract The impact of labour market institutions on both labour supply and job search rates has been exhaustively analysed in *Labour Economics* from theoretical as well as empirical approaches. However, research on the impact of this regulation on self-employment and its composition is limited, that is, the impact of labour market institutions on occupational choice and labour demand. In this context, the aim of this study is to revise the effects of certain labour market institutions on self-employment rates, defining the key dimensions and revising those indicators that could be used for capturing these effects, making an abstraction of the tax system effects.

14.1 Introduction

The impact of labour market institutions on both labour supply and job search rates has been exhaustively analysed in *Labour Economics* from theoretical as well as empirical approaches.[1] Thus, labour market regulations may have significant effects on employment turnover (Bertola 1992, Bentolila and Bertola 1990, Layard and Nickell 1999, Millard and Mortensen 1997, Millard 1996, Nickell 1982), on the levels of employment (Scarpetta 1996, Layard and Nickell 1999) and unemployment (Kugler and Pica 2004), on productivity (Akerlof 1984; Piore 1986), on wages and benefits (Bentolila and Dolado 1994), and on the degree of protection that workers may benefit from (Lindbeck and Snower 1988), as well as the level of self-employment and its composition.

However, research on the impact of this regulation on self-employment and its composition is limited, that is, the impact of labour market institutions on occupational choice and labour demand. The decision to become self-employed is

Antonio A Golpe
University of Huelva
antonio.golpe@dehie.uhu.es

[1] In this sense, the consequences of the duration and quantity of unemployment benefit on the inflow, or the effects of long-term contracts and the dismissal costs on the outflow, are other institutions comprehensively surveyed.

usually the result of an occupational choice problem in which the risks associated to other employment possibilities are weighed. In this sense, the assessment of risk can be determined by the existence of certain labour market institutions. Hence, the existence of such institutions as severance pay, long-term contracts or, even, unemployment benefits, may change the individual's perception of the degree of risk associated to a certain job. This is the reason why the regulation of the labour market and, more specifically, the design of unemployment benefits, severance pay, long-term hiring procedures, or the tax incentives associated to certain types of work, can be determining in solving this problem, as well as for self-employment rates.

Therefore, labour market institutions with disparate purposes may become a hindrance for self-employment, as they can be misleading when choosing an occupation. In the first place, the security that some labour market institutions bestow on paid-employment or wage-work increase the value of uncertainty, which rise the opportunity cost of self-employment.

When the laws that protect employment are very rigid, the risks run by paid-employees are very low. Therefore, labour market regulations can be a handicap for self-employment. We shall pursue this line of thinking in terms of the transition to employment from unemployment. When labour legislation is very protective towards paid-employment, where permanent contracts have prevail, where unemployment compensations and severance pay exist, and there are high salary prospects, the opportunity cost of self-employment increases, bringing about at the same time a higher perception of risk. On the contrary, in the context of a completely flexible labour market, with no elements to safeguard against non-payment, nor unemployment compensation or severance pay, the perception of risk and reward associated to self-employment improves in relation to that of paid-employment. Over the last years, the deregularization of labour markets has made paid-employment more insecure, thus becoming an unexpected stimulus to entrepreneurship.

Secondly, we may consider how the decision of becoming an employer is affected by the existence of adjustment costs. When hiring regulations are too stringent and hefty dismissal costs are imposed, the employer's risk increases, because the cost of workforce reduction adds up to the market fluctuations. Therefore, the existence of long-term contracts and costs of dismissal are constraints that prevent companies from adjusting to demand fluctuations. These adjustment costs can make own-account workers to reject a profit opportunity brought about in a positive demand shock, not because of its feasibility, but because of its possible after effects in case that shock is not steadfast. To illustrate this, let's imagine a self-employed worker considering the idea of becoming an employer. In this decision, this person will have to take into account these adjusting costs, especially if he or she is uncertain as to the permanent or transitory nature of the shock moving them to this transition.

But labour market institutions may also generate distortions in the opposite direction, that is, the transition to self-employment from paid-employment could occur as a way to avoid the most unfavourable constituents of legislation. If we take into account that every agent aims at maximising its objective function, we may acknowledge that both, firms and employees, make some of their decisions according to the design of labour institutions. In this sense, the boost of self-employment has originated a significant distortion, as both employers and employees have "agreed" to certain transfers from paid-employment to self-employment, the former keeping their own activity, in an attempt to cut down their social security contribution and adjustment costs, allowing them to increase the wages of these new "self-employed" and so avoiding the most detrimental elements of labour legislation. In this sense, several countries, at different times, have seen growing numbers of self-employed people who work for just one company, and whose self-employment status may be little more than a device to reduce total taxes paid by the firms and workers involved—the phenomenon of so-called "false" self-employment.[2]

And last, the incentives and policies designed to help some vulnerable groups -such as the unemployed, youths or women- to access to self-employment, can also become a reason for distortion. The self-employment incentives granted to certain long-term unemployed groups and, as a result, somehow stigmatized, can provoke a problem of adverse selection in self-employment, as those who change to it are not the ones with the best opportunities of profit or have the required skills for the job, but those for whom the opportunity cost was lowered proportionally to the diminishing rate of paid-employment offer.[3] In this context, the aim of this study is to revise the effects of certain labour market institutions[4] on self-employment rates, defining the key dimensions in order to capture those effects and revising those indicators that could be used for capturing these effects, making an abstraction of the tax system effects.[5]

---

[2] OECD (2000).

[3] Andersson and Wadensjö (2006) analyse who became self-employed in the period from 1999 to 2002 of Swedish-born men aged 20 to 60 years old, who were either wage-earners, unemployed or inactive in 1998. They found that the unemployed, and even more the inactive, are overrepresented among those who become self-employed. They also studied the economic outcome of self-employment in 2002 for Swedish-born men who were either unemployed, inactive or wage-earners in 1998. Economic outcome in 2002 is measured using income from self-employment and having employees in the firm. The estimations show that those who were wage-earners in 1998 have higher incomes and are also employing other people in their business to a much higher extent in 2002 than those who in 1998 were unemployed or inactive. This indicates that support to unemployed to become self-employed should be implemented with great care.

[4] In particular, employment protection legislation, unemployment compensation and benefits and allowances created to support self-employment.

[5] These have already dealt with in chapter 10 in this book, in which Herbert J. Schuetze revises the relationship between the tax system and entrepreneurship.

14.2 Employment Protection Legislation

All countries of the OECD have a specific regulation that mediates in the employment relationship between employees and firms. Those rules, referred to as hiring and firing practices, are known as Employment Protection Legislation and they usually regulate: i) what kind of contracts are permitted; ii) any special rules favouring certain groups in hiring; iii) occupational standards; iv) the conditions under which workers can be terminated; v) requirements for severance and advance notice for termination; vi) redundancy procedures; vii) special rules for collective dismissal.

Hence, according to their level of employment protection, each country will be placed in a continuum shown in the table below:[6]

Employment protection regulations enhance job security for employees in two ways: by restricting the employer's prerogative to explicitly hire workers temporarily and/or by restricting the employer's freedom to terminate the employee's contracts.

14.2.1 Measurement

Measuring employment protection is a difficult task. Quantitative aspects like the number of months' notice required for individual dismissal or severance pay can be easily computed. But other aspects are more difficult to measure through the interpretations that may arise from the reasons for no-fault dismissal. Besides, it is legal rules that are generally measured, whereas the fact that the quality of the rules enforcement differs widely from one country to another, determine that the above mentioned legal rules provide very little information about what really happens in the work place and the actual effects of regulations. Despite all this, there exist developed techniques to apply indicators to measure the strictness of employment protection legislation. Consequently, data bases have been created in order to estimate the regulation costs (World Bank Doing Business data base[7]), to quantify

Table 14.1 Employment protection continuum

Rigid or protective	Flexible or unregulated
Fixed-term contracting restricted	Unrestricted fixed-term contracting
Temporary agency work restricted	Unrestricted temporary agency work
Hiring standards	No hiring standards
Employer dismissal rights restricted	Unrestricted dismissal rights
Substantial severance and advance notice required	No severance or notice required
Substantial administrative requirements for layoffs	Simple administrative procedures

---

[6] Employment protection regulations. Rules for hiring and terminating the employment relationship. World Bank, Notebooks of Employment Policy. December 2002, n° 1.

[7] Which updates formal regulation measures introduced by Botero et al. (2004) and which we shall review later on.

reform processes (OECD), to categorise reforms in terms of their expected impact on the labour market flexibility and/or its reach (Fondazione Rodolfo Debenedetti Social Reforms Database), to measure *de facto* labour practices (*Global Labour Survey* by Chor and Freeman 2005), or to systematically register and measure different reforms (forthcoming ECFIN LABREF Database).[8]

Going back to the above mentioned enforcement problem, Chor and Freeman (2005) prove that there not exist a correlation between the measurement of the strictness of employment protection carried out by Doing Business and the index on "Employment Regulations and Working Conditions" derived from the Global Labour Survey, which shows that what legal rules transpire is not representative of what actually happens in the workplace. That is to say, the formal hiring and dismissal regulations do not fully contemplate the degree of difficulty of dismissal if legislation is not enforced.[9] This is why some researchers have exploited indexes based on employer surveys. One of these surveys, carried out by the International Organization of Employers (1985) seeks to identify the importance of obstacles to the termination of regular employment and the deployment of atypical workers. In this sense, regulatory constraints were classified as insignificant, minor, serious or fundamental.

Two other employment protection indexes derived from employer surveys have also been used in the literature. An ad hoc survey of some 8000 industrial firms conducted by the European Community at the end of 1985 inquires of the management respondents which of a number of reasons explained their not employing more people at the time of the survey, and asks them to indicate whether each one was "very important", "important", or "not important". One such reason is "insufficient flexibility in shedding labour". The index is obtained by assigning a value of 2 (1) to the percentages of firms responding that this reason was "very important" ("important").

A broader-based survey of employers, the World Competitiveness Report, has been used to provide another measurement of the strictness of cross-country employment regulations.

Di Tella and MacCulloch (1999) exploit one question in the World Competitiveness Report survey to obtain an indicator of labour market flexibility.[10] The survey question asks respondents to rate the "flexibility of enterprises to adjust job security and compensation standards to economic realities" on a scale of 0 to 100, where 0 indicates "none at all" and 100 "a great deal".

The best-known employment protection measurement is maybe the one developed by Lazear (1990), known as the *severance payment*. This defined

---

[8] See Arpaia, Costello, Mourre and Pierini (2005).

[9] As there are no direct measures of the enforceability level of labour regulations, Micco and Pagés (2006) use the variable "Rule of Law" created by Kauffman et al. (2003) so as to account for the different enforceability level in cross-country employment regulations.

[10] The survey covers 21 countries. The number or returned questionnaires varies by year, averaging 1531 between 1984 and 1990. There was no survey in 1987. The flexibility question was changed in 1990, and subsequently dropped.

as the statutory entitlement in months of pay due to a blue-collar worker with ten years of service on termination for reason unconnected with his/her behaviour. The measure thus pertains to no-fault individual dismissals for economic reasons.[11]

Grubb and Wells (1993) identify three elements in the employment protection system: 1) constraints in the dismissal of employees under regular contract; 2) restrictions in the use of temporary contracts; and 3) restrictions in the number of working hours. The first element covers not only severance pay, as in Lazear, but also procedural delays and unfair dismissal provisions. The second element encompasses restrictions on the use of fixed-term contracts and temporary agency work, such as the permissible grounds for their use, the maximum number of successive contracts and their maximum cumulated duration. Finally, hours restrictions cover such things as the length of the normal working week, annual overtime limits, minimum rest periods, and restrictions on night work. Their indicators sum up the strictness of employment protection legislation, and they focused on European Community countries in the late 1980s. The territorial coverage has gradually spread out to EFTA countries and to other non European countries in the OECD.[12]

However, the most widely used measurement is the employment protection legislation overall summary indicator[13] issued by the OECD and developed from 22 aggregated sub-indexes. These basic employment protection legislation indicators are based on an exhaustive revision of the current regulation and the contractual and dismissal laws applying to both regular and temporary employees.[14] These detailed 22 indicators of strictness in the security and protection employment system fall into three main group, one makes reference to the provisions for fixed-term employees or temporary agency work, another one refers to provisions affecting employees with regular contracts and the last one, which was subsequently added, referring to collective dismissals. All of them are shown in the table 14.2 above.[15]

Blanchard and Wolfers (2000) developed an employment protection legislation index[16] combining both OECD and Lazear's data. Another significant contribution

---

[11] These data refer to 20 countries in the OECD during the period 1956–1984.

[12] OECD Jobs Study (1994).

[13] Nicoletti et al. (2000), Boeri, Nicoletti and Scarpetta (1999), Cazes and Nesporova (2003), and Torrini (2005) amongst others use this indicator.

[14] These indicators are certainly affected by measurement errors. The indicators computed for Italy, for example, overestimate the role of employment protection, due to the wrong inclusion in the costs of dismissal of a special type of compensation received by employees, even in case of reinstatement or retirement (Schivardi and Torrini 2003).

[15] Tonin (2005) offer indicators for employment protection legislation following the OECE methodology for Bulgaria, Croatia, Czech Republic, Estonia, Hungary, Lithuania, Poland, Russia, Slovaquia, Slovenia and Ukraine.

[16] These data are available on O. Blanchard's website:http://web.mit.edu/blanchard/www/articles.html.

Table 14.2 OECD synthetic index

Level 1	Level 2	Level 3	Level 4
Regular procedural inconveniences in case of no-fault dismissal Delay to start notice Definition of unfair dismissal Compensation in case of unfair dismissal 20 years of tenure	Procedural inconveniences	Regular contracts	Employment protection legislation overall summary indicator
Severance pay for no-fault dismissal Reinstatement in case of unfair dismissal	Direct cost of dismissal		
Notice for no-fault dismissal Trial period before conditions for unfair dismissal apply	Notice and trial period		
Valid cases other than objective Maximum number of successive contracts Maximum cumulated duration	Fixed-term contracts	Temporary contracts	
Types of work for which is illegal Restrictions on number of renewal Maximum cumulated duration	Temporary Work Agency		
Definition of collective dismissal Additional notification requirements Additional delays involved Other special costs to employers	Collective dismissals		

is that in Botero et al. (2004), who developed a new data base in which they seize different aspects in employment market regulations in 85 countries.[17] Their employment protection measurement stems from 4 sub indexes:[18]

Alternative employment contracts measures the existence and costs of alternatives to the standard employment contract computed as the average of: (1) a dummy variable equal to one if part-time workers enjoy the mandatory benefits of full-time workers; (2) a dummy variable equal to one if terminating part-time workers is at least as costly as terminating full-time workers; (3) a dummy variable equal to one if fixed-term contracts are only allowed for fixed-term tasks; and (4) the normalized maximum duration of fixed-term contracts.

Cost of increasing hours worked measures the cost of increasing the number of hours worked. They start by calculating the maximum number of "normal" hours of work per year in each country (excluding overtime, vacations, holidays, etc.). Normal hours range from 1,758 in Denmark to 2,418 in Kenya. Then it is assumed

---

[17] The resulting data base on employment legislation is publicly available to researchers.

[18] For the 28 members of the OECD the employment protection measures compiled by Botero et al. (2004) can be compared with the OECD labour market legislation indexes. The comparisons between Botero et al. (2004) measurements and the 1998 OECD indexes (OECD 2004) show a positive correlation. However, this correlation is not as strong as expected.

that firms need to increase the hours worked by their employees from 1,758 to 2,418 during one year. A firm first increases the number of hours worked until it reaches the country's maximum normal hours of work, and then uses overtime. If existing employees are not allowed to increase the hours worked to 2,418 hours in a year, perhaps because overtime is capped, it is assumed the firm doubles its workforce and each worker is paid 1,758 hours, doubling the wage bill of the firm. The cost of increasing hours worked is computed as the ratio of the final wage bill to the initial one.

Cost of firing workers measures the cost of firing 20% of the firm's workers (10% are fired for redundancy and 10% without cause). The cost of firing a worker as calculated as the sum of the notice period, severance pay, and any mandatory penalties established by law or mandatory collective agreements for a worker with three years of tenure with the firm. If dismissal is illegal, it set the cost of firing equal to the annual wage. The new wage bill incorporates the normal wage of the remaining workers and the cost of firing workers. The cost of firing workers is computed as the ratio of the new wage bill to the old one.

Dismissal procedures measures worker protection granted by law or mandatory collective agreements against dismissal. It is the average of the following seven dummy variables which equal one: (1) if the employer must notify a third party before dismissing more than one worker; (2) if the employer needs the approval of a third party prior to dismissing more than one worker; (3) if the employer must notify a third party before dismissing a redundant worker; (4) if the employer needs the approval of a third party to dismiss one redundant worker; (5) if the employer must provide relocation or retraining alternatives for redundant employees prior to dismissal; (6) if there are priority rules applying to dismissal or lay-offs; and (7) if there are priority rules applying to reemployment.

14.2.2 Employment Protection Legislation and Entrepreneurship

If we reviewed the literature about the relationship between the employment protection legislation strictness and self-employment rates, our first conclusion would be that this is an indeed controversial matter. Whereas such studies as that of Grub and Wells (1993) and OECD (1992, 1999) found evidence of a positive relationship between employment protection legislation strictness and self-employment rates, more up-to-date investigation, such as Robson (2003) and Torrini (2005), contest the validity of those results.[19]

On analysing the impact of employment protection legislation on employment structure, OECD (1999) gives evidence of a statistically significant and positive relationship between summary measurements of the employment protection system strictness and self-employment rates in OECD countries. The reason for such

---

[19] Contradictory results that may have been generated by the heterogeneous nature of the data in these studies.

a result, previously found in OECD (1992) and Grubb and Wells (1993), is the fact that employers may try to avoid the effects of regulation on their freedom to hire and dismiss employees by subcontracting own-account workers. Paid-employment protection system too strict to regular workers may encourage firms to change to temporary contracts as well as to outsource self-employed workers. If this is so, employers may use self-employment as a tool to undermine the legislation intended effects on employment protection. This leads us to consider that an important percentage of self-employed would be "false", as they would actually be wage-workers under a self-employment contract, so that employers avoid the indirect employment costs.[20] The implications for the employment policy outcome and particularly for the efficiency of those policies designed to foster self-employment, make this a matter worthy of further research. It is very important to know whether the increasing rates of self-employment simply reflect the reaction of employers to higher costs of labour market regulation and taxation and therefore they would be an indicator of growing "false" self-employment, or if they reflect a genuine rebirth of entrepreneurial activity in these countries.

Robson (2003) sheds some light on this matter looking back to the existing evidence of the relationship between the incidence of self-employment in OECD countries and employment protection system strictness. The results of this study lead to the conclusion that previous evidence of the relationship between employment protection legislation and self-employment rates is not consistent. While gross data point at the existence of a positive relationship between employment protection legislation and self-employment rates, this evidence disappear after introducing other control variables for other potential influences on the self-employment rates, in particular, once that the presence of specific fixed effects in each country is taken into account. Thus, this study concludes that the evidence supporting the hypothesis that employment protection system stringency promotes self-employment is very limited.

Torrini (2005) makes use of the above mentioned OECD labour market legislation indicators, published by Nicoletti et al. (2000), and finds out that in a multivaried context there is no correlation between self-employment rates and employment protection legislation. The results are nonetheless sensitive to the model specification.

Robson (2006) uses data assembled by Botero et al. (2004). In particular, he uses two measurements. The first one is a measurement of dismissal costs, calculated as the cost of firing 20% of the firm's workers (10% are dismissed for redundancy and 10% for no cause) with tenure of three years with the firm at least. The cost is calculated as the sum of the mandatory notice period, severance pay, any penalties established by law or agreements reached through collective bargaining. The second measurement is an index of worker protection against dismissal either

---

[20] Pfeiffer (1999b) shows the prevalence of this phenomenon is in Germany. As we will mention in Section 5 of this chapter, some OECD countries have recently adopted measures specially designed to control the incidence of false self-employment.

granted by law or by collective agreements. This measurement takes into account whether the employer must notify or needs the approval of a third party prior to dismissing one worker, due to redundancy or any other reason. He establishes that self-employment rates (employers and self-employed workers) can bear a negative relationship with the strictness of employment protection regulations against dismissal. This evidence is consistent with the idea that more strict employment protection legislation decreases the risk of changing to wage-work in comparison to the risk of changing to self-employment, thus lessening the appeal of the second when compared to the first.[21] Besides, there is no evidence of a significant impact of employment protection legislation on business birth rate.

Hence, if we don't take into account the incidence of "false" own-account workers, an increase in the employment protection legislation strictness may entail a decrease in self-employment rates. On one hand, wage-workers are reluctant to become self-employed in case that the strict hiring and dismissal regulations may prevent them from changing back to paid-employment in case of business failure. Alternatively, an excessively protective employment regulation, although favouring job security, might discourage prospective employers from changing to self-employment. Finally, the coexistence of a high level employment protection and a low self-employment share in some countries is maybe symptomatic of a general contempt for employment instability among risk averse individuals who may be more likely to benefit from regulations than becoming self-employed.

Using data from OECD and Latin American countries, Maloney (1998) finds evidence that employment protection—measured via an index capturing both the difficulty for firing workers and dismissal compensation costs- has a positive impact on self-employment rates. However, the detected differences are negligible.

On the other hand, although related theoretical work does not establish an uncontroversial link between employment protection legislation and the average firm size, the fact that it is differently implemented according to the different firm sizes, makes employment protection legislation a hindrance to entrepreneurial growth, this being measured in terms of employment.

Overall, employment protection legislation is stricter when applied to firms with a bigger number of employees.[22] Garibaldi et al. (2003) and Schivardi and Torrini (2003) study the impact of employment protection legislation both on firm size and the performance of firms of different sizes in Italy, where for firms with over 15 employees it is mandatory to reinstate an employee if he or she proves unfair dismissal, while if the firm is smaller it must only compensate the fired worker with a monetary transfer.[23] This means that crossing the 15 employee threshold may

---

[21] Nevertheless, the evidence is significant only when the dependent variable data belongs to year 2000 and it is not significant for 2001 data.

[22] OECD (2004)

[23] Both of the above mentioned studies find a significant threshold effect, although quantitatively minor.

entail a potential cost for firms, dissuading them from surpassing this number and therefore reducing the entrepreneurial growth as well as the average size of firms. Garibaldi et al. (2003), using data from the Italian National Social Administration (INPS), which incorporates non-agricultural firms with at least one employee, find that firms reaching the 15 employee threshold experience a persistence increase of 1.5 percent points with respect to a baseline statistical model.

Moreover, firms with over 15 employees are more liable to reduce the number of employees than to increase it. Schivardi and Torrini (2003) use the same data for the period 1986–1998, and find that the average size of firms would increase less than 1% if the threshold effect was abolished.

Thus, results suggest that employment protection has a negative impact in entrepreneurial growth, this being measured in terms of employment. However, these findings must be cautiously analysed, and should be completed with the analysis of their effects on the transitions from own-account work to employer.

14.3 Unemployment Benefits

Standard search theory predicts a disincentive effect of benefits.[24] Since benefits are the main source of income when unemployment, when they are exhausted, search intensity rises and the reservation wage falls, so that the opportunity cost of search decreases, thereby leading to an increase in the probability of leaving unemployment.

Some studies have found evidence of a negative relationship between the level of unemployment benefits and self-employment rates in an economy (for example, Staber and Bogenhold 1993; Ilmakunnas and Kanniainen 2001;[25] Robson 2003; Parker and Robson 2004; Kanniainen and Vesala 2005). Nevertheless, in his work, Torrini (2005) suggests that this relationship could be non robust. Using a panel of OECD countries, he finds a negative correlation between self-employment and the replacement ratio between unemployment benefits and wages.[26]

Light (1980) argues that individuals who are disadvantaged in the labour market are more likely to start business. Discrimination may push some individuals into self-employment. In addition, language barriers, ignorance of customs, poverty and unemployment may make self-employment more desirable than available wage work. In order for this theory to make economic sense, it must assume that these disadvantages reduce wage earnings relatively more than self-employment earnings.

---

[24] See Bover, Arellano and Bentolila (1996) for a detailed empirical study, in the context of a duration model, of the effects of unemployment benefit duration and the business cycle on unemployment duration.

[25] Ilmakunnas and Kanniainen (2001) find statistical evidence about the fact that national macroeconomic risks, insurance against social hazard, public sector size and the different structures of labour market have an impact on business creation across countries.

[26] Moreover, he finds that self-employment rates depend negatively on the proportion of workers in the public sector.

For example, unemployed individuals may be viewed unfavourably by employers and will find it progressively harder to acquire a wage work. They may therefore find that their skills produce a relatively higher return in self-employment than in wage work.

Using longitudinal data from the Spanish Continuous Family Expenditure Survey for 1985.I—1991.IV, Carrasco (1999) investigates the effect of unemployment benefits on the probability of accessing to self-employment, obtaining a strong negative effect. Receiving unemployment benefits reduces the probability of accessing to self-employment. This reinforces the previous finding that suggests that the self-employed are poor workers and misfits for paid work. Unemployed not receiving benefits are more likely to change to self-employment, all else equal. This agrees with the disadvantage theory and with the view of some sociologists that "misfits" are pushed into entrepreneurship.

Robson (2006), on the other hand, analyses if the mechanisms designed to diminish individuals' exposure to the risks provoked by economy's shocks, contribute to foster entrepreneurship or if, on the contrary, they are a hampering to it, as they restrict the rewards associated to entrepreneurial success, finding evidence that entrepreneurship rates (measured as self-employment rates) and business-birth rates are negatively related to the level of coverage of the unemployment benefit scheme. However, this evidence is sensitive to the year when the dependent variable is measured.

All in all, the underlying hypothesis in these studies is that high unemployment benefits, particularly when they are high in relation to minimum wages, diminish the willingness of the unemployed to take up jobs and affect negatively the probability to change to self-employment. Likewise, receiving benefits can be a disincentive to change to paid-employment to self-employment, as such transfer entails the loss of this insurance.

In order to assess these hypotheses, the ratio between unemployment benefits and wages—replacement ratio- has been widely used as means to measure the level of coverage or generosity of the unemployment benefit scheme.

However, this indicator only captures this phenomenon partially. Other relevant components are given by unemployment benefit duration and the tightness in applying the requirements that workers must meet in order to be entitled as beneficiaries. Robson's research (2006), based on Botero et al. (2004) compilation, reveals itself as paradigmatic, as it includes a replacement rate measurement combined with strictness indicators of unemployment benefit entitlements, making it possible to develop a synthetic index of the unemployment benefit scheme generosity in a given economy.

14.4 Policies to Promote Self-employment

Particularly since the beginning of the 1980s, governments in most OECD countries have adopted a range of policies to support self-employment, both in its own right, and as part of attempts to foster entrepreneurship. This has taken place in the context of a general trend toward deregulation in many labour and product markets and the persistence of high unemployment (Meager 1994). Policy intervention has been justified by the presence of barriers to access to self-employment, including the existence of capital market failures; administrative burdens associated, particularly, with requirements to report to a number of different administrations; and the lower social security protection of the self-employed relative to wage earners. To counteract these barriers as well as to help people find a job, governments have put in place different programmes and schemes to stimulate self-employment and the creation of new firms. They have also tried to reduce the rate of failure of self-employed businesses, where this is judged to be due to the lack of necessary skills, particularly managerial skills.

The OECD identifies three types of measurements to foster self-employment: policies to help self-employed people develop their businesses, and in particular take on employees when appropriate; policies directed against "false" self-employment and policies to assist unemployed people to enter self-employment and to help young people and women access to self-employment.[27]

Policies to Help the Self-employed Change to Employers

While most governments encourage SMEs in hiring new employees by reducing social contributions through a range of different programmes, few countries address such help specifically to the self-employed. Among those that have done so are France, where the 1989 programme *Exoneration totale des cotisations patronales de Sécurité Sociale pour l'embauche d'un premier salarié* (extended to managers of *Sociétés à responsabilité limitée* in 1990 and to other associations, co-operatives and *mutuelles* in 1992) offered new employers exoneration from social security contributions for up to 2 years; Belgium, where the 1988 programme *Plus un, plus deux* offered a reduction of the employers' social security contributions for the first three employees, declining over a period of three years; Finland, where the 1998 reform reduced and simplified employers' social security contributions in businesses with less than five employees; and Ireland, where the County Enterprise Board promotes the development of micro-businesses at local level, providing an employment grant (of up to IEP 5000) for each new full-time job created.

Policies to Combat False Self-employment

At the same time as introducing policies to foster self-employment, as we mentioned above, a number of governments have been concerned with the possible growth of "false" self-employment (work situations which are classed as self-employment primarily in order to reduce tax liabilities). A primary objective is to reduce the level

---

[27] OECD (2000)

of tax avoidance. While the main policy instruments involved are fiscal ones, labour market policies are also important, because incentives for "false" self-employment may also stem from overly strict labour protection laws. In addition, it has been suggested, for Germany, that policies to foster self-employment, particularly those which foster unemployed people to access to self-employment, may encourage the development of self-employed businesses with relatively low levels of resources and that part of these might be classed as a form of false self-employment.[28]

Special measures were introduced in Germany to control false self-employment. To limit the tendency for wage workers to slide into the category of "false" self-employed, the German government laid down in 1999, more stringent conditions for a person, previously classified as an employee, to become classified as self-employed for social security purposes. According to the new regulation, a person is sorted as an employee if any three of the following five conditions are fulfilled: i) the person does not employ other workers at wages above DEM 630 per month (including family members); ii) the person depends strongly upon one employer over a long time; iii) the person is employed with tasks for which his/her employer or a comparable employer usually employs dependent workers; iv) the person does not act as an entrepreneur; and, v) the person is employed with the same tasks by the same employer for whom he or she previously worked as an employee.

Similar policies have been introduced in a number of other countries, including Greece, where concern over the growing incidence of false self-employment spurred the August 1998 Law on Industrial Relations according to which work agreements between self-employed persons and companies must be notified in writing to the Ministry of Labour within eight days, failing which the work will be regarded as falling within a dependent employment relationship; Belgium, where concern that false self-employment was present in all sectors led the government to introduce a new procedure, through the Arrêté Royal of 25th January 1991, for monitoring the work relations of people accessing to self-employment from wage and salary working; and Italy, where, in the context of limiting the informal economy, efforts to encourage enterprises and workers to "rise to the surface" have been continued in Law 196/97 and particularly by wage realignment contracts. These *contratti di riallineamento* provide for social security contributions to be progressively aligned to normal levels, and concern nearly 90,000 workers since 1997, the majority of whom worked in the agricultural sector.

Policies to Help Unemployed People Access to Self-employment

Over the years, governments in an increasing number of OECD countries have introduced policies to encourage these flows, by converting unemployment benefits into various forms of grants, to help unemployed people become self-employed. While the general approach of the schemes for the unemployed is the same in all

---

[28] Pfeiffer (1999a)

countries, there are a number of important differences in terms of eligibility, mode of financing and payment duration, controls on the viability of the self-employment business and availability of counselling and training. One crucial question is the *survival rate* of the businesses concerned. This seems to depend very considerably on the severity of the criteria applied to the business plan. For example, in Germany, where the criteria are particularly stringent, a study by the *Institut für Arbeitsmarkt und Berufsforschung* of a sample of newly created businesses since 1994 set up by unemployed people who received the "Bridging Allowance" found that, three years after receiving the support, 70 per cent were still self-employed and that on average each recipient had taken on one employee. A very similar result was found in the Netherlands. In Sweden, four years after having received the Start-up allowance, 59 per cent of the unemployed were still in business[29] whereas in France 51 per cent of the enterprises created by the unemployed under the ACCRE scheme were still in place three years after having received the aid, compared with a survival rate of 42 per cent for those enterprises created by the unemployed without aid, and 61 per cent for the enterprises created by workers.[30] In other countries, *e.g.* Ireland, Norway and the United Kingdom, anecdotal evidence suggests that only a relatively small share of subsidised enterprises showed good longer term survivability.[31] However, high levels of survival need to be interpreted carefully before one can assume that the programme in question worked well. High survival rates can be associated with "creaming"—the programme assures success by accepting only the very best candidates. In turn, this raises the likelihood of deadweight costs—such candidates might very well have created their own business anyway.[32] Lower survival rates do not necessarily imply that a higher proportion of the money spent has no long-term effect. Some studies suggest that a higher percentage of programme participants than non-participants succeed in finding long-term employment, even if their businesses do fail.[33]

The research on factors that influence exit from self-employment indicate that those who have accessed to self-employment from unemployment exit to a higher extent than those who have access from paid-employment.[34]

Andersson y Wadensjö (2006) analyse who became self-employed in the period from 1999 to 2002 of Swedish-born men aged 20 to 60 years who were either wage-earners, unemployed or inactive in 1998. They find that the unemployed, and even more the inactive, are overrepresented among those who become self-employed. They also study the economic outcome of self-employment in 2002 for Swedish-born men who were either unemployed, inactive or wage earners in 1998. Economic outcome in 2002 is measured using income from self-employment and having

---

[29] Okeke (1999)

[30] OECD (2000)

[31] OECD (1996)

[32] O'Leary (1998)

[33] OECD (1998)

[34] See Carrasco (1999), and Pfeiffer and Reize (2000).

employees in the firm. The estimations show that those who were wage earners in 1998 have higher incomes and are also employing other people in their business to a much higher extent in 2002 than those who in 1998 were unemployed or inactive. This indicates that support to unemployed to become self-employed should be implemented with great care. However, an interesting result that they obtain is that the unemployed who have a start-up subsidy are doing better than unemployed without a subsidy in different respects (income, number of employees, exit). The explanation may be the result of the subsidy and the help in starting a firm given the employment office, but it may also be a selection effect, i.e. that the case worker selects the candidates more suited for self-employment.

Rissman (2003) analyzes a model of job search and self-employment where self-employment provides an alternative source of income for unemployed workers. In this work, emphasis is put on the fact that there are two divergent views of the self-employed. The first perception is the one of the visionary that is an entrepreneur, an independent worker who accepts risk in return for a greater reward. His independent nature may add to his own valuation of self-employment. He may have some kind of ability or entrepreneurial capital that confers greater returns in self-employment than in wage work. His taste for risk may be different from others'. Alternatively, the self-employed may be a discouraged wage worker who finds his offered wages too low or his employment too sporadic in the wage sector. In other words, he chooses self-employment not because the value of self-employment is so high but because his value of wage work is so low. If self-employment is chosen because of a lack of opportunities in wage work, then supplementing self-employment through tax breaks and less restrictive lending standards may be an inferior way for workers to escape poverty. Increasing their human capital and implementing policies aimed at reducing the cost of job search may offer greater social rewards.

14.5 Conclusions

In this chapter we have reviewed some possible effects of labour market regulation on self-employment rates and composition, as well as on its potential to generate paid-employment. The relative scarcity of research concerning the impact of regulation on self-employment and the difficulty of constructing indicators to capture the features of these labour market institutions, reveal that the shortcomings of the available statistical data—too little samples- can affect the conclusions drawn and should be taken into consideration when gauging the results.

In the present case, along with the traditional measurement difficulties, common to all institutional factor measurements—for example, the problems derived from the differences between legal requirements and their actual enforcement-, the use of qualitative rankings, of little spatial and temporal scope and based on the laws content, should be gradually replaced through the implementation of statistical operations suitable for measuring monetary-equivalent measures of the degree of regulation.

References

Akerlof G (1984) An Economist's Book of Tales. Cambridge University Press, Cambridge

Andersson P, Wadensjö E (2006) Do the Unemployed Become Successful Entrepreneurs? A Comparison between the Unemployed, Inactive and Wage-Earners. IZA Discussion Paper 2402

Arpaia A, Costello D, Mourre G, Pierini F (2005) Tracking Labour Market Reforms in the EU Member States: an Overview of reforms in 2004 based on the LABREF database. Forthcoming ECFIN Economic paper

Bentolila S, Bertola G (1990) Firing Costs and Labor Demand: How Bad is Eurosclerosis? Review of Economic Studies 57:381–402

Bentolila S, Dolado JJ (1994) Labour flexibility and wages: Lessons from Spain. Economic Policy 18:55–99

Bertola G (1992) Labour turnover costs and average labour demand. Journal of Labour Economics 10(4):389–411

Blanchard O, Wolfers J (2000) The Role of Shocks and Institutions in the Rise of European Unemployment: The Aggregate Evidence. Economic Journal 110:1–33

Boeri T, Nicoletti G, Scarpetta S (1999) Regulation and Labour Market Performance. IGIER Working Paper 158

Botero J, Djankov S, La Porta R, Lopez-de-Silanes, Shleifer A (2004) The Regulation of Labor. Quarterly Journal of Economics 119:1339–82

Bover O, Arellano M, Bentolila S (1996) Unemployment duration, benefit duration and the business cycle. Economic Studies, Series of the Banco de España, Research Department 57

Carrasco R (1999) Transitions to and from self-employment in Spain: an empirical analysis. Oxford Bulletin of Economics and Statistics 61(3):0305–9049

Cazes S, Nesporova A (2003) Employment Protection Legislation (EPL) and its effects on Labour Market Performance. High-Level Tripartite Conference on Social Dialogue, Malta, Valetta

Chor D, Freeman RB (2005) The 2004 Global Labor Survey: Workplace Institutions and Practices Around the World. NBER Working Paper W11598

Di Tella R, MacCulloch R (2005) The consequences of labor market flexibility: Panel evidence based on survey data. European Economic Review 49(5):1225–59

Garibaldi P, Pacelli L, Borgarello A (2003) Employment Protection Legislation and the Size of Firms. IZA Discussion Paper 787

Grubb D, Wells W (1993) Employment regulation and patterns of work in EC countries. OECD Economic Studies 21:7–58

Ilmakunnas P, Kanniainen V (2001) Entrepreneurship, economic risks, and risk insurance in the welfare state: results with OECD data 1978–93. German Economic Review 2:195–218

Kanniainen V, Vesala T (2005) Entrepreneurship and labour market institutions. Economic Modelling 22:828–47

Kaufmann D, Kraay A, Mastruzzi M (2003) Governance Matters III: Governance Indicators for 1996–2002. World Bank Policy Research Department Working Paper, World Bank, Washington

Kugler AD, Pica G (2004) Effects of Employment Protection and Product Market Regulations on the Italian Labour Market. Center for Economic Policy Research, Discussion paper 4216

Layard R, Nickell SJ (1999) Labour Market. Institutions and Economic Performance. In: Ashenfelter O, Card D (eds) Handbook of Labour Economics. Amsterdam North-Holland, vol 3E, pp 3029–84

Lazear EP (1990) Job Security Provisions and Employment. Quarterly Journal of Economics 105:699–726

Light I (1980) Disadvantaged minorities in self-employment. International Journal of Comparative Sociology 20:31–45

Lindbeck A, Snower DJ (1988) The Insider-Outsider Theory of Employment and Unemployment. MIT Press, Cambridge, Massachusetts

Maloney WF (1998) Self-employment and Labor Turnover in LCDs: Cross Country Evidence. World Bank Economist's Forum

Meagre N (1994) Self-employment Schemes for the Unemployed in the European Community. In: Schmid G (ed) Labour Market Institutions in Europe. Sharpe, London, chapter 6

Micco A, Pagés C (2006) The economic effects of employment protection: evidence from international industry-level data. mimeo

Millard S (1996) The Effect of Employment Protection Legislation on Labour Market Activity: A Search Approach. Bank of England Working Paper

Millard S, Mortensen D (1997) The Unemployment and Welfare Effects of Labor Market Policy: A Comparison of the US and UK. In: Snower DJ, de la Dehesa G (eds) Unemployment Policy: Government Options for the Labor Market. Cambridge University Press, Cambridge

Nickell SJ (1982) The determinants of Equilibrium Unemployment in Britain. Economic Journal 92(367):555–75

Nicoletti G, Scarpetta S, Boylaud O (2000) Summary indicators of product market regulation with an extension to employment protection legislation. OECD Economics Department, Working Papers 226.

OECD (1992) The Employment Outlook. OECD, Paris

OECD (1996) Enhancing the Effectiveness of Active Labour Market Policies. The OECD Jobs Strategy, Paris.

OECD (1998) Fostering entrepreneurship: Country experiences of what works and what doesn't. ECO/CPE/WP1(98)9, mimeo, Paris.

OECD (1999) The Employment Outlook. OECD, Paris

OECD (2000) The Employment Outlook. OECD, Paris

OECD (2004) The Employment Outlook. OECD, Paris

Okeke S (1999) The start-up grant: a comparative analysis of entrepreneurial survival and growth. Research unit of the Swedish National Labour Market Board, ISEKen 11

O'Leary C (1998) Promoting self-employment among the unemployed in Hungary and Poland. W. E. Upjohn Institute for Employment Research, mimeo

Parker SC, Robson MT (2004) Explaining international variations in self-employment: evidence from a panel of OECD countries. Southern Economic Journal 71:281–301

Pfieffer F (1999a) Self-employment in Germany. Report prepared for the OECD, mimeo, Paris

Pfieffer F (1999b) Business Start Ups and Employment. Centre for European Economic Research (ZEW)

Pfieffer F, Reize F (2000) Business start-ups by the unemployed. An econometric analysis based on firm data. Labour Economics 7(5):629–63.

Piore M (1986) Labor Market Flexibility. University of California, Berkeley, CA.

Rissman ER (2003) Self-employment as an alternative to unemployment. Federal Reserve Bank of Chicago Working Paper 2003–34.

Robson MT (2003) Does stricter employment protection legislation promote self-employment? Small Business Economics 21:309–19.

Robson MT (2006) Explaining Cross-National Variations in Entrepreneurship: the Role of Social Protection and Political Culture. Department of Economics and Finance, 23–26, Old Elvet, Durham.

Scarpetta S (1996) Assessing the Role of Labour Market Policies and Institutional Settings on Unemployment: A Cross-Country Study. OECD Economic Studies 26, 1996/1.

Schivardi F, Torrini R (2003) Firm Size Distribution and EPL in Italy. William Davidson Institute Working Paper 613.

Staber U, Bogenhold D (1993) Self-employment: a study of seventeen OECD Countries. Industrial Relations Journal 24:126–37.

Tonin M (2005) Updated Employment Protection Legislation Indicators for Central and Eastern European Countries. mimeo.

Torrini R (2005) Cross-country differences in self-employment rates: the role of institutions. Labour Economics 12:661–83.

Chapter 15
Financial System and Entrepreneurship: Institutions and Agents

Mónica Carmona, Mario Cerdán and José María Millán

Abstract The availability or ability to access the capital necessary to start an entrepreneurial project has become one of the more deeply explored elements in the empirical research, as it is considered one of the factors that more frequently constitute an obstacle to the decision of becoming an entrepreneur.

This chapter tries to contribute to the measurement of the level in which the financial system and the institutions that regulate them favours or hinders the access to the entrepreneurial function, going over the institutions and mechanisms through which the financial system has an influence.

15.1 Introduction

As stated in other parts of this book, the governments have not hesitated to design measurements to increase the density of the entrepreneurial network, as an attempt to contribute to the economic growth and the employment generation.

Regardless the means set up to achieve this goal, the fact is that this kind of measurements starts from one assumption: the existence of a market failure that should be amended through public intervention. From this perspective, there must be elements in the entrepreneurial factor that prevents from the market clearing, or there must be factors that make suboptimal the resulting level of self-employment.[1]

Monica Carmona
University of Huelva
monica@uhu.es

[1] Verheul et al. (2001), establish a useful range of governmental interventions to increase the self-employment rate, depending on their effect in the supply and demand of the entrepreneurial factor: i) interventions aimed to increase the profit opportunities or to guide them in a particular direction; ii) interventions aimed to increase the number of potential entrepreneurs or to influence on their typology; iii) interventions designed to influence on the resource, ability and knowledge availability among the individuals; iv) interventions that try to change the preferences, values and attitudes; and v) interventions aimed to affect the risk perception related to the performance of the entrepreneurial activity.

Regarding this question, one of the more intensively explored factors is the role played by the liquidity constraints in the decision to become an entrepreneur. To make the self-employment choice feasible as an occupation, the agents have to be able to mobilize productive factors. In this sense, the availability or ability to access the capital necessary to start an entrepreneurial project has become one of the more deeply explored elements in the empirical research, as it is considered one of the factors that more frequently constitute an obstacle to the decision of becoming an entrepreneur.

However, the liquidity constraints tend to decrease as: i) the project risk and innovation level are reduced;[2] ii) the borrower reputation increases; iii) the financial intermediary improves;[3] iv) the local financial market is developing; v) the size of the firm increases; or vi) the competitiveness level in the banking sector raises. Therefore, the development level of the financial market, its efficiency and the institutions that regulate them turn into decisive factors to understand the level achieved by the entrepreneurial activity, and lastly, the growth and the employment.[4]

This chapter tries to contribute to the measurement of the level in which the financial system and the institutions that regulate them favours or hinders the access to the entrepreneurial function, going over the institutions and mechanisms through which the financial system has an influence. This way, we will be able to detect the key dimensions and aspects, and even the possible sources of inefficiency. They will also act as a guideline to design means that favour its deletion.

To achieve this goal, the chapter is organized into five sections, being this introduction the first one. The second section analyses the ability to mobilize the capital factor as one of the determining factors in the problem of the occupational choice, highlighting the role of the asymmetric information and the credit limitations. The third section analyses the financial system institutions and the key mechanisms that influence on the decision to become an entrepreneur or the expansion of the existing firms. The forth and fifth sections present the conclusions and the statistic operations that would show useful indicators to complete a thorough analysis of these institutions role.

---

[2] Here we refer to the situation created when projects of more profitable investment, which have a high level of participation in the economy growth, are those that find more obstacles to access the capital.

[3] Here we refer to the problem of asymmetric information that the investors have to face up in the capital markets.

[4] The level of financial development is considered as a good estimate factor of the economic growth, capital accumulation and technological change rates. In Levine (1997), we find a wide survey on the literature about the financing-growth link.

15.2 Entrepreneurship and Financing

Those individuals having funds to lend, regardless their decision to participate or not in the business property, have to consider and distinguish among projects with a different level of viability, for which, without exception, the information on their viability is asymmetrically distributed. Thus, the entrepreneurs know the assumptions in which the viability for the business plan (for which they offer their participation or capital) is based, whereas the capital owners usually have less elements to value the goodness of the different business plans offered to them. Considering this situation, capital demanders will try to avoid adverse selection problems by the emission of some kind of signals to let the capital owners evaluate the profitability associated to each project.[5] In this sense, the project characteristics and the history of the entrepreneur will turn into facts, in which the assignment of a certain level of credibility to the project is settled. However, the more risky projects, due to its innovative character or to the lack of experience or reputation[6] of the person who is presenting it, will have severe difficulties. Likewise, and in a negative sense, those projects that have been well presented by agents without any previous experience, or by people who had failed in self-employment in previous times, will emit a negative sign that will make the access to financing difficult. A commonly provided solution is the co-participation, that is, the concession of funds for a lower amount than that required. This forces the project promoters to put their own inheritance at risk, guaranteeing this way that the demanded amounts will meet the real needs of the projects, or al least they will present a number of guarantees.[7] Nevertheless, this sort of solution is only possible as far as the entrepreneurial factor has the necessary resources for it. For this reason, the issue of economic viability reports and/or on the part of consultancy firms or independent organizations becomes the only way to emit signs that let the financial system overcome this problem of information and guarantee the access to the entrepreneurial function to the people without the necessary capital or reputation.

The search of financing is even more problematic when the problem of information comes from the innovative project nature itself, and not from the characteristics of its promoters. In these cases, the financing difficulties arise in response to the related uncertainty level. The work of the technological consultancy firms and the research centre is crucial.

In any case, nothing prevents from the emulation in this process. The promoters of entrepreneurial projects can resort to the use of non accurate consultancy firms to issue reports that guarantee the project viability and move the problem

---

[5] We refer to signaling as a solution to adverse selection problems emerging in presence of asymmetric information situations.

[6] In Diamond (1989), we can find a model that explicitly includes the role of the borrower reputation against different levels of adverse selection and moral hazard.

[7] In these cases, the public sector can take part in the process helping in the concession of these guarantees.

of information from the viability aspect to the guarantee aspect of the studies and reports that guarantee such viability.

So, the development level of the financial system and the role of the financial intermediaries when reducing the risk related to the asymmetric information that is always present in capital markets, will be elements to favour or hinder the starting and growth of entrepreneurial projects.[8]

Following this discussion line, the empirical research has tried to clarify how the structure of the capital markets influences not only on the starting of new entrepreneurial projects, but also in the expansion possibilities of the existing ones. To illustrate this kind of literature, let's have a look at the essay of Guiso, Sapienza and Zingales (2004), who demonstrate the importance of development level of the local financial sector over the individual probability to start a business.[9] Likewise, through interactions between the firm size and level indicators of the local financial development, and as stated in the related literature, the authors assert the progressive weakening of the importance of the local bank as the firm size increases. Another conclusion of this kind of works is the existence of certain sector guidelines in the chosen financing, which affects the role of the capital market in every sector (Rajan and Zingales 1998). This kind of literature also analyses how the bank concentration processes turn into an obstacle for the potential entrepreneurs to access the capital markets (Cetorelli and Strahan 2006).

At this point, we could wonder if the market progressive internationalisation and the elimination of the obstacles to the international movements of capital can have any impact on the access to financing by potential entrepreneurs. In a recently published essay, Alfaro and Charlton (2006) analyse the relation between the financial integration level and the business activity level, using information from 24 million firms from 100 countries during the years 1999 and 2004. It explores some of the channels or mechanisms through which the financial integration can affect the entrepreneurship: the role of foreign direct investments and the effects on the credit availability. From a theoretical point of view, the effects of the financial integration on the entrepreneurship are ambiguous. The accelerated process of financial integration (of which we are witnesses), which is an evidence of the exponential growth of foreign direct investments (FDI), has made certain political and academic sectors worry about the possible negative effects of the international capital on the potential entrepreneurs. So, the argument about the expulsion of the internal investment by foreign investment is usual. For example, Grossman (1984) shows how the international capital, and particularly the FDI, can cause an expulsion of the local entrepreneurs. In a similar line, Hausmann and Rodrik (2003) state that the opening can favour low levels of investment and entrepreneurial activity. Another

---

[8] See Boyd and Prescott (1986) or Greenwood and Jovanovic (1990) essays, which are examples of theoretical models about the role of financing intermediaries.

[9] These authors show how, ceteris paribus, the individual probability to start a business has an increase of 33% when passing from a less developed region to the most developed one. It also states that the entrepreneurs are an average of 5.6 years younger in the most economically developed regions. The President of the Italian banking association declared in a conference that "the golden rule in banking is not giving a loan to a client who is more than 4 km away from the office".

discussion, with the same result as the previous ones, makes reference to the fact that the international capital mobility can increase the probability of financial crisis, as it constitutes a source of higher volatility and risk, and it reduces the entrepreneurial and innovation efforts in a country.

However, the access to external financial resources can allow the starting of firms on the part of potential entrepreneurs from developing countries, which have insufficient capital markets and whose entrepreneurs face up liquidity constraints. If funds availability is a determining factor for entrepreneurship and the international financial integration provides the international sharing of risks and favours the competition by reducing the capital cost, the positive effect should be unequivocal. In other terms, in view of the liquidity constraint role, the opening will contribute insofar as the emergence of new opportunities to share risks facilitates the starting of new projects (see Obstfeld 1994; Acemoglu and Zilibotti 1997). Therefore, the crowding-out of the national entrepreneurship can be compensated with the profits that the interaction with foreign firms, in terms of the transfer of previous experiences, knowledge and technology can offer (Alfaro, McIntyre and Dev 2005).

Leaving aside the issues related to the integration level, the financing problems increase if the institutions that control the performance of the financial markets prevent (or do not give enough promotion) from the investment channelling towards the projects of starting or growth of the firms. This way, the taxation on transfers or return on investments, or even the law for bankruptcy and receivership can turn into a negative element if its design is not appropriate. To find out the effects of these institutions, it is necessary to use a comparative analysis of the kind of taxes and the legislative differences.

Finally, the development level of the business angels and, to a lesser extent, the venture capital entities, such as essential institutions for financing firms in seed stage (seeds) or in the start-up stage, make their monitoring and analysis crucial, if we want to find out the effect of the financial system and its institutions on the entrepreneurial network.

15.3 Institutions and Agents

Once the causal link between financing and entrepreneurship is established, we can analyse the role of those financial system institutions and agents with higher influence over the level of the entrepreneurial activity.

15.3.1 Taxation on Transfers and Successions (Inheritance)

There is a huge amount of empirical literature that shows that the absence of own assets, guarantees or inheritance is the more common reason behind the existence of liquidity constraints. In this sense, Cagetti and De Nardi (2002) develop a model of overlapped generations that shows that the taxes on the inheritances reduce the ability to use them as guarantees. This contributes in a negative way to the possibility to switch to self-employment.

On the other hand, if we want to favour the entrepreneurial activity, we can do it by promoting the creation of new firms or improving the continuity of the existing ones. In this sense, the forecasts of the European Union show that around a third of them will change their owners in the next years. Therefore, the tax system of the business transfers will be crucial to guarantee their continuity. The level of this kind of taxes acquires a special importance in the case of transfers among relatives, in such way that the tax regulations about the retirement of self-employed people or about inheritance are essential to guarantee the continuity of consolidated firms and to favour the incorporation of new people to the self-employed people.

The European Commission (2003) has made some suggestions to the member countries, starting from the premise that, in order to promote entrepreneurship, we have to pay the same attention to business transfer as to the creation of new firms. For this reason, the member countries have to direct their actions to the improvement of the markets dedicated to firm transfers and the design of instruments to favour the transfer of the firms (tax, administrative or technical support firms) to third parties, including the employees themselves.

15.3.2 Capital Gains Tax

Capital gains tax (GGT) affects the rate of return on investments and, hence, it influences decisions made by individual investors, financial institutions and venture capitalists to invest in companies. Capital gains should not be punitively taxed, as they are the reward for investments into risky enterprises.[10]

As it may be expected, the tax picture in the European Union is a complex one, varying considerably from one member state to another. Moreover, comparing capital gains taxation schemes in the Member States is difficult, as tax rates, rules, exemptions and qualifications abound.

In this sense, it might be noted that there is no one and only good approach to capital gains taxation. The practical possibilities to improve the situation depend on the design of the existing tax system and the political willingness to change it.

Tax advantage can be implemented in different ways, one of which is to have tax deductions up front. Another is to reduce the CGT rate. The third is to allow the rollover of capital gains; and a fourth one is the possibility of offset losses against capital gains.

---

[10] See Poterba (1989), Mason and Harrison (2000a), Keuschnigg and Nielsen (2002, 2004), and Stedler and Peters (2002).

15.3.3 Bankruptcy and Insolvency

Although the results obtained by the literature seem to agree with the fact that having previous experiences in self-employment increases the probability of becoming self-employed again, this transition depends on the level of success of that previous experience. So, together with the mark effect that can be generated by searching financing when having a negative experience in self-employment, the law for bankruptcy and insolvency can be turned into a complete barrier to self-employment for those who are in this situation, no matter if the new project nature has signs of being successful.

The regulation of bankruptcy situations faces a trade-off: the protection of the creditors' interests against preventing from the starting of new businesses. The issue is especially important if we consider that, sometimes, a successful project is associated with a learning process generated by a number of previous unsuccessful experiences.

In this sense, the regulation of bankruptcy and insolvency can include a period between the bankruptcy and the starting of a new project, while in practice the possibility to mobilize capital through bank loans will be conditioned on the situation of the generated debt.

Governments have a wide range of options in lowering bankruptcy costs such as debt discharge, debt restructuring, and postponement of debt. Debt discharge regulates the uncertainty and the costs incurred during bankruptcy, which in turn affects both the indirect and direct costs of bankruptcy. Restructuring and debts postponement are often carried out prior to an actual bankruptcy and may save viable, yet insolvent companies, lowering the prospects of default in the process.

In a recent essay, Armour and Cumming (2005) study the role of the cancellation of these debts in the entrepreneurial activity in 13 European countries, the United States and Canada. Fan and White (2003) show how the North American Estates with a less taxable law have a higher percentage of entrepreneurs and more tendency to start a business.

Finally, the short number of essays about the existing relation between the entrepreneurial activity and the entrepreneurs who persist in bankruptcy situations does not clarify their connection, not even if there is a training related to bankruptcy phenomena. However, it is obvious that the lack of possibilities to restart a business after an entrepreneurial failure negatively redounds to the starting of new firms directed by experienced entrepreneurs.

15.3.4 Business Angels and Venture Capital

In our review of the financial system and its effects to the entrepreneurial network, business angels and venture capital businesses, they play a decisive role in the mobilization of the necessary capital. Business angels are private investors that directly contribute with their own resources and third party resources to new firms or growing firms. As per the venture capital entities, these investors are going for an entrepreneurial project without getting involved in it every day, but providing an extra value. Nevertheless, these investors are clearly different from the venture capital investors since they provide their own capital, while the venture capital entities usually invest third-party resources. Another difference is the disinvestment period. The venture capital entities usually disinvest before, as they tend to handle temporary funds that they have to give back and achieve a return on them, while business angels do not have this limitation, what lets them invest in less mature projects. The venture capital entities usually consult the stock market, acting on undervalued mature firms with problems and reorganization needs, with the aim of putting them back to the market in a short period.

On their part, business angels fill the gap that prevented the microcompanies from progressing until achieving the necessary dimension to get bank financing and venture capital. Moreover, as business angels invest in start-up (not seeds) firms, they do not compete with the institutional venture capital; on the contrary, they complete it. The financing provided by the business angels is fast and flexible, although limited, so the financing needs generated by the company growth usually exceed the resources that the business angels can provide. This way, the business angels tend to prepare the company to receive institutional investors.

However, the level of development of this financing source is conditioned by the lack of coordination in this market. In fact, business angels encounter problems when they try to find profit opportunities to meet their requirements and their risk perception.[11] On the contrary, and from the point of view of the entrepreneurs, the lack of market coordination prevents from accessing to this financing source. To mitigate this information issues and make the "matching" process more efficient, the European Commission is fostering the development of "business angels" networks.[12]

Nowadays, the monitoring of the level of development of this kind of financing is difficult. So, most of the business angels investments are made without any help from networks and are not recorded. For this reason, and due to the nature of this market, it is not possible for the moment to generate financing flow statistics created this way with a certain level of reliability. However, to progress in the number of successful operations recorded in the networks may be possible if some kind of compensation would be generated in the network, in case the investment was successful.

---

[11] See the essay of Mason and Harrison (1993).

[12] A Business Angel Network—BAN- is an organization aimed to small, medium-sized, new or growing companies to informal and private investors. The business angels networks have two main roles: get together the business angels and increase the efficiency of its process to contact with interesting investment projects.

15.4 Conclusions

The ability to mobilize the necessary capital is an essential requirement to access the self-employment and cause the business growth.

The existence of liquidity constraints and the difficulties to access the capital markets could be a real barrier to carry out the entrepreneurial activity and a severe obstacle for the economy growth.

For this reason, the level of development of the financial system, the law for transfers and failures, and even the opening level to international capital flows, are key elements to favour entrepreneurship. To achieve the appropriate diagnosis and monitoring of the impact of these institutions and the law itself, it is necessary to progress in the search of indicators that let us find out the different aspects we want to measure. Precisely, one of the issues in which the research has found more obstacles to the development has been the lack of the available indicators and statistics. Despite this, we present, in table 15.1, some singular efforts that might be a starting point for the design of homogeneous indicators by the national statistic agencies.

Table 15.1 Financial System Indicators

Credit Indicators
Legal Rights Index
Source: World Bank, Doing Business
Percentage of Individuals With Denied Credit
Source: Survey of Household Income and Wealth (SHIW) Individuals' Savings
Source: OECD
Venture Capital Indicators
Venture Capital Investment
Source: OECD Science, Technology and Industry Scoreboard
Percentage of the High Technology Sector over the Total Venture Capital
Source: OECD Science, Technology and Industry Scoreboard
Venture Capital Investment per Sectors
Source: EVCA Corporate Venturing Survey
Venture Capital Investment per Regions
Source: EVCA Corporate Venturing Survey
Reputation of Venture Capital Managers: Age and Total Capital under Management
Source:
Outflow Opportunities Indicators
Secondary Market Capitalization as a Percentage of the GBP
Source: OECD
Primary Market Capitalization as a Percentage of the GBP
Source: OECD
Tax and Legal Environment Indicators
EVCA index
Source: EVCA, Benchmarking European tax and legal environments
Bankruptcy Law Indicators
Period to Release the Debt after a Bankruptcy
Source: National law in every country

References

Alfaro L, Charlton A (2006) International Financial Integration and Entrepreneurship. CEP discussion paper, London School of Economics

Alfaro L, Vinati D, McIntyre S (2005) Foreign Direct Investment and Ireland's Tiger Economy. Harvard Business School Case 705–009

Armour J, Cumming D (2005) Bankruptcy Law and Entrepreneurship. Berkeley Electronic Press. Berkeley

Boyd JH, Prescott EC (1986) Financial Intermediary-Coalitions. Journal of Economic Theory 28:211–32

Cagetti M, De Nardi M (2002) Entrepreneurship, Frictions and Wealth. Federal Reserve Bank of Minneapolis, Working Paper 620

Cetorelli N, Strahan PE (2006) Finance as a Barrier to Entry: Bank Competition and Industry Structure in Local U.S. Markets. Journal of Finance 61(1):437–61

Diamond DW (1989) Reputation Acquisition in Debt Markets. Journal of Political Economy 97(4):828–62

Fan W, White MJ (2003) Personal Bankruptcy and the Level of Entrepreneurial Activity. Journal of Law and Economics 46(2):543–68

Greenwood J, Jovanovic B (1990) Financial Development, Growth and the Distribution of Income. Journal of Political Economy 98(5):1076–1107

Guiso L, Sapienza P, Zingales L (2004) Does local financial development matter? Quarterly Journal of Economics 119:929–69

Hansson A (2006) The wealth tax and entrepreneurial activity. Mimeo

Keuschnigg C, Nielsen SB (2002) Tax policy, venture capital, and Entrepreneurship. Journal of Public Economics 87:175–203

Keuschnigg C, Nielsen SB (2004) Start-ups, venture capitalists, and the capital gains tax. Journal of Public Economics 88:1011–042

Levine R (1997) Financial Development and Economic Growth: Views and Agenda. Journal of Economic Literature 35:688–726

Mason C M, Harrison RT (1993) Strategies for expanding the informal venture capital market. International Small Business Journal 11(4):23–28

Mason CM, Harrison RT (2000a) Influences on the Supply of Informal Venture Capital in the UK: An Exploratory Study of Investor Attitudes. International Small Business Journal 18(4):11–28

Poterba J (1989) Capital gains tax policy toward entrepreneurship. National Tax Journal 42(3):375–89

Rajan R, Zingales L (1998) Financial Dependence and Growth. American Economic Review 88:559–86

Stedler HR, Peters HH (2003) Business Angels in Deutschland: Empirische Studie der FH Hannover zur Erforschung des Erfolgsbeitrages bei Unternehmensgründung. Fachhochschule Hannover, Fachbereich Wirtschaft, Hannover

Verheul I, Wennekers S, Audretsch D, Thurik R (2001) An Eclectic Theory of Entrepreneurship. Tinbergen Institute Discussion Paper 2001–030/3

Chapter 16
Building a Statistical System on Entrepreneurship: a Theoretical Framework

Emilio Congregado, Antonio Aníbal Golpe, José María Millán and Concepción Román

Abstract The search for a systematic set of indicators to measure the crucial dimensions of the entrepreneurship in relation to its diagnosis, forecast and tracking, has become a very first need for both the economic analysis progress, as well as to obtain an appropriate design, monitoring and evaluation of the public policies.

The main contribution of this study is to present a theoretical framework of reference that may be used as foundation to articulate a statistical subsystem of entrepreneurship indicators, a conceptual general framework that nourishes from the contributions and results, which are the core of the Economics of Entrepreneurship, and that allows us to determine the key dimensions and aspects to be captured by the system.

16.1 Introduction

The search for a systematic set of indicators to measure the crucial dimensions of the entrepreneurship in relation to its diagnosis, forecast and tracking, has become a very first need for both the economic analysis progress, as well as to obtain an appropriate design, monitoring and evaluation of the public policies. Thus, the increasing importance of the entrepreneurial promotion policy in the European area,[1] has a logical inference of starting different kinds of actions to implement this type of statistical information subsystems.

We can appeal to a comparison analysis to show the novelty characteristic of this kind of statistical information. Based on this analysis, we can confirm the short number of institutions and agencies that have real entrepreneurship statistical subsystems, showing important methodological differences among them. This way, at present agencies that implement entrepreneurship statistical systems coexist with

E. Congregado
University of Huelva
congregado@uhu.es

[1] Proof of this statement is the set of objectives derived from the Lisbon Council 2000. These objectives explicitly defend the entrepreneurial promotion policy as a foundation for basing the European Union's growing and employment strategy for 2010.

other agencies that have developed competitiveness subsystems.[2] In these subsystems, entrepreneurship and its dimensions are configured as one of the decisive factors of competitiveness, while the most common fact derives from those agencies that only make some isolated statistical operations, used to try to capture some inner dimensions and aspects of the entrepreneurship.

As starting point, we could wonder about the reason of this situation, we would wonder why the statistical operations designed to measure the entrepreneurship are scanter, and even scanter are the attempts to systemize statistical information. In other words, why a similar statistical development level between labour market analysis and entrepreneurial analysis does not exist?

This situation is, in some extent, logical if we take into account two premises: i) firstly, the economic analysis of entrepreneurship has not been –until recently- a central subject in Economics, which has been translated in a short number of models and theoretical propositions, ii) secondly, the absence of a common framework for analysis implies very different approaches. Consequently, dimensions, indicators and proxies used in research are difficult to be implemented in the same statistical information subsystem.

However, the increasing entrepreneurship integration in Economics through the use of proper models of Labour Economics, the appearing of propositions more robust and verified and the increasing importance of the entrepreneurial promotion policy in the politic action agenda –under the premise that its promotion is an effective way to achieve the economic growth and competitiveness objectives-, imply the following: i) the theoretical framework clarification, with the first efforts to synthesize, and ii) from the statistical point of view, the increasing demand on information and the pioneering efforts to make systematized statistical operations, for them to create entrepreneurship statistical subsystem.[3] In this sense, the search for indicators, and even the articulation of specific statistics have become a crucial need to make a progress in applied research, and in order to design, implement, and assess the different instruments of public intervention on this subject. Thus, the development of a set of indicators that allow satisfactorily capture the different dimensions of the entrepreneurial network for a specific sector or territory –either by using already existing statistical operations, either by implementing new ones- becomes a basic element to favour the progress in entrepreneurship analysis, forecast, and monitoring.

Although analysts, and the agencies themselves have implemented specific statistical operations to measure the entrepreneurial dynamics, and even its stock, those have not been considered as a statistical system, but a set of incoherent operations used to attempt immediately satisfying the increasing demand on entrepreneurial information. This way, and for a short time ago, the only progress in the articulation

---

[2] We can compare, for instance, the Danish Entrepreneurship Index vs. the Competitivity Index of the British Treasure.

[3] We refer here to projects, such as the OECD Entrepreneurship Indicators Project or the pioneering effort of FORA (Denmark).

of indicators -with a certain dose of comparability-, has been associated with both the quantitative aspect measurement of the entrepreneurship, and the creation of Structural Business Statistics.

Therefore, the increasing demand on statistical information about the entrepreneurship, and its actions results, together with the real status of the statistical operations related to entrepreneurship, advice the design and implementation of real statistical information systems on entrepreneurship, for which the dimensions and variables to be captured are determined by some kind of theoretical framework that allows determining which existing statistical operations may be used to propose indicators that help to capture the key dimensions, which ones should be modified for the system objectives, and if no covered dimensions exists that advice the implementation of new statistical operations. Those tasks must have the necessary dose of comparability, which means that they have to be articled based on the use of common methodologies to obtain indicators that should be integrated in the system.

Due to the special features, and the current status of this research subject, the main task may be the articulation of a theoretical framework, and more urgent, to be able to identify unequivocally the dimensions and aspects to be captured by the system, as well as to guarantee the comparability of the systems to be articled in the future. That is why we believe that any proposal to measure entrepreneurship must be established within an orthodox conceptual framework,[4] and must tend to the same international ongoing experiences. In other words, to establish the key dimensions and variables that allow us to capture the entrepreneurship, and the different consequences of its economic actions, we must use the core of the propositions stemmed from the theoretical research on entrepreneurship. We should also take into consideration the most consolidated elements of the implemented or under study statistical subsystems. The main contribution of this study is exactly this: presenting a theoretical framework of reference that may be used as foundation to articulate a statistical subsystem of entrepreneurship indicators, a conceptual general framework that nourishes from the contributions and results, which are the core of the Economics of Entrepreneurship, and that allows us to determine the key dimensions and aspects to be captured by the system.

The chapter structure is in accordance to the proposed theoretical framework itself. Therefore, in Section 2, entrepreneurship is conceptually delimited, and we argue about the need to distinguish entrepreneurship and its determinants from its action results. Once this task is carried out, in Section 3, the model is analysed. In this model, dimensions and variables to be captured by the system derive from determinant factors of entrepreneurship supply and demand, from the entrepreneurial activity itself, and lastly, from this market interrelations to other variables and markets. Finally, in Section 4, we summarize and introduce the dimensions and variables to be configured by the analysed system.

---

[4] This statement should not be understood in terms of rejection of other kind of approaches validity, but as the most operative way to reach a consensus on a theoretical framework of reference.

16.2 A Theoretical Framework to Measure Entrepreneurship

The importance given to entrepreneurship in the policy action agenda has created an increasing demand on statistical information, and as result, the starting of new statistical operations.[5] The first institutions that have tried to create a statistical information system on entrepreneurship face to the difficulty of integrating the different approaches to the entrepreneurship phenomenon. In our attempt to explain the reasons of this situation, maybe the absence of a consolidated research paradigm has caused that action guidelines to capture the statistical information needs have derived from the kind of applied policies. From our perspective, the proliferation of very different origin theories may have impeded the setting of clear guidelines to delimit dimensions and variables to be captured. Because of this, the explanation of a conceptual framework –using models and propositions of the economic analysis on entrepreneurship-, becomes a key element for the development of a statistical system. In this context, the creation of a framework that contributes to delimit factors impacting on the entrepreneurship performance, and on its results and interrelations to other economic variables, represents a optimal strategy to design a statistical system, as well as it may help to solve the diagnosis, design, implementation and validity problems of entrepreneurial promotion policies: a consistent model that may identify all elements useful to increase entrepreneurial network density and quality, and that help us to progress in the international comparability field. Thus, the standardization of concepts, definitions, and forms of measurements must be basic, due to the special characteristics of this research subject.

16.2.1 Systems of Entrepreneurship Indicators Vs. Systems of Competitiveness Indicators

At this moment, we will have a preliminary view of the interest areas for the academy and for policy-makers about the entrepreneurship, areas that may be used as basis to determine if a statistical system satisfies the information needs. However, we do not consider that a statistical information system should be based exclusively on one kind or another type of demand. Therefore, the statistical agencies responsible officers usually declare that the main handicap to articulate a real entrepreneurial statistical system is the difficulty to establish a theoretical framework for the analysis, that help to clarify the dimensions and aspects to capture. Nevertheless, we can state that this approach to entrepreneurship phenomena is not the only possible

---

[5] Without trying to be really accurate, the most used kind of instruments for entrepreneurial promotion are: i) administrative barriers elimination (procedures simplification); ii) economic contributions; iii) establishment of measures addressed to favour education on entrepreneurship; iv) establishment of tax benefits; v) advising; vi) establishment of measures addressed to favour R+D, and technology transfers; vii) favouring scale increases and firm internationalisation; viii) promotion activities; and, ix) favouring network setting.

approach. Thus, a widespread tradition in some statistical institutions and agencies consists in articling entrepreneurial competitiveness indicators systems. In these systems, competitiveness is considered as central element, and the way to determine dimensions and aspects to be captured by the system is based on theories about the competitiveness determinants. We can often find systems based on the wide know Porter's diamond, which is used to list a series of regular propositions to be taken into account for designing a competitiveness strategy. As an example, this conceptual framework is used by the British Treasure to allow the competitiveness and productivity monitoring in United Kingdom. In this framework, a number of indicators are collected in an attempt of measuring the investment, human capital, firms, and competence: all dimensions considered as key elements that influences on the productivity and competitiveness improvements. Under similar parameters, the Global Competitiveness Report,[6] is based.

On the other hand, a statistical system to measure entrepreneurship sets entrepreneurial market as the centre of the system, while competitiveness, growth, its contribution to employment, or innovation level, must be understood as results, i.e., as consequence of its interrelations to other markets within the general equilibrium model framework. How to use this approach will be the result of a number of different considerations. Firstly, because only by using models, propositions and results, we can identify interesting dimensions that may help to the economic research itself, to the entrepreneurial network diagnosis and monitoring, and if applicable, to public policies design. Secondly, designating a statistical system with these features –highlighting the term "entrepreneurship" or the word "competitiveness"-, would only be a terminology digression without interest, if in both cases, propositions derived from economic analysis over entrepreneurship are to be added. In third place, according to the development stage of this kind of systems, we are in a critical moment in order to favour comparativeness. In this sense, the statistical development of indicators on entrepreneurship is a very essential need, for which several governments and national institutions are trying to satisfy. Nowadays, the OECD leads a project to develop a general statistical framework for entrepreneurship. After a previous conceptual debate about concepts and definitions, it is proposed to create a list with required indicators to understand entrepreneurial network and its effects.[7]

In order to contribute to debate, we can take as reference the theoretical framework used as basis for the Danish Statistical System on entrepreneurship, which attempts to fit to synthesis efforts carried out by Audretsch, Thurik and Verheul (Audretsch et al, 2002), and by Lundström and Stevenson (Lundström and

---

[6] 188 indicators are taken as starting point, grouped in the following categories: country added indicators; macroeconomic indicators; technology innovation and divulging indicators; information technology and communication indicators; infrastructure indicators; indicators about public institutions, in terms of regulation and corruption measurement; internal competence level indicators; indicators about clusters development; environmental indicators; entrepreneurial operations and strategies indicators, and finally, indicators about international institutions.

[7] See chapters 4,7 and 8.

Stevenson, 2001, 2002, 2005). This model poses the existence of a number of factors that impacts on the entrepreneurs' supply and demand. Demand is determined by profit opportunities, while supply makes reference to the possibility to carry an entrepreneurial project out. Determinants of supply and demand, together with the incentives structure, and a set of cultural and motivation factors, determine the entrepreneurial activity level of a specific sector or region. Although we share the same framework, there are some controversy elements, that, under our point of view, can be: i) there is no accurate distinction between the productive factor and these agents action results; ii) absence of an incentive structure integration, as a factor of supply; iii) consideration of motivation and culture as something external to the personal decision of being entrepreneur; iv) absence of a exhaustive delimitation about which variables or elements must be integrated in the entrepreneurial activity; and specially, v) mixture of some economical analysis elements for entrepreneurship with other kind of approaches, so pseudo-theories and theoretical models quite accurate have been considered as complementary elements.

Taking into account all previous facts, we consider that designing a theoretical framework that combines academic progresses with the practical requirements may result in an "operative" strategy to detect the dimensions and variables to be implemented in a statistical subsystem on entrepreneurship.

16.2.2 The Entrepreneurial Function, the Entrepreneurial Factor and the Productive Agent

From different theories the economical analysis the entrepreneurial factor is based on, we could agree that the entrepreneurial function performance is configured according to, at least, one of the following functions: i) the entrepreneur is an agent that decreases inefficiencies continuously present in firm (Leibenstein 1969, 1979). His actions must be addressed to search for the optimisation of the factor used by selecting the technology combination more adequate for this objective; ii) he find profit opportunities that permanently exist in the markets (Kirzner 1973, 1979, 1985) by using his knowledge about consumers' preferences, about technology combinations, and about factors markets in order to create a productive combination that satisfies this demand; iii) he faces to the uncertainty of predicting the future (Knight 1929); and, iv) he innovates (Schumpeter 1913).

Thus, an agent carries out the entrepreneurial function and, therefore, he constitutes the entrepreneurial factor if he develops any of the vectors that compose the entrepreneurial functions, regardless: i) the success or luck level with which this task is carried out; and, ii) the link with property. This means that, although the same agent could be capitalist and entrepreneur at the same time, or entrepreneur and paid-employee, we should not overlap the productive factors. Just like the same agent can sell his available time as labour factor, and at the same time contribute with his capital, the same agent can combine the entrepreneurial function performance and the contribution with his capital or labour factor. In this sense, the entrepreneurial function can be carried out by simple paid-employees without any link to capital property –very common case in corporative firms-, just like it can carry out only one of the vectors that configure the entrepreneurial function performance, as this function is done by specialized teams.

With this starting point, for the entrepreneurial factor –just like that for any other productive factor-, a supply and a demand will exist to configure an entrepreneurial factor market, that is to say, available resources and a demand to be satisfied. By clearing this market, expected profits and a specific composition of the network will be generated, that will determine the influence of the market on the entrepreneurial activity results: in terms of competitiveness, the employment creation, the added value generation, and even, the innovation.

The search of both market forces determinants will be our theoretical framework, which must be used to determine the basic dimensions to be included in a statistical information system on entrepreneurship. This system should try to capture all differences in its economic action.

16.3 A Conceptual Framework

According to the premise that any conceptual framework proposal must be based on the most widely accepted propositions, and that it must use the same conceptual schemes that those used on the any other productive factor analysis, the analysis of the entrepreneurial market and its results -if it is either measured in terms of the productive combinations they create or either in terms of its interrelations to other markets-, is a good guide to determine the key dimensions to be captured by a statistical information system on entrepreneurship. Although literature shows an unequal development level associated to the number of contributions from the supply perspective in relation to the analysis of the demand, this fact must not be understood in terms of a complete absence of contributions. Thus, the most frequent way to understand the entrepreneurial factor demand is through this identification with the incentives the economical agents receive if they carry the entrepreneurial action out. This is the idea derived from Schultz (1975) or Casson (1982) theories, who consider that entrepreneur demand is formed by the entrepreneurial profits opportunities. Taking into account this perspective, the entrepreneurial factor demand is conformed by the profit opportunities themselves that each agent is able to detect,[8] so the agent will try to firstly implement the opportunities associated with a higher expected profit rate. This way, the entrepreneurial demand is configured as a decreasing relation between profit opportunities and hours spent on the entrepreneurial function performance.

---

[8] Nevertheless, the profit opportunities are not detected by everybody the same way, since information and knowledge are not uniformly distributed throughout the population. This fact can help us to understand some aspects of phenomena, such us entrepreneurial concentration or productive specializations in specific areas.

On the other hand, the entrepreneurial factor supply must provide the keys about the economical agent will to offer his effort time to perform the entrepreneurial function. At first sight, any agent has the possibility to be entrepreneur. Each agent will have some kind of capacity derived from his knowledge –innate or acquired-, that will allow him to access to a wider or more limited set of opportunities[9]. The same way, a person can be subjected to some –relative or absolute- restrictions that may impede him to choose that selection, although this may be the chosen option in accordance with the expected performance of this option in relation to the derived performance of the paid-employment. This is a problem related to the occupational choice, although with a subjective assessment element determined by the incertitude associated to the entrepreneurial function performance against the safe wage of the paid-employment especially in labour markets in which normative introduce specific guaranties added to the paid-employment.

Just like in other market, the equilibrium will be carried out when for a certain expected profits level, the required entrepreneurial function performance time to capture an opportunity, matches that time agents are determined to offer to the current profit.

If we think in aggregated terms, as result of this dedication to the entrepreneurial function, an entrepreneurial activity level and productive configurations resulting from is action will be generated, i.e., a specific quantitative and qualitative composition of the entrepreneurial network. This entrepreneurial activity level creates certain production levels, employment, some economic results, and even some specific lines of specialization and innovations, depending on the kind of opportunities that have been detected and captured, and on the productive combinations configured based on its actions. Once this general scheme of analysis has been established, we are ready to analyse the supply and demand determinants that must be included as guidelines to determine the dimensions to be captured in a statistical information system on entrepreneurship.

16.3.1 Entrepreneurship Demand

Let's assume there is a continuous flow of profit opportunities set by the general conditions of the external and internal economic environment, although they are probably limited by both the information the individual has according to his knowledge, and by the existence of some institutions that limit the "potential set" of opportunities to be captured. If we, at this very moment, ignore the restrictions set by institutions, the general conditions of the economic environment, i. e., the economy development –that we can identify it with the driving forces of aggregated supply and demand-, will create an atmosphere for the potential development of businesses, influencing this way on the current feasibility of any profit

---

[9] Note that in order to access to a higher number of profit opportunities, it is not necessary condition to access to more profitable opportunities.

opportunity. Thus, shocks –being for offer or demand-, regardless the reasons of their origin or the market that created them, will generate variations on the assessment of each entrepreneurial profit opportunity, and they will also imply that some opportunities may be rejected while other can be created. Therefore, dimensions and variables to be kept in a statistical information subsystem match with statistical operations collected in National Accounting, and specifically the match with the most used statistics for the conjuncture analysis, statistical operations quite consolidated that would be directly integrated in an information subsystem on entrepreneurship. On the other hand, together with these general conditions of the environment, a previous condition to capture opportunities has to be with the deregulation and competence level, with the degree of openness, and even with guideless to knowledge diffusion. This way, the existence of absolute barriers for accessing to certain sectors or the restrictive regulations to exercising some kind of activities may imply that some perceptible opportunities are not feasible, becoming in inexistent profit opportunities. We could follow a similar reasoning in relation to the difficulty elements to diffuse technology, and therefore, they impede some productive configurations and some entrepreneurial projects. Thus, very deregulated economies with a high competence level will show profit opportunities, possibly not as high as in other environments, but they will may suitable to be captured by a great part of the entrepreneurial network. On the opposite site, over-regulated economies, with a low competence level will create a set of profit opportunities, possibly with a very high associated performance, but a great part of the entrepreneurial network will have limited access. Let's pose some examples that will help us to clarify the influence of the economy regulation level, and we will try to make a clear distinction from those that could involve administrative obstacles or institutions that have an effect on the productive factor mobilization. These will be analysed later as obstacles that negatively have an effect on the offer.

Let's assume that there is a specific economic activity, which is regulated so that in order to exercise this activity, it is necessary to have a perceptive license, quantity-limited. In this case, in spite of the existence of individuals that would be ready to capture these profit opportunities, there is an absolute barrier to access to this activity. A phenomenon with the same features would derive from the existence of patents (although, this would only imply a temporary absolute barrier), or from the existence of monopolies, regardless their origin.

This way, the demand of entrepreneurs relates the profit opportunities the entrepreneurial network detects and is able to capture. The general conditions of the aggregated supply and demand, the degree of economic freedom, the guideless to diffuse technology, and the degree of openness will determine the set of feasible opportunities, and therefore, these will be the key dimensions to be kept in a proposal of the statistical system on entrepreneurship. Now we proceed with a brief analysis of the mechanism followed by these factors to influence on the demand, as a way of approaching to the variables and indicators that can contribute to capture these dimensions.

The Macroeconomic Environment

In order to proceed with the detection and capturing of the different existence profit opportunities, the entrepreneurial agent must take into account firstly the analysis of the economic environment, where this entrepreneurial activity is carried out. This environment has two sides: the inner side (internal market) and the outer side (external market), with more o less influence depending on the target market and on the origin of the productive factors. The entrepreneur, as any other productive agent, needs information to detect the opportunities and to face incertitude inherent to any entrepreneurial venture. This way, and just like in any investment project assessment, the forecast of demand, factors to be mobilised and costs related to these factors is crucial. Hence, having a good statistical support to be used in making this forecast and to monitor the macroeconomic environment will be basic to the previous assessment before starting the activity. The main information source to monitor and analyse the macroeconomic and sector situation, including forecasts, will be based on having an economic statistical subsystem to be used to collect the required information in order to foresee, in a more secure way, the consequences of the decisions made. Hence, the result of any decision made about the firm's competitive strategy is subjected to the evolution of the general context of businesses: the aggregate demand level, the factor markets and by the Government intervention. Due to this reason, the entrepreneur must interpret the consequences of the conjuncture on the result of his actions. These macroeconomic conditions (internal and external) –according to the required scale to capture the profit opportunity- are summarized in, what we agreed to call, a macroeconomic framework, in which we collect the indicators that measure the aggregated supply and demand determinant factors, originated from quite standardized statistical operations derived from official statistical agencies. However, one of the vectors that define the entrepreneurial function performance derives from the need of facing to the inherent incertitude of this kind of activity. The results of this entrepreneurial activity are, by nature, uncertain and, therefore, the entrepreneurial factor must make decisions in this incertitude framework. Obviously, the quantity information, the interpretation of this information, the forecasts and the methods used to forecast the future will be different depending on the agents. Thus, the suitability level of the strategic decisions of the firm to changes in the economic environment will be linked to the existence, interpretation, and quality of the statistical information, but also to forecasts. Obviously, not all individuals implied on the strategic decision-making make their own interpretations and conjuncture forecast, but they usually base these on the analysis and forecasts made by the public organisms or institutions. This way, the importance of these analysis, from the entrepreneurial factor point of view, is critical, since they set a number of trends on the agents' expectations and, therefore, on the profit opportunities assessment itself. As it is well known, together with the traditional forecasts based on regular analysis, in the conjuncture analysis, forecasts based on opinion surveys have been introduces. These surveys may be related to the entrepreneurial environment or to consumers' trust, and are done to try to measure the agents' expectations through their interpretation of the economic environment changes when attempting to detect changes on consumption or investment trends.

The way these expectations are formed up and the translation to general climates, favourable or unfavourable, is an increasing in importance element for the current economies development. Once at this point, we consider we have provided enough elements to state that the economic conjuncture analysis is a key element to perceive profit opportunities and to estimate their potential. Therefore, this analysis must be included in a statistical information subsystem on entrepreneurship.

The Degree of Economic Freedom

Defence for competence is considered as an essential element to guarantee the economic efficiency, that is why it is included as rule in the most of modern constitutional texts. From our point of view, the existence of barriers that hinder or impede the access to a specific activity sector not only mean an efficiency loss for the economy, but also they cause a decrease in the available profit opportunities for potential entrepreneurs.[10] But, regardless the assessment of its involvements, our interest is focused on articulating indicators to measure this aspect. In this sense, the existence of absolute barriers to the access is usually valued thorough indicators that measure the legal barriers extension or the number of exceptions to the anti-monopoly legislation. A good example of this kind of indicators is that made by the OECD, where the level of number of competitors limited by legislation, is measured.

The Degree of Openness

The degree of openness should impact directly on the profit opportunities. Let's consider a closed economy, where the existent profit opportunities are those derived from the potential demand of the domestic market, while the productive possibilities are limited to the technologic possibilities and to inner productive factors. In an opposite situation, a complete opening of this economy –let's think about a perfect mobility-, will imply the appearance of new profit opportunities. This appearance is due to the extension of latent demands range and of markets dimension, at the same time that this makes production possibilities feasible, which were not possible before due to technology reasons o to the impossibility of mobilizing the required productive factors in the inner market. Hence, the opening increases the entrepreneurial factor demand. Nevertheless, the final result of a greater opening does not imply necessarily an increase in the inner entrepreneurial activity. Although the opening will create new profit opportunities, this will also imply an increase in the entrepreneur's supply, so the impact can even be the opposite.[11]

---

[10] The point is not choosing having or not a regulation, but being able to assess which elements of the regulation have different effect than those expected.

[11] Given a specific national sector size, the national entrepreneurship crowding-out can be made up by the profits that interaction with foreign firms can provide, in terms of previous experiences, knowledge and technology transfers. From his side, Grossman (1984) shows how the international capital, and specially the direct foreign investments, may imply the expulsion of the national entrepreneurship. In a very similar line, Hausmann y Rodrik (2003) argue that the *laissez-faire*, and specially the opening may create low levels of ex ante investments and self-employment.

Let's ignore, for a moment, these two extreme situations and let's think about an autarchic economy that experiences a progressive opening period. Let's assume, for example, that in this first opening stage, the free movement of capital factor is allowed, but the firm creation from non-national entrepreneurs is forbidden. In this case, the opening would not increase the profit opportunities, but it would favour the entrepreneurs' access to new markets of capital, i. e., it would favour the factor mobilization from the national entrepreneurs' side. This same situation would be also applicable if difficulties exist in order to mobilize labour factor with the desired productivity level and wages, and the arrival of other countries workers is allowed.

Generally speaking, the importance given by governments to the exporting activity of its firms is subjected to its contribution to the economic growth (Lages and Montgomery 2004). These favourable effects have caused that the opening effects analysis has become a subject of increasing interest. The most of these essays argue that countries with a greater number of exporting firms have a global improvement in its competitiveness level, since these firms (either through showing the effect or either by requiring actions to the collaborating national firms) force the remaining activities to make an effort for modernization (Girma et al. 2004). This way, it is widely accepted that an exporting guidance of firms is a favouring factor for the economic growth (Moen 2002), although empirical studies that confirm this are scarce. On the other hand, there are studies that consider exporting firms as more productive firms, with a bigger size and with more probability of survival, while they are capable of paying greater wages than those that do not export (Aw et al. 2000). But, the situation that is not really clear is if the greater productivity showed by these firms is originated in its exporting direction (which allows them to acquire new knowledge, to access to new technologies, and that oblige them to be more competitive), or if the innovation and competitiveness themselves guide these firms towards an exporting activity. To summarize, and despite the relation between the entrepreneurial activity level and the integration level is still a controversial point, the problems in international flows of goods and factors must be subject of tracking and control, and therefore, this relation must be considered in a statistical system that attempts to capture the key dimensions of the entrepreneurship. In this sense, the generally used indicators for the empirical analysis are a good base to act on. This way, the systems should try to capture both integration indicators *de jure*, related to liberalization policies for good and factors movement, as well as indicators *de facto*, related to current flows.

Diffusion of Technology

Innovation, apart from being one of the functions that define the entrepreneurial function performance and one of the entrepreneurial activity output, must be analysed according to the mechanisms used by innovations to propagate throughout the productive system, since these mechanisms are configured as essential elements for its potential conversion to business opportunities. This way, the configuration of the science-technology-industry system is one of the main determinants of entrepreneurship demand, since this determines the way the innovations are diffuse over the productive system. The traditional elements of the R+D statistics, and its measurement indicators of the inputs and results of the research and development process, have no involvement *per se* in profit opportunities. If the R+D activity, even if it is successful, does not have the appropriate mechanisms to satisfy the productive body demands, or if the connections among systems fail, may become a futile activity with no impact on the economic activity. From the outer perspective, the existence of problems in the technological diffusion processes it the main responsible in the failure to fulfil the convergence proposition related to the neoclassical theory of economic growth. We reference here to the fact that a greater opening –even if this would imply a perfect mobility- does not necessarily imply the access to every profit opportunities of the participating countries in the free trade agreement. This way, some profit opportunities will be protected and hence, these would be limited by patents, regardless if they are process or product-derived. Thus, the economies with a lower technological development level will see that some business opportunities will not be capturable; while in other economies, only through royalties payment that will decrease their expected performance, these opportunities can be captured, but economies will be in a disadvantage situation. The dominant role of the country that has the highest relative development level will become an obstacle to capture these profit opportunities from the national entrepreneurs' side.

16.3.2 The Supply of Entrepreneurship

If demand factors are associated to available opportunities, the supply factors must be associated to the necessary requirements. Thus, the entrepreneurial skills, whether innate or acquired, will have an effect on the perception of opportunities. A second requirement to develop an entrepreneurial project is determined by the ability to mobilize these required productive factors. A potential entrepreneur can detect a profit opportunity, but he will not able to exploit it if he has no rights on factors o he has no way to have them. As it has been stated before, an agent will decide to become entrepreneur if the expected utility is higher than the alternative occupation. In other words, if the expected compensation of the profit opportunity that he attempts to capture is higher than the opportunity cost of the alternative activity, which is the paid-employment once taxes and incentives are discounted, plus a risk bonus and dedication bonus that imply some personal features, such as family situation, that may have some impact on this decision. Hence, all those variables that alter the opportunity cost to perform the entrepreneurial function, as well as those personal features (regardless they derive from personal circumstances or from sociological factors) that may affect the assessment of the incertitude linked to the entrepreneurial chance against the paid-employment, will be determinant aspects of the entrepreneurial offer and, therefore, they will have effects on the quantitative composition of the entrepreneurial network. Finally, the institutions of the labour and capital markets may affect the relative assessment of the alternative occupations, affecting then on the decision about the occupation.

The Entrepreneurial Human Capital

In principle, it may be expected that having previous experiences in an activity sector increases the knowledge on product and factor markets related to this sector, allows the knowledge of feasible productive combinations and, therefore, it reduces the incertitude associated to any entrepreneurial change as the quantity of available information increases. Likewise, having knowledge and entrepreneurial skills in the management area or in markets will allow the inefficiency decrease, which is other vector that configure the entrepreneurial function performance. This way, it is possible that, generally speaking, individuals with more experience or those who have acquired a higher level of entrepreneurial knowledge (either by formal educational processes or either by non-formal mechanisms, including those considered as externalities) will have a higher probability of detecting profit opportunities. Then, by contributing to the accumulation of this specific kind human capital, the detection of profit opportunities will be favoured and, probably, the improvement of the already established firms' economic results will be favoured too. This way, the literature about entrepreneurial human capital has not only analysed how the different kinds and levels of human capital have an effect on the decision of being entrepreneur, i. e., on the probability of identifying and pursuing business opportunities, but also it has studied its influence on the entrepreneurs performance in terms of survival and work life span, or even on the activity performance itself. Hence, the design of mechanisms that favour the accumulation of this kind of human capital is considered as one of the most efficient instruments to favour the detection of more and better opportunities. That is way the analysis of the design has an important place in the research agenda.

Generally, economies or sectors with a denser entrepreneurial network, with a wider entrepreneurial dimension or a higher technology development, require that the necessary entrepreneurial human capital level to capture profit opportunities must be higher, sometimes becoming a real access barrier to perform the entrepreneurial function. Likewise, the complexity of some entrepreneurial organizations causes that, even in the design stage of a productive combination, needs the creation of a team with a high specialization level on different areas in the entrepreneurial function. Therefore, if we want to capture the entrepreneurial human capital of an individual, economy or sector, we should try to capture somehow, both the stock of entrepreneurial knowledge and its accumulation processes.

In this sense, it is possible that older workers or workers with a wider previous experience may gather entrepreneurial skills, savings and business relations, being more likely to become entrepreneurs, although we agree that proximity between the indicators and the aspects to be measured is not very accurate.

Another possible accumulation mechanism is determined by the intergenerational transfer of entrepreneurial skills. Based on the parents' labour situation, there exists evidence on the following fact. It is more likely that self-employed people's children become entrepreneurs than paid-employed people's children.[12] This result is supported by the opinion surveys results (Eurobarometer's results) show that self-employed' children are more likely to work as self-employed, than paid-employed people's children.

Apart from these factors, the most intensely studied mechanism of human capital accumulation is that related to the participation on formal educational processes. We do not refer here to the role education may have favouring the existence of a positive social image of the entrepreneurial activity, so education may favour a kind of enterprising spirit,[13] but to the education role in acquiring skills and capabilities that may allow to capture profit opportunities. The economic analysis has intensively studied this relation: Evans and Leighton (1989), Blanchflower and Meyer (1994), and Schuetze (2000) analysis (among others), conclude that there is a positive relation between the educational reached level and the probability of becoming an entrepreneur.

In relation to this question, in a very recent work, Ucbasaran et al. (2006) study in depth this relation, dividing the general human capital effects (education and labour experience) from those of the entrepreneurial human capital (experience as business owner, management skills and technical abilities); effects on the identification and business opportunities, finding evidences to favour both kinds of human capital effects. Parker and Van Praag (2006) try to capture the relative importance of the human capital stock, according the access process to self-employment, i. e., depending on if the access has been by starting a new business or by incorporating into a business already established. This way, it seems that having a higher education level is positively related to the creation of a new business, while by having previous experience in management roles, it is more likely the access to an already established business.[14]

Hence, empirical evidence seems to support the hypothesis, by which the human capital is a determinant factor not only for searching and exploiting business opportunities, but also for the type of access, survival and performance itself. According to these significant effects of the human capital in the entrepreneurial activity results, we consider that a good work guideline to search for indicators that allow us to

---

[12] See Dunn and Holtz-Eakin (2000), Evans and Leighton (1989), Fairlie and Robb (2005) Chapter 1, Laband and Lentz (1983) or Taylor (1996), among others.

[13] However, European public authorities suggest that education is the mechanism to be used to change attitudes towards risks, so education may contribute to promote the entrepreneurial spirit, fostering a favourable attitude, the sensitising for professional opportunities as entrepreneur, and competencies. From their point of view, starting a business requires energy, creativity and persistence, while its development requires an increasing management ability, which implies efficiency, effectiveness and responsibility. Together with this action line, the European Comission tries to spread the entrepreneurial skills teaching, for example, in technical studies faculties, teaching how an entrepreneurial spirit may contribute to the combination of entrepreneurial and technical potencial. Education on entrepreneurial spirit combined with public programs for research gathers the required elements to join scientific excellence and trading of results.

[14] The literature has also analysed the entrepreneurial human capital performance (Van der Sluis et al. 2006), and Bhattacharjee et al. (2006) about survival probability.

measure the analysed aspects in relation to the entrepreneurial human capital, must distinguish indicators designed to measure the stock of this kind of knowledge from those that capture the voluntary accumulation processes, and from those indicators that capture unintentionally acquired knowledge.

Regarding the first mechanism, the stock originated through participation in formal mechanisms, we will find the same difficulties that those traditionally encountered to measure human capital. Then, the most intuitive and common way to tackle the human capital stock measurement at an aggregated level, generally uses the study levels reached by population. An easy way to extrapolate this kind of measurement to the self-employment level, is by crossing the educational level and type of occupation variables, so we can be able to measure the educational level of self-employed individuals against the educational level of paid-employed individuals. Limitations to this procedure are well known: i) this is an imperfect proxy of the real level of knowledge, since acquired knowledge by individuals of the same educational level and type may be different, not only among individuals, but also in regions; ii) not all the same kind of education has the same impact on the productive activities.[15]

These problems leads us to the operations implementation to measure the entrepreneurial aptitudes, as well as to the exploitation of different studies influence, previously defining which studies are related (according to their contents) to having entrepreneurial skills. To control the knowledge stock acquired through other mechanisms, the information gathering about the relatives' labour situation in surveys about labour forces or home panels, together with a possible implementation of new statistical operations, is the master line to be followed by the indicators search, which will allow to increase the measurement accuracy of this aspect.

Productive Factors Mobilization

A second requirement for the development of an entrepreneurial project is being able to mobilize the required productive factors. This way, the access to the propriety rights of the capital factor, or having enough labour factor with the required human capital, are essential requirement to start a business. But, we have to make reference also to the existence of non-excludable factors, i.e., considered as public goods, such as transport or communications infrastructure, which will decrease the necessary factors resources and will favour the factors mobilization in a specific location.

---

[15] We would agree that not all kinds of education, regardless the attainted level, have the same impact on the abilities to capture and to undertake an entrepreneurial project. This way, a priori this is less prone to doubt that with this kind of measurement, two societies formed by the same number of agents, and with the same educational level would show the same measurement of entrepreneurial human capital stock, regardless whether they have a History or Industrial Engineering five years degree.

A) *The Supply of Capital*

Although it is easy to confuse the agent with the productive factor, specially when the capital factor and entrepreneurial factor are provided by the same agent, in order to become an entrepreneur, not only the existence of liquidity constraints is a key variable, but also the difficulty to access to any kind of financing. Due to this, a great part of the empirical essay is focused on analysing the role of these liquidity constraints when deciding to be entrepreneur. Thus, and generally speaking, literature seems to show a solid confirmation of the hypothesis that states the following. It seems that certain kind of entrepreneurial projects, specially those that need big quantities of capital to be developed, depend not really much on the own previous funds, but rather on how accessible the capital markets are, on the accessibility to search for investors, and the development level of the financing institutions.

This way, the quantity of available funds, the number of financed operations, the development level of the different financing institutions and any other indicator that allows us to capture the relative importance of each financing source, are one of the aspect that must be give more focus on, from the design of new statistical operations point of view.

B) *The Labour Market*

A regulated market, with problems that impede the adjustment, or with an unsuitable inadequate human capital, may hinder the starting of any entrepreneurial project.[16] But, the labour market also plays a role, from a different perspective: the paid-employment is the alternative activity in the occupational choice problem. Therefore, the labour market features, either related to the relative remuneration of each occupation, either how this affects to the incertitude level, will be elements that favour or hinder the decision of being entrepreneur.

This way, a highly regulated market, in which the elements of permanent hiring or temporary hiring and high wages will create an increase in the self-employment opportunity cost, both in terms of the rejected wage, as well as to the incertitude level related to each occupation.

Finally, the labour market features have consequences on the localization. The existence of a labour factor with a suitable human capital for the project requirements (professional human capital), and with efficiency and cost levels that make this feasible become essential not only for the project feasibility itself, but this is also basic for the localization of the entrepreneurial activity. Thus, the impossibility to hire labour factor with suitable features for the business nature, with the productivity level according to the business' requirements o with higher wages, may cause that a project may not be feasible in a specific productive localization.

---

[16] Let's consider the effect that some institutions of the labour market, such as the existence of termination costs or permanent hiring formulas may have some effects on the labour factor demand.

Due to the previous facts, we can deduct that usable indicators to approach the mobilisation potential of this factor may contribute to capture, at least, the wage costs, the productivity levels, the human capital and costs related to institutions.

C) Infrastructure

A suitable support for this entrepreneurial activity requires a professional highly qualified consultancy service that may be capable to provide the required information and knowledge (the know-how). Together with this network, the availability of some public goods, such as communication and transport infrastructures or the existence of localizations with specific infrastructures or service firms (industry, technology parks or industry areas) or even networks, decrease the installation costs, create synergies with effects on the efficiency, and favour the innovation. Therefore, these are favouring elements for localization in the places where they appear, and for starting new entrepreneurial projects (Pittaway et al. 2004). Thus, the existence of firms with complementary activities, the existence of firms incubators, the industry parks or the industry networks, and the cooperation centres are some of the elements that form this infrastructure for entrepreneurship, regardless their public or private nature. Finally, cooperation among the institutions of R+D and firms will cause that decisions may be made based on the knowledge sources, which will surely imply a higher effectiveness and suitability level. The structural statistics, related to the communication infrastructures and R+D, have indicators likely to be used to measure this aspect.

Personal Features

Although personal features are not explicitly included in models, the empirical literature confirms that some behaviour patterns may influence on the choice of occupation. This decision depends on the personal features of the entrepreneurial network components, and they are related also to the family core as the decision-maker. Taking the gender into account, women participation rate in self-employment is substantially lower than men's rate. But, this phenomenon is not limited to self-employment. However, the importance of this phenomenon is given by the existence of a bigger difference in relation to paid-employment. The different roles played by women and men in the family core o the higher dedication related to entrepreneurial chances have been some of the hypothesis analysed by literature to explain the phenomenon. If the whole family as a unit makes the decision of the occupation, the family features must have a critical importance when choosing the occupation, due to the implications of this decision on the dedication regime to other activities, and even on the family inheritance itself (Borjas 1986). Likewise, a finding (probably related to the cultural background of specific groups) is given by the high participation of certain groups and ethnic groups in the entrepreneurial network. Thus, it seems that immigrants from certain geographic areas o people from specific ethnic minorities usually chose self-employment against paid-employment.

Costs and Incentives: Taxes and Social Security

A common way of favouring transfers to self-employment is by proving specific incentives (taxes or bonuses in social security fees), so these incentives may decrease the opportunity cost of the alternative occupation. The underlying reason for this kind of measurements is that taxation obligations and costs related to the fulfilment of these obligations must not be an obstacle to create firms nor for their development or consolidation. So, by making the tax obligations lighter and simplifying procedures and requirements associated to its fulfilment, these may be elements that contribute to the firm development, growth and survival. In 1994, Domar and Musgrave suggested using the taxation system as a way to compensate the risk costs related to self-employment through the deduction of the generated losses. The introduction of differences in the taxation treatment of self-employed and paid-employed, in the most of the taxation systems, has moved the interest on the analysis of effects of the taxation on the choice of occupation to the opposite side, i. e., on the analysis of the distortions that these differences may generate over the choice of occupation, given the possibilities of tax evasion related to self-employment. The essays of Watson (1985), Kesselman (1989), Pestieau and Possen (1991), or Jung et al. (1994), Schuetze (2000) or Parker (2004), are only some of the examples of this work guidelines. Using microdata, the empirical essays have identified the different effects of tax regulations on the self-employment.[17] This way, Carrol et al. (2000a, 2000b, 2001) conclude that taxation over personal incomes of self-employed people changes significantly their employment, investment, and expansion decisions. On their side, Blau (1987), Bruce (2000) and Schuetze (2000) find that a high taxation pressure decrease access to self-employment. Parker and Robson (2004) show that self-employment ratio is positive and significantly related to tax rates of the incomes tax. As marginal income tax rates increase, the entrepreneurs tend to expand their businesses slower, and to invest less and to hire less people.[18]

On the other hand, taxes structure also affects to entrepreneurial incentives, and specially, to aspects, such as the linear or progressive nature of taxes, the repayment allowed or the applicable taxation benefits. Generally, both the level and the structure of taxes determine the activity and decisions of the firms, and specifically, those related to the organizational structure, to the combination of productive factors, to financing sources, and to distribution of profits and composition of assets.

But, as well as the taxation charge itself, we should not ignore either the importance of the costs related to taxation fulfilment on the firms' side. This called "indirect taxation pressure" include charges derived from taxation information collection, from demand of lots of taxation charges and deduction at source of different taxes, taxation accounting, consultancy services on the subject, audits and from legal procedures.

---

[17] Bruce (2000) states that an increase of 5 percentual points in the difference between the expected marginal income tax rate of paid-employed and self-employed, reduces the transition from paid-employment to self-employment in 2.4 percentual points.

[18] Holtz-Eakin & Rosen (2001)

Together with tax incentives, some deductions to social costs play the same role when favouring this occupation choice. Steinberger (2005) considers the existence of a negative relation between the size of the Social Security system and the entrepreneurial activity within a specific country. Parker and Robson (2004), on their side, show how self-employment rates are negatively related to social security contribution from employers' side.

Sociological and Psychological Factors

The basic model of choice of occupation shows that a person will chose self-employment if its associated utility surpasses that of the paid-employment. As we have stated before, literature usually makes operative the concept of associated utility of each occupation through its identification with the incomes. However, as stated before, a set of subjective perceptions, such as the desire of personal development or desire of being one's own boss, are psychological factors directly related to the associated utility of each occupation. These psychological factors have been subjected to accurate studies, where emphasis is on intentions, rather than on observed behaviours. This way, we are trying to detect, through the opinion surveys results, the scene of the individuals' preferences. The aim is analysing motivations, different to earnings, that are taking into account when deciding to be entrepreneur. The most surprising result of this kind of studies is the fact that *a priori* the number of individuals that would wish to be entrepreneur almost trebles the proportion of existent self-employed people. This fact has been considered by politicians that it is necessary to clear obstacles that impede this scene of preferences is not showed in occupation decisions. Desire of being one's own boss (the independency), controlling or even choosing this occupation as a mechanism of social promotion, are motivations showed by individuals in relation to the choice of occupation.

From a similar point of view, although focused on the risk perception, the role assigned in different cultures to excessive incomes, the social regard for entrepreneurs, or even the study of higher frequency of entrepreneurial activities in some ethnic groups, are analysed with interest and some measurements are even created to mitigate adverse possible effects of these sociological elements. This way, the promotion of successful entrepreneurs' experiences, or the introduction of elements that diminish the risk perception in certain cultures, are created as essential elements to remove negative possible effects on the decision to be entrepreneur. Although these factors are formed by assumptions, perceptions and elements associated to learning, the key question is creating mechanisms used for these factors to favour the entrepreneurs appearing. Obviously, imposing a new culture that favours these values is not feasible, but it is possible to apply some measurements so social consideration of the entrepreneurial role may change gradually. The entrepreneurial labour promotion of the people who have developed successfully entrepreneurial projects or favouring the leadership culture in formal education through role play, are some of the most commonly used measurements. The Global Entrepreneurship Monitoring is, until this very moment, the only useful source, at European level, to collect indicators that allow us to capture these aspects.

16.3.3 The Entrepreneurial Activity

Following the proposed conceptual scheme, and once the entrepreneurial factor determinants of offer and demand are analysed in a specific sector or area, we will devote this section to the search of dimensions and indicators to capture the supply and demand junction results, which will allow us to: i) quantify the network, either from the perspective of the agents, or either from the productive configurations perspective derived from agent's actions, by using the stock variables; ii) analyse the network dynamics, through the entry and exit analysis or through success using flow variables; iii) diagnose and monitor the entrepreneurial network output, in terms of economic results or according to its interrelations to other markets.

In other terms, if in the two previous sections, we have tried to capture the control factors, which knowledge is essential to the possible therapies application, in this section, we will analyse the result variables, which are the key for the diagnosis and tracking of the entrepreneurial network. To undertake this task, we will firstly introduce a debate about the measurement of the entrepreneurial network from the productive factor perspective, i. e., trying to quantify the number of agents who carry any of the vectors that configure the performance of the entrepreneurial function in a specific sector or area. The measurement of the agents who perform the entrepreneurial function, either as self-employed or performing the management functions in a corporative firm, will lead us to the discussion about the use of Surveys about the labour forces as main source, to the harmonization of the self-employment (business ownership) concept, and lastly, to the analysis of other measurement essays through specific surveys, such as Global Entrepreneurship Monitoring (GEM).

The second approach to the quantitative composition of the entrepreneurial network, in relation to the stock quantification, is carried out from a lightly different perspective, in which the attention is paid on the productive unit (firm or establishment), and not on the agent or agents, who undertake this task. In other terms, attention is moved from the entrepreneurial factor analysis to the productive organizations analysis (derived from the entrepreneurial factor), to the firm analysis. We refer here to the firms and establishments' records exploitation, to the so-called business structural surveys. Without considering which of these perspectives is the most accurate (for being futile), we think that the most positive approach to the phenomenon must be the exploitation of the information from both statistical sources, and try to take advantage of their complementary elements. This must allow us to have a more complete analysis on the entrepreneurship phenomenon, wishing that statistical operations of agencies and institutions move forward the conciliation of both sources.

After the availability, features, potentials and weaknesses of the available sources and indicators to stock approaches, we devote to the analysis of the network dynamics, in terms of flow variables. Afterwards, we focus our attention on the growth and survival capacity, that is, on identifying the key variables, which allow us to clarify the evolution of factors that favour or hinder the entrepreneurial success and its growth. Finally, and as we have stated before, the last approach to the entrepreneurial network is performed in terms of the economic results of the entrepreneurial activity, adding the impacts this activity has on the innovation, employment, and competitiveness of the economy.

The Stock

If we want to approach to the knowing of the quantitative composition of the entrepreneurial network in a specific sector or area, we would need to decide previously if we want to quantify the productive factor or the resulting organizations of its activity. Insisting on the difference is not a trivial question, and this even poses some problems for territory divisions. Let's pose some extreme examples to clarify the previous statement. Let's think on the existence of a territory with a very high entrepreneurial density, in terms of a high number of firms and work centres, but nevertheless, this territory has very low self-employment rates vs. a territory or sector with lots of agents developing the entrepreneurial activity, but where there are a few establishments, as its production centres, or even its organizations, are based in other territories. We will agree that diagnosis of both situations is very different, and that involvements of these entrepreneurial activities will be also different, in terms of impacts on the growth, competitiveness, and employment in that specific territory or sector. Then, we think that combining these two perspectives for the analysis of the quantitative composition of the entrepreneurial network is essential, in order to find accurate diagnosis and tracking of the entrepreneurial network in an economy or sector.

This way, in order to approach to the quantitative composition from the perspective of the productive factor, we will agree that the entrepreneurial network in a specific area (sector or space), is composed of the group of agents who undertake at least one of the functions that define the entrepreneurial action performance. This way, the entrepreneurial network (strictly considered), will be composed of the agents who perform the entrepreneurial function, either in individual firms or corporations, while if we use a wide perspective of the network, this would also include agencies for entrepreneurial promotion, or consultancy agencies, among others. On the other hand, and from the productive organizations point of view –firms, establishments or productive centres-, we can distinguish firms, and firms' local units, it is to say, the sections of each firms located in different places on the firm's account. Hence, we discuss now about the alternative sources and indicators to measure the firms and entrepreneurs stock.

The measurement of the number of self-employed people as proxy of the people who perform the entrepreneurial function in a specific territory is, and has been, the mostly used solution to quantify the number of agents who compound the entrepreneurial network, since this proxy easily derives from the Surveys on Labour Forces, by analysing employed people per professional situation, which allows to distinguish self-employed people (employers with employees and own-account workers), and paid-employed workers.[19] This way, the number of self-employed

---

[19] In this sense, the international guidelines are more in favour of not considering the relatives' help as real entrepreneurs. Because of this, the term "self-employment" makes reference to the

people or the self-employment rate has been a variable chosen for this measurement of the entrepreneurial activity to be operative. This method of measurement has been used to favour the comparative analysis, since (despite the differences) it may be in the labour statistics area where this has progressed the most from the international harmonization of concepts and definitions point of view. Thus, in the European context, the unification of the Surveys on the Labour Forces allows international comparisons about self-employment in the different European territories. The concept of business owner (self-employed) –people who have a firm, constituted or not, and who are not simple investors on the firm, but they work for that firm and receive a wage), used by van Stel, is an example of the harmonization of data derived from the OECD's statistics on labour forces.[20]

It is also remarkable the effort made by the GEM.[21] This project is a research program, began on 1998, conceived to generate annual harmonised data on entrepreneurship, and which main aim is to measure the entrepreneurial activities in their first stages, for each country in order to favour comparison cross-country.[22]

Focusing on the potential indicators derived from the exploitations of Surveys on Labour Forces, these will allow us (through classifications of employed people per professional situation and per occupation) to quantify the number of people who exert the entrepreneurial activity, either by one's own account o by being employed, and to successfully to approach to the quantitative composition of the individual and corporative entrepreneurial activity, strictly considered.[23] Together with these surveys on labour forces, the population surveys, which include in their questionnaires questions about the professional situation (Surveys on Households or Surveys on Family Budgets, among others) become alternative sources to measure self-employment in a specific sector or area. To finish the measurement of the

---

sum of employers with and without paid-employed people. However, this omission probably leads us to underestimate the real role of entrepreneur women, taking into account that some of these women will be classified within the relatives' help, but they should be considered as partners at the same level than that of the business owner (Felstead and Leighton 1992; Marshall 1999).

[20] See van Stel (2005).

[21] For more informatin about the GEM project at international level, please see Web site http://www.gemconsortium.org; see Web site http://www.ie.edu/gem for GEM project in Spain. Information on GEM project in Andalusia may be found in http://www.gem-andalucia.org. For a more accurate description on the research, please see Reynolds *et al.* (2005).

[22] To undertake this task, the Total early-stage Entrepreneurial Activity or TEA-index is created. This index derives from the identification of emerging entrepreneurs (people being 18 to 64 years old who were devoted to starting up activities of new businesses in the previous year of this interview, and who have not paid more than three wages in that very moment), and owners-managers of emerging businesses (less than 42 months). Despite the method differences, having information previous to the starting-up favours the motivations analysis.

[23] This survey allows us to have the classification of employed people per professional situation. According to this criterion, the Spanish LFS divides employed people in this classification: employers, entrepreneurs without employed people or freelance workers, cooperative members, relatives' contribution, paid-employed people, and others. The number of employers and entrepreneurs without employed people is configured with right proxies to quantify the individual entrepreneurial factor, in strict sense.

entrepreneurial factor stock, we have to capture someway those individuals who perform the entrepreneurial function in corporations, it is to say, those cases in which the division between propriety and control implies that it is not the same agent who provide the entrepreneurial factor and the capital.[24] In this kind of firms, the entrepreneurial activity is carried out by manager, sometimes not linked at all to the ownership of the firm. Because of this, if we want to measure the entrepreneurial network, we need indicators which allow us to capture the quantitative importance of this corporative entrepreneurial network.

Once again, the source for this kind of indicators is the Survey on Labour Force (related to employed individuals) together with other population surveys, where social-labour data are collected. The procedure, although imperfect, seems to use the classification of workers per occupation[25]. This way, in the Spanish LFS, when classifying workers per occupation, we have a category in which management members and people of the public administration and directors and managers of firms are included. Moreover, there is a variable in blank for individuals who work in the private sector, and it provides information about the kind of public administration where the individual works, including a category of public firms and public financing institutions. This let us to consider if we may consider the hypothesis about no public paid-employed individual exerts the entrepreneurial function.

Once the measurement of the productive factor if analysed, we will pay attention now to the productive unit: firm or establishment. We refer here to the firms and establishments' records exploitation, to the generally so-called structural surveys of firms. The importance of its analysis lays on that this is a key variable when knowing the features of productive configurations derived from the entrepreneurial factor. The most part of statistical agencies use, as main source to generate structural statistics of firms, the information provided in the firms' and establishments' records, so comparison methods for this data are subjected to the chosen statistical unit, the chosen source, its coverage, the chosen threshold to include or exclude a firm or establishment, or the chosen time to identify entries and exists[26].

---

[24] As we have stated before, if we consider that the delimitation criterion of an entrepreneur is defined by the performance of any of the vectors which define the entrepreneurial function, we will agree that when approaching the number of entrepreneurs through self-employment, we would leaving aside those individuals who perform the entrepreneurial role as paid-employed people.

[25] According to the International Standard Classification of Occupations (ISCO-1988), the major group number 1, includes legislators, senior officials and managers. Managers are specifically divided in two groups: corporative (managers and executive chiefs, production and operation departments managers and managers from other departments), and general managers. The difference between both groups is derived from the existence of entrepreneurial management teams formed by three or more members (the corporative group), while general managers include individuals that perform the entrepreneurial role alone or with the owner help, without having any other help or another manager assistance. For more information about this subject, please visit http://laborsta.ilo.org/applv8/data/isco88e.htlm.

[26] See Vale (2006).

The Flow

Now we will focus on how we can analyse the dynamics of the network, according to the distinction done between the entrepreneurial factor and the productive configurations derived from its action, once the entrepreneurial quantification is analysed based on the stock variables. From the point of view of factors, and through the proposed indicators to measure stock, we can create flow indicators using the vegetative growth calculation and the analysis of the professional situation changes during the permanence of the individual on the sample From the point of view of the firms, the structural statistics of firms provide information about the entry and exit flows.

Success: Growth and Survival

From the analysis of the determinant factors of the entrepreneurial success, expressed in terms of survival and growth, we can find some guidelines to create indicators which allow us to forecast the entrepreneurial network development, either by analysing the survival of the agent, as well as of firms and establishments already built. Detecting success factors for self-employment is not an easy task by using variables and indicators gathered through population surveys. The human capital level, having previous experiences in self-employment, and knowing the activity sector are some of the proxies we are limited to use in the empirical analysis. Because of this, it is required to implement some kind of specific statistical operation to detect the success factors among entrepreneurs, who form the panel during the first years of a firm.

The Output

Finally, and in order to conclude our analysis on the entrepreneurial activity, let's analyse its output, in terms of economy, employment, competitiveness and innovations results. A logical way to act, if we want to measure *ex post* the entrepreneurial activity results, is consulting the analysis on the economic information included in balances. As corporative firms are obliged to show the annual balances in commerce registries, making different statistical operations to exploit these results have been favoured. Thus, in Spain, the Central Registry of Balances of the Spanish Central Bank makes the exploitation of this information, which may be used to know the economic result of the Spanish firms. In this kind of statistical operation, we have to move forward on comparison methods, quite complex issue given the existent differences in the accounting normative.

A second aspect the system should try to capture is collecting the information about the effects of the entrepreneurial market on the labour market. Nowadays, using the available statistical information in population surveys, we can only analyse aggregate elements to confirm whether self-employment and paid-employment cycles move or not following a defined schema. It is possible to make more accurate analysis by using the structural surveys of firms, since these surveys gather information about the variables of employment, linking these variables to establishment.

The third aspect in quantifying the output is delimited by the attempt to measure the entrepreneurial network contribution to the technological innovation processes and by how this network assumes technological innovations. Surveys on innovation of firms are a good reference, since they provide with indicators about the most important variables of these processes, either through the measurement of the input or output of these processes.

To complete our analysis, we should focus now on competitiveness. As we have stated before, capturing certain profit opportunities and their economic results will depend on the junction of factors of offer and demand. Then, the competitiveness of the resulting firms is only one of the consequences of the entrepreneurial network quality and composition. This way, competitiveness is only the result, in comparative terms, of a set of factors that cause the entrepreneurial factor in a specific area performs its function with more or less relative success level. In other words, competitiveness is only a relative concept that makes reference to the capability of doing things better than others, regardless it is done at individual, firm or territory level. Generally, the measurement of competitiveness usually includes the measurement of the costs of factors, of imposition, productivity, labour force creation, or R+D processes. All these dimensions, within our system framework, are determinant factors of the entrepreneurship, already collected in our system.

Due to the previous facts, the measurement of the competitiveness should imply the search for results rates of an economy with regard to its close environment, either through the rate of relative prices (fixed by exchange rates), as well as through any kind of synthetic rate of entrepreneurship, which allows to analyse, in comparison terms, the factors that affect the entrepreneurial factor market.

16.4 Conclusions and Future Agenda

Although there is some kind of general agreement about the importance of the entrepreneurial factor because of its contribution to the processes for generation of employment, innovation, and to the economy growth, and therefore, about the convenience of its promotion, knowing the mechanisms used for the entrepreneurial factor to operate in any of these processes, this agreement is quite weak. In spite of this, governments are focused on designing and implementing entrepreneurial promotion strategies, mainly aimed to "improve" the business environment in an attempt to increase the self-employment rate and, in some cases, the existent entrepreneurial network quality, so this network may be increasingly dynamic in relation to its contribution to the previously mentioned processes. Nevertheless, we will agree there are very few countries and regions that have statistical subsystems with a development level similar to those subsystems designed to analyse the economic juncture, the labour market, or the markets. Generally, analysts, policy makers and statistical information users must resign with more or less accurate approaches (except in very rare occasions) to variables and aspects tried to be measured, based on the exploitation of surveys and records, thought and designed for other aims. This paper has introduced a reference framework to build an entrepreneurship system, detailing the theoretical mechanisms recommended for each dimension studied in the theoretical model, and collecting indicators about any of the considered aspects. The following Table (16.1) summarises the dimensions to be captured by our proposed statistical system on entrepreneurship, and the number of indicators potentially to be used for each considered aspect.

Based on the analysis and exclusively being focused on the objective assessments of the statistical operations usually implemented, the implementation of such a kind of system will require the study of the implementation of statistical operations that allow to provide with indicators to aspects that are not currently covered enough. Specifically: i) move forward through the design of sample exploitations from Social Security, which allow the simultaneous analysis of the productive factors and the productive units, being a good starting point the operations designed by the Statistical Management of Firms of the OECD for this aim; ii) study more deeply the financing statistical field, in relation to the consecution of a system of indicators on financing volumes and sources for new firms and to the development level of financing entities aimed to supply with capital to entrepreneurs and firms; iii) implement operations that allow to capture the entrepreneurial taxation in an harmonised framework with other regions, and in the national and supranational context; iv) study more deeply the sociological and psychological factors, either by directly participating in existent essays (GEM) as well as applying Eurostat Eurobarometer methods; v) study the design of success factor surveys based on the

Table 16.1 Aspects and dimensions

Demand					
Profit opportunities					
Environment					
Legislation					
Degree of Openness					
Technological Diffusion					

Supply					
Human Capital	*Factor Mobilization*	*Characteristics*	*Costs and Incentives*	*Non-economic factors*	*Institutions*
Stock	Capital	Individual	Taxes	Sociological	Labor Market
Investment)	Labor	Family	Social Security	Psychological	Financial Market
	Infrastructure				Administrative Burdens

Economic Activity			
Stock	*Flow*	*Success*	*Output*
Entrepreneurs	Entrepreneurs	Entrepreneurs	Employment
Firms	Firms	Firms	Results
		Innovation	
		Competitiveness	

sampling and tracking of a entrepreneurs and firms panel, from its birth to its first years; vi) move forward on the indicators related to the institutional, and vii) design a synthetic indicator of entrepreneurship (competitiveness), that may be compared to those created by other international institutions.

Acknowledgments Department of Economics and Statistics. We would like to thank to participants to the Workshop on entrepreneurship statistics, held on Punta Umbría, february 2006. Authors would also like to thank for the financial aid received from the *Instituto de Estadística de Andalucía*, and specially, to Juan Antonio Fernández-Cordón, Juan Antonio Hernández, Elena Manzanera, and José Ignacio Merchán.

References

Acemoglu D, Zilibotti F (1997) Was Prometheus Unbound by Chance? Risk, Diversification and Growth. Journal of Political Economy 105:709–751

Acs ZJ (2001) A formulation of entrepreneurship policy. The FSF-NUTEK Award Winner Series

Acs Z, Audretsch D (1988) Innovation in large and small firms: an empirical analysis. American Economic Review 78: 678–690

Acs Z, Audretsch D (1990) Innovation and Small Firms. The MIT Press, Cambridge.

Aguado R, Congregado E, Millán JM (2003) Entrepreneurship financiación e innovación. Revista de Economía Industrial 347:125–34

Ahsan SM (1974) Progression and risk-taking. Oxford Economic Papers 26:318–28

Alba-Ramírez A (1994) Self-employment in the Midst of Unemployment: The Case of Spain and the United States. Applied Economics 26:189–205

Alfaro L, Charlton A (2006) International financial integration and entrepreneurship. HBS Working Paper Number 07–012

Alfaro L, McIntyre S, Dev V(2005) Foreign Direct Investment and Ireland's Tiger Economy. Harvard Business School Case 705–009

Armour J, Cumming D (2005) Bankruptcy Law and Entrepreneurship. Berkeley Electronic Press Berkeley

Audretsch DB (2003) Entrepreneurship policy and the strategic management of places. In: Hart DM (ed) The emergence of entrepreneurship policy – governance start-ups and growth in the US knowledge economy. Cambridge University Press, Cambridge

Audretsch D, Carree M, Van Stel A, Thurik R(2005) Does Self-Employment reduces Unemployment? Discussion Papers on Entrepreneurship, Growth and Public Policy 0705, Max Planck Institute of Economics, Jena, Germany

Audretsch DB, Mahmood T (1995) The post-entry performance of new firms. In: Van Witteloostuij A (ed): Market Evolution Competition and Cooperation Kluwer Academic Publishers, London, pp. 245–55

Audretsch D, Keilbach M (2004) Entrepreneurship capital and economic performance. Regional studies 38(8):949–959.

Audretsch DB, Thurik AR, Verheul I (2002) Entrepreneurship: determinants and policy in a European-US comparison. Springer, Kluwer Academic Publishers.

Austin JS, Rosenbaum DI (1990) The determinants of entry and exit Rates into US manufacturing industries. Review of Industrial Organization 5:211–23

Aw BY; Chung S, Roberts MJ (2000) Productivity and Turnover in the Export Market: Micro-Level Evidence from the Republic of Korea and Taiwan (China). World Bank Economic Review 14(1):65–90

Bates TM (1990) Entrepreneur Human Capital Inputs and Small Business Longevity. The Review of Economics and Statistics 72(4):551–59

Bhattacharjee AJ, Le Pape BN, Renault R (2006) Inferring the unobserved human capital of entrepreneurs. Centre for Research in Economics and Management WP 2006–03

Blanchflower DG (2000) Self-Employment in OECD Countries. Labour Economics 7:471–505

Blanchflower DG (2004) Self-Employment: More may not be better. NBER Working Paper, No. 10286.

Blanchflower DG, Oswald, AJ (1990) What makes a young Entrepreneur? NBER Working Paper No 3352

Blanchflower DG, Oswald AJ (1998) What makes an Entrepreneur? Journal of Labour Economics 16:26–60

Blanchflower D, Meyer B (1994) A Longitudinal Analysis of Young Entrepreneurs in Australia and the United States. Small Business Economics 6(1):1–20

Blau DM (1987) A time-series analysis of self-employment in the United States. Journal of Political Economy 95(3):445–67

Borjas G, Bronars S (1989) Consumer Discrimination and Self-Employment. Journal of Political Economy 97:581–605

Boden RJ (1996) Gender and self-employment selection: an empirical assessment. Journal of Socioeconomics 25:671–82

Böheim R, Taylor MP (2000) Unemployment Duration and Exit States in Britain. ISER working papers 2000–01 Institute for Social and Economic Research

Brandt N (2004) Business dynamics regulation and performance. STI Working Paper OECD

Bruce D (2000) Effects of the United States tax system on transitions into self-employment. Labour Economics 7(5):545–74

Burke AE, FitzRoy FR, Nolan MA (2002) Self-employment Wealth and Job Creation: The Roles of Gender Non-pecuniary Motivation and Entrepreneurial Ability. Small Business Economics 19:255–70

Casson MC (1982) The Entrepreneur: An Economic Theory. Oxford [2nd ed Edward Elgar 2003]

Carrasco R (1999) Transitions To and From Self-employment in Spain: An Empirical Analysis. Oxford Bulletin of Economics and Statistics 61(3):315–41

Carre M, Van Stel A, Thurik R, Wennekers S (2002) Economic Development and Business Ownership: an analysis using data of 23 OECD countries in the period 1976 1996. Small Business Economics 19(3):271–290

Carrol R, Holtz-Eakin D, Rider M, Rosen HS (2000) Income taxes and entrepreneurs. Journal of Labour Economics 18(2):324–51

Casson MC (1982) The Entrepreneur: An Economic Theory. Oxford; Martin Robertson [2nd. ed., Edward Elgar, 2003]

Clark K, Drinkwater S (1998) Ethnicity and self-employment in Britain. Oxford Bulletin of Economics and Statistics 60:383–407

Clark K, Drinkwater S, Leslie D (1998) Ethnicity and self-employment earnings in Britain 1973–95. Applied Economic Letters 5:631–634

Congregado E, Golpe AA, Millán JM (2003) Some Empirical Aspects of Self-Employment in Spain during the nineties. SAE-WP 20, Universidad de Huelva

Congregado E, Golpe AA, Millán JM (2005) Determinantes de la oferta de empresarios. In: García J, Pérez J (eds) Cuestiones Clave de la Economía Española Perspectivas actuales 2004. Comares, pp 165–187

Congregado E, Golpe AA, Millán, JM (2006) Los Autónomos en el mercado de trabajo español. Perspectivas del Sistema Financiero 86:1–19

De Wit G (1993) Models of Self-Employment in a Competitive Market. Journal of Economic Surveys 7(4):367–97

De Wit G, Van Winden F (1990) An Empirical Analysis of Self-Employment in the Netherlands. Economic Letters 32:97–100

Domar ED, Musgrave RA (1944) Proportional Income Taxation and Risk-Taking. Quarterly Journal of Economics 58:388–422

Dunn T, Holtz-Eakin D (2000) Financial Capital Human Capital and the Transition to Self-Employment: Evidence from Integenerational Links. Journal of Labour Economics 18:282–305

Erosa A (2002) Financial Intermediation and Occupational Choice in Development. Review of Economic Dynamics 4(2):303–34

Eurobarameter (2004) no160 Entrepreneurship EOS Gallup Europe: http://europaeuint/

European Comission (2002) Bankruptcy and a Fresh Start: Stigma on Failure and Legal Consequences of Bankruptcy. EU Commission, Brussels

Evans DS, Jovanovic B (1989) An Estimated Model of Entrepreneurial Choice under Liquidity Constraints. Journal of Political Economy 97:808–27

Evans DS, Leighton LS (1989) Some empirical aspects of entrepreneurship. American Economic Review 79:519–35

Fairlie RW, Robb A (2005) Families, human capital, and small business: Evidence from the characteristics of Business Owners Survey. CES 05–07

Falter JM (2002) Self-Employment entry and duration in Switzerland. Working Paper Employment Centre, University of Geneva

Felstead A, Leighton P (1992) Issues, Themes and Reflections on the 'Enterprise Culture'. In: Leighton P, Felstead A (eds.) The New Entrepreneurs: Self-Employment and Small Business in Europe. Kogan, pp:15–38

Frank MZ (1988) An intertemporal model of industrial exits. Quarterly Journal of Economics 103(2):333–44

Flota C, Mora MT (2001) The earnings of self-employed Mexican-Americans along the US-Mexico border. Annals of Regional Science 35:483–99

Fujii ET, Hawley CB (1991) Empirical aspects of self-employment. Economic Letters 36: 323–29

García-Mainar I, Montuenga-Gómez VM (2005) Education returns of wage earners and self-employed workers: Portugal vs Spain. Economics of Education Review 24:161–70

Georgellis Y, Wall HJ (2000) Gender Differences in Self-Employment: Panel Evidence from the former West-Germany. The Federal Reserve Bank of St. Louis Working Paper, 1999/008B

Geroski, P. (1995) What do we know about entry? International Journal of Industrial Organization 13(4):421–440

Gill, AM (1988) Choice of Employment Status and the wages of Employees and the Self-employed: Some Further Evidence. Journal of Applied Econometrics 3: 229–234

Girma S, Goerg H, Strobl E (2004) Exports, Internacional Investment and Plant Performance: evidence from a non parametric test. Core Discussion Paper 2004/09

Golpe AA, van Stel A (2007) Self-employment and employment in Spanish regions in the period 1979–2001. In Congregado E (Ed.): Measuring Entrepreneursgip, International Studies in Entrepreneurship, vol.16, chapter 9, Springer, New York

Grilo I, Irigoyen J (2005) Entrepreneurship in the EU: To wish and not to be. Max Planck Institute Discussion Paper on Entrepreneurship Growth and Public Policy 0105 Jena Germany

Grossman G (1984) International Trade, Foreign Investment, and the Formation of the Entrepreneurial Class. American Economic Review 74:605–614

Grossman G, Helpman E (1991) Trade, Knowledge Spillovers and Growth. European Economic Review:517–526

Guiso L, Sapeinza P, Zingales L (2002) Does Local Financial Development Matter? NBER Working Papers Series WP 8923

Hoffmann A, Nellemann PB, Larsen L, Michelsen NV (2005) Indicator manual. FORA, Copenhagen

Holtz-Eakin D, Joulfaian D, Rosen RH (1994) Entrepreneurial Decisions and Liquidity Constraints. Rand Journal of Economics 25:334–47

Hurst E, Lusardi A (2004) Liquidity Constraints, Household Wealth, and Entrepreneurship. Journal of Political Economy 112 :319–347

Iyigun M, Owen A (1998) Risk, entrepreneurship and human capital accumulation. American Economic Review, Papers and proceedings 88(2):454–457

Jung YH, Snow A, Trandel GA (1993) Tax evasion and the size of the underground economy. Journal o Public Economics 54: 391–402.

Kirzner IM (1973) Competition and entrepreneurship. Chicago, University of Chicago Press

Kirzner IM (1979) Perception, opportunity and profit. Chicago, University of Chicago Press

Kirzner IM (1985) Discovery and the capitalist process. Chicago, University of Chicago Press

Knight FH (1929) Freedom as Fact and Criterion. International Journal of Ethics 2:129–47

Landier A (2004) Entrepreneurship and the Stigma of Failure. New York University.

Laband DN, Lentz BF (1983) Like father, like son: toward an economic theory of occupational following. Southern Economic Journal 50:474–493

Kesselman JR (1989) Income Tax Evasion: An Intersectoral Analysis. Journal of Public Economics 38:137–82

Kihlstrom RE, Laffont JJ (1979) A general equilibrium entrepreneurial theory of firm formation based on risk aversion. Journal of Political Economy 87:719–49

Lages LF, Montgomery DB (2005) The relationship between export assistance and performance improvement in Portuguese export ventures: An empirical test of the mediating role of pricing strategy adaptation. European Journal of Marketing 39(7/8):755–784.

Lazear EP, Moore RL (1984) Incentives Productivity and labour Contracts. Quarterly Journal of Economics 99:275–96

Leibenstein H (1969) Entrepreneurship and Development. American Economic Review 58(2): 72–83

Leibenstein H (1979) The General X-Efficiency Paradigm and the Role of the Entrepreneur. In: Rizzio MJ (ed) Time Uncertainty and Disequilibrium. Lexington, MA, pp 127–39

Lindh T, Ohlsson H (1996) Self-Employment and Windfall Gains: Evidence from the Swedish Lottery. Economic Journal 106:1515–526

Lundström A, Stevenson L (2001) On the road to entrepreneurship policy. In: Entrepreneurship policy for the future series vol.1. Sweden, Swedish Foundation For Small Business Research, 256 pp.

Lundström A, Stevenson LA (2005) Entrepreneurship policy: theory and practice International Studies in Entrepreneurship, Springer, New York

Marshall K (1999) Working Together – Self-Employed Couples. Perspectives on Labour and Income, Statistics Canada 11(4):9–13

Metcalf H, Benson R (2000) From Unemployment To Self-Employment: Developing an Effective Structure of Micro-Finance Support. National Institute of Economic and Social Research, Discussion Paper No 170

Moen Ø (2002) The Born Globals. A new generation of small European exporters. International Marketing Review19/2:156–175

Muñoz PD (2004) Indicators for EU Policy making. The example of structural indicators. Eurostat, www.oecd.org/oecdworldforum.htm

Nziramasanga M, Lee M (2001) Duration of Self-Employment in Developing Countries: Evidence from Small Enterprises in Zimbabwe. Small Business Economics 17:239–53

OECD (1998) Fostering Entrepreneurship The OECD Job strategy. OECD, Paris

OECD (2002) Policy Benchmarks for Fostering Firm Creation and Entrepreneurship. Directorate for Science Technology and Industry, Paris

OECD (2003) Quality framework and guidelines for OECD statistical activities. OECD and Development Statistics Directorate STD/QFS 2003 1

OECD (2004) Fostering Entrepreneurship and Firm Creation as a Driver of Growth in a Global Economy. OECD, Paris

OECD (2005) Micro-policies for Growth and Productivity. Directorate for Science Technology and Industry, Paris

OECD (2005) SME and Entrepreneurship Outlook. OECD, Paris

O'kean JM (2000) La Teoría Económica de la Función Empresarial. Alianza Editorial, Madrid

Parker SC (2004) The Economics of Self-Employment and Entrepreneurship. Cambridge University Press, Cambridge

Parker SC (2005) The Economics Of Entrepreneurship. Foundations and trends in entrepreneurship 1:1–55

Parker SC, Robson MT (2004) Explaining international variations in entrepreneurship: evidence from a panel of OECD countries. Southern Economic Journal 71(2):287–301

Parker SC, Van Praag CM (2006) "The entrepreneur's entry mode: Business takeover or new venture start?" In Entrepreneurship and Human Capital, Amsterdam Center for Entrepreneurship (forthcoming)

Pestieau P, Possen UM (1991) Tax evasion and occupational choice. Journal of Public Economics 45:107–125

Pittaway L, Robertsen M, Munir K, Denyer D, Neely A (2004) Networking and innovation: a systematic review of the evidence. International Journal of Management Reviews Vol. 5/6. Issue 3&4:137–168

Rees H, Shah A (1986) An Empirical Analysis of Self-Employment in the UK. Journal of Applied Econometrics 1:95–108

Reize F (2004) Leaving Unemployment for Self-Employment An Empirical Study. ZEW Economics Studies 25 Physica-Verlag

Reynolds P; Bosma N; Autio E; Hunt S; De Bono N; Servais I; López García P, Chin N (2005) Global Entrepreneurship Monitor: Data Collection Design and Implementation 1998–2003. Small Business Economics 24 (3):205–31

Rodrik D (2003) Growth Strategies. NBER 10050

Schuetze HJ (2000) Taxes economic conditions and recent trends in male self-employment: a Canada-US comparison. Labour Economics 7(5):507–44

Schultz TW (1975) The Value of the Ability to Deal with Disequilibria. Journal of Economic Literature 13(3):827–846

Schumpeter JA (1912) Theorie der Wirtschaftlichen Entwicklung (The theory of economic development). Leipzig: Dunker & Humblot; translated by Dedvers Opie. Cambridge, MA: Harvard University Press, 1934

Steinberger T (2005) Social Security and entrepreneurial activity. CSEF Working Paper n° 130

Stel AJ Van (2005) Compendia: a harmonized data set of business ownership rates in 23 OECD countries. The International Entrepreneurship and Management Journal 1(1):105–23

Taylor MP (1996) Earnings independence or unemployment: why become self-employed. Oxford Bulletin of Economics and Statistics 58:253–66

Ucbasaran D, Westhead P, Wright M (2006) Opportunity identification and pursuit: Does an entrepreneur's human capital matter? Small Business Economics (forthcoming)

Vale S (2006) The International Comparability of Businesses Start-Up Rates. OECD Statistics Directorate, London, UK

Van der Sluis J, Van Praag CM (2006) Returns to intelligence: Entrepreneurs versus employees en Entrepreneurship and Human Capital. Amsterdam Center for Entrepreneurship, Amsterdam

Watson H (1985) Tax evasion and labor markets. Journal of Public Economics 27:231–246